THE MEN WHO INVENTED BROADWAY

Also by John Mosedale

THE GREATEST OF ALL:
THE 1927 NEW YORK YANKEES

THE
MEN
WHO
INVENTED BROADWAY

DAMON RUNYON, WALTER WINCHELL & THEIR WORLD

JOHN MOSEDALE

RICHARD MAREK PUBLISHERS
NEW YORK

070.922
M89m

The author gratefully acknowledges and thanks King Features Syndicate, Inc., for permission to reprint portions of columns written by Walter Winchell and Damon Runyon, copyright © King Features Syndicate, Inc., and Random House for material from *Father's Footsteps* by Damon Runyon, Jr., copyright © 1953 by Curtis Publishing Company, copyright © 1954 by Damon Runyon, Jr. Reprinted by permission of Random House, Inc.

Library of Congress Cataloging in Publication Data

Mosedale, John.
  The men who invented Broadway.

  Includes index.
  1. Journalists—New York (City)—Biography.
2. Runyon, Damon, 1880–1946—Biography. 3. Winchell,
Walter, 1897–1972.   I. Title.
PN4871.M6   070'.92'2 [B]   80-20235
ISBN 0-399-90085-3

For two of my favorite dolls . . .
   Anne Mosedale Cowie
   and
   Helen Buckner Drake

. . . on a day in memory, the summer sun bounced off the northern Minnesota lake.

the two young men, hardly more than boys, this was years and years ago, were returning to the island from town. there were groceries in the boat, soda pop and beer. a mighty three-quarters of a horsepower evinrude elto nudged the boat.

the boy who was steering read aloud from a newly purchased paperback book. he squinted eyes against the glare of the sun from the splendid sky.

he read:

"Ask any of us who jot down notes for the various gazettes in New York, our idea of a big-time, first-rate, grade-A reporter—and eleven times out of ten, the retort will be 'Damon Runyon.'

"Because, among other things, Runyon is the most exciting and spellbinding of historians—whether his assignment is the Kentucky Derby, the Madison Square Garden farces, the current murder mystery or the sitchee-ay-shun in the Orient.

"Damon, I mean to report (oh, get your story in the first paragraph, Winchell) possesses all the necessary attributes that go to make the guy the rest of us on the staff wish we were. . . ."

introduction

ONCE AGAIN the impulse for the book came from Richard Marek, who seven years ago sent me in joyous pursuit of *The Greatest of All: The 1927 New York Yankees.*

This time, in the spring of 1978, he suggested a biography of Damon Runyon. Now you did not grow up loving boxing in my day without knowing Damon Runyon, or reveling in the wild side of American life without reading Runyon's old accounts of rascality, you did not read mass circulation magazines without knowing Runyon's Broadway fables.

There was even a progression from hundreds of comic books to *The Shadow* and *Doc Savage* magazines to Runyon to Hemingway, and there you were as a high school freshman, blinking in the sunlight of literature, in the nick of time.

There already were biographies of Runyon. I remembered reading Ed Weiner's *The Damon Runyon Story* on a train heading east as I sought my first newspaper job. That was a fateful journey, but what places it through the decades is a fearful earache I suffered. The ear *abscessed* as I read about Damon in New York in the Twenties. The modest volume may have saved my sanity.

In the spring of 1978, I discovered Edwin P. Hoyt's *A Gentleman of Broadway: The Story of Damon Runyon,* written in 1964, and, it seemed to me, just about definitive. But I remembered reading and hearing about the friendship between Runyon and Walter Winchell, and that suggested a different kind of book.

Like millions of other Americans, I often had listened to Winchell on Sunday nights, with his famous greeting: "Good evening, Mr. and Mrs. America, from border to border and coast to coast, and all the ships at sea—let's go to press!" I even read Winchell, although how I managed that I'm not sure, since he appeared in the Hearst newspaper in Milwaukee, and I grew up in one of those Republican homes where a Hearst newspaper wasn't allowed. I don't remember sneaking over to a friend's house to sample the forbidden fruit, but somehow I

11

read enough Winchell to be able to imitate his style in a story for the school magazine.

I remember the story dealt with the murder of a fictional columnist on a transcontinental train packed with passengers who had good reason to wish him dead. The plot already was a cliché, but the motive was plausible. "I don't see why Walter Winchell is allowed to live," said Ethel Barrymore, said my father, said thousands of aggrieved readers.

Now I learned that not much had been written about the late-blooming friendship of Runyon and Winchell, those two notoriously difficult men, not even in biographies of Winchell published as recently as the 1970s by Herman Klurfeld and Bob Thomas.

That friendship flowered, as I hope the book makes clear, during one of New York's great periods, the time right after World War II. One survivor, looking back, said that the night life and its talk were comparable to the eighteenth-century London of the coffee houses, although it produced no Dr. Johnson. But its effects lingered. Here is Ernest Hemingway, musing through a concussion suffered in what the press called "a near-fatal" air crash in Africa in 1954:

"I thought of Mr. Walter Winchell and how we used to sit up late together with Damon Runyon, when Mr. Runyon was still a living man and fine companion and not yet a Fund . . ."

The Fund, or the Damon Runyon-Walter Winchell Cancer Fund as it is now called, is both the beginning and the end of their story. It grew out of that friendship formed in the last year of Runyon's life, and as a symbol of the friendship it is where the researcher must begin. Most of the Runyon and Winchell triumphs, being journalistic, are evanescent, but the Fund endures.

And so the first person interviewed for this book was the late Rex Taylor, publicist for the Fund, who directed me to Jewel Baxter, another publicist, whose good offices were enormously helpful, as was the guidance I received from David Walsh, executive director of the Fund, and Robin Harris, Rex Taylor's successor.

Those were the first of interviews which stretched through a year. The persons I talked with are identified in the book except in a few cases where the subjects requested anonymity for reasons I honor if I do not quite understand, perhaps an uneasy feeling that Winchell might return from the grave. He was a hard man to keep down.

(Broadway isn't too hard-boiled to dismiss the Voice from the Grave. Not long after Runyon's death, he wrote Walter's column for him: "Tell 'em to lay off crying, Walter . . . A fellow ought never to cry. When he does, he can't see things clearly. And if he sees things clearly, he won't cry at all.")

Very early in these researches, I decided that both Walter and

Damon, as I came to think of them, were phenomena whose like does not exist today. The reasons for this both puzzled and fascinated me. There is a scattering of journalistic giants today—I am not being ironic—but they are very different from Damon and Walter, better men, perhaps, but very different.

One obvious difference is that newsmen are better educated today. I belong to the GI Bill generation, the first journalistic generation in which a college education was a commonplace, and, incidentally, the last *not* to touch-type. Today, we are told, the influence of Woodward and Bernstein is inducing the best of college youth into journalism. Then why did Damon and Walter, neither of whom got out of elementary school, write a more readable English than do many of today's communication school products? I leave the answer to professors.

As the research for the book proceeded, I found myself concerned as much with history as with personality. Like any serious historian, I borrowed from books by the score. An honest-count bibliography follows the text.

I have spent some of the most industrious hours of my life in the Newspaper Reading Room of the New York Public Library, that national treasure house for anyone truly interested in our past in all its merriment and sorrow, and now I read Damon's columns going back to World War I and beyond, and Walter's from the 1920s on.

Damon and Walter worked for Hearst just about all their working lives. There would have been no Hearst without Pulitzer, and Bennett paved the way for Pulitzer, and the reporter was now in the early nineteenth century in order to try to understand the twentieth-century products, which is how history works.

So what this book became is a social history, the story of what people were doing and saying that is significant to an understanding of the times in which they lived, the music of life rather than its treaties. I hope this book dances a little.

Since the book is a social, rather than a formal, history, I have included sources in the body of the text, rather than in footnotes, remembering John Barrymore's observation that reading a footnote is like being called downstairs to answer the doorbell on your honeymoon.

The New York newspapers for which Damon and Walter worked are no longer with us, gone along with most of their rivals. The Hearst press of the period, and a good many of the opposition newspapers, are recalled with distaste, but their disappearance is a loss in a representative democracy. Do not be mistaken about that. Of all the dangers this country faces, none is more serious than the loss of a voice. A

13

newspaper is considerably more than a commercial enterprise. There always are newspapers that should be in different hands. There is none that should disappear.

This book was pretty much written in the small hours before the start of a work day, and the fact that it got finished at all is due to the love and support shown me by the former Helen Elizabeth Drake and our children, Amy, Laura, Andrew and Michael. My colleagues at CBS News, most of whom were only vaguely aware that I was writing a book, if I worked it right, served as frequent journalistic inspirations.

One person whose comments about the book I anticipated was Eli Waldron, one of the finest writers and most amusing critics I've ever known. He died in an automobile accident this spring of 1980, and it is a terrible loss. I hope he would have liked this book.

What follows begins with memory.

one

LIKE MANY NEW Yorkers, Dr. Marion Nadel worked at a job of some portent unaware of the raffish and improbable events that had contributed to her situation.

This was in the summer of 1979. Dr. Nadel was a Brooklyn native, a slight, dark-haired young woman who was graduated from Barnard and took a Ph.D. in developmental biology from Harvard. Two years earlier, she had been one of 81 youthful investigators selected from a field of 408 applicants to receive a Damon Runyon-Walter Winchell Cancer Fund fellowship, and now she was winding up her second year of research.

As she awoke in her apartment at Eighty-first Street and York Avenue, she was some eighteen blocks uptown from the site of the sixth floor studio of WJZ. She was a few blocks farther from the site of the New York *Daily Mirror*. From both those locations a man named Walter Winchell added considerable stature in the 1930s to his notoriety as a gossip by alerting the American people, at a time when a good many of them had not made up their minds about the New Germany, to the danger of Adolf Hitler and the Nazis, including the domestic variety. Both the fluff and the jeremiads were delivered in the urgent tones of a child who needs to go to the bathroom or were written in a style composed of sass and neologisms.

Dr. Nadel in her apartment was 1,771 miles from Denver, out of which a young reporter and poet who would become a fabulist named Damon Runyon came to New York before World War I. He wrote about sports, covering the Giants and the Yankees, some sixty-six blocks and a trip across town from Dr. Nadel's apartment. He covered the fights at Madison Square Garden, on Fiftieth Street and Eighth Avenue. He reported the horse races from tracks in Queens and Louisville and Saratoga.

Even when he was writing sports, however, Damon was more than a sportswriter. The times were rich in Trials of the Century, and Damon's reputation bloomed in the garden of American journalism as he covered the Hall-Mills case in 1926, the Snyder-Gray trial in 1927, and the trial in 1935 of Bruno Richard Hauptmann for the Lindbergh kidnapping.

"If there ever was a newspaperman's newsman," a couple of history professors commented on all this activity, "it was Damon Runyon."

And those courthouses, ball fields, and racetracks were bridged by destiny to Dr. Nadel's daily journey almost half a century later to Rockefeller University, founded in 1901 as the Rockefeller Institute for Medical Research. As a postgraduate institution, the Rockefeller University fields no football team or marching band and so is not as well known as some academies, but its scientists had earned sixteen Nobel Prizes by 1978, and it lists among its achievements the first demonstration that animal cancers can be caused by a virus, the discovery that DNA is the substance that transmits hereditary information, and the first isolation and successful testing of antibiotics.

With an annual operating budget of about $45 million, the university is a physical manifestation of that faith, called philanthropy on its more exalted levels and charity on its more modest, by which Americans move when government falters. It was a quixotic variant of this faith which supported Marion Nadel in her diurnal round, and you could make an American symphony of it, combining the "Give My Regards to Broadway" bounce of George M. Cohan with the big city melancholy of Gershwin, Kern, and Rodgers.

For what's been called "the quiet charity" grew out of the autumnal friendship between Walter and Damon, each of whom represented a bright strand in the American fabric, Damon the descendant of colonists and the almost mythic pioneers who pushed west, Walter a product of that late nineteenth-century diaspora of Russian and East European Jews which so profoundly affected American culture and commerce.

In 1977, the year in which Dr. Nadel received her fellowship, the Runyon-Winchell Cancer Fund supported initial fellowships at thirty-nine institutions, including Rockefeller University.

Her project title alone, *Messenger RNA of Avian Tumor Viruses,* would have been so much Sanskrit, or spinach, to Damon and Walter, elementary school dropouts both, who lived the clichéd but uncommon American success story of rags-to-riches literally, and who died the death favored by the gloomier American realists, exhausted.

And the great joke is that it is such an *American* story, because almost all of it happened in, and celebrated, New York. It was widely believed at the time Marion Nadel pursued the painstaking hunt for clues to the way cancer works that New York was not part of America.

16

But for more than three decades of a time Marion Nadel was too young to remember, what happened or might have happened in or around a sixteen-block stretch of the street called Broadway, from Times Square to Columbus Circle—Damon's world, Walter's world—seemed part of millions of American lives, shaped American attitudes, and informed dreams.

"Good evening, Mr. and Mrs. North America and all the ships at sea. Let's go to press," Walter barked each Sunday night at nine o'clock, eastern time. He told his listeners who was falling in love ("blazing"), having a baby ("infanticipating") or getting divorced ("Renovated"). He ordered auditors not to miss this play, this movie, this book, or "you'll be listed among the chumps," and it was an article of faith that he could single-handedly create a bestseller, because he did, or a hit play, because he did. For decades he made the Stork Club, run by a bigoted ex-bootlegger from Oklahoma, the most famous nightclub in America.

Walter's news broadcast was frequently in the top ten in the audience survey called the Hooper ratings; sometimes, it was alone at the top. At a time when radio was what television became, there were weeks when more people listened to Walter Winchell than to Jack Benny or Fred Allen. That was only part of it. He was identified primarily as a newspaperman, and by 1940, when his column was carried in 1,000 newspapers, his radio-newspaper audience was estimated at 50 million people in a nation of 130 million.

That was the year St. Clair McKelway in *The New Yorker* magazine deplored the presence of gossip in "the news from Washington and news from abroad." He found gossip in syndicated columns, in the most conservative newspapers, "gossip-writing techniques" in reporting of "important national and international affairs." McKelway concluded that gossip's "presence in American journalism is almost entirely due to the peculiar personality of one man. This man is Walter Winchell."

Speaking of that same period, however, two historians awarded Walter what he called an orchid. In *A Treasury of Great Reporting,* Louis L. Snyder of the College of the City of New York and Richard B. Morris of Columbia University called him "the reporter who has done more to rouse the conscience of America against intolerance and totalitarianism than any other journalist of his time."

Walter was greatly imitated, but he was a once-in-an-epoch phenomenon who moved familiarly among the famous and the infamous, the rich and the powerful, always talking more than he listened, almost always about himself.

Some 230 miles away from the Broadway Walter celebrated, there came a day in Washington, D.C., when Franklin Delano Roosevelt began a private interview saying, "Walter, I've got an item for you."

The gent's room journalist in the Oval Office was almost enough to rouse the Washington press corps from its parochial somnolence, and through much of the Roosevelt presidency, Walter received his share of Washington exclusives to tuck in among rumors of infidelities and pregnancies, while he supplied FDR with gags and Broadway gossip.

Through those years when the nation's press, led by Hearst, McCormick, and Scripps-Howard, not to forget *Time* magazine and the New York *Times,* cannonaded away at that man in the White House, it was Walter, a Hearst columnist, who led the countercharge, and it was through Walter that the President tested the national mood before running for a third term.

Walter called Broadway "the main stem" and "the hardened artery." Along with ruthlessness and a sometimes spine-chilling cynicism, he affected great sentimentality, as well as admiration for any scientific or intellectual achievement he could understand or pretend to understand, particularly if he could tell it in a paragraph.

And so he might have liked the story of his fellow New Yorker, Dr. Marion Nadel, toiling with her coworkers under the direction of Dr. Hidesaburo Hanafusa—"shepherd to us all," says a handwritten sign on the office door—although it is a story with no big payoff yet.

They were studying—like how many researchers in how many laboratories?—what is called transformation, the process by which a normal cell is transformed into a cancer cell. They worked with the Rous sarcoma virus in chickens and chicken embryos. The virus cannot produce a tumor by itself but needs a closely related virus called a helper. To learn about this is slow, painstaking work, full of frustrations and false leads.

The struggle with a disease polite society once didn't even mention is the labor of more than one lifetime. The Rous sarcoma virus was discovered by F.P. Rous at the old Rockefeller Institute in 1911. But the Nobel Prize for that discovery wasn't awarded until 1967, *fifty-six years later,* because lagging technology made detailed study of the virus impossible for most of that half century.

It was in 1910, only one year before the virus was discovered, that Damon Runyon went to New York, to live more than one lifetime, marrying twice, siring two children, making careers as sportswriter, columnist and, most surprisingly, as teller of those tales about Broadway, strange, slight stories, beginning in 1929, when the evocatively named Waldo Winchester, "a nice-looking young guy who writes pieces about Broadway for the *Morning Item* . . . takes quite a number of peeks at Dave the Dude's doll . . . and she takes quite a

18

number of peeks back and there you are, there you are, indeed," igniting "Romance in the Roaring Forties."

The stories appeared in the mass magazines of the period, *Collier's, Cosmopolitan, The Saturday Evening Post,* and *Liberty.* One editor estimated that a Runyon story increased circulation by sixty thousand, a success that helped the critics ignore Damon. This confirmed his opinion of critics.

Not only were the stories collected in hardcover, Damon might have pointed out, but in paperback, and two collections each sold more than one million copies, which was unheard of for short-story collections, and although they were written in a weird kind of American argot, they achieved enormous popularity in England after Lord Beaverbrook printed them in the *Evening Standard.* They induced a degree of enthusiasm in English critics, John Lardner observed, which implied "very plainly that after a long, slow pull, by way of Poe, Whitman, James, Twain, Cather and Hemingway, our culture finally hit the jackpot with Runyon."

Damon affected few pretensions about his fiction. It was a commercial enterprise. He made his own world, selling it to the world, as did, on various levels, Dickens and Balzac and Trollope and John D. MacDonald. Damon wrote about outcasts, dancers on the fringe of society, hoboes, gangsters, soldiers, gamblers, racetrack touts, show girls, killers and, although he never called them that, whores.

Twentieth-century America is a strange society. Damon is often accused of sentimentality, but murder, theft, beatings, cheating, and adultery were incidents in the story line, the way of his world.

What a world it was, the Brooklyn hoods Harry the Horse and Spanish John and Little Isadore, who suffer when there is unemployment because there is no one for them to rob; Big Nig, the crapshooter who, when a monkey carries a baby to a West Side rooftop and seems about to throw the baby off, works the hysterical crowd, offering 7 to 5 against the baby; Hot Horse Herbie and Miss Cutie Singleton, who have been engaged for ten years and will marry as soon as Herbie makes a scratch; Wilbur Willard, the lush whose life turns around after he mistakes a kitten for a leopard; Big Butch, the best safecracker east of the Mississippi River, who takes his baby along on a ten-G job; Bookie Bob, whose head shakes not from palsy but from saying "no" to would-be borrowers, and who will be snatched; Princess O'Hara, a little redheaded doll from over on Tenth Avenue and the adventure that unrolls when Gallant Godfrey, one of the great handicap horses, is substituted for Goldberg, who usually pulls her victoria; Dream Street Rose, the beery and bellicose chambermaid who explains what happened long before in Pueblo, Denver, and San

19

Francisco to make her do what she did in an East Side townhouse; little Lily of St. Pierre, whose pathetic end so moves Jack o'Hearts he cannot finish singing "There's a Long, Long Trail A-Winding," although Broadway morality suggests *he* did what he did to Louis the Lug just to get a place in the male quartet which sings sentimental ballads in the late morning hours at Good Time Charley Bernstein's joint on Forty-eighth Street; the cop-killer Earthquake, who likes to demonstrate his strength by grabbing a man with either hand and holding both over his head, and who dies heroically in Managua, Nicaragua; Joe the Joker, reputed inventor of the hotfoot, whose ultimate gag is a horror, and, of course, Miss Sarah Brown, with the 100 percent eyes, and Sky Masterson, so called because he will go so high betting on any proposition whatsoever, he will bet all he has, and no one can bet any more than that.

Their story, Sarah's and Sky's, became a definitive Broadway musical called *Guys and Dolls* when it opened at the Forty-sixth Street Theater four years after Damon's death, running for an even 1,200 performances. It was transformed into a splashy movie with Frank Sinatra and Marlon Brando, just a little Broadway fable, but it was like striking oil.

If the stories are rich in character, there is not much in the way of what's called "character development." The stories appear to exist on just one level, and yet they have been translated, in spite of their manufactured dialect, into French and Dutch, Italian and Indonesian.

Damon created a common humanity, so much so that more than forty years later, the phrase "Damon Runyon character" meant something from the groves of academe to that low circle where people read nothing at all. The characters are cartoons, but an English commentator said Damon produced "a humanity as new and startling as Lewis Carroll did," and the money rolled in.

Damon spent it about as fast as he made it, in the manner although not on the scale of his primary employer, William Randolph Hearst, who couldn't get by on $15 million a year. Damon spent his money on clothes by the closetful, shoes, gambling, racehorses, apartments in Manhattan, a big house on an island off Miami, and alimony.

He could almost afford this because, in addition to a newspaper contract guaranteeing him $20,000 a year in the 1920s, he wrote those stories for $1,500, later $5,000 each, and in just one depression year he picked up $30,000 in options from Hollywood. Sixteen of the stories became movies in Damon's lifetime, and he believed that was a record.

All of the stories are launched by a faceless, anonymous narrator, who often gets things going as he is standing in front of the evocatively named Mindy's restaurant when, as an example, along comes a sixty-year-old bookie called Sorrowful Jones, holding the hand of a tiny doll who will be called Little Miss Marker and will, in 1934, launch a moppet named Shirley Temple into a world of fame and money some mothers dream about.

In 1979, it was hoped the same kind of gambler's luck would strike six-year-old Sara Stimson of Helotes, Texas, population twenty-five, who, said Universal Pictures, crossing its heart, was chosen from some five thousand little girls interviewed around the country to be the latest Little Miss Marker. The movie, alas, failed, at least in part because it strayed from Damon.

The Damon Runyon character need not be a little doll or a good-looking doll or even a gangster. In "Madame La Gimp," she is a gin-soaked Broadway hag who peddles yesterday's newpapers and secondhand flowers from a funeral home but must, for plot purposes, appear to be a rich woman because the daughter she sent to live abroad is coming home with her fiancé, scion of proud old Spanish nobility.

Hollywood, Walter wrote, made that story "an incessantly robust laugh-provoker named *Lady for a Day*. But this is the lustiest of laughs about that grand flicker. An Academy in Hollywood awards prizes annually for the best this-and-that. *Lady for a Day* copped three of them. One prize went to the director—another to the adapter—and the third to the star. Damon Runyon, the author, didn't rate a nod. Haw!"

Guffaws and a kind of ironic laughter punctuated the careers of Damon and Walter. Damon dramatized himself as "a hired Hessian with a typewriter," and Walter preened as "America's Number One NeWWsboy," but they were company men at heart. Each worked for more than three decades for a publisher who preferred entertainment to news, an experience the venomous Ambrose Bierce said "had all the reality of masturbation."

That sense of unreality distorted their copy. Many of the people Damon and Walter wrote about were creatures of prohibition, which taught millions of formerly law-abiding citizens to break the law, and so broadened the base of organized crime in national life that Americans were still paying off the bar bill for the noble experiment half a century later.

Damon in his fiction and Walter in his columns and broadcasts helped popularize the notion that Broadway's gangsters and bootleggers more or less represented what a later generation would call "an alternative life-style" and were almost regular folks, except more interesting. The glamour was bogus. After a lifetime spent in the glittering lights of Broadway, one columnist wrote, "I never met a professional hoodlum who was a wit, a good conversationalist, showed a likeable personality or gave any evidence of having brains enough to do anything worthwhile." Mark Hellinger, Walter's friend and mentor and fellow columnist, was bored with Broadway by the time he was twenty-six.

Neither Walter nor Damon understood that the cynic knows only half the story. Damon seemed to see himself as an outsider sympathizing with criminals, also outsiders, who didn't do anything much worse than the establishment did.

Yet Damon's sometime Florida neighbor, "Mr. Brown," was Al Capone, whose personal income in 1927 was estimated at $105 million, the largest ever reported—or unreported—in the United States. The money came from bootleg liquor, gambling, and brothels. It financed corruption and violence. There is no accurate count of the murders Capone inspired. Sometimes he delivered personally, as when he dispatched a couple of rivals after an elaborate supper by beating out their brains, at table, with a baseball bat.

Damon's ultimate verdict on Al Capone indicated that Capone was persecuted by the federal government. Walter, granted an exclusive interview with Capone, also was sympathetic. Certainly the moral outrage that informed Walter's broadsides against the Nazis was generally missing from his writing about criminals. He wound up calling them "the UN"—underworld nobility.

Both Walter and Damon knew and admired Arnold Rothstein, the most celebrated gambler and fixer of his generation. Rothstein died, true to the underworld code, after being shot as he emerged from Lindy's one night in 1928, without naming his assassin. He "died game," Damon said, and later adding a few characteristics of Herman Rosenthal, another gambler who was murdered, he created The Brain, evocatively named Armand Rosenthal, "and nobody knows how much dough The Brain has, except that he must have plenty because no matter how much dough is around, The Brain sooner or later gets hold of all of it."

The Brain is stabbed one night leaving Mindy's, and neither his spoiled wife nor his well-kept mistresses offer him room to die in. That beneficence comes from an old woman apple peddler to whom The Brain gave a ten-dollar tip. Damon didn't much like women.

Neither the man who was raised in a West that lived by the laws of expediency nor the man who was reared in the big town ghetto displayed the provincial squeamishness of Nick Carraway. When Gatsby points out a character, also based on Rothstein, rumored to have fixed the 1919 World Series, Nick reflects, "It never occurred to me that one man could start to play with the faith of fifty million people—with the singlemindedness of a burglar blowing a safe."

One of the marvels of Walter's career was that within a couple of years he progressed from being a friend of Owney Madden, a prohibition gang leader, to becoming a confidant of J. Edgar Hoover, director of the Federal Bureau of Investigation.

It was Madden who protected Walter after the columnist aroused the underworld by hinting in his column about the rubout of the psychopathic killer Vincent Coll the day Coll was machine-gunned down in a telephone booth.

And it was to Hoover, in what may have been the gaudiest moment of Walter's career, that on Fifth Avenue at Twenty-eighth Street, Walter personally delivered Louis "Lepke" Buchalter. Lepke was a fugitive from justice and head of Murder, Inc., an extortion ring which bled the city's fur, garment, trucking, and other industries. Troublemakers, reported Meyer Berger of the New York *Times,* were "burned with gasoline, buried in quicklime, shot, stabbed with ice picks, garroted."

Men lived by codes, not laws, on the turn-of-the-century sidewalks of New York and in the foothills of Colorado. It was not easy to tell the good guys from the bad guys and sometimes, in the space of a few bewildering hours, they switched places. The results could be confusing.

Damon happened to be in Chicago in 1934 when Walter was making a stage appearance there. Local thugs were shaking down visiting entertainers. Although he didn't request them, Walter was assigned seven bodyguards. Two came from the FBI, on orders of Hoover. Two were Chicago detectives. Three were gangsters, including a couple of Capone's cousins, assigned from New York by Charles "Lucky" Luciano, the procurer. Each set of bodyguards viewed the others with suspicion. They would not let Damon backstage to visit Walter, shoving him into an alley, and Damon never learned who strong-armed him, the *federales,* the constabulary, or the thugs.

But if Walter and Damon hung around with evil companions, to paraphrase an old song,they had a wonderful time. By the time he reached New York, Damon was a recovered alcoholic; Walter never drank much. But they celebrated the hard-drinking, high-stepping night life of prohibition, the depression, and the war years.

The Stork Club, the Silver Slipper, the Parody, Le Pavillon, the Copa, along with Reuben's and Lindy's—or Mindy's—the neon names of night clubs, restaurants, and delicatessens flashed through their columns. The images burned in the national consciousness until they

23

were as familiar as the neighborhood store, along with the Broadway credo, the wisecrack, the adolescent cynicism and woozy sentimentality, Broadway's smoky torch songs, its putdowns and enthusiasms.

The mores and behavior of a few hundred people in seventeen Manhattan blocks stretching north from Forty-second Street were emulated and talked about in Spokane and Milwaukee and Atlanta. Damon's Florida home, his Hollywood visits, Walter's winters in Florida and his suburban estate aside, Broadway, the street, was their home. "There was something poignant about that," a friend recalled in 1979.

The strictly limited Broadway view of Damon and Walter was part of the lure that attracted thousands of young people to Manhattan—artists and writers and athletes, shopgirls and salesmen and tap dancers and waitresses, all of whom one way or the other saw their names in lights or saw themselves hanging around with those whose names were in lights.

During those decades, remember, New York was a national city in the manner of London or Paris or Rome. "It is to the nation what the church spire is to the village," E. B. White wrote in 1949, "the visible symbol of aspiration and faith, the white plume saying the way is up."

Coupled with that promise, of course, were the pitfalls and violence of the Big Town. This was stuff—bruised bodies and broken butterflies—from which Walter and Damon worked much of their material.

That world, and their vision of it, had to end. They would not recognize Broadway in 1980. Walter said the dying Damon wrote, "You can keep the things of bronze and stone, just give me one man to remember me just once a year." And yet, after the scoops and the gags are forgotten, their monument is a visible symbol of aspiration and faith, a five-story mansion at 33 West Fifty-sixth Street, familiar to both men as one of the city's more celebrated speakeasies.

It is that building which links Damon and Walter to Dr. Marion Nadel, in the most improbable twist in the story, a fable for Damon, a gee-whiz item for Walter.

The mansion, according to *Variety*, was built for the Woolworth family around the turn of the century and was flanked by the town houses of John Wanamaker, the merchant, and Thomas A. Edison, the tinkerer. Damon and Walter knew it as the Club Napoleon, long after it had passed from Woolworth hands, a secluded rendezvous where cocktails for four, plus lunch, cost five hundred Coolidge dollars.

There is a story that Barbara Hutton, the Woolworth heiress fixed by the press as "the poor little rich girl," once visited the Napoleon as

24

a debutante, recognized the bar as her former playroom, and fled in tears.

This anecdote was passed along a few days later to Louis Bromfield, the novelist. Bromfield wrote it as fiction. Paramount made a movie based on his version, *Night After Night,* starring a newcomer named George Raft. Raft arranged a small role in the film for an old friend, Mae West, who entered the speakeasy all a-bulge and awash in jewels. The hatcheck girl exclaimed, "My goodness! What beautiful jewelry!"

"Goodness," Miss West murmured, "had nothing to do with it."

As repeal and the depression approached, speakeasies like the Club Napoleon became more relics than shrines. The town house was then a restaurant called the Casa Blanca, run by a prohibition figure named Larry Fay, a source for both Damon and Walter. Shot dead by a disgruntled employee, Fay did a Jimmy Cagney fall down the sweeping marble staircase that still dominates the foyer.

Number 33 lingered on as the Place Elegante into the 1950s when it was acquired by Dr. Frank Stanton, then president of CBS, and E. M. Simon, a real estate man. In 1962 they presented it to the Damon Runyon Cancer Fund for use as its headquarters. Three times a year a scientific advisory committee meets there to review applications of young scientists like Dr. Nadel, who seek fellowships for research into the disease that killed both Damon and Walter.

The Fund was born in 1946 when Walter made a sudden impassioned plea on his broadcast, shortly after Damon's death: "Will you please, if you enjoyed Damon's genius in the papers, magazines, books, and on the screen, contribute a little or a lot, a dime or a dollar, to get the Damon Runyon Memorial started?"

Something like $75,000 was the original goal, to aid newspapermen stricken with cancer. By the end of 1978, the Fund had awarded $43 *million* in "research grants and post-graduate fellowships in 50 states and a few foreign countries."

It seems improbable, even in a city that celebrates the bizarre, that this work should result from the brief friendship of two classically egocentric and often unpleasant loners.

"I guess I'm just a son of a bitch," Walter sometimes said after savaging a friend in his column. "Runyon was harder to approach than a rodeo bull in a chute," wrote the humorist Bugs Baer, for whom Damon once did a great favor. "There wasn't a time when he wouldn't throw a drowning man both ends of the rope."

Damon and Walter achieved fame in a field where fame flies. Nothing is more perishable than the news, and who remembers the names of dead newsmen? With no more than their typewriters, energy, and talent, they became rich and famous. Each received respectful attention, *postmortem,* in the New York *Times,* Walter's obituary being front page news, Damon's running a full column. Both obituaries were almost accurate.

The Fund may be their finest memorial. It is sometimes a joy to reread their stuff, but browsing in old newpapers is a specialized taste, like Liebling and Trollope, and the masses are meditating or at the disco. In the main, Damon's artful phrases are buried with the box scores, along with Walter's gossip.

And yet in important ways their influence persists. It is not just that Damon's guys and dolls leap and shout on *The Late Show,* or that the personal journalism Walter resurrected is now part of the news flow. They left both journalism and popular culture different from the way they found them.

They were, of course, part of a tribe. There was a whole squadron of Broadway columnists—Ed Sullivan and Louis Sobol, Frank Farrell and Dorothy Kilgallen and Earl Wilson among them; and Damon's colleagues in the press box included Ring Lardner, Heywood Broun, Westbrook Pegler, and Paul Gallico, all of whom also went on to other matters.

But Damon and Walter were the tops, Damon as a sportswriter whose slangy, present-tense reporting defied imitation, as columnist and creator of idiosyncratic fiction; Walter as columnist and commentator whose power and success created rivals but never peers.

It is not that the great machine of American journalism sweat and buckled to produce Walter and Damon, but their lives and work illuminate a society and a craft which was receptive to them only for the moments of those decades. One way to judge a society is by the journalism it creates. Newspapers hold up a mirror to the world and are caught in the reflection.

Walter and Damon serve as metaphor, the very paradigm, of Broadway columnist and observer of the New York and sporting scenes. They carried Broadway with them wherever they went and whatever they wrote about; they made Broadway stand for values and attitudes which remain part of the American perspective, for a way of looking at life, for what is of value, and sometimes the view is through the wrong end of the telescope.

They reported from the observation deck of a rocket. The changes happened so quickly: a mosaic of great events and the trivial. A great war, stupendous ball games, horse races, championship fights, lechers and killers parading, presidents and queens, sex and speakeasies, sleazy nightclubs whose patrons were as gross as the proprietors, wisecracks and blood and wine in the streets, marriages and babies

26

and divorces, the big bull market and the crash, the depression and one-third of a nation jammed up, movie stars and flappers and café society, rat-a-tat-tat goes the tommy gun, dot-dash-dot goes the telegraph key, *Say, don't tell me I'm daffy* goes the lead. *The surrender of public enemy* goes the lead, high-kicking girls and the punch below the belt and another great war and the end.

It is not only the event, of course; it is how we perceive it, what we take away in the collective intelligence.

How we saw those events, what events we saw, a part of what persists in our values, came from the men who invented Broadway, those two demanding, vainglorious, driven, ambitious, peculiar men, Damon and Walter, Walter and Damon, those two.

two

"BROADWAY," RICHARD Harding Davis wrote for *Scribner's* magazine in May 1891, "means so many different things to so many different people."

The cliché is as well worn as old wood;it shines like the mahogany bar in the old Astor House. No truer words ever were written about the street, however. They could have been written a century later. That Broadway and the men who wrote about it stand at a distance that cannot be measured in space and time. Its customs seem as remote as Jefferson's Arcadia.

Davis's Broadway meant one thing to the businessman, another thing to the businessman's wife, and something else to his son. "In this," Davis wrote, "it differs from almost every other great thoroughfare in the world."

To Davis, the Broadway of the Wall Street area was "the great fighting ground of the city, where the battle of business goes on from eight o'clock in the morning . . . until five, when the armies declare an armistice for the day and march off uptown to plan a fresh campaign for the morrow."

The daily arrival of those armies, by ferryboats, by the elevated road, by the Brooklyn bridge, in lots of thousands and tens of thousands "is one of the most impressive sights the city has to offer."

The money that was got on lower Broadway was spent in the shopping district, between Tenth and Twenty-third streets: "The business district is very grim and very real, the shopping district is all color, and movement and variety. It is not the individual woman one sees here, but women in the plural . . . it is apparently a very serious business, this shopping."

But Broadway most moved Davis in the evenings around Madison Square when

> the electric lights shine blue and clear through the black, bare branches, and the lamps of many broughams dance past continually to opera or ball, and give a glimpse through frosty

pane of a woman's figure muffled in furs and swan's-down. There is something exhilarating about this corner of Broadway, where the theatres at every turn are bright with colored illuminations telling of runs of one hundred nights and where the restaurants and hotels are brilliantly aglow and desperately busy.

Davis was an ideal guide to the Broadway of the period. He was at home there, as he was at home almost anyplace in the world, "the knight errant of the nineties," in the court of Nicholas and Alexandra, where he was one of two Americans accredited to cover the coronation, or on any battlefield of the six wars he covered.

He was the most famous foreign correspondent of them all, ineffably dashing and glamorous, and if he is recalled with condescension as a combination Captain Spaulding and Kipling hero, with his pith helmet, binoculars case, and Brooks Brothers uniform of his own design, the fault is with the age. Davis reported for Charles Anderson Dana's *Sun,* later for Hearst's *Journal.* The difference between his employers, and the difference in the readership they sought, reflected the startling new direction of New York journalism.

Davis's achievements were his own. He was not packaged. He was the true golden boy, the greatly beloved son of accomplished parents. He seemed to win effortlessly, even in the mundanities. He scored the first touchdown ever recorded by a Lehigh University football team.

On his second day at work for the *Sun,* the young reporter was accosted by a confidence man in City Hall Park. Davis collared the recreant with a football tackle, then wrote an account of the incident under a period headline: OUR GREEN REPORTER: HE LOCKED HORNS WITH A BUNCO MAN FOR FUN. THEY MET THE USUAL WAY. NOW THE BUNCO MAN IS ON THE ISLAND. A contemporary observed, "From that day, the name of Richard Harding Davis has been familiar to every New Yorker."

Davis wrote slowly, giving an effect of fluency, a practice the *Sun* encouraged. Gerald Langford, his biographer, notes that Davis put his mark on every story, whether the death of a bartender in a rooming house fire, or an interview with Walt Whitman, or the suicide of a *horizontale,* a rich man's mistress.

Davis was the quintessential Wasp, strikingly handsome in a square-jawed, dimple-chinned way. He was, in fact, the model for the escort his friend Charles Dana Gibson drew to accompany the gorgeous Gibson girl. And if Davis inspired jealousy, he created heart-thumping admiration, even among the sophisticates.

"The hero of our dreams was Richard Harding Davis," recalled the iconoclastic H. L. Mencken. Booth Tarkington, the gentleman from Indiana, looked back from eminence as short-story writer, novelist, and playwright to recall the exultation of coming in from Princeton to see Davis "stride into the Palm Room of the just-completed Waldorf.

> Then, oh, then, our day was radiant. . . . Of all the great people of every continent, this was the one we most desired to see. . . . Youth called to youth, all ages read him, but the young men and young women have turned to him ever since the precocious fame made him their idol. . . . He bade them see that pain is negligible, that fear is a joke, and that the world is poignantly interesting, joyously lovable.

It is doubtful that even Davis could have created that kind of response in the last quarter of the twentieth century. For one thing, he was an honorable man, and the historians tell us that honor died in the trenches during World War I. Davis would be regarded as quaint today, or old-fashioned, or perhaps it would be determined that something was wrong with him.

The kind of influence he exerted was more than a regard for careful writing. "It was his example more than any other," according to Langford,

> which ushered out the old-style reporter (who usually had worked his way up from office boy or printer's devil and to whom journalism was a prosaic business) and ushered in the new-style reporter, who, as Richard described him in *The Reporter Who Made Himself King,* was an over-serious young man fresh out of college and possessed of the idea that 'the sun only rises that man may have light by which to read' his paper.
>
> He did not work for pay; his reward was the knowledge that he would have 'crowded the experiences of the lifetime of an ordinary young businessman, doctor or lawyer, or man-about-town into three short years.

Davis wrote enormously, every word his own, then a common journalistic practice. In addition to his reporting, and books about it, he wrote popular stories involving a boulevardier named Van Bibber, by means of which he poked fun at himself. He wrote Broadway hits, including *The Dictator,* a farce in which, a reviewer noted, "Mr. John Barrymore also assists materially and will no doubt be heard from on

30

his own account." Davis knew everyone, the young Churchill, Kipling, all of them.

Hearst paid him a record $500 to cover a college football game. It worked out to 50 cents a word. "Imagine," Davis marveled, "being paid a dollar to write 'For example.'"

He instinctively did the right thing. Among the talents of his period was Stephen Crane, who sometimes wrote for newspapers and wrote *Maggie, A Girl of the Streets,* introducing a new realism into American letters.

Crane encouraged gossip about himself, hanging around with loose women, smoking cigarettes which was regarded as French, and experimenting with drugs. One night in Delmonico's, Davis overheard a loutish photographer announce that Crane was dying of what was then called a loathsome disease. Rather than write an item about it, Davis ordered him to keep still. The photographer sneered. Davis, "blushing furiously," dragged him outside. He returned in a few minutes with a cut lip, asking his friends to forget the whole business.

Davis and the Broadway he observed managed to attract notice unimpeded by the great publicity machine, which was not yet geared up to condemn men to its service. Among the superlatives for which New Yorkers have such fondness, the city counted forty-one legitimate theaters as the century turned, more than any community in the world.

There was theatrical news in the newspapers, of course, as well as in theatrical journals. But the Broadway of Weber and Fields and Victor Herbert, of John Drew and David Warfield, was not entirely convinced personal publicity was a necessity.

The reigning producer was Charles Frohman, considered by some to be the greatest producer of all time. Billie Burke was a musical comedy actress, newly arrived from England, when Frohman "introduced me to New York quietly, avoiding publicity stunts, strictly forbidding me to appear in public or even to see other plays. It was his Napoleonic principle that the illusions of the theatre would be shattered if the public saw too much or knew too much about stars."

This Broadway was the Great White Way. Diamond Jim Brady late one night stepped out after his routine Lucullan feast, surveyed the glare of lights, and announced he found himself on "the Street of the Midnight Sun."

The restaurant may have been Rector's, on Longacre Square, later Times Square. It was the Sardi's of its day. Its proprietor boasted, "I found Broadway a quiet little lane of ham and eggs in 1899 and left it a full-blown avenue of lobsters, champagne and morning-afters. When Broadway sought to sleep, I turned night into day."

The street flourished without multimedia campaigns. There were no gossip columnists in daily newspapers. The talk show had not replaced conversation. About all a publicist could do was plaster the landscape with posters, like the old-time advance man who toured the Orient with a clutch of elderly females, dressing them in sequined tights. He dazzled the rubes of Tokyo, Shanghai, and Hong Kong with placards presenting a rear view of an idealized young woman in the buff and the legend "At 8 o'clock tonight, she turns around."

Much of the time, actresses kept their clothes on while performing, on the old theory that a man may be more intrigued by what he imagines than by what he sees. When Maude Adams retired in 1917 after twenty years of stardom, she was accustomed to making $20,000 a week, keeping her clothes on onstage and her mouth closed off it.

"Her popularity is such that it amounts to almost unreasoning worship," said a contemporary about the woman who was Peter Pan, Chanticleer, and Maggie in *What Every Woman Knows*. "The mere announcement of her name, without respect to the play she is acting in, is enough to fill any theatre in the land."

The glorious Julia Marlowe, too, abhorred personal publicity. Her insistence on a private life did not diminish the ardor of her following, as Allen Churchill noted in *The Great White Way*. A lady's maid abandoned her mistress to serve Miss Marlowe. A compulsive gambler gave up his dice. A theater doorman at whom she smiled maintained a scrapbook of her notices until his death, thirty years later.

A surgeon, called on to lance her cheeks when she was stricken with typhoid, hurled his instruments to the floor, crying, "I cannot do it . . . if I lance this girl's cheeks, she will not be able to act again. I cannot do it!"

She recovered to face down an editor who wanted details of her personal life. "We syndicate our articles," he pointed out. "What you say will be printed in one hundred seventeen newspapers tomorrow."

She answered, "That is one hundred seventeen reasons for not doing it."

But Frohman's War, as it might be called, was soon lost. Publicists must eat, too, a press increasingly soliciting the masses was avid for the juicy detail, and stars revealed their thoughts, which tended to be commonplace, on love and the meaning of life.

There is no age of innocence, and the Victorians did not devote themselves wholly to the pursuit of high art and guileless enjoyment. The history of the double standard, and the double lives led by many of them, along with the scandals reported in the sensational newspapers, indicate that they were as randy as their descendants. Sex did not dominate their novels, plays, and discourse, however, suggesting that selective hypocrisy is not without its merits.

Davis in his 1891 article for *Scribner's* wrote about the lonely working girl who joins the Broadway parade for some sense of companionship.

"But she may read how great her danger is in the face of the young woman who passes her with alert, insolent eyes, and who a year before was what she is now, and who sees nothing in the lighted shop window before which she stops but the reflection of the man who has dropped out of step with the procession and is hovering at her side."

For Broadway, in a phrase of the day, was also the primrose path. O. Henry's city of *The Four Million,* his Bagdad-on-the Subway, also bred slums worse than those slums which spurred the London correspondent of Horace Greeley's Whig-turned-Republican New York *Tribune* to write *Das Kapital.*

In an age of laissez-faire capitalism, poverty was indiscriminate. Half a million immigrants passed through the city annually; many of them stayed. A dollar twenty-five was a good wage for a twelve-hour day. Fathers stupefied by work, if they did not pause at the corner saloon, might return home to a kitchen shared with a dozen families and send a child out to fill the beer growler.

Wives and daughters worked in sweatshops for $4.50 a week, which could be reduced for minor mistakes. The luckier sons got jobs as newsboys; a compassionate legislature passed a law restricting them to a sixteen-hour workday, beginning at 6 A.M. Boys who were not so blessed became street Arabs, sleeping in doorways or on park benches.

For many of them, parents and children, there seemed no way out of the monotony and hopelessness. It was society that bred rapacious capitalists, prizefighters, entertainers, and whores.

In *Park Row,* Allen Churchill quotes an anonymous observer's comment:

> . . . romance lurks in every doorway, and vice, horrible yet fascinating, stalks all the byways. Life is freer, wickeder, bolder here than anywhere else. Crowds, the rapid pace, and the everlasting struggle, whether for supremacy or mere existence, seem to create a different sort of being from those who amble through life in a smaller town. For the outlander, there is always the thrill of excitement in the very atmosphere of the colossus.

The titillated tourist stood with an obdurate upper class. In the establishment, the bland led the bland. Politicians and the police profited by vice; the clergy, except for a few excitable redoubts, dwelled on higher matters.

A lower matter frequently assailed by the clergy was the growing influence of the newspaper, which had gradually assumed the powers of the pulpit in the nineteenth century.

Wiser heads had predicted this might happen. Johann Gutenberg no sooner had invented movable type in the fifteenth century than authority moved to control it, by licensing and censorship. The first newspaper published in the English language went to press, not in England where the Crown regulated printing, but in Holland, where religious dissenters produced a newssheet in December, 1620, the month and the year the Pilgrims landed at Plymouth.

Fifty years later Sir William Berkeley, governor of Virginia, expressed authority's fear at the very idea of an unlicensed press. He wrote a famous letter to the home office:

"But, I thank God, we have not free schools nor printing, and I hope we shall not these hundred years. For learning has brought disobedience and heresy and sects into the world, and printing has divulged them and libels against the government. God keep us from both."

Providence, inscrutable as always, nodded. The American press was established in the same painful and romantic manner as the emerging nation itself. Before the appearance of newspapers, newsletters from abroad and from important towns like Boston and Philadelphia informed a minority of the literate. They were written by men of affairs or professional letter-writers. Ballads based on news events encouraged a deplorable tendency toward folk music.

A Boston hustler named Benjamin Harris published the first colonial newspaper, *Publick Occurences, Both Foreign and Domestick,* on September 25, 1690, to be "furnished once a moneth (or if any Glut of Occurences happen, oftener.)" The first issue, of three pages, combined that mixture of piety and human interest which would characterize much of the nation's press.

There was an item that "Christianized Indians in some parts of Plimouth, have newly appointed a day of Thanksgiving. . . . Their example may be worth Mentioning." The human side of the news was represented by "A very Tragical Accident," an old man who hanged himself after the death of his wife, whose "discretion and industry had long been the support of his Family."

This modest beginning was too much for authority, which four days after *Publick Occurences'* publication suppressed the paper as containing "Reflections of a very high nature: As also sundry doubtful and uncertain Reports."

34

It was fourteen years before the first continuously published American newspaper appeared, the *Boston News-Letter,* on April 24, 1704. By 1735 there were five newspapers in the colonies' largest community. Newspapers appeared in Philadelphia in 1719, and in New York six years later.

New York, of course, was the scene of the colonies' first great press challenge to authority. John Peter Zenger, publisher of the New York *Weekly-Journal,* which he founded in 1733, repeatedly zapped the autocratic royal governor and his faction. Claiming "seditious Libels" which "with the utmost Virulency have endeavored to asperse his Excellency and villify his Administration," the authorities clapped Zenger in jail, from where he continued to edit the paper.

After a trial which echoed through the colonies and England, and before a courtroom packed with the "common people" he wooed, Zenger was acquitted. Scoundrels and patriots ever since have cited the principles established in that little court, "the admissibility of evidence as to the truth of an alleged libel, and the right of a jury to determine whether publication is defamatory or seditious."

The revolutionary war fed a disputatious mood in the press which battened with the emergence of political parties. The newspapers which previously had been not much more than a printer's sideline now trumpeted the truths of Jefferson and Hamilton and mortal men.

They reflected a roistering and brash society that was feeling its oats. So personal and scurrilous were their partisan bleats that Frank Luther Mott, the newspaper historian, called the early nineteenth century "the Dark Age of American journalism." It was not a time of great editors.

From the beginning, newspapers gasped for editorial matter. Serial fiction and feature material turned up as early as the Revolution. Periodicals devoted to gossip anticipated Walter. In 1826 the New York *Hawk and Buzzard,* "edited by a nanni-pigeon," boasted, "Our gossip-birds shall keep a bright look-out/And show the world what folly is about."

But the *daily* newspapers aimed for middle-class respectability. Rich in mercantile and shipping news, they were sold to men of affairs by subscription. Single copies, when they were available, cost a Spanish real, worth six and a quarter cents and called a sixpence in New York where foreign currency was sound.

The idea of a cheap newspaper to be sold on the street was a novelty to just about everyone except the young Horace Greeley. No idea would ever be novel to Greeley. In 1833 he was involved with a short-lived paper that cost only a penny.

But on September 3 of that year, a printer named Benjamin H. Day established the *Sun* as a penny paper, and it embarked on a long, sometimes brilliant career. Borrowing from the London *Morning Herald,* the *Sun* made the police court a centerpiece of its reporting. The accounts are not quite gossip, being matters of record, but the remorseless listing of who misbehaved and where is part of the literary pedigree of Walter and his tribe:

> Margaret Thomas was drunk in the street—said she would never get drunk again "upon her honor." Committed "upon honor."
>
> William Luvoy got drunk because yesterday was so devilish warm. Drank 9 glasses of brandy and water and said he would be cursed if he wouldn't drink 9 more as quick as he could raise money to buy it with. He would like to know what right the magistrate had to interfere with his private affairs. Fined $1—forgot his pocketbook and was sent over to Bridewell.
>
> Bridget McMunn got drunk and threw a pitcher at Mr. Ellis, of 53 Ludlow St. Bridget said she was the mother of three little orphans—God bless their dear souls—and if she went to prison, they would choke to death for the want of something to eat. Committed.
>
> Catherine McBride was brought in for stealing a frock. . . .

The great day of New York journalism dawned in 1835, when James Gordon Bennett, then forty years old and with a capital of $500, founded a penny paper called the New York *Herald.* He all but invented what Americans think of as a newspaper. He was spicy and saucy, two of his favorite adjectives for his paper. He freed the daily press from prudery and subservience to political party. He was sensational, publishing detailed coverage of crime and sex scandals. He also reported Wall Street activities with a fierce independence and society news with skepticism.

Bennett sanctified sports events as the stuff of daily journalism, reporting the big fights, horse races, and ball games. In 1862 the *Herald* hired Henry Chadwick as a baseball writer, the first to appear outside the pages of a sporting publication. Chadwick invented the box score, reaping immortality as the only writer in baseball's Hall of Fame in Cooperstown, New York.

After Joseph Pulitzer bought the New York *World,* he established the first sports *department,* pointing the way to the proliferation of sports coverage, which hard thought may find difficult to justify as news.

There is a collateral line from Bennett's hiring of Henry Chadwick in the Civil War period to Damon's observation in 1927: "Increased circulation is the only return newspapers can hope to realize from the money and space they devote to sports. If a sports writer can't deliver circulation, he isn't worth a dime."

For the penny press, as Mott observed, "pandered to the masses by emphasizing the trivial and easily understood at the expense of the economically and socially significant." This established a tension which continues to trouble journalism: how to balance the editor's perception of what the reader needs with the perception of what the reader wants. The intelligence, intellectual curiosity, and sophistication of the reader are seldom overemphasized.

By Richard Harding Davis's time, the great newspapers of the city spoke for Fifth Avenue. Until recently, no newspaper had reached for the newly arrived masses. But the laborer had found his champion, and the discovery changed the course of American journalism.

The newspapers of the nineties were clustered around Park Row, also called Newspaper Row, "just a little street with only one side and no square corners," as Allen Churchill wrote, the western side being City Hall Park.

"Newspaper Row bounds the eastern side of the square with the workshops of the great dailies," Davis noted in the *Scribner's* article:

> They rise, one above the other, in the humorous hope that the public will believe the length of their subscription lists is in proportion to the heights of their towers. They are aggressively active and wide-awake in the silence of the night about them.
>
> The lights from hundreds of windows glow like furnaces, and the quick and impatient beating of the groaning presses sounds like the roar of the sea. "There she is—the great engine—she never sleeps. She has her ambassadors in every quarter of the world, her couriers on every road. Her officers march with every army, and her convoys enter into the statesman's cabinet!"

Even as Davis looked at it, Newspaper Row must have seemed a phantasmagoria, shimmering in the change of a city gathering steam. The *Sun,* which was under Dana's stewardship from 1868 to 1897, was the newspaper any reporter with literary pretensions aimed for, the first newspaper consulted in city rooms across the land.

The *Sun*'s city room was on the third floor of the shabby old Tammany Hall building. The first practical typewriter had been patented in 1868 by a Milwaukee *Sentinel* editor, but thirty years later, many reporters believed the contact of pencil to paper was needed for the finest effect, and the *Sun*'s reporters, most of them bearded, generally wrote longhand, their hats square on their heads against light-fingered visitors.

The spirit of camaraderie among *Sun* reporters was strong. Will Irwin wrote, "The organizaition with its peculiar democracy, its freedom and its good will of man to man is probably the most admirable thing about . . . the *Sun*." It was like a college, he said, with "the same respect for tradition, the same general good will, the same cohesion of effort and the same voluntary acceptance of a certain set of ideals."

"Life was not a mere procession of elections, legislatures, theatrical performances, murders, and lectures," a historian wrote of Dana. "Life was everything—a new kind of apple, a crying child on a curb, a policeman's epigram, the exact weight of a presidential candidate, the latest style in whiskers, the origin of a new slang expression, the idiosyncrasies of the City Hall clock, a new fourmaster in the harbor, a vendetta in Mulberry Bend. . . ."

In the decade before Davis's ruminations, in the 1880s, Newspaper Row offered an almost solid front, in spite of the papers' fulminations against one another. The *Tribune* was adjusting to life under Whitelaw Reid after the death of the irreplaceable Greeley on November 29, 1872; the erratic *Herald* wobbled as it bestrode the globe under a great publisher's son, James Gordon Bennett, Jr.; lapping at their heels and the *Sun*'s was a watery collation including Albert Pulitzer's *Journal*, "the chambermaid's delight"; the once-respected *Times*, "feeble and failing, dead from the neck down"; the intellectual *Evening Post* and such others as the *Star*, the *Mail & Express*, the *Commercial Advertiser*, and the *World*, which was published by Jay Gould, the financier.

All that changed in 1883 when a thirty-six-year-old hurricane named Joseph Pulitzer, Albert's older brother, blew into New York and bought the *World* from Gould, paying $346,000 "for a press franchise and a bad name." Pulitzer was a native of Hungary who came to the United States as a Union Army volunteer and journeyed to St. Louis at war's end, working as a reporter for a German-language newspaper and honing his English. He worked with the reformer Carl Schurz, who lectured him on social conscience, and he built the St. Louis *Post-Dispatch* from the merger of two struggling papers into a crusading, sensation-peddling journalistic monument, destroying his health in the process.

Pulitzer's *Post-Dispatch* prospered through enlightened editorials mixed with such stories as an interview with an unhappy hooker headlined A WELL-KNOWN CITIZEN STRICKEN DOWN IN THE ARMS OF HIS

MISTRESS. Pulitzer carried the formula in his head. The invaluable W. A. Swanberg, biographer of Pulitzer and Hearst, likened Pulitzer's editorial approach to the performance of a hula dancer before a cathedral, the dancer attracting the audience to the editorials.

Pulitzer served in the state legislature, shot and nearly killed a lobbyist and, when his editor shot and *did* kill a political foe in the *Post-Dispatch* office, found St. Louis confined quarters.

Pulitzer ostensibly was headed for a European vacation, with wife and children, when he bought the *World*. For all the ominous ownership of Gould, the sedate *World* was "the gentleman's newspaper of New York."

Pulitzer intended to shake things up. He saw that more than five million immigrants had entered the country since 1870, that the city had grown by half a million in a decade, and that masses of Jews, Germans, Irish, and Italians read no newspaper at all.

He assembled the *World*'s staff. "Heretofore you have all been living in the parlor and taking baths every day," he said. "Now I wish you to understand that, in the future, you will all be walking down the Bowery." Some staffers, the more fools they, resigned on the instant.

The new approach must have been a shock for the *World*'s fifteen thousand subscribers. One day they read a newspaper with headlines like AFFAIRS AT ALBANY, OUR CABLE LETTER, and BENCH SHOW OF DOGS. Pulitzer took over, and the next day the headlines read WARD MCCONKEY HANGED—SHOUTING FROM UNDER THE BLACK CAP THAT HIS EXECUTIONERS ARE MURDERERS; MARRIED AND TAKEN TO JAIL—A CEREMONY WHERE CONGRATULATIONS WERE RATHER TOO PREVIOUS; and A FORTUNE SQUANDERED IN DRINK.

The headlines rolled on—MADDENED BY MARRIAGE; GOING TO THE BOW-WOWS—while from the cathedral the editorial voice called for taxes on large incomes, inheritances, monopolies, and corporations, took up the cause of immigrants and union labor, assailed the robber barons with their "odor of codfish and the mustiness of age."

The *World* attacked Assemblyman Theodore Roosevelt, igniting a battle with fateful consequences, for opposing on the grounds that it was communistic a bill reducing the eighteen-hour day of horse-cab drivers. It reported infant mortality in the slums. It asked, "Does Fifth Avenue forget that it is flanked by the tenements of Eleventh Avenue and Avenue B, and outnumbered 1,000 to 1?"

Pulitzer's *World* picked up 6,000 readers in two weeks; in three months, the press run was 39,000, little of it coming from the other newspapers, although they kicked at him. He reached people who had never read newspapers, feeding them the simplest human interest stories. In fifteen months, circulation topped 111,000. "Workmen who could not spell his name," Swanberg wrote, "considered him the greatest of men."

One veteran of the previous regime returned from vacation. "It seemed as though a cyclone had entered the building," he said, recalling the lanky, bearded, bushy-haired man with the glinting pince-nez and beaked nose, Adam's apple bobbing. Pulitzer rushed about, crying, "Condense! Condense!" and "Accuracy! Accuracy." He demanded "provocative headlines, short sentences, violent verbs and tight writing."

Pulitzer paid a price for his success. His health was never restored. He was subject to violent headaches. And he was going blind. On the day before what should have been his greatest triumph, the opening in 1980 of the Pulitzer building with its golden dome, looking down on all the other Park Row newspapers and City Hall, he sailed for Europe, in bits and pieces.

But where there had been one inconsequential *World* eight years earlier, there was the authoritative *Morning World,* the sensational *Evening World,* and the simply stupendous *Sunday World.* A. J. Liebling wrote, "From their city room, the men of [the] *World* could look over and beyond the North River and out to sea, as well as at Brooklyn, across the only high bridge there was over the East River at the time. All Manhattan was visible at their feet, and it only accentuated their cockiness."

Not for long. Those who stayed shortly found themselves on war footing. Many men of the *World* went over to the enemy. A struggle for mass readership produced golden hours, a dark age, and a journalistic influence that persists.

For Hearst had come to town.

three

WILLIE, AS only his mother called him, was the definitive spoiled child, still spending her money when he came to New York at thirty-one.

He was born in San Francisco, April 29, 1863, the eve of the battle of Chancellorsville. He was the only child of a semiliterate, fabulously rich mine owner, George Hearst, forty-one, and a pretty former schoolteacher, Phoebe Apperson Hearst, nineteen. There was so much money coming from the Homestake Mine and Anaconda Copper that Willie could never quite spend it all in the course of a long and profligate life.

He was expelled from Harvard in 1885, his junior year, after majoring in the study of Pulitzer's *World*. He already had acquired a mistress, and he hastened his departure by sending his instructors chamber pots engraved with their names on the bottom.

He worked as a reporter for the *World* and then, in 1887, his father *gave* him the San Francisco *Examiner,* a struggling newspaper George Hearst had picked up to further the political career that sent him to the United States Senate, even as he allegedly demanded, "If b-u-r-d doesn't spell bird, what in hell does it spell?"

Willie, or W.R., or Mr. Hearst, as he soon came to be called, was something of a radical at twenty-four. He went after the interests, particularly the railroads. He won a reduction in water rates.

He also knew what he wanted. One day he circled the names of the principal American cities on a map, with a double circle around New York. "George," he told an aide, "some day, a paper here and here and here."

In San Francisco, he immediately applied the *World's* formula to the *Examiner's* front page, a sensation a day, relying on creative thinking if no sensation occurred. Amid murders, fires—"leaping higher, higher, higher, with desperate desire"—and other calamities, the *Examiner* gave over much of the front page for the Kaiser's ninetieth birthday celebration under a big headline: HOCH! HOCH!

Examiner reporters escorted Sarah Bernhardt on a tour of China-

41

town, including a visit to an opium den. *"C'est magnifique,"* exclaimed the Divine Sarah, *"Il rêve."* Posing as a lunatic, an *Examiner* reporter spent a week in a state asylum, which he found suitably horrid. A girl reporter pretended to collapse in the street, denouncing the city's rescue system when assistance was tardy. Readers were wrenched by a tearjerker about an orphaned newsboy, McGinty, sole support of his younger brothers, none of whom, alas, existed.

"Examiner young men go up in balloons," a rival commented. *"Examiner* young men jump off ferryboats to test the crews. . . . *Examiner* young men swim to save fishermen marooned on rocks."

"What we're after," said a Hearst editor, "is the gee-whiz emotion." Swanberg notes that this appraisal was too modest. "Any issue that did not cause the reader to rise out of his chair and cry 'Great God!' was considered a failure."

Hearst was a giant who became an ogre. Sensational in San Francisco, outrageous in New York, he became a bore when he hollered through the megaphone of thirty newspapers, so that it is easy to forget that he must have been exciting to work for in his younger days, paying top dollar, belting the interests, an energetic, enthusiastic man, more than six feet tall, with piercing blue eyes and a voice, said Ambrose Bierce, "like the fragrance of violets made audible."

"In the strict sense," Swanberg notes, "the Hearst papers were not even newspapers at all. They were printed entertainment and excitement—the equivalent of bombs exploding, bands blaring, firecrackers popping, victims screaming, flags waving, cannons roaring, houris dancing and smoke rising from the singed flesh of executed criminals."

The *Examiner* was talked about but was just turning the corner financially when Hearst invaded New York. He wasn't concerned about money. George Hearst had died, leaving his wife $18 million, but the figure was deceptively low, since most of it was in mines and real estate, which kept giving promiscuously. After some nudging, Phoebe Hearst presented her son with $7.5 million, to see how that would do in Big Town.

Hearst was seeking power, for he anticipated Frank E. Gannett and Henry R. Luce in the touching faith that any American publisher can grow up to be president. He never came close and settled down to become kingmaker, although when that happened in the fourth decade of the twentieth century, it only proved the puissance of the Chinese curse: May all your dreams come true.

After looking over the *Times* and other properties, Hearst settled on the *Journal*. Not even New York had been big enough for two

Pulitzers. The brothers quarreled violently, and in 1894 Albert sold his chambermaid's delight to a Cincinnati publisher who made the paper respectable, losing its audience. The circulation was 77,000 when Hearst bought it at the end of the year for $180,000.

The *Journal* lacked an Associated Press franchise, which put it at a serious disadvantage in coverage of national and international news. Many of those stories were cribbed from its hated rival, giving rise to a city-room couplet: "Sound the cymbal! Beat the drum!/ The *World* is here! The news has come!"

Hearst's ambition was to beat every newspaper in the city. Big stories sent the entire staff, dubbed "the Wrecking Crew" by Park Row bystanders, rushing from the building. Staffers commanded hansoms and bicycles to charge to the scene of adventure, small boys and barking dogs in their wake. Pulitzer tried to compete, but if he sent five reporters, Hearst countered with ten. If another story broke during the exodus, the man left to cover the city room went to neighboring bars and park benches to commandeer a free-lance staff. Stephen Crane and Theodore Dreiser picked up work that way.

They were all children at the circus. An editor, noting unwonted calm in the city room, cried, "Get excited, everybody!" Motion, copy paper flying, typewriters busy, reporters hollering. When things went well, Hearst inspired the staff with his enthusiasm, which he sometimes demonstrated in strange ways.

"Hearst suddenly spread the proofs in precise order on the floor," an employe recalled, "and began a sort of tap dance around and between them . . . with lively castanet accompaniments produced by his snapping fingers." Even when he was older, employes remembered Hearst spreading the papers on the floor and turning the pages thoughtfully, with somewhat prehensile toes.

With his seven million-plus dollars, Hearst was determined to drive Pulitzer to the wall. He didn't know this man, but there is no question that he damaged Pulitzer. He demonstrated early that he was willing to spend money without scruple, altering the old saw to read, "If you can't lick 'em, get 'em to join you."

Hearst's first target, the *Sunday World,* had a circulation of more than 450,000 and advertising revenues about equal to those of the parent newspapers. Its magazine was edited by a Dartmouth man named Morrill Goddard, who had established himself as an imaginative reporter by interviewing James G. Blaine, the presidential candidate, then hustling to the kitchen to interview Blaine's servants. Goddard was a student of human psychology and his studies led to the first comic strip, "The Yellow Kid," about the adventures of a bald, snaggle-toothed slum urchin.

"Are Sea Serpents Real?" the *Sunday World* magazine asked. "Cutting a Hole in a Man's Chest to Look at His Intestines and Leaving a Flap That Works as if on a Hinge." "Science Can Wash Your Heart." "How It Feels to Be a Murderer." "Eight Stage Beauties." The great masses responded to Goddard's mixture of pseudoscience, crime, and sex. So did Hearst.

What finally fetched Hearst, according to Swanberg, was Goddard's handling of a stag party tossed by Stanford White, the eminent architect and rakehell. Out of a huge pie in White's studio stepped a sixteen-year-old model, "covered," the *Sunday World* reported, "only by the ceiling."

Always covetous of treasure, Hearst hired away Pulitzer's entire Sunday staff. Pulitzer hired them back, but only for a day. Hearst opened the checkbook a little wider. Pulitzer was furious. He had raided other newspapers, seducing a reporter or two at a time, but he regarded Hearst's all-out assault as a kind of rape.

Viewing the war of headlines and checkbooks, including a struggle for "The Yellow Kid," a rival editor called it "yellow journalism." Pulitzer cringed; Hearst was delighted.

Hearst had taken the initiative, and Pulitzer found himself imitating his imitator. The *Journal* at a penny a copy lost money with every sale, but Hearst didn't mind. Pulitzer lowered his price to meet the challenge and lost advertising. "When I came to New York," he said later, "Mr. Bennett reduced the price of his paper and raised advertising rates—all to my advantage. When Mr. Hearst came to New York, I did the same. I wonder why?"

It's been observed that if Pulitzer courted the underdog, Hearst went after the *under*-underdog. To the unscrupulous politician, saber-rattling may be a vote-getter; to the unscrupulous editor, it may be a circulation-builder. Oswald Garrison Villard, the editor and critic, recalled "the devilish work done by the *World* and the Hearst press in bringing on the war with Spain. . . Mr. Pulitzer was willing to outdo Hearst in shameless and unwarranted sensationalism lest Hearst inflict on his papers irrevocable injury."

Theodore Roosevelt, who had reason to be grateful, called it "that splendid little war," and Hearst, at the front, would exhort a wounded correspondent, "I'm sorry you're hurt, but wasn't it a splendid fight? We must beat every paper in the world." But men died in the war; boys were killed.

The Spanish-American War approached, like most wars, with slow, stone strides. Cuban guerrillas, sniping at Spanish rule, apparently had no thought of winning their freedom, hoping instead to attract the United States to their cause. Hearst, like many other Americans, sympathized with the rebels and wanted to see Spain out of American waters. He also saw a chance to break Pulitzer over his hip.

The rebel leaders were artful propagandists. Hearst and Pulitzer printed without question their versions of rapes, suffering, hunger, infanticide, and other imaginative atrocities. The *Journal* elevated a beautiful young subversive into a "Cuban Joan of Arc"; it identified a Spanish general, blameless as generals go, into "Butcher Weyler." In a famous episode, Hearst sent the artist Frederic Remington to Cuba, and when Remington complained there was no action to illustrate, Hearst cabled, "You furnish the pictures. I'll furnish the war."

Spain temporized. President-elect McKinley, already under Hearst's fire as a creature of the trusts, suggested, "We want no wars of conquest. We must avoid any temptation of territorial expansion." The *Journal* called his words "vague and sapless." Congress equivocated. Opportunities for peace abounded. Hearst, Pulitzer following, would have none of it. Not for the first time, but seldom so foolishly, the *idea* of war became a kind of lust.

Petitions protesting the imprisonment of the Cuban Joan of Arc proliferated, flowing in from the women of America in their Volumnia mode. President McKinley's *mother,* General Grant's widow, Jefferson Davis's widow, Julia Ward Howe, the Sisters of Notre Dame, thousands of women demanded the girl's pardon. Just before Spain was able to oblige, a *Journal* reporter rescued her from not much security and hauled her to the United States, where she was jerked from one wretched triumph to another.

The *World* printed Buffalo Bill's boast that thirty thousand Indian fighters could chase Spain out of Cuba. The *Journal* proposed a regiment of athletes including heavyweight champions Bob Fitzsimmons and Jim Corbett, baseball's Pop Anson and wrestling's William Muldoon. "They would," claimed the *Journal,* "overawe any Spanish regiment by their mere appearance."

No fewer than forty American "war correspondents" languished in Cuba in January 1897 with no war to report. Davis sent well-written, inflammatory stories to the *Journal,* including a vivid account of three Cuban girls stripped and searched by the Spanish as suspected spies. In New York, Hearst editors rewrote the story to have the searching done by male detectives while the humiliated girls cowered. The *World* crowed when that version was exposed as a fake. Characteristically, Hearst was unperturbed.

The *World* regarded the arrest of one of its correspondents for obtaining a false police pass as an insult to the flag; the mysterious death of a Cuban dentist who was an American citizen was seen by the *Journal* as an even greater insult to the flag.

45

The battleship *Maine,* apparently by accident, blew up in Havana harbor on February 15, 1898. The Spanish general who had succeeded Weyler burst into tears when he heard the news. "Please spread the story all over the front page," Hearst ordered. "This means war."

The *Journal* thoughtfully reported the views of mothers of the dead sailors. "How would President McKinley feel, I wonder," one of them was made to say, "if he had a son on the *Maine* murdered as was my little boy? Would he then forget the crime and let it go unpunished while the body of his child was lying as food for the sharks in the Spanish harbor of Havana?"

Hearst and Pulitzer did not stoop alone, of course. The *Sun* joined them. Four-inch headlines pushed relentlessly for WAR WAR WAR. Hearst, Pulitzer, and the *Sun* built a joint circulation of 1,650,000, and the wires spread much of their fiction nationwide. The *Herald,* the *Evening Post,* the *Tribune,* and the *Times* were voices of moderation, but, dwarfed by numbers, they were like a professor in a barroom brawl, attempting to stop the fight with intellectual arguments while the bottles and fists fly.

The *Evening Post* expostulated, "No one—absolutely no one—supposes a yellow journal cares five cents about the Cubans, the *Maine* victims or anyone else. A yellow journal is probably the nearest approach to hell existing in any Christian state."

Johnny got his gun, in this case, on April 19, 1898. The atmosphere of carnival persisted. Pulitzer furnished correspondents by cutter; Hearst by yacht. For a couple of particularly tasteless days, the *Journal* carried an ear reading, "How do you like the *Journal*'s war?" The *Journal* recorded the death of Colonel Reflipe W. Thenuz, an Austrian artillerist. The *World* picked up the story the next day. The *Journal* joyfully pointed out that, carefully rearranged, the letters in the colonel's name suggested, "We pilfer the news."

In the week after the *Maine* explosion, the *World* had sold five million copies, which it called "the largest circulation of any newspaper printed in any language in any country." For a time, both the *World* and the *Journal* saw their circulations soar.

But cautionary tales of the kind often overlooked by newsmen emerged from the Spanish-American War. While Pulitzer and Hearst tossed dollars around as carelessly as facts, the *Herald* made do with the restrained and accurate reporting of Richard Harding Davis, who had abandoned Hearst for distorting his dispatches. The *Herald* enjoyed a new vigor and gained a new respect.

The *Times* had been purchased in 1896 by a young publisher from Chattanooga named Adolph Ochs. Lacking the resources of Hearst and Pulitzer, he relied on Associated Press dispatches from Cuba and concentrated on local news coverage and cultural matters. He cleaned up the typography and cloaked the product in respectability. The establishment purred. In two years, circulation climbed from 25,726 to 76,260. It was a lesson Ochs seemed never to forget. He would be called a merchant of news, both as praise and pejorative, but the *Times* seldom clowned around.

The Spanish-American War proved no path to glory for either the *World* or the *Journal,* ending for both on a dying note. Hearst's correspondents were banned for their hijinks by the United States Army, and Hearst suffered the ignominy of being repeatedly scooped on his own big show.

When Stephen Crane wrote for the *World* that the 71st New York Volunteers had performed less than valiantly at San Juan, Pulitzer reeled under charges he defamed the courage of our brave boys and abashedly set up a subscription to a memorial for them.

So Hearst and Pulitzer, two giants like knights exhausted as much by the weight of their armor as by the combat, sued for peace about the same time Spain did.

Pulitzer even ordered the four-inch headline type melted down. The order didn't last long. When he saw the *Journal*'s continued success with the billboard, he allowed the type restored in the *Evening* and *Sunday World,* which he regarded only as moneymakers anyway.

Both the *Journal* and the *World* remained nominally Democratic, crusading, and sensational. But the *Journal* fed Hearst's political ambitions. It was shrill and vindictive. The *World* spoke through what Swanberg calls "the nation's most carefully edited editorial page." The *Journal* was a broadsword. The *World* was a rapier.

Pulitzer was now blind. His nerves were tortured by extraneous sound, from the scrape of a knife on a plate to the beat of a horse's hoof. He sailed the seas and searched the health spas of Europe for a peace he never found.

Not long before his death, Pulitzer commented, "As Mary Stuart said about her heart being left in France as she sailed for Scotland, my heart was and still is in the editorial page." This was not rhetoric. The Pulitzer papers still trumpeted and, rebounding from the fiasco of the war, triggered in 1905 a state investigation into the scandalous mismanagement of New York's great insurance companies. It was, said one commentator, "a master stroke of public service."

Hearst was a weather vane. "Thus," Villard wrote in 1926, "true leadership cannot be his. Indubitably he has fought . . . many a good battle—no one can advocate so many things over a long period of years as he has and not be right sometimes . . . but it is all tarnished by self-interest, by self-seeking and arouses the never-failing and justified suspicion of his sincerity."

The war experience taught Hearst nothing about excess. One of his stunts literally backfired. He rented Madison Square Garden in 1902 for a Democratic party victory celebration. A nine-inch fireworks bomb exploded, touching off others. Eighteen persons died in a hail of shattered glass, some one hundred persons were injured, and the lawsuits dogged Hearst for decades.

He was dogged by worse. The end of the war with Spain had brought no truce with President McKinley. Hearst cartoons were vicious. A Hearst editorial called McKinley "the most hated creature on the American continent." Another editorial suggested, "If bad institutions and bad men can only be got rid of by killing, then killing must be done." Hearst stopped the presses and removed the line, but he did nothing about Ambrose Bierce, who marked the assassination of Governor-elect William Goebel of Kentucky with a quatrain the *Journal* published February 4, 1900:

> The bullet that pierced Goebel's breast
> Cannot be found in all the West;
> Good reason; it is speeding here
> To stretch McKinley on his bier.

Bierce later explained that he meant the verse as a warning that the President needed better protection; a likely story. When McKinley was shot on September 5, 1901, Hearst told an editor, "Things are going to be very bad," and they were. Rival newspapers savaged him. Hearst newspapers were seized by angry crowds and burned. He was hanged in effigy.

He may have become "the most hated creature on the American continent." His reputation never fully recovered from the judgment of the muckraker Lincoln Steffens: "To give us better government, he would make us a worse people."

Hearst and Pulitzer represented the end of the line of New York's outsize publishers—Greeley of the *Tribune*, Dana of the *Sun*, and the elder James Gordon Bennett. The journalism of Pulitzer and Hearst anointed the reporters with a new celebrity. Urban journalism assumed the role of town gossip. From the international scoop to the homely local feature, the reporter became part of the story, a not unmixed blessing.

Irvin S. Cobb, who came from Paducah, Kentucky, in 1903 to write for the *World,* observed, "The time of the great editor had waned and faded; the time of the great reporter succeeded it." It was Hearst, not Pulitzer, who scattered his newspaper with bylines, but Pulitzer, from the days he made his staff the best paid in St. Louis, recognized the importance of the reporter. "Every reporter is a hope," he said, "every editor is a disappointment."

Cobb went on to fame as a short-story writer and entertainer, but almost half a century later, Damon recalled Cobb as one of the great reporters, a master of the rococo. Cobb wrote 600,000 words about the first Trial of the Century, that of Harry K. Thaw for murdering Stanford White, "enough to make eight novels." He never forgot Evelyn Nesbit, the former Florodora girl who was no better than she should have been but who ignited Thaw's jealous rage with "a head that sat on her flawless throat as a lily on its stem; eyes that were the color of blue-brown pansies and the size of half dollars, a mouth made of rumpled rose petals."

There were others, of course, who by their flair ended the reporter's traditional anonymity. Frank Ward O'Malley, a brilliant feature writer for the *Sun,* was credited with coining the word "brunch" for the morning newspaperman's first meal of the day and with coining, too, the sentence "Life is just one damned thing after another."

The columnist Franklin P. Adams eulogized Lindsay Denison of the *Sun* and the *Evening World:* "He, more than any other reporter I ever heard of, was considered New York's best reporter."

The elegant young David Graham Phillips, one of Pulitzer's chosen, scooped the British press with a spectacularly resourceful account of the sinking of the battleship *Victoria* and, before quitting journalism to write fiction, proclaimed, "I would rather be a reporter than president."

Will Irwin of the *Sun,* for eight days with only fragmentary reports, relied chiefly on his prodigious memory to write "the city that was," an account of the earthquake that leveled San Francisco, "the gayest, lightest-hearted, most pleasure-loving city of this continent."

Herbert Bayard Swope of the *World* almost single-handedly cracked the Rosenthal murder in 1911, sending police lieutenant Charles Becker to the electric chair, District Attorney Charles Whitman to the governor's mansion, and introducing a gaping public to the prototypical hit men Gyp the Blood, Whitey Lewis, and Lefty Louie. Swope's later fame as editor and windbag enabled some to forget that he received the first Pulitzer prize for reporting and was ranked by the British press tycoon Lord Northcliffe "the greatest reporter in the world."

Julian Ralph, whose account of General Grant's funeral for the *Sun* ran fourteen thousand words, described the wedding of Consuelo

Vanderbilt and the Duke of Marlborough for more than three tightly packed pages of the *Journal* as "a story so intimate it might have been the bride's diary."

The goateed globe-trotter James Creelman of the *World* and the *Journal,* whose account of Japanese atrocities at Port Arthur swung American opinion about the Russo-Japanese war, also interviewed Count Leo Tolstoy and Sitting Bull.

As a twenty-year-old free lance for the *Herald,* Stephen Crane, stubborn and sure of his destiny, "could not report. Apparently he did not want to report," according to Thomas Beer. Crane preferred to describe the scene, not the fire, and the sordid stuff of urban life unimpeded by names, addresses, numbers, although the brightness of those New York City sketches for various newspapers endures. He won, so to speak, his own red badge of courage in Cuba, capturing a village single-handed, throwing a celebration after dividing the populace into "good fellows" and "bad fellows."

He rode up San Juan Hill with Teddy Roosevelt. He captured, too, war's dominant force in reporting the death of Surgeon Gibbs: "Every warm vibration of his anguish beat upon my senses. He was long past groaning. There was only the bitter strife for air which pushed out into the night in a clear, penetrating whistle with intervals of terrible silence in which I held my own breath in the common unconscious aspiration to help. I thought this man would never die. I wanted him to die. Ultimately he died."

And, of course, there was Richard Harding Davis, without whose presence no war was official. He noted that as the *New York* bombarded Spanish shore batteries in Cuba, the ship's orchestra played Wagner—the Prize Song from *Meistersinger*—and the effect was "like watching the burning of the Waldorf-Astoria from the Brooklyn bridge."

Ned Brown, who abandoned medical studies after solving a splashy murder for the *Journal,* and later became a boxing writer for the *World,* looked back on the era: "Being a newspaper reporter gave you stature then. . . . A first-string reporter on any recognized paper had a lot of prestige. *Civis Romanus est.* He was a citizen of no mean state." The reporter at century's turn became a byline. He would become a columnist and, in the time of Damon and Walter, a celebrity, the newsman as star.

The state lost more than another citizen when Pulitzer died in 1911. His name, like Nobel's, is forever associated with a famous prize, but the money came from a different explosive, compounded of sensationalism and a democratic ardor.

The first quality is easy to imitate: A few million dollars and access to a printing press, microphone, or television camera and you are in business, free to shock and scandalize. Pulitzer and Hearst polished Bennett's concept that a newspaper "should not instruct but startle."

But Pulitzer represented a crucial distinction. People cared about the *World*'s opinion. The *World* elected presidents, governors, mayors. Pulitzer's tax proposals, deemed radical in the 1880s, passed into law. Swanberg asks, "Who could tell how many thousands, how many millions had joined the largest of all classes—learned their political lore from this page appearing 365 times a year in the 27 years since the professor had opened his New York academy?"

And almost with his dying breath, Pulitzer took on the president of the United States and whipped him.

WHO GOT THE MONEY? the *World* asked, charging that the federal government paid $40 million for the Panama Canal, and $10 million for the newly created Panama republic, not to the French government but to J.P. Morgan and Company. The *World* asserted that President Theodore Roosevelt, to protect members of his administration, lied repeatedly about the financing of the canal.

On his last day in office, Roosevelt instructed lawyers to seek a federal indictment of the *World* for criminal libel under a remarkable interpretation of an 1825 statute. The government argued the newspaper could be prosecuted on each of 2,809 federal reservations in the United States. The suit was clearly designed to ruin Pulitzer. A similar suit against the Indianapolis *News* already had been dismissed, drawing from Roosevelt, whose strong suit was never maturity, the verdict that the judge was "a jackass and a crook."

Roosevelt, bounding off to Africa full of vigor to kill animals, clearly wanted the ailing Pulitzer jailed. The *World* answered him: "Mr. Roosevelt is mistaken. He cannot muzzle the *World*."

Pulitzer decided to challenge the government's jurisdiction rather than fight the charges. If the *World* lost its case, Swanberg commented, "the privilege of the press to criticize public officials would virtually have been abolished."

The *World* did not lose. It is probable no other publisher and no other newspaper would have undertaken the long and costly fight, but the newspaper was vindicated on every count. The *World* called the unanimous Supreme Court decision "the most sweeping victory won for freedom of speech and of the press since the American people destroyed the Federalist party more than a century ago for enacting the infamous Sedition law. . . ."

That was the shining face of what Silas Bent called the gargoyle journalism ushered in by the Spanish-American War and urbanization.

The leering saffron face of that journalism was addressed by an unusual woman, the mother of Richard Harding Davis.

Not the least of Davis's accomplishments was that he outshone remarkable parents, rather than shriveling in their shadow. Clarke Davis was called "the premier in American journalism as editor of the Philadelphia *Public Ledger.*" Rebecca Harding Davis wrote stark, realistic fiction in 1861, six years before Zola published his first novel.

She continued writing long after her son's fame eclipsed her own. In 1902 she looked at yellow journalism for *Independent* magazine, asking "What Does It Mean?" She examined press coverage of the death of a young girl at the hands of a burglar. The lives of the girl's family, Mrs. Davis wrote, "were held up to the greedy curiosity of the whole nation; we were told how they dressed, how they ate, how they prayed. The old mother was forced to describe for us again and again her child's death."

Mrs. Davis asked, "Can it be that the American appetite demands such food?" The question, of course, has been answered no more fully than "Who Got the Money?" Mrs. Davis's belief was that yellow journalism and cheap fiction created the appetite.

There was an almost immediate retort from Arthur Brisbane, a Hearst editor who had come over from Pulitzer. "I am the yellowest journalist in the world," he said. "If not, I wish to be. . . . The papers pander to a depraved appetite because the people demand it. They do not, however, create this appetite, and when there is an improvement in the people, it will be accompanied by an improvement in the papers, because the newspaper will always be on the watch for such a change."

The issue did not trouble the sleep of eleven-year-old Walter Winchell, who hawked the yellow journals on the streets of Harlem for two dollars a week.

And for one newcomer to the city the year after Joseph Pulitzer died, the changes rung by the journalistic wars were helpful. It is impossible to imagine him in the stately, pipe-smoking city room atmosphere of the old *Sun,* but Alfred Damon Runyon soon would be right at home with Hearst.

four

HE WAS thirty years old when he arrived in New York, a newspaperman, versifier, writer of magazine articles and fiction, Spanish-American War veteran, and, until recently, a drunk.

New York had sent him no summons. He was talented, ambitious, and hopeful, and so he obeyed a law of American journalism: Go East.

His stock was as American as a white man can claim. He was descended from pre-revolutionary war settlers on both sides, as Edwin P. Hoyt notes in his sympathetic biography *A Gentleman of Broadway*. Seven Renoyan brothers, French Huguenots, settled in Pennsylvania and New Jersey shortly before the War of Independence. William Renoyan, a journeyman printer born in New Jersey, headed for California in 1852, a national imperative, with a group of eighty families. They boarded a steamer in Cincinnati, ran aground at the Blue River in Kansas, decided the hell with it, and built a settlement they called Manhattan.

William Renoyan worked as a printer and farmer. He had changed the spelling of his last name to "Runyan" by the time his son, Alfred Lee, was born in 1851. Alfred Lee became office boy for the Manhattan *Independent,* then enlisted in the 19th Kansas Volunteer Cavalry to fight the Indians, serving six months under a showboat commander named George Armstrong Custer, whom he despised.

He called him "Custar," according to Ed Weiner in *The Damon Runyon Story*. Custar, said Alfred Lee, "may gain a name for making long marches in short periods, but he wears out men and animals in doing so. He has few friends among the privates of the 7th and 19th."

With Custer, Alfred Lee took part in the battle of Washita River, which qualified him as an Indian fighter, a subject of his barroom oratory the rest of his life. He was mustered out at the end of a six months' enlistment.

In 1876 he married Libbie J. Damon, a descendant of John White, who landed in Massachusetts Bay in 1638. Their son, Alfred Damon, was born on October 8, 1890. (The men in the Runyon narrative are Alfred Lee, Alfred Damon, and Damien, or Damon, Jr. Like much else

53

in Damon's story, the nomenclature is easily tangled, and for purposes of clarity, the men will be called Alfred Lee, Damon, and Damon Jr.) Three daughters followed Damon's birth.

Alfred Lee was a short and short-fused redhead. He became editor and manager of the Manhattan *Enterprise*. His temper, however, broke up two partnerships, and he was sole proprietor when he sold the newspaper with a parting shot: "I haven't gone broke to make the paper the best in the state, and have not gotten rich by cheating its patrons of a reasonable return for their money."

He failed with two newspapers in Clay City and one in Wellington, the last scuppered by a libel suit. Libbie's health was precarious; she suffered from diphtheria and tuberculosis. On medical advice, Alfred Lee moved his family to the high, dry ground of Pueblo, Colorado, in 1837, when he became a printer on the *Chieftain*. Libbie was homesick and took her daughters back to visit relatives in Kansas. She returned, alone, to Pueblo and died.

Al, as his father called Alfred Damon, was thus free to grow up on the streets, quite literally a motherless child; he remained in a sense very much a street kid all his life, a loner. His father was no family man, preferring the camaraderie of the barroom. They shared a bed in a boardinghouse for a time, the son taking over the night shift, the father sleeping in the day after his work on the morning newspaper.

Alfred Lee Runyan drank too much, a family failing. Financial pressures pushed father and son to a shack in a district called Pepper Sauce Bottoms. The fine, open spaces for Damon, fishing in the river, the tattered child left to his own devices—it was like Huckleberry Finn, only worse.

Damon hated school. In Montaigne's phrase, he "just nibbled the outer crust of learning." He was a hell-raiser and hookey-player, leader of a street gang. On a dare, he sauntered into the street near his father's newspaper and lit up a cigarette. He was nine years old. It would be six years before bartenders knew him well enough to take down his brand of whiskey as he marched into the saloon.

His father was a character out of a frontier Dickens, a big talker with a foot on the rail of the Arkansas Saloon, full of tales about Indian fighting and the relatively new pastime of baseball. Damon crept in to be with the old man, a dusty kid who thus picked up early the habit of listening in saloons.

Alfred Lee also fed Damon odd scraps of classical poetry and the names of the great figures of literature. It seemed part of the tramp printer's equipment in the nineteenth century.

What Damon learned on the streets and in the saloon was at least as much a part of his educational luggage as what he was taught formally before being kicked out of the Hinsdale school in the fourth or the sixth grade. The last straw apparently was an intercepted note to a girl.

He would always have woman trouble, rooted perhaps in the kind of advice his father gave the ten-year-old Damon who was "composing a confession of sweet emotions to a beautiful girl of nine who went to the same school I did. 'Don't write,' my father said. 'Send word.'" Bum advice also was in the family tradition.

"The loss of a mother, and the lack of a real father at so early an age, made him wary of forming close relationships for fear of losing them. The man grew up silent, since there was never anyone in whom to confide his inner thoughts."

That sounds glib, but it is based on folk wisdom and it came, not from a literary psychologist, but from a *De Profundis* called *Father's Footsteps*, written by Damon's son. Without much other guidance, young Damon acquired a sense of expediency on the Pueblo streets which helped shape his character.

It came with the territory, as Daniel Boorstin noted in *The Americans*. "The distinctive disorders of the cattleman's West did not arise because people refused to live by the Ten Commandments or to obey the simple rules of justice," he wrote. "The new problem was not dishonesty but ambiguity. Many of the violent struggles of those days, explained far from the scene as a fight between 'Law' and 'lawlessness,' were, in fact, not that at all. On the scene, both the rights and wrongs seem divided."

Damon recalled asking his father, seeking the right and wrong of it, if idealism led Alfred Lee to fight the Indians.

"'No,' replied our old man. 'If he had ideals, he would have been fighting on the side of the Indians. What he fought for was $12 a month and cakes.'"

Damon often cadged *his* cakes at the homes of friends. How else was he to eat? He remembered sleeping so often on the pool tables of Mr. Baer's emporium that "the balls all ran down into pockets at certain ends from a break, a great advantage to the local sharks."

He ran errands for newspapermen, sometimes in Pueblo's red-light district, and then he began contributing to the paper, one version holding that his father published two stories Damon wrote when he was thirteen. Damon later recalled that his first *big* story was written for the *Evening Press,* an account of the lynching of a bandit, and he covered murders, holdups, and other frontier violence with neutrality, while sounding early the grace notes of the newsman's obligatory cynicism.

Damon was given a two-dollar raise when he referred to an enemy

55

of the newspaper as Judge Johnnyhmitchell, a reference which so pleased Damon's publisher that it went into the stylebook. He needed the money because he wanted to dress like a dude, emulating a Harvard man who worked on the newspaper. Damon wanted, according to Hoyt, "more clothes than he could wear in a week and so many pairs of shoes they would never look worn."

The money also went for whiskey to coax Damon out of his shyness. He was fifteen when he went to work for the *Press,* with a teenager's determination to be a man by emulating man's more lamentable habits, and in the dissolute atmosphere of mining town journalism and the saloon, a man bellied up to the bar, although Damon later conceded, "Liquor only gave me delusions of grandeur that got me into trouble. It never made me happy and bright and sparkling as it does some people. It made me dull and stupid and quarrelsome. It made me dreadfully ill afterwards."

But Damon already was demonstrating those qualities of industry, intelligence, and loyalty which characterized his career. About this time, a printer misspelled his last name. Damon liked the way it looked, and when his father said the name originally had been spelled with an "o," he became Alfred Damon Runyon.

He was a bona-fide reporter, just a few months shy of eighteen, when the Spanish-American War broke out. The patriotic flames so fervently fanned by Hearst and Pulitzer half a continent away burned brightly on the frontier, too, and by lying somewhat about his age, Damon enlisted in the 13th Minnesota Volunteers as a bugler, although the typewriter was his only musical instrument. Out of a common vanity, he later in life lied more about his age, creating a myth that he enlisted at fourteen and was the youngest soldier in the Spanish-American War.

On July 31, 1898, the 13th Minnesota Volunteers reached the Philippines. Two days later Manila fell to the Americans. The company was billeted in Sampoloc, the city's red-light district. The Spanish-American War ended in September but, as is often the case, the armstice did not bring universal peace. Insurgents were determined to establish a Philippine republic, and the Americans were hard pressed to put down the dream. Damon became a reporter for the soldier's newspaper, the *Manila Freedom,* and he wrote stories and verse for the *Soldier's Letter,* an illustrated magazine.

Like many servicemen, Damon re-created his war. He later told stories of being wounded, although there is no record of that, and of training Chinese troops near Peking, which simply was not true, and he wrote about the Battle of Manila as though he were a participant, although his regiment fought the battle before he arrived. Those were all the harmless stretchers which are part of many soldier's memories, just as the war fought by a man in his youth remains forever *his* war and is the lens through which he views others.

"Has no one a few minutes to spare for an old soldier's recital of another taking of the city of Manila?" Damon wrote plaintively after General MacArthur's troops wrested the city from the Japanese in 1945.

> We did not have nearly as many men, nor as many guns as Douglas MacArthur but, by grab and by gravy, we gave the people a blamed sight better show when we took the town.
> We had a band.
> Yes, sir, a band.
> Off to the left of the advancing line, right behind the skirmishers, it marched on Manila, one of the spare bandsmen lugging an American flag and another toting the regimental colors. . . .
> Yes, sir, and it played:
> When you hear those bells go ting-a-ling
> Oom-pah, oom-pah, oom-pah
>
> . . . there was something comfortable in the familiar strains that they sent floating across the muddy rice paddies on that misty morning 46 years ago:
>
> All join hands and sweetly we will sing,
> Oom-pah, oom-pah, oom-pah. . . .

> Ah yes, it was a little war, but it was such a brave little war, such a jaunty little war, with a handful of rank greenhorns 10,000 miles from a base, marching behind a band into a battle that was to take an empire.
> Occasionally, a man in the advancing line pitched forward on his face and lay quite still. The dead never know the size of their war. . . .

Not bad, for a man who wasn't there.

Much of the 13th Minnesota Volunteer activity involved horseplay, drinking, gambling, and girls, the customary release of the marginally involved.

"Her name was Anastacia Bailerino," Damon wrote about "as lovely a maiden as ever came down the pike." They were an item, Damon, Anastacia, her pet pig, Otis, and her pet python, Alexander. Damon claimed it was a romance until Otis vanished on one of the army's meatless days after the company cook's eye fell on the pig as it followed Damon back to camp. Anastacia then signaled the end of the affair by taking a shot at Al, "but I have always denied and I still do deny the story that in my hip pocket the sad day Otis attended me to camp, leaking at my every step, was a packet of corn."

Some of the soldiers married natives and settled down. Damon remembered an enlisted man called Baldy who was wounded in a battle with the insurgents and was nursed back to health by a "Filipino lady named Maria something." Romance bloomed, and they were married "with Maria's father in close attendance . . . with a bolo to see that [Baldy] did not back out at the last minute."

Maria's simple dowry included a water buffalo Baldy christened Theodore "after a well-known United States government executive of the period." Damon later affected regret he was not one of the soldiers who followed Baldy's "matrimonial example . . . especially when I learned that any work Maria was unable to handle was taken care of by Theodore the buffalo, and that all Baldy had to do was recline in the shade of a mango tree and eat mangoes. I always did like mangoes."

Disease was a bigger military problem than ordnance. Damon escaped "the No. 1 big terror, the black smallpox, and the reason I did not get that was because I had a mild form of smallpox back in my old home town of Pueblo and so was immunized. . . . So I did not have to run for cover, like the other fellows, when the mournful cart with the quicklime-laden coffin came through the Poco district of Manila en route to the cemetery with a Filipino runner out front, crying the nature of the load."

But Damon suffered damnably from a mysterious tropical ailment called the dobie itch "and holy Toledo, how it itched!" Army doctors had no concept of cause or cure "and anyway in those days when soldiers got anything the matter with them, the croakers had only two things to give them: salt and iodine."

Almost half a century later, Damon wanted to return to Manila "to see if they have repaired a certain stone corner of Bilibid prison . . . where I was on guard one night and which I wore down from a sharp projection to a mere nubbin, backing up to it and scratching the dobie itch between my shoulders."

The regular army relieved the volunteers, and Damon and his companions sailed home, an unwashed and restive troop that arrived in San Francisco after a month on the high seas, and after palely loitering in the Presidio for a month, Private Runyon received his honorable discharge October 3, 1899.

The military influence stayed with Damon all his days, contributing to his sympathy for the enlisted men of life long after he was rich, famous, and bitter. His son recalled Damon "going through the *Manual of Arms* with a shotgun, or saber drill using a cane or other suitable substitute, barking commands to himself."

Or Damon would stand ramrod straight in his New York apartment and recite his own "To the Colors":

It isn't on th' firing line you feel th' battle thrill,
An' it isn't dodgin' bullets wot you know are meant to kill:
An' it isn't when th' bandmen play some patriotic air
That you feel th' fever in yer blood an' wanter rip an' tear—
But let th' ole familiar break come in th' tune they play;
A silence for a moment an' you hear th' captain say:
"Port Arm" an' then th' air is split as though by shrapnel shell—
"To th' Colors" sing th' bugles an' it's then you wanter yell.

Hoyt notes that a clouded period followed Damon's discharge from the army. Damon himself was vague, almost amnesiac on the subject. Apparently he stayed in San Francisco long enough to get drunk and lose all his money. He seems to have returned to Colorado as a Knight of the Road, inaugurating a series of forays in hobo camps, learning something of the way of the hobo. It was a subject to which he often returned.

He befriended a 'bo called Kid Swift. "It was in one of these camps outside Provo, Utah, on what the 'boes called the bread and milk route that I saw a man crouched over a tin can in which something was brewing over a fire. He kept skimming the top of the substance in the can and afterwards Kid Swift told me that the fellow was boiling dynamite and skimming off the nitro with which he intended to blow a safe. Kid Swift said the fellow as a John Yegg, which meant a real tough hombre."

Jean Wagner, a professor at the University of Grenoble examined Damon in a monograph called *Runyonese: The Mind and Craft of Damon Runyon*. He wrote, "Perhaps it was an early sympathy with rebellion which . . . drove him into the hobo jungles out West." Wagner wondered "if there did not at heart exist some secret affinity between his own stray impulses toward rebellion and the spirit of those other rebels from the underworld. . . ."

And Damon, reviewing one of his own books, remarked, "I tell you, Runyon has subtlety but, it is the conviction of the reviewer that it is a great pity the guy did not remain a rebel out-and-out, even at the cost of a good position at the feed trough."

Not likely. Damon wanted that good position at the feed trough, no matter how romantic the idea of hoboing might be. He wanted success, and it was material: "a beautiful wardrobe," his son said, "and a woman to match."

The twenty-year-old Damon worked briefly for the *In-It Daily,* a newspaper named for the outdoor swimming pool in Glenwood Springs, Colorado, before returning to Pueblo and finding work on the *Chieftain.* There, in addition to his reportage, he contributed derivative verse. He was called "the Colorado Kipling":

> What do the horses' hoofses say
> Poundin' on the road?
> Raisin' a blanket o' dusty gray,
> Complainin' o' their load?
> Listen, an' hear 'em talk—
> Gallop or trot or walk,
> This is what the hoofses say
> Poundin' on the road:
> "A mile! A mile! A mile!
> Boot 'em along an' smile!
> The sabers clank to the plankety-plank—
> A mile! A mile! A mile!"

Or, writing about the Moro, the Philippine insurrectionist, Damon reflected the soldier's jaundiced view: "He may be a brother of Big Bill Taft, but he ain't no brother of mine":

> Oh, do not hurt the Moro, boys:
> He's Uncle Sammy's child;
> An' when you speak, be sure your tones
> Are soft an' low an' mild;
> Oh, do not mind his knife, my boys;
> He's just a little child;
> An' do not hurt th' Moro, boys—
> He's Uncle Sammy's child!

His rhymes achieved a certain popularity, the kind of verse damned as "poetry for men," turning up in military and prison publications for years, often as contributed by Anon. There was no chance Damon considered poetry as a career. There is no money in it.

Damon sometimes disappeared. He resumed, or continued, his

60

acquaintance with the hoboes: Cincy Skin, Peoria Shine, Cheyenne Red, Reading Blackie, and A No. 1, "the King of the 'Boes," who could board a train when it was moving thirty-five miles an hour.

Damon heard about a John Yegg who was brutalized by a shack, a railroad cop. The Yegg cooked up some nitro, poured it in a vial, and placed the vial in his hip pocket. He found the shack, taunted him, and ran from him along the top of a moving train. When the shack caught up, he delivered a mighty kick to the seat of the 'bo's pants. Up they went, the two of them, into the air, across the landscape, into atoms. A story with a satisfactorily ambiguous moral about the hobo who is the outsider versus the despotic representative of society.

Damon was drinking too much, and he wrote a haunted verse about that life:

> I'm roostin' here like a Shantyclear on a rod the size of a
>   match,
> With an open view on either side an' a box-car floor for a
>   thatch;
> An' I hope the shack don't find me, for me face is all he could
>   punch,
> As I'm beatin' my old friend Vanderbilt and eaten his ballast
>   for lunch.
> Oh, the ground slips by like a river,
> An' me nerves are all a-quiver—
> For I've bin out on a sort o' bat, an' the rail-points sing to
>   me:
> John Barleycorn! John Barleycorn!
> John Barleycorn! John Barleycorn!

Damon learned one night that his drinking was about to cost him his job. He called a friend on the Colorado Springs *Gazette,* who was in the same difficulty, and they agreed to exchange jobs. Damon moved to Colorado Springs. It was, curiously for the West of its day, a temperance town, which meant that Damon had to go to the trouble of visiting the back room of a drugstore to find liquor. He found it. His disappearances continued. At least once he had to be taken to the hospital for repairs.

The management tired of this, although Damon already was a good reporter and a good writer. He was encouraged to find a job with the St. Joseph, Missouri, *Gazette,* where his duties included a spell as sports editor, but Pueblo called, and two years after he left it, he was home.

He landed a job with the *Chieftain,* sold a poem to *Collier's* in 1904, and continued his hell-raising. A busybody called the mother of another reporter to say he'd been seen with Damon the previous night at Nellie White's in the red-light district.

"All right," said the mother. "How would you like it if I ask Chester to call on your daughter when he gets off work at two o'clock in the morning?"

The frontier edition of *Journalistic Ethics,* a fancy, of course, was a pretty short book, and few expected a reporter to preserve his objectivity by rejecting outside sources of income. The idea never caught on with Damon. He saw no reason to change, not even when he was a great man, from the kind of arrangement he worked out in Pueblo, where he supplemented his eighteen dollars a week by writing publicity for ball clubs, traveling shows, and businessmen.

His commitment to Pueblo proved casual, and he moved on to Trinidad, Colorado, working for the *Advertiser* and managing a semiprofessional baseball team. He seemed to be trudging along his father's path as a tramp newsman.

But for a reporter of energy and talent early in this century, there were only two newspaper towns in the West: San Francisco and Denver, and in 1905 Damon stepped into the center ring.

Denver was consumed by a circulation war matching the establishment *Rocky Mountain News,* owned by Thomas MacDonald Patterson, a millionaire senator, and the upstart Denver *Post,* owned and operated by an improbable pair, Frederick G. Bonfils, a West Pointer and Kansas City real estate man, and Harry H. Tammen, "the little Dutchman," a former bartender who owned a profitable curio shop.

Between them, they raised the *Post*'s circulation from a questionable six thousand when they bought it in 1895 to sixty thousand in 1905. They borrowed from the great preceptor of sensational journalism, the elder Bennett, who believed "no editor could break the mental and monied monopoly held by the old newspapers, except by adopting an extravagant style."

"Give 'em a show," Tammen cried. "Laughs, tears, wonder, thrills, tragedy, comedy, love and hate." The *Post* boasted red headlines and an unbelievable standing order that the front page each day contain no fewer than twenty-one stories, each headline in a different typeface. The *Post* provided scandal and relentless giveaways, promotions, stunts, and sideshows, including a circus it called Sells-Floto. The second name honored *Post* sports editor Otto Floto, because Tammen thought that was the most beautiful name he had ever heard. The *Post* was parochial. "A dog fight on Sixteenth Street," Bonfils said, "is a better story than a war in Timbuktu."

Damon joined the *Post* after a brief spell on the *Republican,* a third newspaper in the mix. He was in fast company. In addition to its other attractions, Denver was an asylum for hard-living newspapermen ordered to its mile-high climate as restorative.

The paper's slam-bang staff included the Honorable Lyulph Stanley Ogilvy, younger son of the Sixth Earl of Airlie. Lord Ogilvy, as he was called, was the paper's farm editor. He endeared himself to his peers by driving a pair of horses into the Windsor Hotel and breaking up a banquet by lassoing the toastmaster.

The life-style suited Damon, but he wasn't ready as a reporter. In a collection of his columns called *Short Takes,* Damon remembered that one day Josiah Ward, "the grand-daddy of all city editors," beckoned him to his desk, waving two-foot shears.

"'Come, come, Runyon,'" Ward said, speaking in the elaborate prose style Damon always substituted for formal speech. "'Kindly eliminate this aroma of new-mown hay, this note of good evening, neighbor. I have looked up your record and find you were a messenger boy in the red-light district of Pueblo most of your youth, and I fear you acquired a worldliness that unfits you for playing the joskin in the large city.'"

For one of those surveys of human nature favored by the proletarian press, Ward assigned Damon to offer passersby a ten-dollar gold piece for five dollars.

"I think Joe felt the people of Denver were too distrustful of each other for their own good," Damon wrote, "but strangely enough, the first fellow that came along bought my tenner. The incident might have revived Joe's faith in humanity had not the purchaser later been disclosed as a red-headed reporter pal of mine . . . and the eventual repository of the tenner Vaso Chuchovich's saloon on Larimer street."

In any event, the stunt is not the sort of assignment given a front-line reporter, and not long thereafter Damon was fired. It must have been a hard blow. This time he could not find solace in the disgrace of being fired for drinking. He was let go for incompetence rather than intemperance, and he fled the city.

But he was not about to return to the minor leagues. He set out for San Francisco, although he hedged his bet and bought a round-trip ticket. He landed a job with the San Francisco *Post.* He was upset, according to Hoyt, when he was told the newspaper wanted only a brief account of an apartment house fire he had covered, lots of smoke, flames, and heroics, and people routed from their beds.

"Maybe you have heard about a fire we had in San Francisco," he was told. "It takes a BIG fire to make a story around here."

Later, Damon repeated the old newspaperman's boast that he had never refused an assignment. But in San Francisco, when he was asked to go over to Oakland and pick up a story that an exhausted luminary had worked on through the night, he bridled.

"Not me," he said. "I follow no man's story."

The star was able to exact his revenge by blocking Damon's chance to become sports editor, and the same year Damon left Denver, he returned. He landed a job on the *Rocky Mountain News,* writing stories and verse, and in 1907 he published his first fiction, for $35 a story.

Because he knew the price of everything, and because the early fiction was not as polished as his later writing, Damon didn't think much of those efforts. But four decades later, John Lardner cited two of the stories, "Two Men Named Collins" and "The Informal Execution of Soupbone Pew," as "fresh and vigorous in a way that nothing he wrote afterwards is."

"Collins," which appeared in *Reader* magazine in September, deals with two soldiers bearing identical names. It is told by one of them, a disenchanted brute who kills his favored namesake for trying to desert. For reasons the narrator cannot articulate, he gives the dead man's parents a certificate of heroism he himself had won.

Apart from its quality as a page-turner, the story starts out in the present tense: "I know some things all right if I could think of them. These guys say I'm crazy—crazy in the head like a sheep, but I'm as happy as if I had good sense.

"I hear 'em talking in the barracks when they think I'm not around, and I know what they say . . ."

There is recurrent debate over Damon's use of the present tense. Gene Fowler claimed Damon got it from Arthur Brisbane, via *The Rime of the Ancient Mariner;* a recent biographer hears it as a kind of tape recording of the Broadway low-life Damon wrote about, but there he was using it at the dawn of his career, and for good reason: It is a traditional mode of speech for the underclass, the peacetime soldiers, the hoboes and criminals populating his fiction.

"The Informal Execution" is a chilling little story about some hobo's revenge on a sadistic shack. Along with "Fat Fallon," "As Between Friends," and "The Defense of Strikerville," the stories reflect what Lardner called Damon's "thorough first-hand knowledge of Army life and of hobo life."

The *News* paired Damon with a cartoonist named Frank Finch, called Doc Bird because he signed his art with the figure of a bird with an enormous beak, the kind of self-caricature often favored by cartoonists. Finch was undersized and even thinner than Damon, and they shared a gigantic thirst and otherwise hit it off. Doc Bird drew pictures, Damon supplied humorous commentary, and they worked up a popular chalk talk they took around to fairs and grand openings, to their gain and the glory of the *News*.

Gene Fowler, the newspaperman, author, Hollywood screenwriter, and Merry Andrew, was a teenage schoolboy when he met Damon on a visit to Colorado Springs. Young Fowler was suffering from poison oak, and he remembered Damon looking up from his beer long enough to advise him to eat poison oak each summer to build up an immunity. Damon might have been advising homeopathy, or perhaps it was that streak of cruelty which was part of his character, a big small-town joke.

"As Mr. Finch says," Damon wrote about their traveling show, "we pass this way but once, the people are always on the lookout after that to see we don't repeat."

"Under no circumstances does he get good-natured until noon," Doc Bird said of his friend. "He is a lovely traveling companion if he happens to be in the next coach. The only time he laughs is when someone mentions money. That always makes a big hit with Mr. Runyon."

Damon wrote of more than "Me and Mr. Finch," and what he wrote was in that indigenous booster spirit which transforms the cowtown into metropolis, routine events into press-stoppers, and every merchant into Maecenas. He would always be careful about his targets.

As mined by Edwin Hoyt, Damon's Denver journalism hints at the versatility which later made him, in Red Smith's phrase, "a good, all-around man for Hearst."

Damon wrote sports, covering a fight between a local and an easterner, "and for thirty minutes [they] engaged in a duel that was about the most rapid-fire occurrence which has been seen in Denver in some time"; reporting football: "Like a soft smoke, the dusk drifted across the field, and forms were taking on phantom shapes yesterday afternoon when the shrill note of the referee's whistle signaled taps for the greatest football battle ever fought in Colorado, and the Silver and Blue of the School of Mines shot upward, triumphant, with the Silver and Gold of Old Colorado trailing," and he wrote the requisite series about local businessmen who also were advertisers.

In a Christmas issue of *Lippincott's* magazine, Damon was represented by a poem, "The Spirit of You," allegedly based on a wartime memory, the death of an ornery soldier who clutched a locket:

> We laid him out there as he wanted—McSweal of the
>   Battery, dead.
> With a blanket of perfumed blossoms; and the guidon under
>   his head;

With the locket still clasped in his fingers—we gave him a
    volley or two,
And we left him there as he wanted—to talk with the Spirit
    of You.

Wiping away a manly tear, the author of those sentiments continued to be seen, quite often, in the company of low women. He was
called "the Demon" in the Denver Press Club, and it was not just a
play on his name. Periods of sobriety were followed by tumultuous
carousals, from which he would rouse himself, sick and shaken.

He recalled swallowing just in time a note from an amorous
waitress as a jealous switchman approached to search Damon for
evidence. "I do not now remember the full contents of the letter," he
wrote, "but I do recollect that it carried a touching postscript that
said, 'I shall love you forever and always, and I wish you would lend
me ten dollars as my room rent is due.'"

Damon's benders sometimes ended, in a journalistic tradition at
least as old as two sheets of paper in the typewriter, in some waitress's
bedroom or in a bordello, to which emissaries of the *News* were
dispatched to fetch him for the day's round of reporting the world
made new.

It was around this time that he met on assignment Ellen Egan, a
society reporter for the *News*. Her father, Damon's son wrote on a des-
cending scale, "was a railroad superintendent, a high and mighty position in those days when the snorting iron horse represented power in the
fast sprouting West. If he didn't rate society, he was just a cut beneath."

On any social scale, Ellen and her family were several cuts above
the likes of the alcoholic Damon. But women tend to improve men in
whom they are interested, and it was noticed that Ellen publicly
disapproved of Damon's drinking, to no immediate effect.

As a Christmas promotion, the newspaper announced that Santa
Claus and Doc Bird would participate in a motorized parade and
giveaway for Denver's children. Doc Bird was attired, Gene Fowler
recalled, "in baggy trousers with stripes three-quarters of an inch
wide, a red vest, a bright red tail-coat and a red stovepipe hat" above
his papier-mâché beak. Santa Claus wore an ill-fitting suit obviously
bolstered by a vagrant pillow. Santa was Damon.

It was an unusually temperate day, and both men had been
drinking heavily to ward off the warmth. Doc Bird hid a bottle inside
his giant beak, and when he felt the need of a booster, turned his head
to the sky "like a turkey in the rain," according to Fowler. Damon
recited one of his verses, about a Mexican whose sister was seduced by

a gambler, the chorus running, "What happened to my seester, meester?"

Well, Santa Claus fell asleep, midparade, and so did Doc Bird, and when the kiddies clambered aboard the shiny red vehicle for their presents, "Santa Claus began kicking and cursing," and *News* office workers hustled out to distribute the presents and to protect Santa and Doc Bird from parents favoring the law of Judge Lynch.

Newspaper publishers were not so touchy in those days, and the affair did not seem to count heavily against the two men. The *Post,* in fact, promptly hired Doc Bird away, for more money, and tried to lure Damon. He turned them down. The affable Doc Bird was able to drink more, with more money, and he died in a few years.

Damon found no similar spirit to replace Doc Bird. Irascibility surfaced. Other reporters respected him but steered clear of his dark moods. At a rodeo, he sent a photographer out for crowd shots, a variety of "types." A girl reporter thought that was a terrific idea. "Charlie," Damon scoffed, loudly enough for the photographer to hear, "wouldn't know a type if he saw one."

But Damon was very much the star, covering labor disputes, Frontier Day celebrations, murder trials, even the Democratic National Convention in Denver in 1908, which nominated the shopworn William Jennings Bryan for the third time.

Damon began paying court to "the gentle Ellen." It was not a course paved smooth. Damon's son wrote that a girlhood friend and Ellen "came upon [Damon] trying to thrash the dust from his clothes. . . . He'd just been tossed out of the city room. A binge had left him with battered face from some bout at the bar.

"He felt so badly at being seen in such a condition he didn't want to walk down the street with the girls. My mother wasn't one to let that bother her. They got on a horsecar together, but then my father wouldn't sit with her."

When sober, Damon called on Ellen at her home, "a chesty house on a so-called good street," according to Damon, Jr., "a sprawling box of many rooms set on a broad lawn where you could hit a baseball without breaking a window. . . .

"In summer nights, the neighbors sat under bold shade trees big enough to defy the sky. The elders rocked and fanned while the younger set played croquet. . . . When darkness moved in, they took to the drawing room for a big evening of singing around the family piano."

Sam the Gonoph and Benny South Street might have been as at home in that setting as their creator, but nevertheless, Damon

67

proposed. Ellen turned him down. Not so long as he drank, she said. *Men have died from time to time,* Rosalind observed, *and worms have eaten them, but not for love.* And, although it is romantic to think otherwise, the alcoholic does not quit drinking for love.

Damon and Ellen remained rather engaged to be engaged while he cemented his position as star reporter of the *News,* exposing land fraud, writing politics, writing sports, covering Billy Sunday, the reformed drunk and baseball player. Damon demonstrated early foot as a trial reporter, as in the case of a seer who bilked old women:

"'Money, money, money—all around and about you I see money; nothing but money; you should never work again,' is the clairvoyantly conjured picture presented to weary women, worn from endless labor, by Mrs. W. W. Wheeler to run their tiny hoard of money into her own pocket, if the extraordinary stories related in West Side Criminal Court yesterday by wet-eyed victims are true."

Old Denver hands insisted that Damon was storing up his Broadway characters even then, that Nicely-Nicely Johnson and Nathan Detroit were rooted in Denver's pool halls and cigarette stores.

Ah, the cigarettes. The boy who smoked publicly at nine was now a chain-smoker who claimed that sucking a troche kept his sensitive throat from tickling, even though he smoked from arising to bedtime.

His verse continued to attract a national audience. Clark Kinnaird, a Runyon authority, claimed, "No poet since Kipling was taken to heart by so many ordinary men." With "The Sky Marines," written for *Century* magazine in 1908, Damon joined Nostradamus, Tennyson, and Da Vinci as a prophet of air power:

> With a dynamite bomb in me hand
> A-sailin' the deep blue sky,
> You'll reckon with me on land or sea
> Sometime in the sweet bye and bye.

Damon was elected president of the Colorado State Baseball League at a bibulous meeting in Pueblo and was present shortly thereafter when it collapsed in a sea of red ink and red-eye in a saloon. By this time, Ellen had accepted him. Just as soon as he quit drinking.

One night she and a friend attended a band concert when she thought she saw Damon sitting up front with two women. She sent her friend to check. It was Damon, all right, drunk and with a couple of whores. He wobbled shamefaced back to Ellen.

"Go away," she said, "and take those two women with you."

He obeyed, but Hoyt says this time the night did not end before Damon's shrieks so alarmed a room clerk that he summoned a doctor. The doctor quieted Damon's delirium tremens, and the next day he told Damon that his heart could not stand another drinking bout.

Damon quit drinking.

Although he would spend much of the rest of his life in nightclubs and in sporting circles with people for whom drinking was the point of the game, the best evidence is that he never took another drink. He quit cold. It was an astonishing act of discipline.

Sometimes, asked about it, he tapped his chest and said, "Ticker." It may have been a tricky heart, the result of rheumatic fever or typhoid in childhood.

But the real reason was more likely the one he set down decades later in a letter to his son:

> I quit because I saw that I was not going to get anywhere in the world if I didn't, and I was determined to go places. I was sorely tempted many times, usually in moments of elation over some small triumph, or when I was feeling sorry for myself, a strong characteristic of the drinker, but I managed to stand it off.
>
> It was never taking that first drink that saved me.
>
> I never took any bows for being sober. It was selfish on my part. I wanted to be successful, and I had to put booze out of my life to achieve that end. I never felt I was doing anyone a favor by staying sober except myself.

This is an almost perfect attitude for a recovered alcoholic. Damon wanted success more than he wanted to drink. That was the stupendous simplicity of it. But if the success now included Ellen Egan, it no longer included an evening around the piano with the fans and lemonade.

A reporter named Charles E. Van Loan had gone from the Denver *Post* to New York to write for Hearst. He quit to write short stories for the *Saturday Evening Post* and other magazines. Knowing something about Damon's talents, he offered him room in his home in Flatbush, while Damon tried to make good as a writer, the trade-off being that Damon would supply Van Loan with plots.

Ellen remained in Denver, waiting Damon's call when he would be putting money in the bank.

Damon set out for the Emerald City with no more substantial prospect than that, willing to be lucky, and riding hope like a boxcar.

five

THE TWO Henrys—Adams and James—were masters of nuance and description; confronting New York City early in the twentieth century all but winded them.

Henry Adams, coming up the bay in 1904, found

> the outline of the city became frantic in its efforts to explain something that defied meaning. Power seemed to have outgrown its servitude and to have asserted its freedom. The cylinder had exploded, and thrown great masses of stone and steam against the sky. . . . Prosperity never before imagined, power never yet wielded by man, speed never touched by anything but a meteor, had made the world irritable, nervous, querulous, unreasonable and afraid. All New York was demanding new men, and all the new forces, condensed into corporations, were demanding new types of man. . . .

Three years later, Henry James, examined the

> power of the most extravagant of cities, rejoicing, as with the voice of morning, in its might, its fortune, its unsurpassable conditions, and imparting to every object and element, to the motion and expression of every floating, hurrying, panting thing, to the throb of ferries and to the plash of waves and the play of winds and the glint of lights and the shrills of whistles and the quality and authority of breeze-borne cries—all, practically, a diffused, wasted clamor of *detonations*—something of its sharp, free accent and, above all, of its sovereign sense of being "backed" and able to back.

There is more.

Walter Winchell, himself something of an explosion and an unsurpassable force, who would devote much of his life to explaining the city, although in shorter sentences, was born amid all this *tsimmes* on April 7, 1897, in a three-room flat in Harlem—about the time Damon Runyon went off to the Spanish-American War.

Walter's parents had emigrated to the United States from Russia in 1893. They were ripples in one of those vast waves of immigration so often upsetting to settlers whose forebears arrived a generation or two earlier. (Westbrook Pegler, whose own father emigrated from England, suggested late in World War II "it isn't fascism or racism to suggest that, until things settle down and we are able to adjust our differences between ourselves, the plush rope be stretched across the Battery and Golden Gate supporting a polite sign reading 'Full up.'")

The Winechels, as an early spelling had it, spun off what Irving Howe calls "a turning point in the history of the Jews as decisive as that of 70 A.D., when Titus's legions burned the Temple at Jerusalem, or 1492, when Ferdinand and Isabella decreed the expulsion from Spain."

Howe referred to the assassination of Czar Alexander II, called by Disraeli, "the kindliest prince who ever ruled Russia." The accession of Alexander III triggered a series of pogroms which, over the next thirty-three years, led to the flight of one-third of Eastern European Jews from their homelands, two million of them settling in the United States, chiefly in its larger cities.

Walter's paternal grandfather, Chaim, was a cantor and a rabbi, reputedly a powerful speaker, a writer of poetry and even something of a renegade, attending a lecture by Colonel Robert Ingersoll, the eminent atheist. And on the Sabbath, when the devout are enjoined from using public conveyances, Chaim sometimes took the subway from Harlem to within a few blocks of his Lower East Side congregation, before getting out to walk.

Chaim fathered eleven children by two wives. His sons included George, who rose to distinction on Wall Street, and Walter's father, who was less successful. Jacob was a salesman and a small, very small, businessman, a trim figure with a dainty mustache, sometimes calling himself Jack de Winchel. Walter recalled that his father was in the silk business with a man who absconded with the goods one night. Jacob, like Damon Runyon's father, concluded "No partners!"

Most pictures of Jewish life in New York City around the turn of the century center on the Lower East Side, but there were Jewish settlements in Williamsburg and Brownsville in Brooklyn, and the Harlem of the period was called by the *Jewish Daily Forward* "a Jewish city, inhabited by tens of thousands of Jews . . . as busy and congested as our East Side, with the same absence of light and air."

71

The streets between Lenox and Seventh avenues were, indeed, "the aristocratic Jewish neighborhood of New York," but Walter was raised in no hothouse atmosphere.

Jacob or Jack de was something of a ladies' man. He married Janet Bakst, called Jenny, when she was sixteen and he was twenty-one, and when business was slow, he took his mind off economics by consulting other figures. Walter later said, "That's when my mother told him to get out of her life."

In a contentious series of articles written for *The New Yorker* in 1940 and later published as *Gossip: The Life and Times of Walter Winchell,* St. Clair McKelway indulged in the pop psychology even then subverting American letters and discovered "an atmosphere of disillusionment bordering on bitterness" shaping young Walter's character.

> Like many Jews, the elder Winchells were visionary, impractical, Christlike folk [he wrote, although "Christlike" was not the adjective that sprang to Walter's lips, or as far as the record shows, anyone else's, in describing Jacob Winchell.] Their ancestors in central Europe had been forced into business and commerce against their natural inclinations because the professions, the arts and even the pursuit of agriculture were made inaccessible to them by their Aryan overlords.
>
> They had come to this country expecting to find racial equality and a spiritual culture and had been rudely disenchanted by numerous unpleasant experiences with the intolerance and materialism of the Yankee civilization. Winchell's father was no more capable of competing successfully with the native-born American businessman than the typical Jewish patriarchs who can still be seen on the Lower East Side— impecunious, Old World Hebrews who live there because they have never been able to make enough money to live anywhere else.

This surely is naive. Plenty of Jacob Winchel's landsmen not only played the Yankee game but excelled at it, sometimes creating friction.

"The economic and social conditions of the elder Winchells," McKelway argued, "offered the boys a chance to work out a philosophy which holds that the world is full of grabbers and schemers and that in order to survive one must adopt aggressive characteristics and subdue one's scruples." As McKelway conceded, this theory may fit

72

Walter nicely, but it did not explain his brother, who became an accountant of diffident mien.

It is a moot point whether Jenny dismissed her husband or whether he decamped. This was early in Walter's childhood and no dramatic departure. Jacob seems simply to have eased out of family life. His surrender wasn't just to the charms of a cutie or cuties but was a withdrawal from commercial life. He gave himself over to pinochle "with other defeated men" of upper Broadway, not the success on that street his son would be. Walter said, "My pop wasn't much of a businessman, but he was a hell of a pinochle player."

Walter lived with his grandmother and with other relatives and with friends who could be persuaded to put him up for a couple of nights. It was his recollection that his mother tried to impress him with the importance of education. But like the young Damon, he soaked up much of his learning from the streets, the economics of hustle. His first job was waiting in the rain with an umbrella at subway stops. He escorted people home for a dime. He delivered chickens for a nickel or a penny tip, hawked newspapers and magazines.

There are few childhoods without a close call, and one winter evening Walter and a friend were riding a sled that skidded into a horsecar at Lenox Avenue and 116th Street. The accident left Walter sprawled and bleeding. His panicky friend disappeared into that crowd that gawks.

Then Walter ran, his leg bleeding, looking for help. He tearfully asked a policeman in a drugstore if he were going to die. The policeman asked him how many accidents he'd had.

"This is my first one," Walter recalled saying.

"Well," answered the policeman, "you have to have one hundred accidents before you can die." Walter claimed he was a long time forgetting the policeman's reassurances but an even longer time getting over nightmares about the accident.

Walter was not above the kind of we-were-poor-but-we-didn't-know-we-were-poor smugness affected by some ex-poor boys. One day he took a sentimental journey through Harlem with Herman Klurfeld, his most authoritative biographer and for decades a skeleton in his closet as the ghost of columns Walter wished the world to believe Walter wrote.

"The tough life was not so tough," the rich and famous journalist said. "Harlem gave me something money can't buy. It cost me a lot, but I learned plenty. It wasn't all bad. Not bad at all." But another time he told Klurfeld, "The trouble with poverty is that it's so damned boring."

73

The boredom, for Walter, centered on Public School 184. "I was the school's prize dunce," he remembered, before slipping into the royal third person. ". . . we excelled in spelling, geography and history. We failed miserably at arithmetic. How many times 28 goes into 1446 was over our head."

He escaped the failures at school, the street brawling and the emotional insecurity of growing up in a variety of homes by sneaking into vaudeville houses and nickelodeons. He picked up some routines. He hammered iron strips into the toes and heels of his shoes and practiced tap-dancing over outbursts from neighbors who would have settled for a beginning saxophonist next door.

When Walter didn't play hookey, he entertained his fellow pupils with a little song-and-dance, a little patter. The prize dunce and by no means the toughest kid on the block, the slim, blue-eyed, blond boy found a way to grab the spotlight. "I can still remember the way I felt when the other kids watched me dancing," he said. "It was a kind of excited, breathless feeling. And it was more fun than playing cops and robbers."

One of the neighborhood kids was George Jessel, later a singer, toastmaster, and professional patriot. Jessel's widowed mother was a ticket-taker at the Imperial Theater, and she got her son and Walter jobs as ushers. They were asked to entertain during intermissions, and Walter and George obliged with "Swanee River" and period pieces like "The Lobster and the Wise Guy" and "Pony Boy." They performed from the orchestra pit because something called the Gerry Society cracked down on managements permitting underage performers on stage.

The singing didn't augment the four dollars a week the boys earned as ushers, but show business pointed to a new direction in Walter's vagabond existence. He and Jessel were joined by a third boy named Jack Weiner and became The Imperial Trio as Lawrence, Stanley, and McKinley, names Walter dreamed up to add a touch of class. They were optimistically billed as The Little Men with the Big Voices.

Weiner couldn't sing worth a lick, and Jessel's voice later furnished material for comedians, but Walter apparently was an adequate tenor who provided the harmony. Magazine articles and at least two biographers record there came a day when Walter didn't show, the other two boys raised quavering and uncertain voices and were showered with the traditional rotten fruit and vegetables.

The theater bouncer, Gyp the Blood—yes, these stories insist, the same Gyp the Blood later convicted of murdering Herman Rosenthal—bounced up to the balcony, where he found Walter locked in embrace with a neighborhood waif.

74

"It's a good story," Walter told Kurfeld, "but it never happened. I missed the performance because I was sore at my partners. Maybe I was too busy selling papers."

Walter was not quite thirteen when the Imperial Theater dismissed the trio. He also learned that he was about to be held back in the sixth grade for a third time. It was getting humiliating. The great educational advance known as social promotion had not yet been developed by the pedagogues.

The Imperial Trio hired on with a vaudevillian named Gus Edwards, who also recruited Eddie Cantor, Lila Lee, and George Price, and who is remembered primarily as the composer of "School Days."

The act that included Walter, which was called The Newsboy Sextette, opened at a crummy little theater in Union Hill, New Jersey, but it was all more than life-size in Walter's memory. "To us kids," he recalled, "Gus Edwards is more than the name of a songwriter—more than the name of a man. It is the name of our earliest education. We got it at the stage door—not in college. We got our schooling trooping from town to town all over the United States, in all-night day coaches."

Walter's vaudeville career was never distinguished. But, like Damon's apprenticeship on Colorado and California newspapers, it shaped both the kind of journalism Walter would practice and much of his attitude toward life, the sense of what he thought was important.

Herman Klurfeld in 1979 told a listener vaudeville was the single most formative influence in Walter's career.

"I asked him twenty times why he became a writer. He was uneducated. 'What made you become a writer?' I asked. He didn't know. He never could explain what drove him in that direction. My interpretation is that it was directly connected with vaudeville, which was full of gags and gossip. It may all have been a fluke."

A piece of doggerel Walter later wrote included corroborating lines:

Broadway bred me, Broadway fed me,
Broadway led me—
to a goal.

Walter was the scowling villain in The Newsboy Sextette, wearing a turtleneck sweater and a cap, carrying a rolled-up newspaper with which he swatted his fellows as he dashed about the stage. As the curtain opened, the boys and girls raced around and hollered. That seems to have been pretty much the act. The teacher entered, and the

75

class calmed down long enough to sing, "School days, school days, good old golden rule days. . . ."

The teacher attempted to call roll, triggering bedlam. Walter, in the center of it all, cried, "Aw, shuddup!" The act ended, mysteriously, with a rendition of "There's a Garden Down in Italy."

If it had all the sophistication of *Laverne and Shirley*, it, too, found an audience, and it toured for four years on small-time circuits, playing communities where "they sit down and devour their young." Vaudeville introduced Walter to America and to the world of show business with its chatter, slang, and gossip, its backstage romances and bitchiness. Walter developed a worship of stars, the successful ones who displayed "class," and he developed a contempt for small-timers.

He was a good-looking young man with blue eyes and what McKelway later called "an expression of questing intelligence like a fox terrier's." Charlie Chaplin who, with Fred Karno's English pantomime troupe, traveled the same circuit, remembered Walter as "a rather attractive scalawag who looked small for his sophisticated manner. He had a mania for gambling with cigarette coupons. . . . He was an extraordinarily fast talker."

Another vaudevillian of the period said Walter "talked very little about himself. He didn't engage in the usual roughhousing. He seemed very alone and aloof." If that memory is accurate, it covers the only period of self-effacement in Walter's life, since all other recollections have him borne out of the cradle endlessly talking.

A memory shared about Walter as the act bounced from city to tank town, living in side-street boardinghouses, concerns his energy and drive and will to succeed. "While the rest of us were fooling around, he was occupied with some project or other," Eddie Cantor recalled. "He never knew when to quit. I hardly ever remember seeing him relax. He didn't have any definite direction, but he was all motion."

He noticed everything, new acts, a *shtick*, rivalries, feuds, friendships. Life opened up. "Hello, ma, here I am in San Diego," he scrawled on a postcard. He later said he educated himself "meeting people everywhere and reading newspapers in every city. I read the editorial page to find out what the news and happenings meant. I became interested in the world around me."

Memory deludes us all. Walter's interest in the great world would be decades in showing up. The more evident limits of his interest were sharply defined by vaudeville. What he learned that became a permanent part of his equipment was how to grab an audience and hold it, what people wanted.

He formed the almost obligatory, casual liaisons with women. He

76

was, after all, making fifteen dollars a week, and it is a truism that two can sleep as cheaply as one. But he formed no enduring friendships in his vaudeville days. An old headliner noted bitterly more than sixty years later, "When he became famous, he had no time for the rest of us." He had never had time to grow close to anyone, of course. He was living around as a child, going to work after school at six, on the road at thirteen. The sharpest poverty of his youth was emotional.

Like Damon, he got the name he made famous by typographical error. Somewhere along the line, an extra "l" made it "Winchell" on a theater marquee, and he liked the spelling and adopted it.

Life on the road teaches a young man to look out for himself. Looking out for himself, Walter prepared for the day he would outgrow the act. He studied sand-dancers, who shuffled gracefully to soft music, occasionally tap-dancing, after scattering sand on the stage. He locked himself in the bathroom, "the only place I could get peace and quiet," outlining a song-and-dance routine.

The act broke up in 1914 or 1915. Walter recalled his last night with the troupe: "I was more than a little afraid . . . I couldn't sleep that night. But I wasn't alone. One of the dolls in the show kept me company."

It understandably was tougher than leaving what had never been a home. He was, as the saying is, at liberty. He returned to New York, with all its humiliations for the jobless, taking a room in a theatrical hotel on West Forty-fourth Street.

A new patriotic fervor burst across the land in 1915, and Walter wrote a song called "The Land I Love," added an oration, and hit the trail. Jingoism is always a crowded bandwagon, and Walter soon was back in New York, looking for work. He thought about an act dancing on roller skates, but he set the skates aside when he saw a chimpanzee doing it better than he ever could. He hung around with other vaudevillians who were out of work.

He was on what Damon called "Dream Street," where, "the gab you hear sometimes sounds very dreamy indeed. In fact, it sometimes sounds very pipe-dreamy . . . vaudeville actors, both male and female, are great hands for sitting around dreaming out loud about how they will practically assassinate the public in the Palace if ever they get a chance."

I often stood in front of the Palace for hours swapping lies [Walter told Klurfeld]. There were always jobs we turned down because the agents were either too stupid to appreciate us or unable to meet our prices. I used to wait at the Palace,

77

hoping to meet a friend rich enough to invite me to join him across the street for a cup of coffee and a sandwich. It was all so damn frustrating and humiliating.

The strange part of it was that none of us ever thought about trying another job or getting into another field. It was like a religion. We were in show business and we intended remaining in it, even if it meant we had to starve to death. There is something about the pride of actors that is hard to understand. I guess you have to be an actor to understand it. It certainly isn't anything rational.

At eighteen Walter was a little old for the kid stuff, but he even thought about another "Schooldays" act. That field proved crowded, too, including a company that featured the Marx brothers.

One of the young women he saw around and about was an ambitious young dancer named Rita Green. What they talked about was mostly show business, and eventually they decided to get an act together, putting it on the road in 1916.

Walter re-created the act for Klurfeld and a few guests in the studio after a broadcast during World War II. It was an eerie retrospective for a handful just after he had barked his view of the world to millions. Klurfeld described the scene in his biography, *Winchell:*

"'If you please, professor, bring me on with "Give My Regards to Broadway" with lots of brass.' I danced out with my cane, straw skimmer and white flannels."

His feet swished against the carpeted floor.

"I waited for the opening applause. It wasn't always there. The second curtain parted . . . and . . . my partner sat on a replica of a wall, gazing soulfully at the sky. She looks my way and then we duet—a love song for the act, which I named 'Spooneyville.'"

Winchell gazed upwards as if searching for the balcony's reaction.

"Then we danced together for a short time, a bit of cakewalk, continuing to give out with the romantic duet. And don't forget that blue spotlight. Oh, how I waited for the sound of applause. . . . After that duet, my partner exits. I take the stage solo. . . .

"I then sang a war song, just to get the chill out of their bones. I wrote the lyrics." He glided from one side of the studio to the other, miming a song. "Then my partner returned to the stage for her solo dance. A twirly-whirly. When she was finished, she pretended she was breathless. The hard breathing was a popular bit. It helped milk applause."

Walter flapped his arms. "Then I bounced back onstage for an exchange of gags with my partner. Oh, those jokes. . . . 'Are the oysters healthy?' 'I never heard them complain.' Yockety-yock-yock. Then there was, 'You can drive a horse to water, but a pencil must be led.'"

A quick jig and another swish-swish-swish on the carpet. . . .

"The act finished with a double bit of wild tapping." Winchell leaned over and moved his feet and arms briskly in an effort to recall the mounting intensity.

"Segue into two choruses of 'Swanee River' pizzicato and pianissimo—until the last four bars. Then bring it up fast and forte to the exit and the bows."

Then he commanded with harsh emphasis, "Applause, you bastards."

That's all there was, there wasn't anymore. And it remained a deuce act, meaning it never progressed beyond the second spot on the bill, following the animal act, jugglers, or acrobats who opened the show with something fast and simple to settle the audience down.

Winchell and Green worked steadily at vaudeville's lower levels, the Sun Circuit, a midwestern chain; the Sullivan-Considine chain in the Pacific Northwest, and the Pantages Circuit, including a half dozen West Coast theaters. They earned between $50 and $75 a week. A contemporary said, "It wasn't sensational, but it was pretty good. It had good potential. Walter was a cocky kid. And many of us believed he was going places."

"Spooneyville's" literal and figurative high point probably was a week at the American Roof in New York, where a *Variety* reviewer called it ". . . a promising start. Theirs is a sort of bench turn, but it has dialogue, song and dances. . . . The first two numbers appear to be written and were helped by the naive manner of Miss Green. The turn isn't one to bring forth any volume of applause, but it's pleasant. . . ."

But "war came along, and everything went blooey," Walter recalled. As Americans busily kicked dachshunds and rechristened sauerkraut "victory cabbage," enlistments cut into the ranks of performers and audiences alike, theaters were closed one day a week, and Walter returned to New York and enlisted in the Navy. "Politics or philosophy had nothing to do with it," he told Klurfeld. "And I was damn proud."

He performed yeoman service, assigned as an admiral's receptionist at the New York City customs house. There is a widely reprinted anecdote that one day, while melting wax to seal correspondence, Walter was so intent on eavesdropping, he set his nose on fire. When Klurfeld asked him about this, Walter said, "Never spoil a good story by trying to verify it," an unfortunate philosophy for a newsman.

He and Rita were exchanging love letters, and when the war ended they were married in a civil ceremony in New York. They resumed the act.

She: "What's your idea of a good time?" He: "Watching a shipload of second lieutenants sinking." He: "Why is a corset like a three-day old beard?" She: "I don't know." He: "Because they're both stiff." Music up to cover the silence. The question has never been settled whether it was jokes like that or the fast-growing movie industry that doomed vaudeville, but there was no doubt that it no longer seemed the entertainment wave of the future.

The flame of Walter's curiosity continued to burn. "He always knew everything about everybody in the show," a fellow vaudevillian said.

One day backstage in a Chicago theater—a day that might be commemorated with that day on which the elder Bennett set up shop in a dingy basement at 20 Wall Street or with that day when Joseph Pulitzer came to town—Walter tacked up on the bulletin board a typewritten sheet of gossip about his fellow performers.

He called it *Newsense*. No one asked him to do it, no one paid him to do it. He suddenly found that he liked to write gossip. No issue of *Newsense* survives, but the sheet looked into the private lives of vaudevillians. "He would tell who had a beer with who," according to one who was there. To Walter's delight, it was an instant success. Klurfeld told an interviewer, "Suddenly Walter realized he had a species of clout."

The sheet appeared wherever Winchell and Green were on the road.

> Occasionally actors or actresses would become irritated at his intrusions on what they considered their privacy [McKelway wrote], but when this happened, it was also to be observed that almost everybody backstage was titillated. . . . Winchell padded out his writing with jokes ("You tell 'em, Ouija. I'm bored"), verses and vignettes, but the body of the column was gossip."

> Though the author of the column was not exactly popular, he was respected, sometimes feared, and assiduously read [according to McKelway]. Frequently, one member of the troupe would tell Winchell something about another, and

Winchell noticed that these contributors appeared to experience a pleasurable sense of self-importance when they saw an item in Winchell's column and realized the little furor it caused backstage.

"People like to tell tales," Winchell has said. "If I take the rap for what they tell me, they'll tell a lot."

He rode that principle to the stars, trailed by a flotilla of imitators. Although McKelway and other critics implied that Walter created this unpleasant impulse, he simply rediscovered and popularized an element of journalism the elder Bennett had seized on to make his *Herald* the most widely circulated newspaper in America. But then, as Pulitzer liked to observe, quoting Goethe, "Everything has been thought of before . . . the difficulty is to think of it again."

The young man who was one-half of a deuce act became something of a press lord backstage. If the actor within lacked an appreciative audience onstage, vanity was gratified by the attention he got through *Newsense*.

He stitched out a career with two fingers at a typewriter. He began contributing notes to trade publications. He was rejected more often than not, but soon *Billboard,* an entertainment weekly, began accepting some of his submissions, paying him space rates for "Stage Whispers."

His first check for journalism was $6.90. "Imagine being paid for something you would do for nothing," he said, revealing that fatal weakness which has depressed newsmen's salaries through the ages. "I later received fancier paychecks, but no reward gave me the glorious feeling I had just then."

"Stage Whispers" was pretty tame stuff, but it showed promise of malice: "Sign outside of a Cleveland movie theater: Geraldine Farrar, supported for the first time by her husband. . . . Most actors are married and live scrappily ever after. . . ."

Walter also contributed to the New York *Vaudeville News,* a house organ published by the tyrannical Edward F. Albee, the vaudeville impresario. Albee was warring with the always independent *Variety,* the show business authority. *Variety* supported a vaudevillians' union called The White Rats—"rats" as in "star" spelled backwards. Albee was attempting to crush the union.

It is unlikely that Walter bothered himself about the politics of the thing. There is no evidence he was antilabor. What he was, as friendly biographers have pointed out, was pro-Walter.

It is good he was finding a new career. Winchell and Green continued to drift, professionally and personally. They joined the

Butterfield Circuit, but that centered on Michigan, which had not yet developed Motown to build theatrical legend.

What apparently cut it for Walter was a cancellation in midweek when "Spooneyville" was playing Birmingham, Alabama. The act was left with just enough money for one ticket home. Rita took the coach. Walter earned his way back to Big Town by feeding a boxcar full of chickens.

He sought out Glenn Condon, editor of the *Vaudeville News* and beseeched him for a job. He was signed on for $25 a week and a commission on ads he solicited. He wrote *Newsense* type of gossip, stood with a camera outside the Palace, taking photographs and the show biz pulse.

He wrote a friend:

> I am writing to tell you what a wonderful proposition has been made to me from the Keith Exchange to be assistant editor of the *Vaudeville News*. . . .
>
> You no doubt don't blame me, because you have heard me mention that I would love to become a figure in the world, preferably in the news game. I have always had an inclination toward it, and at last have had my wish granted. . . .
>
> I also realize that when I tire of this (if I do), I can always go back to being an ordinary actor, can't I?

That may have been Walter's last reference to himself as "ordinary," and there was no question of "going back." When the young newsman suffers that stroke—"imagine being paid for what you'd do for nothing"—it is too late to call the doctor.

In what was almost a symbolic act, Walter and Rita were divorced in 1920. The marriage had been built on dreams of show business, and now Walter was dreaming along different lines.

six

THE NARRATOR in O. Henry's story leaves his girl sitting on the stoop while he seeks "The Voice of the City."

"Other cities have voices," he argues. ". . . Chicago says unhesitatingly, 'I will'; Philadelphia says, 'I should'; New Orleans says, 'I used to'; Louisville says, 'Don't care if I do'; St. Louis says, 'Excuse me'; Pittsburgh says, 'Smoke up'. . . ."

But he receives only unsatisfactory and conflicting answers from a bartender, a cop, a poet, and a newsboy, and he returns to find Aurelia still sitting on the stoop in the moonlight:

> And then, wonder of wonders and delight of delights! our hands somehow touched, and our fingers closed together and did not part.
>
> After half an hour, Aurelia said, with that smile of hers:
>
> "Do you know, you haven't spoken a word since you came back!"
>
> "That," said I, nodding wisely, "is the Voice of the City."

O. Henry died in 1910 in the Irving Street flat from whose window he had watched the shopgirls and clerks and cops he invested with romance in stories that often were sad but never despairing. The search for the city's voice did not die with him.

Gene Fowler went to New York at Damon Runyon's suggestion in 1917. They were riding in a taxi after watching a ball game.

"Runyon sat back, chain-smoked in silence for a while, then said as though to himself 'Just listen to it roar!'" Fowler wrote ". . . My friend was speaking of the ever-lasting roar of the city. He had the solemn look of a child that holds a conch shell to its ear.

"'Just listen to it roar!' he said once again."

Like Damon, Fowler went to New York from Denver and was a reporter of outsize talents. But in all other important ways, they were opposites. Damon wrote, "Money has a tendency to buy happiness."

Fowler said, "Money is something to be thrown off the platform of moving trains."

Where the young Damon was slight and often silent, Fowler was a lanky, big-eared, outgoing bravo, a hard-drinking, woman-loving legend whose profile, in a north light, somewhat resembled that of his friend John Barrymore. Jack Dempsey called him "the greatest barroom fighter I ever laid eyes on," and while that may have been a friend's flattery, Fowler's habit of laughing maniacally in combat sometimes shattered the enemy.

He married one of the most understanding women in history. Setting eyes on the dewy Agnes Hubbard back in Denver, he announced, "Whatever your name is, you are going to be the mother of my children." She was understandably discomfited by this, but after she learned the proposition included matrimony, she yielded, and, in due course, along came Gene, Jr., Jane, and Will.

Fowler loved his wife and children. He was never lost, only strayed. Men loved Fowler, too. Hearst, forgiving him his trespasses, called him, "That young man from Denver." Ring Lardner called him, "The last of the Bison," and the choleric Westbrook Pegler said, "He was never able to hate anyone. Laughter always got in the way."

Fowler was a morning star on the Denver *Post* while it built its reputation as what John Gunther called "the most lunatic newspaper in America." His copy attracted interest beyond his hometown, fueled by such leads as "She laid her wanton red head on her lover's breast, then plugged him through the heart." To prospective employers, that gaudy talent outweighed Fowler's wild boy act; besides, such behavior was not uncommon for newsmen of an era before they sublimated it in tennis and seminars.

"It is possible I knew [Runyon] longer and better . . . than any other writing man now alive," Fowler reflected in *Skyline,* his final memoir, although it was a friendship at arm's length.

Fowler went to New York thinking of it as Rainbow's End and the Promised Land, and in 1917 he noticed that Damon already spoke of it "as if he had been born there instead of that much smaller town of the same name, Manhattan, Kansas. . . . He talked about New York, especially Broadway, as if he were its discoverer."

Damon told him, "The greatest thing about New York is a blade of grass. This is not prize grass, but it has moxie. You need plenty of moxie in this man's town, or you'll find yourself dispersed hither and yon."

Damon could speak with authority, since he had covered plenty of ground in his six years in the city. The live-in with the Van Loans did not last long. He supplied Van Loan with short-story plots, all right, taking the cash and letting the credit go to Van Loan, but Damon was not an easy man to share a roof-tree with. Anyway, he had written to Denver, asking Ellen to join him. She held out; she expected him to find a steady job.

He was not exactly the nest-egg type. He had fallen behind on his board bill when he sold a story to *Munsey's* magazine under his own name, but he blew the $65 he got for the story on a shoe trunk that called to him from a Fifth Avenue luggage shop window. It was yellow leather with brass fittings, and it held separate compartments for eight pairs of shoes, which was seven more than he owned at the time. It was that extravagant, impulsive waste of money which makes life merry.

Damon rationalized the purchase by saying the trunk served as goad, inspiring him to work to get the money to buy the shoes to fill the trunk. And in later life he wrote, "Whenever I have felt disposed to beef about some foolish action on the part of anyone, I have said to myself, Runyon, remember the shoe trunk."

This did not put butter in the Van Loan larder, however, and in the spring of 1911 Van Loan played golf with a Hearst executive who urged him back to the fold. Van Loan was content writing short stories. He suggested Damon as a prospect. The executive said he would take a look. Damon had kept a scrapbook, in the manner of most reporters who are proud of their work, the editors liked what they saw, and he signed on with the *American,* now the name of the morning *Journal,* for $40 a week.

His hiring was no more complicated than that. Newspapers were run more along journalistic than, say, banking lines then, and prospects were signed up for their promise. There were no batteries of psychological and other tests favored by up-to-date newspapers of later decades. It is possible that Damon, Fowler, and certainly Stephen Crane would have flunked such tests; it is hard to picture an old city room manned by psychologically integrated personalities.

The *American* was the flagship of the Hearst fleet. It greeted the New Year of 1911 with a front-page box claiming for the *Sunday American* "the fourteenth consecutive year of undisputed leadership both in circulation and display advertising," equaling the *combined circulation* of the New York *World* and the New York *Herald,* and it claimed that the *Morning American* gained more daily circulation in the previous year, its best, "than all other morning newspapers in New York *combined.*"

Damon was assigned to the sports department and, once his desk was pointed out to him, there seems to have been no apprenticeship. He acquired the name he would make famous when Harry Cashman, the sports editor, decided Alfred Damon Runyon was too long and drew a blue pencil through Alfred; the three-name byline was becoming the province of women reporters.

The big story involved a missing American heiress in Italy: DOROTHY ARNOLD/BELIEVED TO HAVE VISITED/GRISCOM IN DECEMBER. The *American* continued its attack on "the fire insurance trust." Cholly Knickerbocker wrote, "'Charity' in letters of light blazed across one end of the ballroom at the Waldorf-Astoria last night, where once a year their magic attracts society for the time-honored charity ball."

A Washington correspondent noted that with the change from the Roosevelt to the Taft administration, "Helen pink has taken the place of the long-popular Alice blue." An editorial argued that "Hearst's radicalism becomes Andrew Carnegie's conservatism" in calling for the regulation of rapacious business.

A local story reported that "Mrs. Donald Stuart, widow of a noted Boston artist and one of the notable women of New York society" was injured when her cab hit "a deep hole in the pavement, one of those evidences of apparent official neglect which have aroused public protest within the last few weeks."

And there, on March 21, is Damon Runyon stirring a potpourri as though he had been part of the sports scene since the century's turn. He led off with a rhyme, "The Language of the Gloves":

> Shufflin' mah feet in de rawsum, waitin' de soun' o' de gong
> Seems to me lak ah heahs a voice—yo'll say dat mah haid is
>   wrong.
> It comes from de gen'man's cohnah, a whisperin' soft an' low
> An ah heahs dat gen'man's right han' speak an' it say to de
>   lef' jes' so
> It saiz:
> "Ka-bam! Ka-bam! Ka-bam!"
> Thas all. . . .

Damon followed with a note about a German fighter intimidated by his foe: "He no go ous, me go ous." And, speaking with the authority of a man with no experience of big league baseball, "If spring training dope accounts for anything, and history relates that it does not, the Chicago White Sox, aged overnight from a corps of youngsters into an aggregation of astute veterans, will cut a very considerable figure in this American League season. . . ." (They finished a distant fourth.)

Big-time professional sports in 1911 meant baseball and boxing, and the *American*'s sports page was just that, a page, with room left over for a comic strip, usually "Mutt and Jeff," and display ads: "606/ To the Public/ A Few Words of Advice/ About Professor Ehr/ Lich's Great Dis/ Covery—Salvarsan" and "Wonderful/ 3-Day Cure for/ Drink Habit."

Damon was sent to interview the fearsome John L. Sullivan, former heavyweight champion. He was advised to "just mention Arthur Brisbane to him. That will soften him up."

> [Damon] found the aging John L. in a Broadway hotel bundled up in bed, and I was still trembling from his resounding roar "Come in," when I said mendaciously:
> "Mr. Sullivan, I was sent to you by Arthur Brisbane."
> "Arthur?" queried Sullivan. "How is Arthur?"
> "I said Arthur was all right, which was correct as far as I knew for to tell you the truth, up to that moment I had never clapped eyes on the mighty journalist, and I went away with my interview devoutly hoping that he and John L. would not meet before the latter's memory of my visit faded."

Years later, Brisbane told Damon that in 1888 he had covered the famous bare-knuckle fight in Chantilly, France, between Sullivan and Charley Mitchell, a little Englishman. There were thirty or forty witnesses. There was no purse; only side bets. "The men fought on the turf and wore shoes with sharp spikes, and Mitchell stepped on the American's foot and sank his spikes to the bone. Sullivan drew away, eyed Mitchell reproachfully." He said, according to Brisbane, "Charley, can't we fight like gentlemen, you dirty son of a bitch?"

Damon hadn't much more than learned his way to the office when he was dispatched to San Antonio, Texas, to cover the New York Giants in spring training. These were the Giants of the splenetic manager John J. McGraw, Little Napoleon, a familiar on Broadway and a veteran of two-punch fights, the second punch being the one that decked him. McGraw would lead this team to three straight pennants, only to find Philadelphia or Boston waiting.

These were the Giants, too, of Christy Mathewson, "Big Six," in Jonathan Yardley's phrase "the real Frank Merriwell," winner of 37 games in 1908, 373 lifetime, who pitched three shutouts in the 1903 World Series. It was the team which inspired second baseman Larry Doyle to exult, "It's great to be young and a Giant."

With stars like Mathewson, "Chief" Meyers, and Fred Merkle shining, Damon chose to specialize in the life and works of Arthur L.

Raymond, called Bugs although he was no entomologist. There was a lot of human interest in Bugs, the kind of color a young sportswriter could build a reputation on.

Bugs was an unreconstructed alcoholic who died at thirty, a McGraw reclamation project. He threw a spitball at three speeds, but made a habit of slipping from the ballpark to the nearest saloon, where he would trade baseballs for drinks, hurrying back before McGraw marked him absent. Damon got to know Bugs during rainy days in Texas hotel lobbies and wet nights in saloons.

As the team worked north, Bugs issuing bartenders bogus passes to the Polo Grounds, Damon wrote of Bugs crawling on hands and knees from bullpen to pitcher's mound, Bugs saving up meal tickets to splurge on one deluxe room service breakfast.

Damon detoured to pay a final visit to his father, who was dying of tuberculosis in Arizona. The two swapped shop talk, according to Weiner in *The Damon Runyon Story*. It was not a demonstrative family, but Damon was so moved by the sight of his father near journey's end that he wrote a poem which concluded:

> So we kneel when darkness comes and pray—
> (There's very little that we can say,)
> "Lord, Oh, Lord, Give us this day—
> Be with us;
> Stay with us!"

But mainly Damon was busy making Bugs Raymond a Damon Runyon character and, in just a little more time than it took Lord Byron, Damon awoke to find himself just a little less famous, scarcely an exaggeration since in 1911 only the newspaper reported what was undisputedly the national pastime.

Ellen came to New York in May. Damon took her for a cab ride up Fifth Avenue. The great houses of the street won her. Damon promised her they would live there someday. They started more modestly. They were married in Charles Van Loan's house in Flatbush and took rooms in a boardinghouse in Flushing, gloriously confident that this was only a beginning, a first step. There are few persons more gloriously certain than a working newsman newly come to New York with a bride on his arm; life is spread out before him like a great sunny plain, it is all prospects, no valleys.

Forty dollars a week was not life on a shoestring then. John Wanamaker offered seventy-cent shirts and neckties for fifteen cents. During World War II, Damon was reminded by an old friend that in the New York of the 1900s "you could get three good meals in nice joints for thirty cents."

There was a ten-cent breakfast at Coddington's on Seventh Avenue near Forty-third Street.

> At noon we went to Dowling's saloon, same locality, for a beer, turned to the free lunch counter and had a nice beef stew with bread *for free*. The beer was a nickel. . . .
>
> At 4 P.M., to Frank Geraghty's at 46th and Broadway. . . . You bought beer for a nickel and had your fill of those miniature Welsh rarebits for which the place was noted. . . .
>
> At 7 o'clock, we went to Mack's at 46th Street and Eighth Avenue. You went into the 46th Street entrance, paid ten cents for a double jott of beer, and a guy handed you a plate of horse doovers that you had to hold in both hands. You were supposed to have the main dish afterwards and pay your check for the dinner on the Eighth Avenue side, but if you were smart, you never went to the Eighth Avenue side but backed out of the 46th Street door because one of the Mack boys was near-sighted and you made him think you were coming in.
>
> I've been eating all day long, and the tab is 30 cents. If you had a dame and wanted to splurge, you went to Guffanti's at 26th and Seventh Avenue. The big spaghetti dinner with the old red was 40 cents.

Only later generations, ignorant of the American past, believed there was no such thing as a free lunch. There are snakes even in situations of paradise, however, and Damon was quickly involved in the busyness and socializing of sportswriting, away from home for long hours, sometimes on the road. In the beginning Ellen understood because it was understandable.

Baseball boasts the most considerable literature of any sport. In 1911 the game still retained its bucolic flavor, but it was covered by men of some sophistication—Bozeman Bulger of the *World,* Grantland Rice of the *Mail,* Sid Mercer of the *Globe,* who, Damon said, "showed me the baseball ropes when I first came to the big leagues."

Franklin P. Adams, no baseball writer, already had composed "Tinker to Evers to Chance," and in Chicago, Ring Lardner covered the Cubs and the White Sox and, in a few years, would give literature Jack Keefe, the ignorant busher of *You Know Me Al.*

Damon quickly staked out his territory. All his life he was famous for arriving on the scene early and leaving late, the ground around him littered with crumpled paper, evidence that he had searched for the lead. Once he found it, he typed steadily away, chain-smoking. He was seldom in a rush to give you the results. What he often gave you was a fresh approach. He was free to choose the day's big game among the Yankees, Giants, or Dodgers.

Thus, on July 5, 1911, readers in the midst of a heat wave that had claimed twenty-nine lives the previous day could refresh themselves with the following:

> Well, by the bend in the great horn spoon, we've got a greater population than Philadelphia, anyway!
>
> The Metropolitan Tower is taller than any building they've got in Quakerville.
>
> Our main street is wider, in spots, than any thoroughfare they can boast over yonder.
>
> Our climate is more climatic. The end-seat hog is not so pronounced in our subway than he is on their street car. Our ventilation and acoustics are much nicer. Our policemen are handsomer. Our scenery is more easily seen.
>
> In fact, we have it over Philadelphia in many ways, here in Gotham, and everybody present being agreed on that proposition, why, let them go ahead and buther our baseball team to make a Pennsylvania holiday, if they insist.
>
> But there is such a thing as going too far.

There are five more paragraphs before Damon writes: "The Declaration of Independence of Philadelphia was again read at the Hilltop yesterday morning and afternoon, as follows, to wit:

Athletics 7 11

Yankees 4 9.

Damon's approach was not always so leisurely: "Mathewson pitched against Cincinnati yesterday. Another way of putting it is that Cincinnati lost a game of baseball. The first statement means the same as the second."

The Reds, as Damon shortly explained, hadn't beaten Big Six in three years.

Reporting the first major league baseball he had ever seen, Damon clearly loved the game and its characters, but it was a long season, at that, and by October 11, his pulse didn't pound as he noted the Dodgers beat the Giants, 2-1:

> It is rumored that there was a game of baseball over in Brooklyn yesterday afternoon, the offending parties being the

members of the champion New York club and Bill Dahlen's Boosters. . . .

This afternoon, the dreary schedule drags painfully back to the Polo Grounds, and the game goes on and on. It may be that the Athletics will be completely petered out from the fatigue of waiting by the time they get a crack at the Giants for all that dough.

Damon's enthusiasm returned by the time the Series rolled around. New York won the opener, 2-1, and Damon would never become too jaded to reach for a bottle of the old hyperbole: "Christy Mathewson, the greatest of his kind, held the Philadelphia Athletics, champions of the world, in the hollow of his mighty hand yesterday afternoon and the Giants scored first blood." It was "a baseball battle that will live forever in the memory of the enormous throng that saw it."

The opening day crowd of 38,281 was indeed a World Series record, and Damon wrote in the spirit of the period. According to a Hearst laureate named James J. Montague:

To get a country big enough for that great game today,
Columbus sailed across the sea and found the U.S.A.

For Giant fans that was the high point of the Series, unless it was a rain delay which postponed the inevitable for nearly a week. But "Just as everybody was half out of rumors," Damon wrote, "the sun came slinking in apologetically and announced it had not taken the veil, as was commonly supposed."

Philadelphia proceeded to win the championship in six games.

"Baker hit the ball over the right field fence for a home run in the sixth inning," Damon wrote on October 17. "Let the portcullis fall! The story ends there."

The next day he wrote, "Pitching with consummate craft, Christy Mathewson, the master workman of baseball, held the champion Athletics runless for eight wonderful innings at the Polo Grounds yesterday afternoon; then, in the first half of the ninth inning, with one out and a victory at the Giants' fingertips, Frank Baker, the Maryland butcher boy, slashed a home run into the right field stands. . . ."

Home runs in consecutive World Series games made J. Frank Baker forever "Home Run" Baker. Damon was enthusiastic: "It was such a game as sends blood boiling through the veins. It was a game as makes baseball great. . . . The home run drive, when hope is dead, is the big spectacular play of baseball."

91

The 1911 Series also proved a cultural landmark because John N. Wheeler, a baseball writer for the *Herald*, became the first acknowledged ghost-writer for a professional athlete, turning out stories for Mathewson. A couple of World Series later, Wheeler was spinning tales for eight stars.

Later in the century, of course, the output of the athletes' amanuenses contributed significantly to the Gross National Product, although Senator William Bradley (D-N.J.) observed, when he was playing in the National Basketball Association and a hot-shot rookie announced autobiographical intent, that the last twenty-one-year-old whose life was worth examining was Mozart.

With the end of the baseball season, Damon immediately demonstrated the versatility of a good utility man. On November 11 the Horse Show opened at Stanford White's Madison Square Garden, aptly named because it was on Madison Square and was topped by a garden. Twenty-three hundred orphans attended, the guests of A. G. Vanderbilt. And Damon marked the occasion with a verse, "Mr. Deeters of Cheyenne":

> Son, call that man in the hard-boiled bib
> An' order me one more snort;
> My name is Deeters if I failed to say; I'm a
> Well-known Cheyenne sport.
> Does I know the hawses? Well, son, I does,
> I savvies hawses right well—
> For I won the buster belt one year ago
> On a critter they call O'Hell—
> An' son I been to that Madison Square an' I
> Seen that hawses show.
> Well, I'll mention free, I'd admired to see
> How they cut them blankets low—
> The hawses?
> No, cuss it, no!
> I'm speakin' about the show! . . .
> . . . they ain't no harm,
> but a heap o' charm
> in cuttin' them blankets low . . .
> . . . and they'd freeze in the range
> from the sudden change
> if they cut them blankets so low . . .
> Why, I'm proud to state

That we'll agitate
For to keep them blankets low . . .

Then Damon was off to Harvard Stadium:

> Once this afternoon, opportunity rapped at the door of Yale, but stepped aside to avoid a poor snap from center on a try for what seemed a perfect field goal; once it beat a loud tattoo at the Harvard portals and then dodged back before a forward pass.
> Whereupon opportunity came no more to the gate, and the annual battle between Harvard and Yale ended in a scoreless tie.
> Nothing could be fairer than nothing to nothing.

But it was primarily as a baseball writer that Damon built his early reputation, a baseball writer with humor. By the time the 1912 World Series rolled around, the industry founded by John Wheeler was practically automated. The "greatest galaxy of baseball stars to write for the *American*" included Mathewson, John "Chief" Meyers of the Athletics, and Rube Marquard. Damon commented on the semitough competition: "Scanning the field of battle with glassy eye this morning, we discover the opposing forces assuming the crouching position made famous by James J. Jeffries and resting on their typewriters. One amanuensis attached to the pitching staff fell dead over his notebook yesterday. It was nothing serious, however. . . ."

The Giants lost that series to the Red Sox in eight games, the second being an eleven-inning 6-6 tie. To Damon, it was nothing like kissing your sister: "Pitching with the cunning of an old fox brought to bay, fighting with his back against the wall, Christy Mathewson, he who has been called the greatest of his kind, beat back the slashing Boston Red Sox today and held them to a drawn battle. . . . It was a drama of the world of sport done into eleven innings of baseball playing, it was a drama that men may dream about and talk about in years to come. . . ."

By the time of the following World Series, the *American* identified him as "Expert Damon Runyon," and he was taking the long view, like a Washington pundit before a primary:

"There is an old, old saying that the third time is the charm. John J. McGraw and his New York Giants are about to put that ancient claim to a severe test. . . .

"If the Giants fail for a third time, they can have no excuse.

93

"Two years ago, they were fairly beaten after a hard fight, and last year they slipped on a fluke."

The following day, he wrote: "The smack of a bat meeting a ball in the fifth inning of the first game of the World Series yesterday afternoon, followed by the dull boom of forty-thousand voices, was the sound of history raucously repeating itself."

"Home Run" Baker had struck again, and the A's beat the Giants in five games. "Far be it from us to flag the subway or the elevated train of your thoughts with inane observations on such a morose morning as this," Damon write, "but we simply cannot refrain from triumphantly remarking—we told you so!

"That's to say, we told you there was to be a World Series. There was."

Damon later confessed to sometimes assuming a "half boob air" in his writing. This pretty well concealed a darker strain, a kind of native determinism present in another writer of the period, who is all but forgotten.

In 1914 there died in New York City a newspaperman named Alfred Henry Lewis, like Damon a native of Kansas and, like Damon, the author of fiction about the New York underworld. Comparing the two men, Professor Wagner wrote in *Runyonese:* "Especially striking is the use to which both writers put their underworld characters to protest social inequality." Lewis's underworld is more sinister than Damon's, but a simple cynicism expressed by Lewis in a short story called "Baby Fingers" summed up Damon's emerging philosophy: "All over New York City, in Fifth Avenue, at Five Points, the single cry was, Get the Money! The rich were never called upon to explain their prosperity. The poor were forever being asked to give some legal reason for their poverty."

Get the Money as imperative—Damon would polish that touchstone to his death. He was industrious, and he was building a reputation in 1914 and prospering in the modest journalistic manner, and for a time that seemed sufficient.

"There was happiness in our home then," Damon Runyon, Jr., wrote of his parents' early married life. "My father was going places with hard work, and he had a smart-looking woman to take with him. Ironically, the higher they stepped together, the more they lost that original glow of the cozy home."

Damon was far, far from home early in 1914.

"Covered all over with foreign labels and all chattering away like Baedekers," he wrote from Paris on February 18, "the Giants–White Sox party of sixty-seven—count 'em yourself—breezed into this sedate little village tonight with firm and determined intention of playing a few nights' stand."

He had joined "almost at third base" an around-the-world tour of the two teams. His presence was promoted on the front page of the *American*. "The famous baseball writer (and celebrated humorist)" would accompany the teams to "Paris, London, Glasgow, Edinborough, Dublin and other towns where they play."

At a time when most Americans stayed put, the young man from Pueblo had sailed his second ocean. His countrymen are notoriously innocent of history and geography, and this showed up in a composite interview he did with the ballplayers.

They already had witnessed the mysteries of the Orient, but their most vivid memory when Damon joined them was the voyage out to Japan. The waves were "about ten or twenty times as high as the Metropolitan Tower." And "much to our amazement and surprise," they were quoted, "when we reached Italy, we discovered that the country was heavily populated by Wops."

Baseball management is routinely obtuse, and with spring training already at hand, the tour still faced more than three weeks of exhibition in a chill and rainy European winter. Not much ball was played.

Damon accompanied McGraw to the tomb "of the man whose name the Giants' chief made famous in America, the name being Monsieur Bonaparte, the deceased promoter of the Federal 'outlaw' league of his time . . .

"'I, too, met the Duke of Wellington,' said McGraw, 'only his name was Connie Mack.'"

The group attended a party given by Mr. and Mrs. George Kessler of New York at their Paris home, where Mrs. Kessler wore pearls she announced were worth half a million dollars, and Larry Doyle and Hans Lobert "and other diamond stars were introduced to the mysteries of the 'Maxixe,' the mazes of the 'Furianz' and the 'slides' and 'steps' of other new Paris dances."

The teams departed, the White Sox being "especially sorry to leave Paris. They say it is the Chicago of Europe." The troupe headed for London to "meet British nobility. . . . But all patriotic Americans may rest assured that it will not be baseball that recoils from the shock."

It seemed a time when nothing could dampen Damon's spirits: "The weather today was grand. The sun could almost be seen several times, which is said to be a record in this vicinity. . . . Some of the players today came up with heavy colds, the results of sleeping in the terrible draught which was created by the news that the hotel charges extra for heat."

There were tours of Buckingham Palace, the Tower of London and all that. Then:

> Across an English football field in the heart of historic old Chelsea, boomed the weird war chant of the American, while His Majesty, King George of England, and 20,000 of his subjects sat listening today. They saw the White Sox beat the Giants, 5-4, in an eleven-inning game.
>
> . . . So entranced was his Majesty that he did not even dodge when Eagen's foul broke a window in the Royal box and glass fell all about him. In fact, he captured a piece of the glass and is keeping it as a souvenir. . . .
>
> His Majesty canceled half a dozen engagements in order to be present. . . . Mr. Churchill, the King's second valet, was really responsible for the Royal presence."

Mr. Churchill, Damon explained, became infatuated with baseball while visiting America and told the king "it was much more spectacular than football," a minority view in the mother country to this day.

Finally putting their ears to the ground, the White Sox–Giants leadership heard the baseball season approach, and they cut short the tour and headed for home. If they had listened closely, they might have heard a great thunder.

ENGLAND AND GERMANY DECLARE WAR the *American* announced on August 5. Damon was noting that day that the Giants won a game although McGraw was sitting out a suspension after arguing with an umpire: "With all their affairs in the hands of a committee of three . . . the New York Giants nobly withstood the opening run of the Chicago (Ill.) Cubs. . . . At the close of business, the Giants seemed to have four runs, and the Cubs one. Which is as it should be. Scientific management must prevail."

Well, the sportswriter's job is to write sports. He spends his professional life in the shallow end of the pool. The principle was further tested on August 24, when Ellen Runyon gave birth to Mary Elaine, premature and weighing only two pounds. Damon's son wrote, "Mother, always dramatic, cried, 'If I'm going to die in childbirth, I'll do it at home! No hospital for me! Besides, imagine being born in a hospital!'"

Damon was not present for the birth. He was at the ball park, where he confessed:

The writer of this piece could not stop a ground ball with a fish net, and that's the honest truth. The writer of this piece could not catch a fly in a bushel basket, or hit a flock of balloons with a tennis racket.

He could not run once around the bases in ten minutes flat, to save his life. . . . He would steal second with the bases full as a matter of instinct. . . .

Nevertheless and notwithstanding, the writer of this piece is about to tell a lot of intelligent, well-paid, gentlemanly, professional baseball players how they should have played that pastime at the Polo Grounds yesterday.

With that high-powered hindsight through which we view so much of our parents' behavior, Damon's son commented bitterly that his father did not attend Mary's birth because "He was busy edifying the public about a more world-shaking event, a baseball game."

The father's presence in the delivery room is not a requirement of nature, and little Mary survived her father's absence at her debut. Ellen soon was noting the baby's first words, first step, and other remarkable signs of progress in a baby book.

This is not to say that Damon was domesticated. "My father held that he was keeping his end of the marriage deal if he won all the bread a breadwinner could win," the younger Runyon wrote. "The rest was left to the wife. Raising children, managing a home and such workaday chores were out of his province, and he viewed them with the detached air of an innocent bystander. . . ."

Damon also viewed the Giants faltering that season; perhaps they suffered from what's been called Montmartre in the legs. A morning-afternoon doubleheader with the onrushing Boston Braves, the Miracle Braves who came up from the cellar in mid-July, drew seventy thousand to the Polo Grounds, which Damon called "high tide in the history of baseball" and the Giants had to be satisfied with that modest achievement.

The Braves went on to sweep the mighty A's in the World Series, an event Damon found anticlimactic:

This thing today, when the Boston Braves won the championship of the baseball world, was like watching an old, old play, with familiarities precluding the possibility of surprise, and with no prospect of variety. . . .

The result almost seemed a foregone conclusion. The score of 3 to 1 would indicate a close game, but it did not seem

97

close. . . . It was a rather curious culmination of the greatest feat in the history of baseball. . . .

Damon was now being promoted as "The real literary treat the *American* offers." He turned his attention to an event as riveting for its sociological as for its sporting implications.

Nascent Ph.D.s and other troublemakers looking for evidences of racism in our history will find plenty to deplore in yesterday's newspapers. Blacks, Orientals, Germans, the Irish, Jews—all were the butts in comic strips, verse, and whimsical articles. The humor appeared good-natured, but it clearly reinforced, where it didn't create, stereotypes.

This manifested itself early in the century with the search for a "white hope," a phrase that passed into the language. The search was so determined that one fight manager sought a white hope among the peasants of China. The search was aimed at a reckless black named Jack Johnson, who was heavyweight champion of the world. No black had held that title. Johnson was no invisible man but a mouthy, high-living, hard-drinking champion who took a white wife and frequently taunted the white men he beat down in the ring.

Johnson won the championship from Tommy Burns in 1908, after shagging him all the way to Australia. He humiliated former champion James J. Jeffries two years later and still wasn't breathing hard. Sought for violation of the Mann Act, he departed the country for the good life on the boulevards of Europe. Damon encountered him in Paris during the Giants–White Sox tour: "The conqueror of Jeffries actually blocks traffic when he goes about. He is apparently rolling in money. He has a valet, secretary, chauffeur and three new cars. His new wife, who is constantly attended by two maids, has Jack completely under her thumb."

In April 1915 Johnson defended his title at a Havana racetrack grounds against the latest white hope, a relatively amiable former cowpuncher from Kansas named Jess Willard, called The Tall Pine of Pottowattamie. Willard was bigger and younger than Johnson, but it took considerable suspension of disbelief to make him out a bomber, even though he had killed a man in the ring.

Damon didn't think much of the fight in prospect. The day after his daughter's first Christmas, he called the idea of a Johnson-Willard match ". . . a gloomy thought to add to the mental depression of the morning after." He discussed rumors "that Willard is fixed to win on a foul or otherwise . . ." and another rumor "that the likelihood of some excited Texan shooting John Arthur if he is winning from the white man."

On the scene in Havana, he thought neither man appeared to be in good condition. A few days before the fight, he reported a dramatic development: "Opinion on the big fight among Americans here has been almost completely stampeded to Willard during the past twenty-four hours. . . . This sudden general sentimental switch is based on no hint of fake, either. . . ."

The fight itself has been recast for more than half a century now, fed by Johnson's imaginative recounting, in which he claimed that he took a dive so that authorities would allow him to return to the United States to visit his dying mother. Johnson also claimed that a German zeppelin once shadowed him through the streets of London. He was a fine man but seldom under oath. The fact seems to be that Willard simply wore him down and knocked him out, but as with Germany after the Great War and the post-bellum American South, there are those who prefer the losers' versions.

As Damon noted in his account from ringside, there was honor enough for the thirty-seven-year-old Johnson in going almost twenty-six rounds under a broiling sun. It is the longest heavyweight title match ever fought with gloves.

"Tonight, Jess Willard, a gawky, green-looking Kansas farmer cowpuncher is heavyweight champion of the world, with all the world before him," Damon wrote, "while Jack Johnson, late lord of the pugilistic realm, is just a portly, middle-aged colored man, browsing on the record of one of the greatest battles ever made by a man of his years."

Damon noted that between the twenty-first and twenty-second rounds, Johnson told his corner that he was getting weary and could not go on much longer. "I want you to get my wife out of here," he was reported to have said. But it was the twenty-sixth round before that emissary we all rely on at the crossroads of life found Mrs. Johnson. Her husband was dropped before her eyes.

"She exclaimed, 'Oh, my God,' then disappeared in the mad crush of 18,000 people suddenly gone mad," Damon wrote. "Something approaching a race riot followed. Thousands of people began parading the track, yelling, 'Viva la Blanca!' while the blacks drew off in little groups."

Persons close to Willard promptly announced that he would "draw the color line and stick to it," i.e., not defend the title against a black, Oriental, or red man. There was precedent. John L. Sullivan simply said, "I never fought a colored man. I never shall," and no one regarded this as a taint on his claim to be champion of all the world that walks on two legs and more or less talks.

Rumor surfaced immediately that the Johnson-Willard fight was fixed. Damon addressed himself to the question for the rest of the week. He quoted a black heavyweight who served as a Johnson sparring partner as "pointing the finger of suspicion at the fight." Damon said, "We do not wholly agree," but he passed the testimony along in the interests of fair reporting. He expressed his feelings on the racial hullaballoo by calling the fight "the recent triumph of the noble white race."

By the end of the week, he was writing, "We believe . . . the fight was strictly on the level. If it wasn't, then we were as badly fooled as anyone else. We believe that it was not only on the level but, for the big man, a great fight. . . . There is nearly always a whispering of fake after a big fight. . . . There is nearly always a whispering of fake after every great sporting event."

The concern over color seemed peculiarly unfortunate in a nation about to bleed making the world safe for democracy. But it was not confined to the sporting mob.

Herbert Bayard Swope, then city editor of the *World*, "had a low opinion of most full-time sports writers," according to Swope's authorized biographer, E. J. Kahn. "He thought them infantile." Swope took himself to Havana. He noted that Willard, like John Brown, came from Pottowattamie, "but he certainly had no love for the colored brother." Swope reported the crowd "begged for Willard to wipe out the stigma that they and hundreds of thousands of others, especially in the South, believe rested on the white race through a negro holding the championship."

Swope told his readers about Mrs. Johnson, who was pretty "in spite of the paint on her cheeks and the rouge on her lips. . . . She seemed fairly to enjoy her importance as she entered, and equally she seemed to bitterly resent her slide into obscurity as she left. Her transition was abrupt—from the wife of the world's champion, fawned upon and adulated, she had become merely the white consort of a fat and unusually homely, middle-aged and very dark negro. The women present had eyes for her and frowns for her when she left."

Concern about the rising tide of color was not restricted to blacks. Hearst, who was accused of pro-German bias, also saw the war as opening the west to a sinister oriental dominance. A fellow looking mighty like Dr. Fu Manchu leered over an *American* editorial in which Hearst warned "Europe is committing hari-kari on the doorsteps of Asia. . . . Asia sees the chance awaited for centuries. Civilization commits suicide and murders civilization. And Asia *waits*."

Having produced an inflammatory film about a Japanese plot to overthrow the United States government, Hearst turned his thoughts toward Mexico. He owned property there, and it had been despoiled by the guerrilla leader Francisco Villa, called Pancho.

"The was to IMPRESS Mexicans is to REPRESS the Mexicans," the *American* editorialized. "The way to begin is to say to them, 'We are no longer planning to catch this bandit or that. We are GOING INTO MEXICO. And, as far as we'll go, we'll *stay.*"

That was easy enough for Hearst to say. When Villa and his band crossed the border in 1916 and killed eight soldiers and nine civilians in Columbus, New Mexico, Washington ordered General John J. Pershing to capture Villa and restore order on the border.

Damon was detached from the Giants' spring training camp in Marlin, Texas, to cover the action. It would be conventional to suggest that he "graduated" from the sports page with the assignment, as though sports reporting were a kind of prep school for what Pulitzer regarded as a university. But whether there is greater challenge in covering another war or another session of Congress than in covering another World Series is a judgment call.

"Moving as swiftly and unerringly as a homing pigeon, Francisco Villa continues his flight eastward and southward toward the mountains of his boyhood country," Damon reported. The pursuit was hard going.

Slipping quietly and peacefully along the dusty roads of northern Mexico, General Pershing's flying columns are now covering a wide stretch of territory in pursuit of Villa. . . .

The heat on the dusty roads worked hardship on the troops, especially the infantry at first. But they are gradually becoming seasoned. . . .

Fires were burning on the mountainsides. Someone had probably accidentally touched off the dry grass, which grows at this season of the year as high as a man's waist. . . .

Villa used to light fires as signals, but there is no chance that Villa was responsible for this particular fire. With his sore and jaded horses, Pancho could not take a 24-hour start on the American cavalry and hope to get away.

There were fewer fires in the camp than usual because after a gorgeous day, the night was fairly warm. When a bunch of newspaper correspondents turned on the lamps of an automobile to furnish illumination for their literary efforts, the two shafts of light split the darkness with startling effect. . . .

The army never did catch up with Villa, but it dispersed his troops, and Damon clearly had caught the editorial eye as someone other than a sportswriter. In September 1916 he was in Chicago for Teddy Roosevelt's last hurrah at the Republican National Convention. Damon was so dazzled by "ante-convention stuff and preparedness parades" that one of his stories was not much more than his notes:

Weather, ok., clear skies, etc.
Limpid lake, etc.
Bands out early.
Streets decorated.
Pretty girls.
Enthusiasm, patriotism, etc.

He was there for the convention's single combustible moment:

Teddy's name may have missed fire . . . Thursday, but today it almost blew the roof off the Coliseum.
Senator A. B. Fall of New Mexico, who nominated Mr. Roosevelt, never really got the full name of his candidate before the house.
"I offer for your consideration," said the gray old legislator from the Far West, aiming a long, lean finger at his audience, "the name of Theodore—"
A woman in the gallery screamed hysterically. There was a masculine gasp and gurgle, and after that, for the space of 45 minutes, the place was given over to an uproar.
It was an uproar that was furnished largely by the spectators, however. . . .

After that bit of color, the convention went on in great tedium to nominate Charles Evans Hughes. Roosevelt bowed out of politics. The principle was established that when the occasion demanded Damon would be in the front row for spectacles other than sporting events.

Gene Fowler, newly arrived from Denver, caught up with Damon in 1917.

Fowler rode free to New York, accompanying the remains of an elderly woman he called Nellie, which he was assigned to deliver upstate. There were alcoholic delays, he misplaced the corpse a time or two, he got involved with Ben Hecht and Charles MacArthur and other journalistic rascals in Chicago, but after shedding Nellie completed the last lap of his trip by Hudson River Dayline, washed in memories of Washington Irving.

"It seemed like the most beautiful valley in the world . . . [and] the river boat's engine beat like the heart of an Irish queen," he wrote.

102

"Gray clouds moved slowly overhead, but the sun kept breaking through. The Hudson then became a silver sash across the July-green breast of the storied land. Three hundred years of history sailed with me from the portals of the Catskills to the rise of the Jersey Palisades and between banks of wondrous imaginings in the valley of the Dutch."

Damon showed Fowler around. They witnessed the funeral procession of former mayor John Purroy Mitchel, killed in a flight training crash. Damon introduced Fowler to a seedy character Damon called Dr. DeGarmo. "'I have deposited Doctor DeGarmo right here,' he said. And he tapped his brow with a well-manicured finger. 'Locked up tight, right here. Money in the bank. The Runyon Savings and No-Loan Bank.'"

For obscure reasons of youth, Fowler had elected to make his Big Town debut affecting a pince-nez he didn't need, a flowing necktie, and a walking stick he carried "like an oar out of water." Damon chewed him out. "You are getting off on the wrong foot in this man's town," he said. He told Fowler a reporter must be a spectator, not a spectacle, "until he has proved himself." Damon was always chewing Fowler out. In what was almost a journalistic tradition, Fowler left New York thinking unprintable thoughts about the city, but it was only a lover's quarrel.

World War I, which evolved into a nightmare, a stalemate of trench warfare and poison gas, had opened with notes of Chaplinesque burlesque. The *American* carried a front-page bulletin reporting SIXTH BOMB DROPPED ON PARIS: "A German bi-plane passed over Paris at 4:30 this afternoon and dropped a projectile. It did not explode."

Damon foresaw the suspension of boys' games played by men: "There will be little or no professional sports of any kind practiced for hire in this land if the war continues. . . . The time is probably not very far distant now when a baseball bat, a golf stick or a tennis racket in the hands of a man of serviceable age and physical ability will be an insignia of discredit."

Damon, Jr., was born June 17, 1918. Coincidentally, Damon that day offered a column by A. Mugg which is rich in insight for readers-between-the-lines:

> My young one is around the other evening with another book under her arm wanting me to read it to her, although I am busy thinking what a terrible sap I am to be betting on such a beetle as War Cloud and wondering if I am ever going to beat a race again in my whole life.
>
> Anyway, after the bawling out I get from my old lady when

she hears me telling the young one the story about Cinderella, I figure I am better off letting my young one do her own reading, but when young ones are only three years old, or some such matter, it is very hard to make them take a hint and go away and leave papa alone.

Finally I take her book and look it over and find it is a most interesting yarn. . . .

Once upon a time, or so it seems, there is a little dame who is called Little Red Riding Hood, because she always gets herself up in a red hood and red cloak, which, as I explain to my young one, may be a swell-looking outfit on Broadway, all right, but is not so good to wear across a pasture, where there may be a bull. . . .

The story is recounted in tough-guy terms before Damon's windup.

My young one says that he is a very bad wolf, and I tell her he is worse than that. I tell her he is certainly nothing more or less than a stinker, but pretty soon I hear her telling my old lady about a dirty old wolf which is a stinker, so I go downtown because I figure my old lady will be around after awhile, asking questions about where my young one gets that new word, and I cannot always be explaining things to dames.

Damon was going downtown a good deal. Broadway was becoming his real home. Ellen, Hoyt wrote, "did not yet understand that she was losing her husband to a street." The difficulty was more profound, as Gene Fowler learned on his return to Rainbow's End, this time accompanied by Agnes. America was at war now and, family or no family, Damon was itching to get overseas as a correspondent. He had recommended that Fowler replace him in the sports department.

Moving up in the world, Damon had moved his family from Queens to Manhattan. Ellen found the Fowlers a ground-floor apartment on 112th Street and Amsterdam Avenue, just south of the Runyon home, near the cathedral of St. John the Divine.

Fowler irritated Damon by holding out for a $100 salary from Hearst instead of accepting the $60 management offered. After Fowler got his money, an *American* veteran told him he'd been smart—"Mr. Hearst," he explained, "hates bargains."

The women, of course, got together. Ellen told Agnes of her growing loneliness. Damon spent nights away from home, often in the company of chorus girls. He told her, straight-faced, this was research.

Fowler got drunk on his first out-of-town assignment for the

American and arrived penniless at the Runyon home for dinner. Agnes was glad to see him. At the end of the meal, Damon exploded. "Well, all I've got to say is that I wish Ellen would overlook my mistakes like Agnes does yours."

Damon became a war correspondent. He warmed up by reporting the recruits' life with a verse called "The First Night at Yaphank," which begins:

> I'm there with two thin blankets,
> As thin as a slice of ham.
> A German spy was likely the guy
> Who made 'em for Uncle Sam.

One byproduct of World War I was a lasting literature, from *All Quiet on the Western Front* to *A Farewell to Arms,* and it also produced first-rate journalism, perhaps symbolized by Richard Harding Davis's account of the German war machine rolling through Belgium:

> The entrance of the German army into Brussels has lost the human quality. It was lost as soon as the three soldiers who led the army bicycled into the Boulevard du Regent and asked the way to the Gare du Nord. When they passed, the human note passed with them.
>
> What came after and twenty-four hours later is still coming, is not men marching, but a force of nature like a tidal wave, an avalanche or a river flooding its banks. At this minute, it is rolling through Brussels as the swollen waters of the Conemaugh Valley swept through Johnstown.
>
> At the sight of the first few regiments of the enemy we were thrilled with interest. After they had passed for three hours in one unbroken steel-gray column, we were bored. But when hour after hour passed and there was no halt, no breathing time, no open spaces in the ranks, the thing became uncanny, inhuman. You returned to watch it, fascinated. It held the mystery and menace of fog rolling toward you across the sea.

Damon's reporting from the front did not achieve that level. He saw only about a month of combat, sailing from New York in September for a war that ended November 11. The proud war machine of mystery and menace in 1914 was largely reduced, four years later, to ranks of broken and disillusioned men who only wanted the thing to end.

For a correspondent, there were lighter touches. Damon ran into Sergeant Alexander Woollcott, the drama critic, who told him an

American offensive "reminds you of a big first night because you see everyone you know." Damon encountered plenty of sports figures, including Hank Gowdy, the catcher, and pitchers Christy Mathewson and Grover Cleveland Alexander.

He had written a jingo verse about American might:

> The types that tell the story
> Sing Glory! Glory! Glory!
> They seem to be an echo of the guns—
> The Yankee guns!
> Each line a bar of music—
> Of sweeping, swelling music—
> Glory! Glory! Glory!
> To our God and to our guns!

The reality, he found, was different. The glory was aching feet as he covered the war on foot, hiking, he said, "from Etain to the Rhine." He wrote of rain "as finely woven and as clammy as a funeral garment" and of doughboys pulling themselves from the muck in which they'd slept "with a noise like yanking a rubber boot out of the mud."

Damon remembered to write home. "He's only being polite," Ellen told Agnes Fowler. "And he's farther off than France from me. He might as well be in Siberia, even when he's in New York."

After the Armistice, Damon traveled with the army as it occupied German territory. He interviewed General Pershing and Marshal Foch and the American ace Captain Eddie Rickenbacker, the beginning of a lifelong friendship. Damon's clock remained set to Broadway time. He followed up the day's round with visits to restaurants and nightclubs. With Webb Miller, a United Press correspondent, he requisitioned one of the better rooms in the finest hotel in Coblenz, to cover the arrival of the American troops.

They didn't get their wake-up call.

> The first I knew of the historic crossing of the Rhine [Miller wrote] was when I heard the tramp of feet, jumped to the window and shook Runyon awake.
>
> "The troops are starting to cross the Rhine, they're marching down the street. Get up!"
>
> "I'll be damned if I'll get up," Runyon grumbled. I argued with him . . . but he was obstinate. I sat in the open window, shivering and only half awake, describing the crossing in staccato phrases while he lay in bed. . . . Runyon wrote by far

106

the best story of any correspondent. He told how he stayed in bed within a few feet of the ceremony while I described to him the happenings.

Miller called his memoir, published in 1936, *I Found No Peace,* and the title might serve as epitaph for a considerable number of his generation. For many, the mood of disillusionment set in with the Armistice. For sports fans, the symbol of the end of innocence was the 1919 World Series, which, being fixed, proved that there were times when baseball was no longer a boys' game.

The 1919 Chicago White Sox were a great baseball team, often compared to the 1929 Philadelphia Athletics and the 1927 New York Yankees, the greatest of all. The Cincinnati Reds had heart and strong pitching.

The Series, stretched to nine games by vote of baseball's National Commission, opened in Cincinnati in an atmosphere of carnival, although Prohibition technically had set in.

"Fans looking for tickets. Fans looking for rooms," Damon wrote.

> Fans looking for drinks. Fans who have found drinks. Much jabber. Much walking up and down. Much walking back and forth. Many sore feet. More excitement than the time old John Morgan, the rebel son-of-a-gun, came riding up the Ohio on that raid. . . .
>
> Dope favors the White Sox but gives the Reds a great chance. Not much betting. Cincinnati folks want odds. Sox folks don't want to give odds. . . .
>
> "You rather lean to the Reds, don't you?" asked a gent who burst in on us out of the parched night.
>
> "Well, we may lean some, but don't nobody get to pushing."

In retrospect, every line written about the Series illumines the hoax. But if you leaned to the Reds, as Damon did, Cincinnati's 9-1 win in the first game was not suspicious.

Chicago's Ed Cicotte "'had nothing' as they put it in baseball parlance," Damon wrote. "The magic of the right arm that carried Chicago . . . through to a pennant had vanished. The spell of the so-called 'shine ball,' at which Cicotte is supposed to be the master, and which seemed to enthrall the batsmen of his own league, was impotent before the Reds."

Chicago's wonders couldn't pitch, hit, or field. They ran the bases clumsily, misjudged flies, threw to the wrong base. After the second game, Ring Lardner and a couple of other embittered Chicago newspapermen gathered in a roadhouse and wrote a lyric to a popular tune:

> I'm forever blowing ball games,
> Pretty ball games in the air,
> I come from Chi,
> I hardly try,
> Just go to bat and fade and die. . . .

The poignance behind the bitterness of that lyric is deep. There is a disputed theory that Lardner, who would descend into alcoholism and early death, never recovered from the shock of witnessing the sellout. That may be oversimplification, but gamblers and eight White Sox indeed had *played with the faith of fifty million American people.*

"There was a little more betting last night and today than at any time since the Series started," Damon wrote after Cincinnati won the second game, "with Reds fans taking even money where a few hours before they were asking odds. Not a great deal of money was bet, at that. Not a great deal of money ever is bet on these World Series. . . ."

Too much, it turned out. When the Reds won the eighth game and the Series, Damon wrote, "Even at best, the game was a burlesque."

In a way the Series served as a fitting epigraph for the vulgarity of the next decade, the time of what was called Flaming Youth in what was called the Roaring Twenties. A different kind of journalism reported that world, and the time of Aurelia and her fellow holding hands on the stoop in the moonlight already seemed remote, innocent, and almost laughable.

seven

"WE WANT what one may call canons," the editor of the Richmond *Commercial Compiler* wrote in 1817, "for the management of the press, a sort of 'codification,' as Jeremy Bentham calls it, of those *rules,* which ought to guide the conductor of the press—to regulate its *liberty* and restrain its *licentiousness.* Not rules enacted by the laws of the land, but *rules,* drawn from the sound principles of discussion and forming a sort of moral legislation for the press. . . ."

That idea's time has never really come.

To be sure, there are publishers and editors associations, where executives make speeches and tear them up, but no thoughtful man regards them seriously, and the American press has remained pretty much free to develop on impulse. It is not the best of all possible worlds, since the founder of a newspaper enterprise needs cash as well as inspiration, but the professor was not entirely Panglossian who wrote that the press "operated well enough for society as it is"— unless, of course, the reader regards society as anywhere near perfect.

Impulse certainly figured in what Stanley Walker in 1936 called "the most significant trend in American journalism since the war . . . the rise of the *Daily News,* the New York tabloid."

There was even a screwball symbolism in the birthplace of the *News.* It was conceived near a manure pile in a farmyard near Mareuil-en-Dôle, France, on July 20, 1918, and a pungent earthiness if not quite the odor of the *fumier* informed its great moments.

The founding fathers were two rich young men from Chicago, Captain Joseph Medill Patterson of Battery B, 149th Field Artillery, Rainbow Division, and Colonel Robert R. McCormick of the 61st Field Artillery, both scions of a fortune built on newspapers and other endeavors.

Patterson recently had spent a furlough in London, where he was impressed by Lord Northcliffe's *Daily Mirror,* a pictorial tabloid with a circulation of eight hundred thousand. He talked things over with the British press lord, who suggested New York would be fertile ground for a kind of American cousin. Patterson and McCormick agreed.

109

The *Illustrated Daily News,* as it was called when it first appeared on June 26, 1919, was neither the first American tabloid nor the first picture paper. The trick was to think of them again. The first illustrated daily in the world, according to the historian Silas Bent, was the *Daily Graphic,* published in Park Place in 1872. It was somewhat larger than the conventional tabloid, called itself "the greatest newspaper enterprise of the day," and perished in 1889.

Two years later Frank A. Munsey, the newspaper murderer, merged a couple of papers into the *Daily Continent,* believing "a smaller sheet with the news presented concisely would be more convenient than the conventional blanket-size newspaper." But the experiment didn't last six months.

During a visit to New York, Lord Northcliffe got out the January 1, 1901, issue of the *World,* in tabloid form. Circulation that day jumped by 100,000, but Pulitzer's nod was Homeric, and the episode is another "what if" of journalistic history.

The *Daily News*—it soon dropped the *Illustrated* as redundant—achieved swift success, not without some financial struggle. Circulation topped 230,000 in a year and 1,000,000 within six years before becoming the largest in the annals of the daily American press.

The difference between that success and earlier failures seems to have been Patterson. Bent scorned the paper's reliance on "piety, patriotism and prurience." Patterson himself said, "The *News* built its popularity on legs. When we got the circulation, we put stockings on the legs." Plenty of publications have tried that dodge without lasting long enough to order the stockings.

The *News* was saucy and tough. Patterson had the common touch. In its first issue, the paper promised "the appeal of news pictures and brief, well-told stories will be apparent to you as it has been to millions of readers in European cities. . . . The story that is told by a picture can be grasped instantly. . . . No story will be continued on another page. . . . You can read it without eye-strain."

News pictures made news, from exclusive, first-photos of the Wall Street bomb explosion on September 16, 1920, to exclusive, first-photos of Christine Jorgensen, the ex-GI who underwent a sex change operation in 1950. One picture never has been worth a thousand words to the literate, but until the advent of television, the news photograph gave the looker—as distinct from the reader—his sharpest sense of being there.

Patterson pioneered in Hollywood coverage. He promoted secretaries to movie critics and theater writers. At one to five dollars an acceptance, the *News* enlisted contributions from readers: "My Most Embarrassing Moment"; "Bright Sayings of Children"; "My Motor

Experience"; "The Queerest Boss I Ever Worked For." It invited "Real Love Stories" from readers, explaining, "No attention will be paid to literary style," and it offered $10,000 to "The Most Beautiful Girl in New York" (Alice Louise Secker, a corset factory girl).

For decades, conventional wisdom held that "more than any other feature, the comic strip is responsible for holding readers to a newspaper." Patterson dreamed up or promoted "The Gumps," the first comic with a story line; "Gasoline Alley," the first comic in which characters aged; "Harold Teen," which greatly influenced American youth with its bell-bottom trousers, autographed raincoats, and such slang as "Fan mah brow"; "Dick Tracy," the progenitor of all comic-strp cops, and, of course, "Little Orphan Annie," the reactionary gamine.

The *News* was best when it was irreverent, which was most of the time, whether headlining an opera singer's death at the Metropolitan —SINGER CROAKS ON HIGH C, or explaining a presidential refusal of financial aid to New York—FORD TO CITY: DROP DEAD—which some analysts believe lost the President the state in the ensuing election.

Patterson died an isolationist, but he had done a lot of thinking in his lifetime. He embraced socialism in his youth, and it was no casual liaison as he reviewed his capitalistic heritage with wonder and scorn:

> My income doesn't descend on me like manna from heaven. It can be traced. Some of it comes from the profit of a daily newspaper; some of it comes from Chicago real estate; some from the profits made by the Pennsylvania and other railroads. . . .
>
> It takes to support me just about twenty times as much as it does to support the average working man or farmer. And the funny thing about it is that these workingmen and farmers work hard all year around, while I don't work at all.
>
> I have better food, better clothes and better houses than the workers who supply me with money to spend. I can travel oftener. I have horses to ride and drive, domestic servants . . . the best physicians. . . . My children will never go to work in a cotton mill or a sweatshop. In short, I live a far more civilized life than the working people.

He vowed, "I shall go to work and try to produce hereafter at least a portion of the wealth which I consume." He wrote novels. *A Little Brother of the Rich* included an attack on society girls which might have been written by a vulgar Shaw: "They can't sing, they can't dance, they can't act, they can't paint, they can't sew, they can't cook,

111

they can't educate. They are inept, unthorough, inconsequential, rudderless, compassionless, drifting. They don't know life because they haven't lived life. . . . They delegate all their functions in life save one—and even that they don't do well enough or often."

He wrote plays. In 1909 Broadway saw his collaborative effort, *The Fourth Estate,* with a finale that featured two linotype machines pounding on stage. As the curtain fell, ushers distributed copies of the crusading editor's "extra."

By the time Patterson founded the *Daily News,* he had discovered that socialism was somewhat worse than a bad cold. But the arteries of the *News* never hardened into the senescent reaction of Colonel McCormick's Chicago *Tribune,* and Patterson supported Franklin Roosevelt through most of three terms.

He did not rely on marketing experts before founding the newspaper; surely they would have warned him off. There were seven other morning newspapers and ten afternoon dailies in place. Patterson operated with not much more than his own conviction, as had Pulitzer forty years earlier.

Arthur Brisbane was regarded as a high-octane thinker, a kind of Walter Lippmann of the proles, and, like Lippmann, he often guessed wrong. He didn't think the *News* offered Hearst much competition. He saw it as "pictures and vaudeville for the unintelligent masses" and didn't believe it could succeed without Hearst's genius—Brisbane—behind it. Time would demonstrate the extent of his error.

When the *News* passed half a million in circulation, the *American,* under orders to fight at all costs, announced a lottery with a grand prize of $1,000. The following day, the *News* answered with its own lottery and a prize of $2,500. The *American* doubled that. The *News* went to $10,000.

Prizes were awarded to persons holding coupons whose number corresponded to those printed in the papers. Maddened crowds gathered where circulation trucks distributed the coupons—in Times Square, Columbus Circle, the Battery. Police were called out. No one, not even the staffs, paid much attention to other events of the day, wars, murders, politicians. When the *News* raised the ante to $25,000 the *American* editor all but collapsed. By agreement, Patterson and Hearst executives prevailed on postal authorities to chastise them and stop the contest.

The decade of the 1920s was made for the *News,* for tabloid journalism, for the gossip column and the stardom of the sports reporter. It is recalled in terms of big events like Lindbergh's flight and Teapot Dome, big trials like the Hall-Mills case and Snyder-Gray, outsize sports legends like Dempsey, Ruth, Grange, Tilden, and Bobby Jones, Hollywood stars like Valentino and Mary Pickford.

Broadway itself was changing. Speakeasies supplanted restaurants. Ziegfeld began glorifying the American girl in 1907, and by the time of *The Passing Show of 1914,* FPA noted it featured "a large number of handsome girls. But they . . . had too little clothing to be alluring, and I was minded to think on Percy Hammond's observation that the human knee is a joint and not an entertainment."

It didn't take much to wow the Americano. Behind his world of bathtub gin, fast cars, and the snappy rejoinder hinting at sophistication stood Mencken's credulous boob. In the words of a French observer, writing about New York receptions for royalty, channel swimmers, heroes for a day: "The soul of the crowd is in large measure the soul of a race. Here one saw the American people replete with a facility of juvenile admiration, with a collective and docile infatuation for anyone who can boast of having accomplished something."

Walter Winchell was ideally suited to report that decade and to help make popular its values. In *The Night Club Era,* Stanley Walker commented, "Winchell brought to his job the perfect equipment—great energy, an eager desire to know what was going on, a lack of conventional breeding and experience, a mind delightfully free of book learning, and an unquenchable desire to be a newspaperman. If his background had been different, he would have been so befuddled by the canons of what some people call good taste that he would have been revolted by some of his best stuff."

Walter never worked for the *News.* But the birth of the picture tabloid provided his access to daily journalism. He already was beginning to gray in his and the decade's early twenties, as he hustled for Albee's *Vaudeville News,* writing columns called "Merciless Truth" and "Broadway Hearsay," making acquaintances not only among show business professionals but among men like State Senator James J. Walker and Herbert Bayard Swope.

He already had developed the technique of suggesting the unpleasant possibility—"One of the Vanderbilts is about to be Renovated. . . . Are the Jerome Astors of High Sassiety tossing it out the window?"—and the technique, too, of writing the blind item: "A blondiful sextress is asking for trouble, fooling around with married men. Are there any other men? Hehehehe," which was irresponsible since it raised the possibility that anyone who could be called a blondiful sextress—what *is* a sextress? an actress in a salacious production? an actress of easy approach?—was "fooling around" with

113

someone else's husband. This is not a quibble. The blind item is written with a poison pen, and with sophistication it would damage reputations more substantial than that of a sextress.

If Walter was attracting attention, he still needed assistance.

Billy Koch was a bookmaker and Walter's uncle. He helped support Walter's father, who came around just about weekly, always dapper and well groomed, always talking of business prospects, accepting whatever was in the envelope Billy passed him. Billy advanced Walter money with which to buy a Speed Graphic camera for his work. But it wasn't photography that promoted Walter's career.

Getting a mention in his columns began to mean something. The *Vaudeville News* had been a throwaway, but he talked management into charging a nickel for it. He became advertising manager with a commission of 20 percent for ads he solicited. He gave favorable mention in his columns to restaurants or performers who bought advertising. Some weeks he made as much as $100, more than his editor.

Walter separated his items with three dots, setting the style for his imitators. "I originally used dashes when I was writing 'Newsense,'" he told Klurfeld. "But the dash key got stuck, so I used three dots. I don't know why it was three. It just looked right, I guess."

Much of the glamour of the 1920s was seen through a glass of prohibition liquor, darkly. But there was a sort of license for romance, and it seems a time when boy met girl cute, as they said in Hollywood.

The first scandalous murder of the decade occurred June 11, 1920, when a person still unknown shot and killed Joseph Elwell, clubman and reigning bridge wizard, in his West Side brownstone, *plugged him through the head*. Investigators found a card index listing the names of fifty-three women, many of them pillars of society, an assortment of lingerie, and, for the Lothario himself, a closetful of wigs and corsets.

Arriving late on the scene was a young reporter named James Westbrook Pegler, not long since bounced from the European front for baiting generals. He was a son of Arthur Pegler, who is credited by some with *inventing* the Hearst style, which the senior Pegler likened to "a screaming woman running down the street with her throat cut."

Bud Pegler, as James Westbrook was then called, was filled in on developments in the Elwell case by a young woman reporter for the *News,* Julia Harpman. Not long after, she was seriously injured in a street accident. The courtship took place in the hospital, they married, and until the day she died in 1955, his concern and devotion to her were the marvel of all who knew Pegler as a man who instinctively went for the jugular, including Walter's. Not long before Julie's death, Pegler had the wife of his fictional alter ego say "nobody knows how crazy I am about the most wonderful husband of all. Frantic, insane, frenzied. I said I know, I know, I know. And you know what she did? She cried."

Walter, in the beginning, was almost as lucky. He received a tip about a young dancer who had taken in an infant and was struggling to support it. He hustled over to a theatrical hotel on West Forty-sixth Street and knocked on the door whose number he had been given. There was no answer. He knocked again.

A sleepy voice asked, "Who is it?"

Walter identified himself. The name did not yet open doors. He explained his mission. The young woman either told him over the transom that she was simply caring for a friend's child or, in another version of the story, pushed a baby carriage into the hall and said, "Talk to the baby if you want the facts so badly."

In either case, on that day Walter first saw June Magee, a blue-eyed, red-haired young woman who had left her native Mississippi as half of a girl dance act called Hill and Aster, found little success, married and divorced. Walter said, "I fell in love with the sound of her voice." She was almost as impressed by Walter as he was. He put a photo of her dance team on the inside cover of the *Vaudeville News*.

They were married, according to Walter, three weeks after they met, renting an apartment down the street. Walter took her to openings at the Palace, to the new night life of the city, but she seldom wanted to be a party to that and didn't often accompany him on his rounds.

The specific culture that spawned Walter's career was Prohibition.

"There was a spirit of lawlessness, of revolt from both unreasonable reform and from Victorian convention, reasonable or unreasonable," McKelway wrote in *Gossip*. "There was the hysteria of elation which precedes a depression, and a tolerance everywhere which amounted to abnegation."

According to the Broadway historian Louis Sobol, Manhattan suffered for about twenty-four hours after Prohibition's arrival on January 16, 1920, before the borough's first speakeasy was in business. It was the 50-50 Club, located over a garage at 129 East Fiftieth Street, with a membership of fifty men who paid $100 each as initiation fee. Members stored their liquor in private lockers.

It remained for a progenitor named Perkins to set up the first illegal bar, in a brownstone on Fortieth Street east of Fifth Avenue. The words "speakeasy" and "bootlegger" were imported from the rural south, which had a long history of circumventing Prohibition laws, and soon bootleggers were supplying speakeasies like the Club

Napoleon, Jack and Charley's, the Stork, and the Park Avenue, which boasted a bar that cost $50,000.

No record of the meeting survives, but it would be surprising if Walter's path did not cross Damon's on the nightclub circuit of the period, since both spent considerable time there. It is not likely that Damon would have noticed the young gossip, who was just getting the wind to his back.

Although Damon still covered sports in the early twenties, he was free to comment on more general matters. Sometimes "A. Mugg's" column turned up in the *American* on a news page, and one of those columns sounds like a man clearing his throat in preparation for the kind of story Damon later made famous. It also reflects the genial "spirit of lawlessness" which accompanied Prohibition:

> Well, sir, I have to laugh when I think about it now, ha, ha, ha, ha, ha! but I am not laughing so much at the time it comes off, because, at the time it is no laughing matter.
>
> What I am talking about is a proposition the other night up here in a joint on Broadway and what I am doing there is something that must not be misunderstood. I am there by accident.
>
> I am standing on a corner thinking of nothing much in particular, except maybe what a terrible town this is since there is no place to go, when along comes a friend of mine by the name of Shorty something, who is called Shorty because he is about eight feet high.

Damon explains that Shorty is a "flat hopper" or "someone who knows where there are many flats with liquor."

"Well, personally, I am not interested in hooch," he wrote, "because it is years since I take a drink, what with my stomach going back on me and one thing and another, but where there is a flat full of hooch, there is always likely to be other propositions so, of course, I go along."

But a knock on the door so terrifies the drinkers assembled in the apartment that seven of them jam themselves into a small closet. The knock was a false alarm. The guests resume their drinking. And the narrator discovers that without panic as a spur, only four men can fit in the closet.

Even as semifiction, the column is interesting, with its excuse of the bad stomach for not drinking—and Damon always ate heartily—and the comment that there are other "propositions" in a "flat full of hooch." Broadway already was commenting on Damon's string of ponies, and Ellen Runyon spoke to her closest confidante, Gene

116

Fowler's wife, "about the chorus girls Alfred would sit with all through the night."

"He was looking for characters," the loyal Fowler explained.

"That's one way to put it," said Agnes Fowler.

No siren's song was required to call Damon from the hearthside. Along with Irvin S. Cobb, Bozeman Bulger, and a few others, he "acquired a pot-bellied old boat in which we voyaged out of Seaford on Long Island, fishing in the Sound in the summer and shooting shore birds in the fall and ducks and geese in the winter. We would sleep and eat on the boat and sometimes get frozen in by ice for days at a time, but Cobb was always all the entertainment we needed."

Damon was eulogizing Cobb, but, of course, he was also writing about himself: "I never knew Cobb to be unavailable for a hunting trip, and I do not think it was because of any great love of the chase. I think it was because he enjoyed male companionship and the life of the camps. He was at his best in boots and canvas clothing before a roaring fire in the woods surrounded by hairy-chested guys who could eat and drink in quantity."

For more extended trips, the group acquired a hunting lodge in Georgia called Dover Hall. Damon would pass on the fishing, but he enjoyed the hunt.

His son recalled that Damon once

> hung a string of duck corpses out the window of the 95th Street apartment when my mother banned them from the icebox. A neighbor below yelled bloody murder. Blood from the deceased birds had dripped down and was absorbed by an expensive coat she had put out for an airing on her window sill.
>
> My mother told my father in no uncertain terms that hereafter she would take care of the food department by going to stores like civilized people did—never mind the big hunter act.

In addition to the hunting trips and the intervals with the chorines, duty called Damon far from home. He reported political conventions, adventure—boarding the navy ship that accompanied a quartet of army around-the-world fliers—and the big sports stories.

His interest had shifted from baseball to boxing, thanks primarily to yet another Coloradan, Jack Dempsey, whom Damon christened the Manassa Mauler. Damon thought a plasterer from Rochester, Minnesota, named Fred Fulton was Willard's heir apparent, but Dempsey took care of that in one round. Fulton's manager later told

117

Damon that Fred's heart "sometimes swelled up to the size of a pea."

By the spring of 1919 Damon was building up the Dempsey-Willard title match with a series called "A Tale of Two Fists: The Life Story of Jack Dempsey," which appeared sporadically in the *American* over a two-month period. Damon later confessed that because he wrote so much, there was a good deal of water in his stuff, and the "biography" is full of digression and philosophy, stories of Dempsey's hobo life that are clearly as much Damon as Dempsey, and the confession: "I want to warn you that I may not get Jack Dempsey's early ring battles in their chronological order. I may forget to put one in exactly where it should occur in his history . . . but that's not my fault. It's due to Jack's captious memory. His mind does not work in a groove. It bobs about. Every time I see him, he says, 'Hey, I forgot to tell you about. . . .'"

Dempsey recalled an early fight with one Johnny Sudenberg. Sudenberg knocked him down seven times in the first round, three times in the second, twice in the third. "Finally, Johnny got sort o' weary knocking me down, and then I commenced knocking him down. I knocked him down so often I lost count. I guess I evened up the knockdowns. Anyhow, the referee called it a draw."

His manager spent all but $10 of that $150 purse "entertaining the town," Dempsey recalled, "but he was a good guy, at that." Dempsey said, "It looked as if I'd never learn to box. I was a terrible mug. I couldn't get over the idea that I ought to fight a man like I'd fight him in the street."

That was Damon's kind of fighter. He went to Toledo, Ohio, in June for the Willard match, although the fight didn't take place until July 4. There wasn't much doubt in his mind about the outcome.

"Jess Willard reminds me of nothing so much as a businessman grown a bit flashy and flabby on the treadmill of trade," he wrote, "working out in the gymnasium of his club in a mild effort to restore some of the physical form of his youth."

Willard was six inches taller than Dempsey, outweighed him by some sixty pounds and expressed concern that he might kill the challenger. But Damon noted that Willard "by his own admission is eleven years past [Dempsey's] twenty-four, and, after watching the two men at their training, one can almost imagine they see those eleven years standing, grim and grisly, like old dead trees among the brief stretch of roadway that separates the two camps." Besides, he learned that Willard was sleeping late.

Ohio was one of those states with its own Volstead act, prohibition taking effect July 1, and Ring Lardner marked the blow with a dirge of his own composition:

118

I guess I've got those there Toledo Blues,
About this fight I simply can't enthuse,
I don't care if Dempsey win or lose
Owing to the fact I've got Toledo Blues.

There seemed to be no shortage of liquor. Damon noted that Lardner lost a round of golf to Rube Goldberg, the cartoonist. "They took advantage of Lardner in getting him up early, however."

Damon believed that "Between things human, it's never 4-1; it's mostly 6-5," but he also believed in Dempsey to the extent of "laying the chunk," that is, betting all he could get his hands on, that Dempsey would knock out Willard in the first round. In one of the most ferocious rounds in heavyweight history, Dempsey almost did that, dropping Willard seven times and breaking his cheekbone.

Willard was sitting when the referee counted ten, and Damon and other longshot bettors were mentally squandering the money when they learned that the referee had failed to hear the bell at the count of seven. Willard lasted two more rounds with the arm-weary Dempsey.

Dempsey went to New York with the traditional retinue. Another Hearst bard, George Phair, described for all time the athletic king and his court:

Hail, the conquering hero comes,
Surrounded by a bunch of bums.

Until the advent of Joe Louis heavyweight champions were not expected to busy themselves with title defenses. Dempsey did not face a major challenger for two years, and even the importance of that fight was a tribute to the sportwriters' imagination, if not their greed. Georges Carpentier, called the Orchid Man, was a French war hero and a fine fighter who had worked his way up from the lighter weights, but he was not much more than an overblown middleweight when he faced Dempsey on July 2, 1921, in Boyle's Thirty Acres in Jersey City.

The buildup for the fight was prodigious. Dempsey's promoter was a close-mouthed gambler from the gold fields named Tex Rickard. He did not spend a penny on advertising his fights, but he gave newspaper employes tickets it would cost $10,000 to buy, according to Silas Bent, and he told *Editor and Publisher* that he spent $65,000 a year "entertaining" boxing writers. Gene Fowler had picked up fees refereeing fights in Denver; when he got to New York, he learned there was money for a reporter in boxing that didn't require the effort of playing third man.

119

Damon was closer to Dempsey than to any other sports legend of the twenties. But the sporting press's interest in Dempsey's fight with a challenger one observer called "the frayed French light-heavyweight" was fanned by money under the table.

In *The Daily Newspaper in America,* Alfred McClung Lee recalls an exposé touched off by Jack Kofoed, a sportswriter for the *Post:* "Rickard called in the boxing writers who had taken money in the past and told them what he wanted. The price varied according to the promoter's estimate of their value to him. Five hundred to one. One thousand to another. . . . Bit by bit, interest was steamed up. Even men who refused the Rickard gratuity wrote column upon column about the fight."

All that helped produce boxing's first million-dollar gate. "I never seed anything like it," Rickard remarked of the crowd, which was tony, dotted with Hollywood stars, society figures, and reputedly respectable women. What they saw was not much of a fight.

"Our Mary once had a delicate little French doll, all lacy and frilly and very pretty to look at," Damon wrote. "One day the bull terrier pup got hold of the doll. The sight of the little doll after the terrier got through with it kept recurring to mind this afternoon as Georges Carpentier of France lay on the canvas floor in the fourth round, mauled by 'Iron Mike,' the right hand of Jack Dempsey."

Arthur Brisbane called it a fight "between a thoroughbred and a percheron." H. L. Mencken, on assignment for the *World,* concluded, "It was simply a brief and hopeless struggle between a man full of romantic courage and one overwhelmingly superior in every way."

As a central figure in the Golden Age of Sport, Dempsey was eulogized in a *World* editorial as "a sort of legend with us, a superhuman colossus of brawn."

This sort of thing was laminated gold leaf. A midwestern editor of the period lamented that the newspapers had created a Frankenstein monster of public interest in sports and then worshiped their own handiwork. Excess often results in calamity, and on July 4, 1923, Dempsey participated in one of sports' stranger episodes, which John Lardner called "the rape of Shelby, Montana."

Dempsey won a fifteen-round decision over a light-punching boxer named Tom Gibbons, in a fight promoted by boosters hoping to put the old hometown on the map. The bout was an artistic and financial failure, leaving the customers dissatisfied and the community broke.

Damon called it a fight between a coyote (Gibbons), "one of the wiliest, fastest and shiftiest animals of the plains," and a greyhound, "strong, alert, speedy, dangerous," and pretty much let it go at that.

Dempsey almost immediately redeemed himself against an Argentine slugger named Luis Firpo, amid scenes of bedlam in New York.

As Damon described it under a front-page bannerline on September 15:

> Seven times the tiger man, Dempsey, knocked the 'Wild Bull of the Pampas' to the floor in the first round in the Giants stadium last night; seven times the 'Wild Bull' struggled to his feet, punch drunk, glassy-eyed and reeling.
>
> Then out of the wildest, maddest flurry of human fists that men have ever seen in the prize ring, out of a brawling, crazy struggle that had 85,000 men and women on their feet screaming, the 'Wild Bull,' Louis Angel Firpo, clubbed Dempsey to his knee—clubbed him clear out of the ring.

Dempsey climbed back in the ring and flattened Firpo in the second round. Brisbane sniffed, "It is a pitiful exhibition of bloody, awkward maulers. . . . Two good ditch diggers were ruined when they became inferior prize fighters. . . . Put the two men in a locked room and Firpo would have killed him." But that was a minority view, and the Dempsey-Firpo fight entered the books as epic.

One of Damon's finest pieces of sportswriting centered on another legend. The New York Yankees won their first World Series, but they lost the opening game to the Giants on an inside-the-park home run by Casey Stengel, and not the least interesting thing about Damon's marvelous lead is the fact that he was calling Casey Stengel "old" in 1923:

> This is the way old Casey Stengel ran yesterday afternoon, running his home run home.
>
> This is the way old Casey Stengel ran running his home run home to a Giant victory by a score of 5 to 4 in the first game of the World Series of 1923.
>
> This is the way old Casey Stengel ran, running his home run home, when two were out in the ninth inning and the scored was tied and the ball was still bounding inside the Yankee yard.
>
> This is the way—
>
> *His mouth wide open.*
>
> *His warped old legs bending beneath him at every stride.*
>
> *His arms flying back and forth like those of a man swimming with a crawl stroke.*
>
> *His flanks heaving, his breath whistling, his head far back.*

121

Yankee infielders, passed by old Casey Stengel as he was running his home run home, say Casey was muttering to himself, adjuring himself to greater speed as a jockey mutters to his horse in a race, that he was saying: "Go on, Casey! Go on!"

Spectacle was everywhere in the twenties. The war, historians tell us, left Americans avid for sensation and release. Some of that was supplied by sportswriters like Damon. He responded to the mood of restlessness, and in 1922 he developed a new and abiding interest, horse racing. The affair bloomed in Saratoga, a mirage in upstate New York, and it inspired perhaps his single most famous piece of writing.

Damon's column of August 1 recalled a drunk who attended a fight in Coney Island that lasted eighty-eight rounds. The drunk fell asleep in the fifteenth round and awoke in the fiftieth round and muttered, "Say, I've seen these fellows fight somewhere before."

That was how he felt, Damon wrote, after going to bed at the old United States hotel without seeing a familiar face and then awakening in the morning.

> We had a vague sense of having taken a long journey the night before that carried us back from strange parts to familiar haunts.
>
> We were back on Manhattan Island with the same bunch you see in front of the Astor in the early evening or up at Reuben's along toward morning, dapper, soft-collared, knowing-looking gentry, scattered around. . . .
>
> Between suns, the old town of Saratoga has come to life, the life it leads for one brief month every year when the horse races come here and which revives to some extent the glory that was Saratoga's in the days when it was one of the most brilliant spots on the American continent. . . .

That mellow mood animated what proved to be a kind of heroic song cycle. On Sunday, August 13, in a column of comment called "Saratoga Chips," Damon paid homage to jockey Earl Sande:

> Sloan, they tell me, could ride 'em,
> Maher, too, was a bird;
> Bullman was a guy to guide 'em—
> Never worse than third.
> Them was the old-time jockeys;

122

Now when I want to win
Gimme a handy
Guy like Sande
Ridin' them hosses in.

There are two more hypnotic stanzas, insistent as hoofbeats. Two
weeks later, Sande won on a horse called Edict, and Damon's lead
was:

McAdoo knows them horses,
Ensor's a judge of pace;
Johnson kin ride the courses
In any old kind o' race.
All them guys are good ones
But, say, when I want to win
Gimme a handy
Guy like Sande
Bootin' a long shot in.

Damon was not a man to let a good line, lines, or idea die, and when
Sande won a big stakes race at Belmont Park on September 12,
Damon offered a variation on the theme:

Kummer is quite a jockey,
Maybe as good as the best.
Johnson is not so rocky
When you bring him down to the test.
But, say, when they carry my gravy—
Say, when I want to win,
Gimme a handy
Guy like Sande
Bootin' them horses in.

Two years later, Sande was badly injured in a fall at Saratoga and
announced he would not ride again. Somehow, Damon found words for
the occasion:

Maybe there'll be another,
Heady 'an game an' true—
Maybe they'll find his brother
At drivin' them hosses through.
Maybe—but, say, I doubt it.

123

Never his like again—
Never a handy
Guy like Sande
Bootin' them babies in!

Sande, it developed, was not through, and Damon was not through with Sande, but the various versions of the verse, as Damon's anthologist Clark Kinnaird pointed out, already had become popular enough to stir barroom debate over whether Damon said "Ridin' them hosses," "Bootin' a long shot," or "Bootin' them babies in." All hands were right.

Damon clearly had mastered his craft. In a single paragraph, he came closer than most tacklers to capturing the elusive Galloping Ghost of the University of Illinois: "What a football player—this man Red Grange. He is melody and symphony. He is crashing sound. He is brute force."

Damon was all over the newspaper, prospering and, if not yet quite famous, well known. No matter how varied the assignments, Damon carried with him the street upon which he pounced, in Gene Fowler's phrase, "like a prospector jumping a claim." Covering the Democratic convention in San Francisco in 1920, Damon wrote:

There's a little touch of Broadway wherever you go. . . .

"Wild Jim" Riley fell into our palatial quarters last night, uttering the war-cry of the Ninety-Sixth Street and Broadway clan. . . .

Col. William C. Lyons of Denver, Colorado, whose attire includes Palm Beach suit, white shoes, Panama hat, sword cane and John Roscoe, or six-pistol; without his sword-cane, the Colonel would not be able to pick his teeth. Without his John Roscoe, or smoke rod, he would catch cold. . . .

But he pines for Broadway. The colonel assuredly pines. Not even one of the most elaborate suites in the St. Francis and much honor and acclaim from the multitude can take the colonel's thoughts entirely away from his beloved Broadway. . . .

Al Jolson, Bert Kalmer, the songwriter. . . .

There's a little touch of the roaring forties wherever you light. . . .

It was perhaps harder to sense a Republican presence along Broadway, and at the GOP convention in Chicago, Damon complained, "After listening to the chatter of politicians and political experts for four days, one is finally forced to the conclusion that the Republican nominees will be Messrs. Hem and Haw." The party did only somewhat better, nominating Messrs. Harding and Coolidge.

But the correspondent with the sometimes chilly eyes and often mirthless smile was no unreconstructed romantic. On March 14, 1921, Damon wrote an editorial page column opening with a long quote from Dickens' *American Notes,* which described pigs rooting on the nineteenth-century Broadway.

> Since Mr. Dickens' time [Damon observed], the pigs of Broadway have changed only in form, having taken on the semblance of humans. . . .
> You can see them today in streetcars and subway trains, pushing and grunting their way to seats while women stand clinging to the straps. You can see them wandering along Broadway, old hogs familiar with every sty in the city, and young porkers just learning the ways of swine, their little eyes eagerly regarding every passing skirt.
> Of an evening they gather in cabarets, wallowing in illicit liquor and shouting through a conversational garbage made up of oaths and filthy stories and scandal.
> A pig is a pig even when it wears evening clothes. . . .
> The pigs of Mr. Dickens' day served one useful purpose. As much cannot be said of the Broadway pigs of today. They fatten on the rottenness of human existence, but few of them ever grow to be worth the killing, save for the sake of getting rid of them. . . .

There is an evergreen quality about the stricture, even if it seems overheated. More than half a century later, the street remained a long, long trail removed from the Broadway of Richard Harding Davis.

The same day that column appeared, Damon also was represented in the *American* by a column on the tortures of making weight, as experienced by Babe Ruth; a sports-page editorial on the strangeness of six-day bicycle racing, and a column of comment from readers concerning an earlier article by Damon asking why more Jews didn't play major league baseball.

"Damon would write you out of the paper if he could," Bugs Baer told Hoyt bitterly in the 1960s.

If pigs grunted on Broadway and Americans demonstrated the once-proud spirit of rebellion with a hip flask, life in the United States seems simpler in retrospect than it would become. Buster Keaton, the silent film clown, joined Damon for a World Series game in Washington in 1924.

They lunched with a Washingtonian, his wife, and their three-year-old daughter. After the meal, Keaton invited the husband to come to the ball game. He said it would be nice if the woman could join them, but she undoubtedly had to take the child home.

"Oh, I'll go with you," said the woman. "I'll send the baby home in a taxi."

"Thereupon," Damon recalled, "she had the doorman call a taxi, plumped the little girl in the seat, gave the driver the address, and away he went, with the little girl waving from the back window to us standing there on the sidewalk.

"'It shows you family life in this town is secure,' said Buster."

It depended, as always, on the family. Damon and Ellen seemed to baffle each other; familiarity did not breed content. She complained to Agnes Fowler that Damon came home only to change his clothes, which he did twice a day. "Ellen used to wonder how a man could spend all that time in the bathroom."

Ellen was complicated, proud, slender, and vivacious. She bought her shoes at I. Miller and spent "a small fortune on perfumes," and when a bottle was half empty, she poured the remainder into a pint-size, cut-glass bottle, creating her "extra special mixture." That would seem nothing to be sniffed at, but Agnes said the special perfume was both alluring and distinctive.

"I think it had something to do with her character, always improvising, changing, mixing, looking for something magical. Going to fortune-tellers and asking me not to tell [Damon]. He always hooted at her superstitions. They were both looking for somthing."

The two young women took their children for rides on the double-decked Fifth Avenue buses. Ellen liked to study the mansions and wonder "how the millionaires lived."

She told Agnes she "had been deeply in love with Alfred," as she always called Damon, "but the coolness began about a year or so after Damon, Jr., was born. Not all at once, the coolness," said Agnes. "No one was to blame for this, I suppose."

Damon certainly bore his share of the blame. Part of the problem was his attitude toward women, shaped, his son wrote, in the old West. Damon was courtly toward women, but for the wrong reasons: "A woman was a dear and priceless luxury, to be handled with care, an ornament for the arm, a treasure to show off to the boys. Any ideas or comments she might have, say, on the state of the union, were to be taken lightly, like a musical comedy."

Ellen was an independent spirit, not likely to accept patronizing.

126

Women had the vote, bobbed their hair, shortened their skirts, smoked if they felt like it, and drank, got around and about. She was more in touch with the new freedom than was Damon, who seemed to yearn for an old order.

Damon, Jr., recalled his father's observation that women were "nice to have around, especially if they're not bad-looking, if they don't get any ideas. Sometimes I just like to listen to 'em prattle along, you know, the way they do when they're not really saying anything. I just like to listen to their voices and look at 'em. But sometimes"—his face clouded—"I wish they'd go jump in the river. This, of course, is just between you and me."

Out of his accumulated wisdom, Damon told a friend, "Give a woman a couple of kids and she'll leave you alone." Ellen was intelligent, and she had some experience of the world beyond the boudoir and the kitchen, and the likelihood she would adjust to that small misogyny was remote.

Being a father demands more than fertility. Damon ran a tight ship, in the manner of Captain Bligh. The household "had to be grimly quiet" until he awoke around noon, the morning newspaperman's dawn.

"He spent an hour emitting groans and other agonized noises," his son wrote, "and trying to sneak back to oblivion. He was impossible to deal with during this hassle with himself, and the children were warned away. Finally, he would face the new day and fling open the bedroom door, announcing to whom it might concern, 'I'm up.' The communiqué would filter down to us through channels. . . . Then we would go whooping in."

Damon chatted with the children while he shaved. Breakfast had to go perfectly "or a storm would break. The eggs had to be done exactly three and one-half minutes, the bacon and toast just so."

In his sister's baby book, Damon, Jr., said, their mother noted that day when the infant Mary "could by crawling and holding to the wall visit her daddy's room and knock at his door." In later years, the son commented, "such a disturbance would be rewarded by whacks."

It was self-indulgent for a newsman to enter himself in the Proust sweepstakes, since journalism offers no corklined quarters. Damon, who started working in the boiler room of a newspaper office when he was fifteen, was enforcing a double standard. He wrote at ringside, after all, in press boxes, in political arenas.

Gene Fowler wrote:

> I cannot recall . . . that occupational hardships, the sardine conditions . . . the hullabaloo of the crowd, or anything else

bothered [him]. He seemed well-insulated at all times. He would find a place for his typewriter, a feat comparable to pouring a quart into a pint bottle. . . . He would glance at his copy paper as though it had just told him an off-color story and puff awhile at his cigarette. Now he would pull his hatbrim low over his spectacles, readjust his necktie, then . . . bingo!"

Damon's reputation as a humorist surprised his son. "He had the habit of going around with a long face," Damon, Jr., recalled, quoting an old-timer who said, "Around the office he appeared very moody, as if he was all burning up inside. But then he would stop and talk and be very courteous and pleasant."

The tragic mask at home convinced the son his father was angry with him. "I was forever trying to figure out what I might have done to displease him. I feared to talk to him in these moods. . . ."

Damon was full of advice and aphorisms, many of them bad. "Women," he sighed to his son. "You can't live with them, and you can't live without 'em."

"Don't drink," he said, "and don't get married." Since the second admonition seemed bootless, it may be that Damon, Jr., saw no reason to consider the first.

"'Don't gamble,'" Damon said, "turning away from a Saratoga dice table where he'd just dropped $800 in an hour," according to his son, "and $10,000 in one month."

"'Watch your lungs,'" he said, although he was a chain-smoker. "How was one to figure such advice?" the son wondered.

Damon told his son all about the sucker punch but nothing about sex. "I figure you pick up such details around and about, as young fellows do," he explained, "and you probably know as much or even more on that score than I."

Psychology is a tool of the century, explaining everything, and Damon was a troubled spirit, but at least part of his problem may have been physiological. Between the cigarettes and "ten to fifteen cups of coffee" at a sitting, his central nervous system undoubtedly was Broadway at rush hour.

Damon and his family were on the move—from 111th Street and Amsterdam to 116th, then 95th and Broadway, 102nd and Riverside Drive, and finally Bronxville. Each move was a step up, his son recalled. Damon said his favorite was the seventh-floor apartment at 95th and Broadway, overlooking "one of the haunts of bootleggers and gangsters of the period."

In 1980, Broadway and 95th Street is one of the least attractive crossroads in the metropolis, given over to winos and junkies, the wild-eyed, dangerous, and ultimately boring, awash in litter and those transistor radios tuned to static that would not soothe a civilized breast. Its subway stop is rated one of the ten most dangerous in the city.

But in the 1920s it furnished Damon with inspiration for his stories. "Later it came to be believed that 'Damon Runyon characters' were inspired by the Broadway set around Lindy's," his son wrote. ". . . the Lindy's circle provided inspiration for later characters, but the real originals were from uptown Broadway."

The Upper West Side also served as gastronomic inspiration. During World War II, Damon sat in Reuben's restaurant in midtown one night, birthplace of the famous sandwich. He remembered Arnold Reuben's "little delicatessen store and restaurant at 74th Street and Broadway, which he opened in 1915, suddenly and inexplicably becoming the seat of Broadway night life in the hours after midnight. There was always a mob scene there going on in the dawn's early light . . . and in a few years, he had an imposing establishment on Madison Avenue."

After Damon became known to the seedy, sporty clientele at the Ninety-sixth Street intersection, one of them told him, "If you ever miss anything upstairs, leave me know. I will see that you get it back." The 95th Street apartment represented the midpoint in his financial climb. "The man on the top of success has to worry about staying there," Damon, Jr., pointed out.

Damon's arrival near the top was marked by the move to 102nd Street and Riverside Drive, a seven-room apartment with new furniture, a Steinway grand piano, and the passionless comfort of separate bedrooms. Damon was getting the money. "The kids are your job," he told Ellen.

While her friends remembered her as charming, generous, and vivacious, to her son she was "a tyrant with a hairbrush for a scepter." She believed in corporal punishment, and she didn't believe in vaccination: "I'm not going to stand for my children being injected with germs and poisoned." She was strong-willed. Fowler recalled that "she liked very much to solve the problems of others, whether or not they wanted her to do so."

And then, in one of those damnable twists of life, Ellen Egan Runyon became a drunk. Having forced sobriety on Damon as a condition of marriage, she began sneaking drinks. As early as 1919, Agnes Fowler remembered, Ellen was going to the clothes closet and taking down a bottle, a subterfuge that must have fooled Damon for twenty-three seconds.

There soon were episodes of conduct puzzling to the children. "She would act silly, or make seemingly incoherent statements," Damon Jr., wrote, "or fawn over us with evil-smelling breath, or teeter. If we asked what was wrong, she would grab her bosom, roll her eyes and groan dramatically, 'Oh, my poor heart. I'm not well.'"

Ellen was not a woman who clung; from the earliest days of their marriage, she had shown Damon she could function socially without him. This seemed to violate some obscure code of the hills in his mind.

She did not approve of Damon's raffish companions. When he was overseas, she observed tartly that if he died, she would not know a soul at the funeral. She found her own set, revolving first around others with Denver backgrounds, then around the motion picture crowd. Movies were being made in New York City and its environs, mainly in Long Island studios, and Ellen sometimes took the children along to watch the filming and, in those nonunion days, she sometimes played a walk-on role. She made her own world, discrete and indiscreet, and the drinking grew worse.

It did not appear to be a matter of pining for her straying husband. Their son believed that in some dim way Damon wanted her back. But by the mid-1920s Damon and Ellen shared not much more than a roof and a name while, as Agnes Fowler observed helplessly, each searched for something.

Damon was to boast that he stole "from the greatest writers that ever lived to entertain and instruct my parishioners. . . . Sometimes I wonder if youse appreciate me. I steal from Plato, Socrates, Woodrow Wilson, Shakespeare, Montaigne, Mr. Dooley, Euripides, Nat Fleischer's All-Time Ring Record Book, Lincoln's speeches, Ingersoll's lectures, La Guardia's readings of the comic strips, Caesar (Irving and Arthur and Julius), Butler (Nick, Ben, Sam, and Bill), Dickens, Cato, Thoreau, Emerson and Whitman. . . ." The list continues, but Damon apparently felt a particular affinity for Montaigne. Ellen had given him an eight-volume edition of the French essayist's work in 1918.

Montaigne, surveying sixteenth-century France with a Gallic eye, could be hard-boiled, and elements of his philosophy would be comfortable to the Colorado kid grown older. "I find that the highest places usually are seized by the least capable men," Montaigne observed, "and that great fortune and ability are seldom found together." Damon could agree with that at least three days a week.

On February 1, 1924, Damon reminisced: "Montaigne says, 'Nor alive nor dead, it doth concern you nothing. Alive because you are. Dead because you are no more. Moreover, no man dies before his hour. The time you leave behind was no more yours than that which was before your death, and concerneth you no more.' Yet it is always depressing to learn of the passing of old friends. . . ."

Damon had learned of the death of Harry Tibbetts, a veteran waiter at Jack Dunstan's celebrated all-night restaurant on Sixth Avenue, and the death, too, of Johnny Toner,

> a grand chap with the courage of a lion. In more tempestuous times, the night crowd that roared through Jack's between midnight and dawn often grew unruly. A touch of a "buzzer" at the cashier's desk quickly alarmed the once celebrated "flying wedge" of waiters, Johnny at the peak, and no disturbance lasted long. . . .
>
> Actors and actresses, rich brokers, polo players, song writers, newspapermen, authors, artists, pamphleteers, poets, prize fighters, ball players, promoters, "grifters," hotel keepers, jockeys, billiard players, horse owners, chorus girls, gunmen, gamblers. . . .
>
> For in the heyday of Jack's no night was a complete night that did not finish at Jack's.
>
> This writer is not old, nor yet young. . . . Today, tonight will never return, and it is most depressing to feel that old friends called by death are gone forever.

The mood was three o'clock in the morning. But it was transitory. For Damon and for Walter, the hour was more like one minute after midnight of a new day, with few "cannons" to regulate the *liberty* of an exuberant press or to restrain its *licentiousness*.

eight

THE TUG of New York in the twenties was both palpable and emotional; it was like an unforgettable woman.

Prosodists turned to poetry. "It gushes up," wrote Le Corbusier. He visited the city in 1920, in 1926, and in 1928, writing a book about the metropolis he called *When the Cathedrals Were White*. "I cannot forget New York, a vertical city, now that I have had the happiness of seeing it there, raised up in the sky."

He was distressed by lesser buildings. "What are these small buildings doing in dramatic Manhattan? I haven't the slightest idea. It is incomprehensible. It is a fact, nothing more, as the debris after an earthquake or bombardment is a fact." But these were only rough drafts, part of "a provisional city. A city which will be replaced by another city."

This sense of impermanence and change stirred Scott Fitzgerald, who in 1919 had found himself "mediocre in advertising and unable to get started as a writer. Hating the city, I got roaring, weeping drunk on my last penny and went home [to St. Paul, Minnesota]."

He returned in six months, having completed *This Side of Paradise*. Now ". . . the offices of editors and publishers were open to me, impresarios begged plays, the movies panted for screen material. To my bewilderment, I was adopted, not as a Middle Westerner, not even as a detached observer, but as the arch-type of what New York wanted."

Fitzgerald believed a new urbanity existed. "If this society produced the cocktail party, it also evolved Park Avenue wit and for the first time an educated European could envisage a trip into New York as something more amusing than a gold-trek into a formalized Australian Bush."

He had everything, the girl, fame, and money. "Within a few months after our embarkation on the Metropolitan venture we scarcely knew any more who we were and hadn't a notion what we were. A dive into a civic fountain, a casual brush with the law, was

132

enough to get us into the gossip columns, and we were quoted on a variety of subjects we knew nothing about."

The world's work remained to be done, but for Fitzgerald and others life seemed a round of cocktail parties and suffering,

> a luncheon in the cool Japanese garden at the Ritz with the wistful Kay Lauren and George Jean Nathan, and writing all night again and again, and paying too much for minute apartments and buying magnificent but broken-down cars. . . .
>
> At last we were one with New York, pulling it after us through every portal. Even now I go into many flats with the sense that I have been there before or in the one above or below—was it the night I tried to disrobe in the *Scandals* or the night when (as I read with astonishment in the paper the next morning) "Fitzgerald Knocks Officer This Side of Paradise"?
>
> . . . And lastly from that period I remember riding in a taxi one afternoon between very tall buildings under a mauve and rosy sky; I began to bawl because I had everything I wanted and knew I would never be so happy again.

This sort of thing was enough to inflame the tough guy in Westbrook Pegler, who would growl about the time "when Scott Fitzgerald's few were gnawing gin in silver slabs and sniffing about the sham and tinsel of it all." But Pegler himself, whose cultural depth may be measured by his choice of *Snow White* as his favorite movie, christened the decade "The Era of Wonderful Nonsense."

The nonsense existed on several levels, most superficially in the round of parties and speakeasies, when "the Montmartre was the smart place to dance and Lilian Tashman's fair hair weaved around the floor among the enliquored college boys," as Fitzgerald recalled. "The plays were *Déclassé* and *Sacred and Profane Love,* and at the Midnight Frolic you danced elbow to elbow with Marion Davies. . . ."

Until recently, historians have tended to treat the twenties kindly, embracing the decade as though it were a returned veteran and murmuring that the nation deserved a break after the great responsibility of the Great War. One ringmaster for the circus, as much symbol as any president, was the one-hundredth mayor of New York, James J. Walker.

He was of the Greenwich Village Irish, "clean favored and imperially slim" in Edward Arlington Robinson's phrase, and often saved by

133

a wisecrack. Stanley No Relation Walker called him "the Dream Prince," and he was "Beau James" to Fowler.

As a state legislator, Walker sponsored legislation regulating boxing in New York. He killed a Clean Books bill commenting, "I never heard of a man or a woman who was ruined by a book." He spun a lifeline for a thousand pale imitators, cracking "A reformer is a guy who rides through a sewer in a glass-bottomed boat," although it would be the reformers who got him.

As a young man, Walker wrote the song "Will You Love Me in December As You Do in May?" and the city's affection for its night mayor never seemed to wane. Walker achieved that office in 1925 through the efforts of Governor Al Smith, with whom he shared a race, a party, a church, and nothing else.

Walker often turned up at Broadway first nights or the prizefights arm-in-arm with Betty Compton, a dimpled darling of the musical stage, while the amiable Mrs. Walker sat home in St. Luke's Place, back in the Village. This was not socially acceptable behavior in the America of the period, and Walker professed a great love for his church as for his city, but a good time was had by all, and when the mayor welcomed the comely Queen Marie of Rumania on her goodwill tour of the country, a voter cried as they passed in a moment of unaccustomed silence, "What's the matter, Jimmy? Can't you make her?"

Stanley Walker fixed a reception in 1926, when the city honored a gallant seaman, as the occasion on which Mayor Walker first called New York "the most cosmopolitan city in the world." Later that year he had so planed the phrase that it fit snugly into the scaffolding of his rhetoric, as in his introduction of the queen: "We have thousands of Rumanian stock in this world city, in this most cosmopolitan city of the world, and today . . . may I not beg to assure you that Rumanians have made as fine citizens as this country has within its borders? They have done much for the building of the city of New York."

As the other Walker pointed out, the mayor "was always glad to say the same thing about Turks, Syrians, West Indians, Armenians, Greeks, Serbs, Croats or Basques."

It didn't much matter for whom the reception was held, whether it honored Trudy Ederle the Amsterdam Avenue butcher's daughter who swam the English channel; Ramsay MacDonald, who was announced as "the Prime Minister of the United States" before his stage whisper was heard, "Britain, old boy, Britain"; Admiral Byrd, who flew over the North Pole, thirty-five Blackfeet Indians, or various golfers, pugilists, and soccer players.

There would be a parade up Broadway from the Battery with a

ticker-tape shower, arrival at City Hall a little after noon, thus assuring a crowd of thousands on their lunch break to demonstrate that one of the wonders of New York is that it boasts more gawkers than Zenith.

But, as Stanley Walker noted in *Mrs. Astor's Horse,* the whole nation gawked. Adulation for Queen Marie in 1926 drove Sir John Fraser to write in London's *Evening Standard* that "the United States should buy a King. . . . Americans are a nice people and do not repress their feelings like decadent Europeans. The Americans must get a King and Queen of their own. They will never be happy until they do."

As Americans prostrated themselves before the queen, an English editorial writer recalled that when the late King Edward visited the United States as the Prince of Wales, New York women bottled the water in which he washed his hands. Now Americans seemed "the richest and least responsible people in the world . . . all dressed up and no place to go." A Minneapolis alderman called Queen Marie "an international gold digger," grumbling "Rumania is only about the size of Duluth, anyway," but reporters from *four* news agencies accompanied the royal train and, rather typically, the Denver *Post* gave over just about its entire front page to her arrival in that city.

Walker danced gracefully to this music. He was a natural leader, in the same dangerous sense as the Pied Piper. Bankers and businessmen were impressed with his grasp when he could be brought to pay attention, but he suffered as badly as the most acquiescent woman from an inability to say no.

All of this, the receptions, the tours, the cutie on the arm, and the pace-setting high life, was wonderful stuff for the New York press. Editorial writers grumbled, but City Hall reporters and feature writers loved him.

The New York press sank to the occasion of the times. Never again would so much newsprint be expended on so little. The tone was set by a suddenly crowded field of tabloids. Hearst, who had trifled with the idea but waited too long, envied the success of the *News.* He produced his very own tabloid in 1924, calling it the *Mirror,* although it never joined Lord Northcliffe's paper on the summit of popular taste and, indeed, never caught up with the *News.*

Has it been noted that Hearst was in some ways a strange man? There is no indication he was troubled by a lofty journalistic idealism; he built his empire on sensationalism, entertainment, and stunts, but although he spent millions on the *Mirror,* he viewed it, to borrow from Booth Tarkington, in the manner of a duchess beholding a bug, for his name never graced its masthead.

He trotted out Albert J. Kobler, an executive with the *American*

135

Weekly to formally buy control of the *Mirror,* but there was no doubt it was a Hearst paper. For one thing, it announced its policy as 10 percent news, 90 percent entertainment, "a sort of printed sideshow of curiosities, scandals and sensations."

And it produced a sideshow by which the decade is remembered. The production began with a good man's infatuation for a woman, one of those comedies that dissolves in farce and ends in tragedy.

The *Mirror* seemed lucky when it acquired Phil Payne as its managing editor. He was a native of Canada who was raised in New Jersey, a boy wonder as city editor of the Hudson *Dispatch.* Patterson discovered him and brought him to the *News,* where he quickly became city editor, then managing editor. Payne seemed to sense just the balance of crime, pictures, and sex Patterson and the public wanted.

He was a stocky fellow in horn-rimmed glasses, who owned one suit at a time, wearing it until it all but fell apart, although he changed shirts daily. He would have been 100 percent newsman but for a susceptible heart.

He had married his childhood sweetheart. They lived simply, planning to build a castle on the Palisades, and Payne's success had brought that within reach when his wife died. Payne was inconsolable. He lost himself in his work and was otherwise reclusive. He went to live with his mother-in-law so that he could sleep in the bed his wife had slept in, stopping each night to pray for her in a church across the street, which kept its doors open for him.

His mother-in-law and a newspaper buddy named Francis Farley urged Payne out of his depression. Farley shepherded him around and about Broadway, the theaters, restaurants, and speakeasies. Slowly Payne discovered that, what the hell, there was a whole world out there. He became something of a fashion plate.

He also came upon Peggy Hopkins Joyce, who would be described for decades as "a former *Follies* beauty," a sweetheart of the press because she glittered when she walked in a sheen of jewelry, and because she was frequently married, frequently not. She and Payne were soon an item. There was talk he might marry her, or she him. Stories about her appeared rather too frequently in the *News* for Patterson's taste.

One night Payne took her to the office. She was wide-eyed at the wonder of it all, the electric clamor of the newsroom, the progression of the great god news from typewriter to linotype to the massive presses. Payne showed her, little her, the button that would set the presses rolling. Might she? A tiny finger, undoubtedly jeweled, set leviathan roaring.

136

Patterson heard about it. He was, as publishers go, good to his staff, but he didn't approve of monkeying around. He didn't even want his editors *associating* with actresses. He fired Payne.

Hearst immediately hired him to make the *Mirror* the *News*. This could not be done. Perhaps the problem was that Hearst couldn't also hire Patterson. Payne, the good newsman, came up with a wow of an idea, perhaps kindled by his New Jersey background, his knowledge of that state's little secrets. He dispatched reporters and private detectives heavy with Hearst cash to snoop around the New Brunswick area and sound out the locals.

On a September morning four years earlier, which is to say in 1922, under a crabapple tree on a lover's lane adjoining an abandoned farm, there had been discovered the bodies of the Reverend Edward W. Hall, rector of the Episcopal church of St. John the Evangelist, and a singer in his choir, Mrs. Eleanor Mills, who was the wife of the sexton. They had been shot. Her throat had been cut and her vocal cords removed. Scattered over the bodies were fragments of love letters, pretty hot stuff, they had been exchanging for some years.

Silas Bent called this a second-rate case because it involved "an obscure clergyman and a janitor's wife." But it gripped the attention of a nation which, admittedly, didn't have much on its mind. Alexander Woollcott noted that Jeanne Eagels was even then rehearsing for *Rain,* "at which, through five seasons, the American playgoer watched a hot-eyed missionary overwhelmed by his passion for a rowdy harlot he had thought he was trying to redeem. Such little slips by the clergy always fascinate the urchin hearts of the laity. . . ."

Mrs. Hall, who had been older than her husband, came from money. Along with their distressing fascination with the fall from grace, people like to think the fix is in for the rich, as it often is, and these twin suspicions, under Payne's prodding, helped reopen the Hall-Mills case.

The books had been closed with the customary "by a person or persons unknown" after what appeared to be a desultory and inept investigation, compounded by the circumstance that De Russey's lane ran along the border between two jurisdictions, each of which hoped, in the thrifty Coolidge manner, that the other would follow through.

Poking around, the *Mirror* was able to get New Jersey to indict Mrs. Hall, her two brothers, and a cousin, and to bring to trial the first three on the charge of murdering Mrs. Mills. The authorities were even thoughtful enough to arrest Mrs. Hall in her home at midnight on a Saturday; only the *Mirror* knew the arrest was to be made. The other tabloids suspected something was stirring when the *Mirror* did not print an early edition and posted a special policeman at its door to keep out snoops. The *Mirror* scored a rare, clean scoop.

The Hall-Mills case was not a feast served up exclusively for readers of the picture papers. Silas Bent noted that the London *Times* reported the Battle of Waterloo in about three hundred words, "whereas to report the Hall-Mills case, a single newspaper required twice as many words as Will Durant needed to tell *The Story of Philosophy*."

That newspaper was the New York *Times,* which, by Bent's reckoning, devoted 528,300 words to the case, more than twice as many as did the *News.* The *American* made do with 347,700 words, most of them, most memorably, by Damon Runyon.

He set the scene on November 3, 1926:

> In this pleasant looking little town of Somerville, in the heart of old New Jersey, and in a pleasant looking little court house, all white and trim, the trial of the century starts this morning at ten o'clock.
> . . . the thing has taken on some of the aspects of a big sports event. In fact, the telegraph switchboard used for the Dempsey-Tunney fight has been installed in the courthouse and forty-seven telegraph instruments have been hooked up. An enterprising radio outfit will unofficially broadcast the proceedings, play by play, so to speak.

He described the characters, "such a cast as David Belasco might revel in," with detail no camera could capture:

> My mental picture of Mrs. Hall based on what I read of her, was as a proud, cold, emotionless woman, of immense hauteur and hard exterior. With that sort of picture in mind, I was scarcely prepared for the entrance of the real Mrs. Hall.
> . . . She slipped in through a rear door with her brothers, a solid-looking woman in black hat and black cloth coat with a collar of gray squirrel. Under it she wore a black dress with a low collar edged in white. Her shoes were black. In her hat she had a bright silver ornament. She suggested what she is— a wealthy widow. . . .
> Her face is large, her expression set, almost graven in its seriousness. Her complexion is white to pastiness. Her skin is fairly smooth but there are folds under her chin. Her hair, such as showed around her temples, is sprinkled with gray.

She looks more than the fifty-one she admits. Willie is around fifty-two. Henry is fifty-eight. . . .

Willie seemed more interested in the proceedings than did his sister or brother or anyone else in the court room for that matter. They say Willie is not quite all there mentally. He loves to hang out in fire houses, and the clang of engine bells is music to his ears.

Willie is a heavy-set man with thick, bushy hair, which stands up on his head straight and stiff like quills upon a fretful porcupine that Mr. Shakespeare wrote about. It gives Willie a startled appearance, which is increased by a pair of thick, black, arched eyebrows and wide open staring eyes. . . .

He wears spectacles with heavy lenses. A heavy dark mustache, shaped like bicycle bars, sags over his mouth. He has no great amount of chin. He has a thick neck, heavily ridged in back. Take him in all, Willie has a rather genial appearance. He somehow made me think of a successful delicatessen dealer. . . . Henry Stevens, who is said to be the man the State expects to prove fired the shots . . . has thick, flat, iron-gray hair and wears a mustache and spectacles. His complexion is ruddy. He looks like a doctor. He wore a dark suit and white linen today with rather a fancy four-in-hand tie. Willie frequently beamed and grinned, but Henry Stevens' face maintained a stern, implacable expression.

As the trial moved along, the State's case, while circumstantial, appeared moderately damning. The high point was the testimony of Jane Gibson, happily identified by the press as "the pig woman," a former circus bareback rider "who farmed a lonely patch of ground and raised her pigs and chickens outside the little city of New Brunswick, friendless but unafraid. She has been a drifter along the rocky shores of life in her time, no doubt of that. She has seen much, and some of the things she has seen she wants to forget."

Her story was that on the night of the murder, she rode her mule Jenny out in search of corn thieves and, hearing sounds, investigated and saw by their flashlight the Stevens clan huddled over the bodies under the crabapple tree. Newspaper artists, as may be imagined, made the most of that tableau.

Gravely ill, the pig woman was carried to the courtroom on an iron hospital bed, attended by a nurse and a doctor and a hospital air. The packed courtroom hushed:

139

"I heard voices, mumbling voices, men's voices and women's voices. I stood still. The men were talking, and a woman said very quick, 'Explain those letters.' The men were saying 'G— — d—— it,' and everything else. [She would not speak the oaths.] Somebody was hitting, hitting, hitting. I could hear somebody's wind go out and somebody said, 'Ugh.'

"Then somebody said 'G—— d—— it, let go.' A man hollered. Then somebody threw a flashlight toward where they were hollering. Yes, and I see something glitter, and I see a man, and I see another man, like they were wrestling together. The lights went out and I heard a shot. Then I heard something fall very heavy, and I run for the mule.

"I heard a woman's voice say after the first shot, 'Oh Henry,' easy, very easy, and the other began to scream, scream, scream so loud. 'Oh my, oh my, oh, my,' so terrible loud. That woman was screaming, screaming, screaming, screaming, trying to get away or something, screaming, screaming, screaming, screaming, and I just about got my foot in the stirrup when 'bang, bang, bang,' three quick shots."

That was her story, but she wasn't through for the day. As the court recessed, and after the jury had left the room, the attendants bundled the pig woman up for her ambulance ride back to the hospital.

From under the bed covers came a white hand, pointing at Mrs. Frances Noel Stevens Hall [wrote Damon].
"So help me God, I told the truth!" cried "the pig woman."
"You know I told the truth," she cried, still pointing at Mrs. Hall.
Blood rushed into the pallid countenance of the woman who is accused of being a party to the murder of her husband and the choir singer. She was surrounded by relatives, the group including not only her brothers, but a number of the women members of the rich Stevens-Carpender family. One of the women laughed a light, tinkling laugh.

The defense, of course, attacked the credibility of the State's witnesses, including that of the pig woman, whose mother testified she was unreliable. The defense noted that in the week after the bodies were discovered, the pig woman "visited the Mills' house, and spent an evening there and then she becomes a witness. Then she hears all these things and sees all these things. And then the chorus is

140

formed to fasten this crime on the Hall family, and 'the pig woman' looms on the scene."

Damon noted that the defense played strongly on local pride. The Somerset County jury seemed to resent the prosecution of the case by Hudson County authorities, reflecting that historic suspicion of the outsider common to the primitive tribe. The prosecution produced affidavits that the jurors were "gabbing loquaciously about the case outside of the courtroom and slumbering in their chairs inside the room," defaming the prosecution and predicting it wouldn't take twenty minutes to reach a verdict.

"You can get 100 to 1 that [the accused] will walk out of the court house free of [the] charge within the next few days," Damon wrote. "The price was never shorter than 2 to 1 and has steadily gone up."

Perhaps chastened by the prosecutor's threat that he would go to the "Supreme Court immediately at the conclusion of the trial and ask for a 'foreign jury' to try these same defendants," the jury was out, not for twenty minutes, but for five hours and four minutes before exonerating the defendants.

Damon simply recorded the verdict but Hoyt noted that he had been "obviously convinced that [the prosecutor] was on the right track" and that the local eminence of the Stevens clan weighed on the jury. "As far as Damon was concerned," Hoyt wrote, "it was another bitter lesson in the way of the world." Tom Clark, whose biography of Damon appeared in 1978, commented that "Damon and the other byline writers scoffed among themselves at the verdict, exchanged I-told-you-sos, and then folded their typewriters and headed home."

But Alexander Woollcott, who made something of a study of the matter, commented ". . . the preposterous case . . . relied almost entirely on the testimony of a raffish and cockeyed old girl named Jane Gibson. . . . Such nuts volunteer as witnesses in all sensational cases and, if necessary, will even confess to the crime. . . . At the trial this farrago of transparent nonsense . . . made the acquittal a foregone conclusion."

Far from going to court again, the authorities quashed all charges the day after the trial ended. Perhaps the most important thing about the Hall-Mills case is that in 1926 it seemed so important. Mrs. Hall, who apparently lived in another century, a time of comity that never was, announced, "I don't think it is fair, or good Americanism, to make snapshot pictures of unwilling persons and print them. I think that is stealing, just as much as stealing one's personal property."

She whispered in a gathering wind. No one was listening. When she sued the *Mirror* for libel and the case was settled out of court for an estimated $50,000, "Even so comparatively scrupulous a newspaper as the New York *Times*," Woollcott wrote, "which, while the case was news, had wallowed in it for countless columns, made only a microscopic report of the settlement and printed that report as inconspicuously as possible."

Hearst apparently was not bothered by the affair. Fifty thousand meant little to him. But Payne brooded.

Then he announced a great new publicity plan, a transatlantic flight to capitalize on the aviation mania of the day, "aware," as Swanberg wrote in *Citizen Hearst*, "that if the editor of the *Mirror* flew to Rome it would be a Hearst scoop that would gather in more readers."

Two British fliers were hired as pilots, but the plane was called *Old Glory*. Hearst was at first enthusiastic. Much was made of the preparations. Mrs. Hearst joined a trial flight over Manhattan and then equipped the instrument panel with an emerald-studded St. Christopher's medal.

In the international scramble over aeronautic derring-do and its proven power as a circulation-puller, Hearst already had sponsored a flight to Hawaii, and it was lost with two pilots. He suddenly cooled on the *Old Glory* idea, asking Payne to call it off. Payne answered, "You have been a great Chief to work for. I honor you and love you, and I know you will forgive any mistakes I have made."

That was Hearst's first indication that Payne himself planned to take part in the flight. Hearst frantically telephoned from California and ordered the flight stopped.

Payne's faithful friend Farley was with him at the airfield. Payne asked him to buy him a pint of whiskey. Although Payne was not a drinker, Farley obliged. Payne took a phone call from an editor who relayed Hearst's order to abort the flight. Payne asked, "Is that all?"

He shook hands with Farley and said goodbye. Farley said he meant *au revoir*. Payne said, "Oh, no. This time it is goodbye."

He climbed into the plane, sitting near a trapdoor. *Old Glory* lumbered off. In *Sauce for the Gander*, Frank Mallen advances the theory that somewhere over the Atlantic, fortified by liquor, Payne dropped himself through the trapdoor. That would be enough, the theory went, to allow a violent rush of air into the cabin of the plane.

Old Glory was never heard from again.

If the circulation stunts were sometimes like schoolboy pranks that suddenly go terribly wrong, the fact was lost in the bawdy, brawling atmosphere of gargoyle journalism.

A couple of cub reporters for a rival tabloid did important legwork the morning the *Mirror* reported the Hall-Mills indictments. They were pressed into service because there was no one else around the office when the *Mirror* hit the streets. Walter Winchell hustled out to New Brunswick and came back with copy an editor later called "exciting and thorough . . . moving and dramatic. It covered the highlights and the little human interest facets, too." Ed Sullivan, a sportswriter, obtained an exclusive interview with the pig woman, rousing her from bed, and also interviewed Willie Stevens, who wore a nightgown and tasseled cap.

Then Walter and Sullivan were pulled off the story.

The editor who praised their efforts could not understand that, but then, few things were understandable about the paper for which they worked. It was the *Evening Graphic,* not to be confused with the nineteenth-century tabloid, not to be confused with anything else ever seen on the journalistic moonscape. In a crowded list, it was the most bizarre daily in the history of New York journalism, a goofy experiment which to everyone's astonishment lasted eight years.

The *Graphic* was the brainchild of Bernarr Macfadden, who changed his Christain name of Bernard because he wanted "something out of the ordinary." He was a Missouri farmboy, orphaned in youth and often sickly. He built himself up. Then he tried to build up the rest of mankind through exercise, vegetarianism, and sound sex lives. At the suggestion of a friend who knew some Greek, he called himself a kinistherapist.

Macfadden opened a "studio of health" in New York where weight-conscious fat men ran naked around the gym keeping balloons in the air by blowing at them. Then he invented a pulley-exercising machine.

He published a pamphlet celebrating its virtues, illustrated with near-nude photos of himself. The pamphlets became the magazine *Physical Culture.* Readers wrote him telling of their physical problems and sometimes about difficulties in love and marriage. These letters inspired the magazine *True Story,* which soon reached a circulation of two million.

Macfadden staffed the magazine with the kind of people who read it—manicurists, barbers, clerks. The minute a staff member showed literary ambition, he was fired. One day an editor stopped off for a haircut. The barber addressed him by name. "I've seen you at the office," said the barber. "I used to be on the staff of *True Story.*" Had he said "seed," his editorship might have been secure.

Macfadden often ran afoul of authorities at a time when a kind of prurient prudery streaked the culture. Washington authorities confiscated Macfadden posters boosting a physical culture exhibition in

1901 because they portrayed young women in bloomers or black tights. In 1905 he was arrested in New York for promoting a beauty show with posters showing men and women in union suits. In 1907 he was fined and sentenced to prison for publishing an article called "Growing to Manhood." None other than President Taft canceled the prison sentence but not the fine, saying that although some of the narrative was "improper," the article's advice was wholesome.

Macfadden was canny enough to promote himself as well as his principles. He attracted attention through the years with barefoot walks, frequently hiking the twenty-one miles from his home in Nyack to his office in New York. In 1935 he led a swarm of forty hikers on a 325-mile walk to Dansville, New York. Two grandmothers and an eighty-three-year-old man were among the starters. Thirty-eight of the starters, including Macfadden, finished after fifteen days on the hoof. Macfadden subsisted on cracked wheat, raisins, and brown sugar.

With his fascination with body and self, his faddism and solemn egocentrism, Macfadden would have been right at home in the America of the eighties. As it was, most thoughtful people earlier in the century regarded him as something of a nut.

Reporters might have scoffed as Macfadden hectored them about physical culture principles, but his was not entirely a workaday life. At sixty-nine he was sued for alienation of affections by a doughnut maker named Satir C. Adams. None of this is fiction. Abbie Reinhardt Adams conceded the intimacy. She said she enjoyed Macfadden's hikes, nature talks, money, and "technique." She said, "I was honored."

Macfadded died at eighty-seven, anticlimactically enough in Jersey City, New Jersey, but four years earlier, in 1951, he had celebrated his birthday with a 2,500-foot parachute jump into the Hudson River.

Not even the bravos of the press scoffed at the financial side of the Macfadden empire. In 1928 he controlled a $15-million business, including 13 magazines and 10 newspapers with a combined circulation of more than 220,000,000. It was a time of uninhibited worship of Mammon, a time when professors believed that all the country needed was a good sound business administration, and Macfadden hit the Baal right out of the park.

His idea was to publish a New York tabloid called *The Truth*. He bought the old *Daily Mail* building, saw that the desks were dusted off and the rust chipped from the presses. The project was put together in great secrecy, with the result that everyone in the business knew about it, even before Macfadden took out ads in other newspapers for his publication, now called the *Graphic* at the insistence of an executive who feared daily publication of something called the *Truth* "would result in nothing but disaster."

"A NEW EVENING NEWSPAPER FOR NEW YORK CITY," Macfadden proclaimed.

"I intend to publish a newspaper that is human all the way through. . . .

The paper will be unlike any that you are now reading. It will shatter precedent to smithereens. . . . It will flash across the horizon like a new comet."

In a sense, Macfadden delivered on that promise. His notion was to publish every story in the first person. A grabbag of *Graphic* headlines included:

I KNOW THE MAN WHO KILLED MY BROTHER

FRIENDS DRAGGED ME IN THE GUTTER

I KNOW THE MAN WHO KILLED MY GIRL

I AM THE MOTHER OF MY SISTER'S SON

LET'S BE LESBIANS URGES CULT WOMAN

THREE WOMEN LASHED IN NUDE ORGY

"Nothing But the/ TRUTH," the paper boasted in a front-page box adjoining a headling: POOR BOY, 19/ FACING NOOSE, CRIES/MUST I DIE? In a signed editorial, Macfadden announced, "I am entering the evening newspaper field as a crusader. And I expect to make a few million dollars for myself and associates."

This hope was never realized. The *Graphic* first hit the streets, or gutter, on September 15, 1924. Curiosity fed a circulation of 400,000. At the end of the second week, it was down to 83,000. It later soared, but big advertisers ignored the paper, and only Macfadden's stubbornness and millions kept it afloat.

Along with professional newsmen, Macfadden's physical culture devotees turned up to lend a hand. An editor one day discovered a man "hanging by his long black hair from water pipes across the ceiling. He said he had the strongest hair in the world." To get to their desks, reporters had to pause and feel the biceps of strangers with tape measures. A thoughtful secretary jotted down figures of increased chest expansion. A man drove spikes through boards with his bare hands. It was difficult to keep telephone books around since nascent Samsons tore them in half to show off. It was too bad that Damon did not wander by, Montaigne in hand, "'To have stouter legs and arms is the quality of a porter,'" he might have reminded the strong boys, "'not a sign of valor.'"

But the *Graphic*'s great contribution to gargoyle journalism was the faked picture. The cosmograph, as it was called, is what brightens the *Graphic* headstone in the graveyard of deservedly dead newspapers.

Head shots of the famous, notorious, or briefly celebrated were attached to the bodies of models who posed in re-creation of the news, or non-news, event. The gallery included a bride who bared herself to the waist to prove that her dim-bulb socialite husband could not have failed to know she was black; the silent screen star Rudolph Valentino going under the knife and, perhaps most imaginatively, Valentino and Enrico Caruso together in heaven, according to a medium's vision, toga-ed like extras in the yet-to-be-seen *The Green Pastures,* as they offer benedictions to the fortunate few.

The *Graphic* printed no foreign news to speak of and little national news. It is true that with a mayor who seemed to function best after sundown and who took seven extended vacations his first two years in office, and with an excess of nonsense to choose from, much of the social history of the 1920s seemed written by a *Graphic* man with a hangover.

Daddy Browning and Peaches, for example, were cosmographs in the flesh.

Edward West Browning, a New Yorker and Columbia University man from a respectable family, labored mightily the first forty years of his life and piled up a fortune in real estate. Then he set eyes on and quickly married a file clerk. They adopted two daughters.

He built a mansion in the sky on West Eighty-first Street for his wife and the girls, featuring what Stanley Walker described as "a collection of bronze spiders, dogs, frogs, owls whose electric eyes blinked on and off, turtles, dragons and other disquieting apparitions." Some of the devices contained push buttons which opened doors, announced callers, or illuminated fountains.

Outside the living rooms, Browning constructed a lake deep enough to float a rowboat, with 250 goldfish, some 10 inches long. The lake was bordered with flowers and gravel paths sprinkled with semi-precious stones.

"It makes me ill when I think of it," he said about the cost of all this. But what Edward W. Browning wanted was publicity. "He would rather appear as a person who has been put upon, deceived, outraged and fooled beyond all belief than not to appear at all," said a friend.

Browning sued his wife for divorce, naming a dentist as correspondent. "A dentist of all people!" he exclaimed. "How can any sensible woman fall in love with a dentist, particularly with the dentist who has done her work? The idea is preposterous."

Browning understood "preposterous" well. On July 5, 1925, he

Walter in 1929, the year he left the Macfadden zoo for the Hearst circus. When the *Daily Mirror* folded 34 years later, he recalled, "I walked right in this place, and I was ready to swing." He swung.

Damon looking dapper around the time he joined Hearst's New York *American* in 1910. The Colorado Kid never forgot his western heritage, but he was immediately at home on the newspaper, in the city and on the Broadway he made his own.

Damon on the SS *Mauretania* in 1922 with the celebrated Peggy Hopkins Joyce, who was married as often as not, and an unidentified woman. This was the age of the great ships and the year of Damon's most famous verse, "Gimme a handy/guy like Sande."

Just a couple of Colorado boys looking to make good in Big Town. Damon with heavyweight champion Jack Dempsey in the early Twenties. There is a certain wistfulness in the proprietorial grasp— the heavyweights Damon actually owned were more valuable chauffeuring the Runyon family car.

Damon and Patrice, his second wife, at the Tropical Park track in 1935. For a time, just a time, Damon was happy, and when he called Florida "the land of sand in the shoes," he made it sound like fun.

Hollywood in the Thirties: Walter imitating a hunk of man, Clark Gable imitating a gossip columnist, and Carole Lombard going along with the gag. Walter praised and panned movies he'd never seen; Hollywood feared him.

Walter with Jimmy Walker, "the night mayor" of New York, who is dressed for work. It seemed all right for a saloon columnist to comment on Walker's activities, but when Walter began reporting from FDR's White House, traditionalists winced.

Damon, Walter and Sherman Billingsley, proprietor of the Stork Club in August, 1946. The trio represented a good deal of New York's night life, but it was just about closing time.

At ringside, the ball park, the political arena and the courtroom, this was a familiar sign—Damon at the typewriter. He sometimes fumbled for the lead, observers said. After that, it was an artillery barrage.

Damon, in constant pain, had only five months to live. He'd already identified Death as "a large and most distinguished looking figure in beautifully tailored soft white flannels."

Walter in a characteristic pose. His mouth is open and working. People listened. This picture was taken in 1947, the year after Walter made his first appeal for money to fight cancer in Damon's name. He was looking for thousands; he got millions.

The 1940 opening of *Tight Shoes,* one of sixteen movies made from Damon's short stories in his lifetime. Also in the picture: Nick Kenny, the Hearst laureate who wrote that "snow is the dandruff of God"; Broadway Rose, "a Runyon character" in the flesh; and Milton Berle.

Walter and Rep. Martin Dies (D. Tex.) moments after they teed off on each other over the radio. Dies personified the politicians who almost persuaded some critics to love Walter for the enemies he made.

Walter loved the Navy, in which he served during both World Wars. But he was a sea dog without a ship, whose greatest danger came from congressional torpedoes. He didn't know much about football, either, but that didn't prevent Lieutenant Commander Winchell from huddling with Coach George Halas and quarterback Sid Luckman back when the Chicago Bears really were the Monsters of the Midway.

He couldn't name his first-born Walter, Jr., so he named her Walda. As a Broadway ingenue, she was not going to rely on the family name, so she called herself after her favorite British politician—Toni Eden. If, like many fathers, Walter was sometimes baffled by his daughter, he doted on her, as this 1954 photo makes clear.

Hand in hand in the Miami Beach sunshine, Walter and Walter, Jr., seemed the happy father and son in 1940, but they were headed for a sea of troubles. The burden of growing up as "Winchell's kid" proved to be too much for young Walter, who became a problem that ended in tragedy.

advertised in the *Herald Tribune* for a "pretty, refined girl, about fourteen years old" he wished to adopt. He received some twelve thousand letters from around the nation from little orphan Annies and their ambitious mamas, looking for Daddy Warbucks.

He chose one Mary Louise Spas. Browning uncharacteristically tried to keep her address a secret, but resourceful reporters located her home in Queens. "My feelings," said her mother, "are not for the world."

"Of course they were for the *World*," Bent noted bitterly, "also for the *Times,* the *Herald Tribune, Daily Mirror* and hundreds of other papers." The parents wished to keep the news from another daughter, who was critically ill in Denver. A reporter found her, told her the whole story and, a short time later, she died. That was probably an unfortunate coincidence.

Meanwhile, Browning posed with Mary Louise for pictures, passed out cigars and was seen dancing with her around town. She called him Daddy, giving him his public name before the transports of delight collapsed. Records appeared indicating Mary Louise was twenty-one; she grew hysterical and said she wanted to go home. Daddy moved to invalidate the adoption.

The aging roué, or worse, then created a sorority which he christened Phi Lambda Tau, designing its pin and official seal. He sent one of its members, Frances Heenan, whom he called "Peaches," to finishing school, preparatory to marrying her when she was sixteen. He was fifty-one.

And so they were wed. An avid press corps, to Daddy's delight, tormented them with attention. Fleeing in a blue Rolls-Royce, Daddy paused to make sure he was being followed, kissing the bride. To no one's shock and apparently everyone's interest, the two soon filed separation suits against each other.

Daddy insisted he had always been a gentleman and, what's more, had given Peaches two hundred bunches of flowers, fifty boxes of candy, twenty boxes of fruit, one ermine coat, one fox-trimmed coat, one Russian sable coat, one other fur coat, sixty dresses, et cetera, et cetera.

Peaches charged Daddy had driven her to a nervous breakdown by asking her to breakfast in the nude, by buying an African honking gander which he led around on a string, by fooling around with a rubber egg and trick spoons in a hotel dining room, by setting off an alarm clock under her ear, and by crawling around on hands and knees barking "Woof! Woof!"

Graphic cosmographs, which fed on this rich banquet of pathology

147

and greed, included a gander squawking "Honk! Honk! It's the Bonk!" Damon covered the court hearings for the *American,* identifying them as "the great moral opus entitled 'The Saps of 1927.'" He did not think much of the litigants. Daddy, Damon wrote, "has dark eyes that are constantly shifting in their gaze. Daddy's eyes remind me of the orbs of Mr. Harry K. Thaw, that other celebrated connoisseur of feminine youth. I say this with all due respect for both Daddy and Mr. Harry K. Thaw."

As for Peaches, she "is large and blonde. Her hair is a straw color. She is one of those expansive, patient-looking blondes, who are sometimes very impatient. She has blue eyes which contain an expression of resignation. She has stout legs. I hesitate to expatiate on so delicate a matter, but they are what the boys call 'piano legs.'"

Damon committed a famous line: "A rattle of applause broke out among the spectators as Daddy Browning came down an aisle, walking first on one foot, then on the other." But he theorized that the gods on Mount Olympus "must have guffawed . . . as they saw a court room jammed with men and women and young girls, with their ears distended, and a street packed with people almost rioting in their desire to get a peep at the principals in a duel of defamation."

The court decided for Peaches. She was only one in a gallery of silly girls who furnished spectacle for the *Graphic* and its peers. A cosmograph depicted a notorious backstage party tossed by Earl Carroll, an impresario of the flesh, at which a seventeen-year-old showgirl named Joyce Hawley sat nude in a bathtub filled with champagne, from which the invited stags, including Thaw, the comedian Frank Tinney, and Irvin S. Cobb, were invited to drink. The poor mortified creature fled in tears before many whistles were wet, but she tarnished the image of innocence wronged by quickly turning up in the Greenwich Village *Follies* as "The Queen of the Bath" and offering interviews for $100, one picture for $50, a five-picture film strip for $200, and so on.

A Federal grand jury investigated, primarily to see if the girl bathed in wine, thus violating Prohibition laws. Among the witnesses was Walter Winchell, who testified he was there, all right, and saw several politicians, including Senator. . . . At this moment, he was excused.

Carroll went to prison for committing perjury when he denied that the bathing incident ever happened. Joyce in the tub, Carroll incarcerated, both made cosmographs.

The *Graphic* sponsored contests in search of readers, or viewers. It sent Miss Courtesy in search of polite New York men who would give up their seats on the subway or open doors for her. Successes were headlined, but the politest, or whatever, man she found was Fulton Oursler, executive editor of Macfadden publications; she married him.

The *Graphic* also sponsored an annual Lonely Hearts Ball, where the unattached could attach. Its sports dinners at the Hotel Astor attracted such guests of honor as Jack Dempsey, Gene Tunney, Sophie Tucker, Babe Ruth, Bernard Gimbel, Al Jolson, Mayor Walker, of course, and at one of them Rudy Vallee introduced "The Maine Stein Song."

The tabloid promoted a search for ten American Apollos and ten American Dianas "to encourage the wedding of the physically fit." Photos of candidates left the minimum, for the day, to the imagination. The *Graphic* offered a thousand Coolidge dollars as a wedding gift and $500 for each child born in the first five years of marriage. Mussolini was fooling around with the same principle over in Italy, but the *Graphic* campaign failed when not enough American Apollos could be found.

With its excesses and odd campaigns, the tabloid was soon tabbed the porno-*Graphic*. If its semidraped females and its emphasis on sex seem more vulgar than obscene in the 1980s, that may be a judgment on the 1980s. You did not have to be fastidious to object to the *Graphic* in the silliest decade of the century.

When Rudolph Valentino died on August 26, 1924, the grief was international and extravagant. Stanley Walker noted that hundreds of women and girls gathered at a high mass in Rio de Janeiro; in London a dancer swallowed poison and left a note requesting a friend to "look after Rudolph's picture." In a New York tenement a twenty-year-old mother of two gulped iodine, shot herself twice, and collapsed over a heap of Valentino photographs.

Thirty thousand people tried to jam into Frank E. Campbell's funeral parlor, where the silent film star lay in state; a plate glass window shattered in the crush. Mounted policemen tried to restore order. Women wanted to touch the dead actor's face, to snatch a button. On the first day, the gentlemen of the press drank $273 worth of Campbell's bootleg liquor. He switched to a cheaper brand.

The *Graphic,* of course, savored this meat. It turned loose squads of bootjacks, hearties whose specialty was to hawk extras. They earned as much as $100 a day. The *Graphic* managed a cosmograph-in-advance, showing the pallbearers bringing the body out of the chapel; even as they emerged in the flesh, they saw bootjacks peddling their picture. It was enough to call the quality of Campbell's liquor into question.

But beyond all the cosmographs and the first-person confessions of lust and violence, the *Graphic* is studied in Journalism 102 chiefly because it introduced Walter Winchell to the general public.

A mutual friend had introduced him to Oursler, who was making do with I KNOW THE MAN WHO KILLED MY GIRL and THREE WOMEN LASHED IN NUDE ORGY en route to *The Greatest Story Ever Told*. Oursler was familiar with Walter's column in the *Vaudeville News* and, indeed, had sent him a poem which Walter rejected. Oursler complimented him on his taste.

Walter telephoned Oursler at two o'clock in the morning, wanting to know if he had the job. Half asleep but wide awake, Oursler hired him at $100 a week plus a percentage from advertising he solicited. Walter was amusement writer, drama editor, drama critic, amusement-advertising manager, and Broadway columnist.

Oursler later recalled, "The funny thing is that I hired him because I believed he would be a good source of stories. . . . The column was secondary. Originally, the *Graphic* wasn't column-minded. Its big attraction was human interest."

But not even the *Graphic* was ready for Walter's brand of the new journalism. He told the city desk, for example, that an aging actor was about to leave his wife to marry the ingenue in his latest play.

"Has his wife filed suit for divorce?" the editor asked in his old-fashioned way.

"No, but—"

"Then it isn't news," said the editor.

Walter skulked away. "That son of a bitch," he complained, "won't ever take anything I give him."

His column, "Your Broadway and Mine," was tame stuff in the beginning, sparked by neologisms like "cinemagic" that became his trademark and just about every imitator's payment of tribute. The early columns were mostly show biz: "This town of ours . . . Longacre small talk places Luther Reed as the NY *American's* next dramatic reviewer . . . Trader Horn once colyumed for the Alleghany *Times* and the Rocky Mountain *News* . . . J. Kaufman commences *Morntelly* activity August 1 . . ."

There were the blind items: "What very well-known moom pitcher actress secretly abrogated her marriage in Paris last winter?" There were the plugs: "Recommended for diversion seekers . . . Rosita and Ramon at the St. Regis roof . . . Lundy's at Sheepshead Bay for seafood . . ." There were the inaccuracies: "Ernest Hemingway, they say, has agreed to furnish *Cosmopolitan* with his entire output for fifty grand a year, which was the title of one of his best-sellers."

One day, the story has it, he sat down to write his weekly column and found he had no jokes or quips. What he had were the sort of notes the desk had been tossing back at him. He put them on paper in desperation: "Helen Eby Brooks, widow of William Rock, has been plunging in Miami real estate . . . It's a girl at the Carter De-Havens . . . Lenore Ulric paid $7 income tax . . . Fanny Brice is betting on the horses at Belmont . . ."

Not yet the kind of thing to arch eyebrows, but within two months of joining the *Graphic* Walter was drawing more mail than any other contributor. Heywood Broun said Walter was the only thing in the paper worth reading. Walter was encouraged to write gossip by the *Graphic*'s managing editor, a mercurial figure named Emile Gauvreau, who left a vivid memoir called *My Last Million Readers,* which described his barely placable dislike for Walter:

> And in a corner sat a hunched figure with a white lean face of deceptive humility, looking up occasionally, startled. He pecked a typewriter nervously, with a frenzied determination, but from the machine a form of gossip was beginning to appear which he himself never dreamed could be accorded the benediction of print in a daily paper. When his column, *Your Broadway and Mine,* became the talk of the town, no vestige of humility remained in him. . . .
>
> No stranger phenomenon has yet appeared in the news-paper business. Gossip acquired such a tangibility, such a grip on his life, chiefly from the bare nucleus of a slim fact that, many times, he was more often cleverly wrong than monoto-nously correct. . . .

Gauvreau, in the newspaper tradition of the day, grew up in humble circumstances. He had been crippled in a boyhood accident. He learned the business on Connecticut newspapers. He read om-niverously and so, unlike most self-educated men, he did not have a fool for a teacher.

Walter drove him crazy. Walter wrote that Paris was a seaport. Walter wrote that Emile Zola was a woman. Walter's "lack of newspaper experience when I began to handle his copy; his refreshing *insouciance* about the difference between a subject and a predicate, became an ironical asset which preserved his personality and may have had the virtue of saving him years of learning to be like everybody else."

Walter and Gauvreau soon became, in Walter's coinage, don't-

151

invites, their dislike ripening into hatred, the first of Walter's famous feuds.

At the same time, Damon's private life finally fell apart.

These troubles made little difference for Damon and Walter. Their careers arched toward apogee like rockets across the strange skies of boom going bust, and each of them understood that the career came first.

nine

"JOURNALISTS! PEEKING through keyholes! Running after fire engines like a lot of coach dogs! Waking people up in the middle of the night to ask them what they think of Mussolini. Stealing pictures off old ladies of their daughters that get raped in Oak Park. A lot of lousy, daffy buttinskis, swelling around with holes in their pants, borrowing nickels from office boys! And for what? So a million hired girls and motormen's wives'll know what's going on."

Thus speaks Hildy Johnson in *The Front Page,* which Ben Hecht and Charles MacArthur sent rolling down the corridors of eternity at the Times Square Theater on August 14, 1928.

For all their womanizing, cursing, cynicism, and drinking, Hildy and his colleagues, even the Mephistophelean managing editor Walter Burns, are innocents. Part of the play's charm is the newsmen's single-minded devotion to their strange calling.

The big story is always a murder, a fire, a hanging, and yet the element of play is strong in *Front-Page* journalism. The veteran newspaperman-turned-critic Silas Bent wrote of faking a story when he was a young reporter. He found himself unwilling to wangle a statement from a teenaged girl whose father had just poisoned himself. Bent fooled the office.

"Thereafter I became thoroughly hard-boiled, and looked at such incidents as a game," he recalled. "Most reporters speak of newspaper work, you will observe, as 'the game.' Perhaps they have not been permitted to learn it in such a way that they can think of it as a profession."

Well, that might be in error, too. When a newsman speaks of journalism as a profession, he is likely to point out that it is the second oldest. The disputatious might question Kipling's remark to Herbert Bayward Swope that a good reporter is the noblest work of God, but a good reporter feels a sense of mission.

At the top of his form in 1927, Damon covered a quintessential *Front-page* story with a missionary zeal. Here's how he managed in three lead paragraphs to paint the broad outlines of a case that transfixed the nation even more deeply than did the slaughter in De Russey's Lane:

A chilly looking blonde with frosty eyes and one of those marble, you-bet-you-will chins, and an inert, scare-drunk fellow that you couldn't miss among any hundred men as a dead set-up for a blonde, or the shell game, or maybe a gold brick.

Mrs. Ruth Snyder and Henry Judd Gray are on trial in the huge weatherbeaten old courthouse of Queens County in Long Island City, just across the river from the roar of New York, for what might be called for want of a better name, The Dumbbell Murder. It was so dumb.

They are charged with the slaughter four weeks ago of Albert Snyder, art editor of the magazine, *Motor Boating,* the blonde's husband and father of her nine-year-old daughter, under circumstances that for sheer stupidity and brutality have seldom been equalled in the history of crime.

That last was another belt of Runyon hyperbole. Crimes as brutal and senseless as Snyder-Gray frequently turn up in the station houses. But it was a decade of extravagant claims and the year, according to Gene Fowler, marked the two-hundredth anniversary of the cuckoo clock. Once again Silas Bent deprecated the great fascination with the case, arguing "there was no element of mystery . . . nor any pronounced element of suspense," the only doubt being whether the once red-hot lovers would go to the electric chair.

The Hall-Mills case, Bent noted, was a dud from the standpoint of circulation. And yet editors, always slow to learn, assigned 120 reporters to the Snyder-Gray trial, "more than represented all the American newspapers and news agencies in the Far East, at that moment a tinder-box into which might be dropped purposefully the spark of another World War. Not only reporters were assigned to the murder trial, but, among others, Mary Roberts Rinehart, Billy Sunday . . . David Wark Griffith, Peggy Joyce, and the Reverend John Roach Stratton."

In a kind of amendment to Parkinson's law, the significance of the event expanded to justify all that newsprint and ink. Alexander Woollcott and other armchair sociologists averred that Americans were fascinated with the case because to Everywoman, Mrs. Snyder was the little lady across the breakfast table, and there was a sexist disbelief that a mere woman could be guilty of such a crime.

That said, Damon's trial coverage was brilliant, including his comment after Gray demonstrated how he bashed the unfortunate Snyder with a sashweight: "He is a right-hand hitter."

If Damon was cynical about Jersey justice, the crowd at the Snyder-Gray trial, and its behavior, appeared to strengthen Damon's growing sense of disillusion. He wrote on April 30:

> It seems a pity that old man Hogarth isn't living to depict the crowd scene at the courtroom yesterday.
>
> . . . Some strange-looking characters almost fought for a chance to leer at the principals in the trial. Apparently respectable men and women showed court attendants cards, letters, badges, birth certificates and automobile licenses in an effort to impress the guardians of the portals with their importance and the necessity of their getting into the courtroom.
>
> Dizzy-looking dolls said to represent the social strata of Park Avenue—the upper crust, as I understand—were there, not a little proud of their heroism in getting out so early. Some were escorted by silly-looking "muggs" wearing canes and spats.
>
> But also there were men who might be business men and women with something better to do, standing chin deep in the bloody scandal of this bloody trial and giving some offense to high heaven, it seems to me, by their very presence. . . . The women outnumbered the men by about three to one. They stood for hours on their tired feet, their eyes and mouths agape.

Damon came back to the crowds again and again. On May 6, he commented, "This remains the best show in town, if I may say so, as I shouldn't. Business couldn't be better. In fact, there is some talk of sending out a No. 2 company and 8,000,000 different blondes are being considered for the leading female role. No one has yet been picked for Henry Judd Gray's part but that will be easy. Almost any citizen will do, with a little rehearsal."

When the trial wound up, Damon wrote, "In some ways it was a disheartening spectacle, if one happened to think how many spectators would have been attracted to Long Island City to hear a few pleas for the Mississippi Flood sufferers."

Amid all the sordid sideshows, the press only occasionally was forced to indulge in the painful process of self-evaluation. The *Graphic* acknowledged that with its cosmographs and columns it might have

155

gotten carried away with Daddy and Peaches, although "it never stooped to wallow knee-deep in the mire and filth that a certain phase of the case represented."

Not long after, however, as Stanley Walker noted, the paper advertised, "Don't fail to read tomorrow's *Graphic*. An installment that thrills and stuns! A story that fairly pierces the heart, and reveals Ruth Snyder's last thought on earth; that pulses the blood as it discloses her final letters. Think of it! A woman's final thoughts just before she is clutched in the deadly snare that sears and burns and FRIES—AND KILLS! Her very last words! Exclusively in tomorrow's *Graphic*."

As it developed, Mrs. Snyder's last words were in the public domain. "Forgive them, Father," she began, before the current quieted her. A *News* photographer with a camera strapped to his leg snapped a picture of Mrs. Snyder in the electric chair.

But a few thousand words may be better than any picture, and H. Allen Smith more than fifty years later recalled standing popeyed in front of a teletype machine in the city room of the Denver *Post* as Gene Fowler's account of the execution came pounding out. A *pastiche* reveals as much about the social attitudes of the times as it does about the wretched pair's final moments:

> They led Ruth Brown Snyder from her steel cage tonight. Then powerful guards thrust her irrevocably into the obscene, sprawling oaken arms of the ugly electric chair.
>
> That was about 30 minutes ago. The memory of the crazed woman in her last agony as she struggled against the unholy embrace of the chair is too harrowing to permit of calm portrayal of the law's ghastly ritual. . . .
>
> The formal destruction of the killers of poor, stolid, unemotional Albert Snyder in his rumpled sleep . . . was hardly less revolting than the crime itself. Both victims of the chair met their deaths trembling but bravely. . . .
>
> Brief as was the time for the State to slay Ruth and Judd, it seems in retrospect to have been a long, haunting blur of bulging horror—glazed eyes, saffron faces, fear-blanched that became twisted masks, purpling underlips and hands as pale as chalk, clenching in the last paroxysms. . . .
>
> And as these woeful wrecks passed from life, the shadows of attendants, greatly magnified, seemed to move in fantastic array along the walls, the silhouettes nodding and prancing in a sepulchral minuet. . . .
>
> The tired form was taut. The body that once throbbed with

the joy of her sordid bacchanals turned brick red as the current struck. Slowly, after half a minute of death dealing current, the exposed arms, right leg, throat and jaws bleached out again. . . .

At the first electric torrent, Judd's throat and jaws were swollen. The cords stood out. The skin was gorged with blood and was the color of a turkey gobbler's wattles. Slowly this crimson tide subsided and left his face paler, but still showing splotches of red, which were mosaics of pain. The electricity was put on just as the chaplain got this far with his comforting words:

"For God so loved the world . . ."

Even as Damon and Fowler prospered, the relationship between them was as much shadow as sunshine. Damon had said Fowler came to New York "with a wild gleam in one eye and a still wilder gleam in the other." Damon had been angry when Fowler, his protégé, held out for a higher starting salary than Hearst first offered. Damon identified himself with the Hearst interests, however cynical his attitude, and he may have been trying to prove that he was executive material by holding down salaries.

Fowler said, "I always took into consideration how Damon counseled me, and then I did just the opposite. Strangely enough, it always turned out."

Fowler was celebrated for his imaginative expense accounts, perhaps most famously for the bill he submitted after an Alaskan adventure, when he entered an item for the funeral of a lead dog on the dogsled team and, when that didn't quite balance things, added an entry for "flowers for the bereft bitch."

Damon did well with expenses, too, although he conceded Fowler was his superior. When he needed a few dollars to get him out of the red, Damon simply wrote, "Spent while going around and about." Bugs Baer once adopted this tactic, "Spent while going around and about like Damon Runyon," but it was disallowed.

Hearst, in a moment unguarded even by his standards, named Fowler managing editor of the *American* in 1924. Fowler at first declined, explaining he didn't like editors. Neither did he, said Hearst, but he made it clear that Fowler would be doing him a favor. An *American* managing editor walking into the city room in that period sometimes met himself walking out, "giving rise to the rumor that there was a mirror in the entrance," according to Damon.

Damon said Fowler was "climbing the thirteen steps to stand on the Jim Julian," the name of the gallows back in Colorado. Fowler did not last long as managing editor, being easygoing and a creative sort. He spent much of his time with his feet on the desk, trying to master the concertina. The experience did not slow his career; after all, he was one of six managing editors at the newspaper in three years. Circulation continued to drop. People were calling it "the vanishing *American,*" and Hearst sent Fowler on a Mediterranean cruise as a reward for being fired. This must have further irritated Damon.

Damon sometimes brought his son to the office, "a sinister-looking rookery busy with the noisy confusion attending the printing of a big city newspaper," Damon, Jr., wrote. "At night, when my father would be muttering over his typewriter, the place was frightening for a child. . . ." People already were asking the boy if he was following in father's footsteps. "At an early age, I'd grown weary of the question, mainly because I couldn't think of a suitable answer besides a blunt 'no.'"

Damon and Ellen were together only in theory. The Riverside Drive apartment was in his name, but he usually slept at the Friars Club or in a room above Billy LaHiff's many-storied tavern on West Forty-eighth Street. Ellen continued on her literally dizzying round of partying.

One night Mary awoke her younger brother. She said their mother was lying on the floor "in Daddy's study. What'll we do?" The two children, clinging to each other, tiptoed through the dark and silent apartment to investigate. They could barely make out the form of their mother's fur coat on the floor.

"Do you suppose she's dead?" Mary asked.

The trembling children urged each other forward. Finally, Mary, as the eldest, advanced. "Why," she sighed, "the coat's empty." They found their mother in her bed, sleeping it off. "She was getting out of control," her son wrote, "and it was a fearful experience when one of the giants got out of control."

Young Damon was often sick. He was hospitalized with various childhood ailments but seemed to perk up after a doctor prescribed an "iron" tonic. Years later, after he learned he was an alcoholic, he saw a bottle of the magic restorative in a drugstore near the Lydia Pinkhams and found it was richer than wine in alcohol.

Mary, in an effort to win some of the attention devoted to her sickly brother, raised moderate Cain. "I just don't know what I'm going to do with that child," Ellen complained. Then she figured it out: Hand the problem over. When Mary was ten, she was sent to the Convent of St. Vincent in the Riverdale section of the Bronx.

Her brother and mother accompanied her to the convent, and years later Damon, Jr., recalled her pathetic screams, "Please, don't send me away! Mother, please don't! Please don't leave me here! I'll be good, honest, I will. Mother, just please don't leave me here. . . ."

Damon, Jr., derived a lesson from his sister's banishment. He withdrew. "Such a good boy," said Ellen. "So quiet." Ellen was not deliberately cruel. She took young Damon to Broadway shows and movies, to see movies made, to the scenes of the big stories—the house where the Snyders lived, the sidewalk where Arnold Rothstein bled. . . .

Rothstein.

William Fallon, the celebrated criminal lawyer who would be disbarred but whom Gene Fowler called The Great Mouthpiece, characterized Rothstein as "a man who waits in doorways . . . a mouse, waiting in the doorways for his cheese." Damon knew Rothstein, just about everybody on Broadway knew Rothstein, show business figures, athletes, sportswriters, and Herbert Bayard Swope who was a prodigious gambler. Rothstein sat at tables in Broadway restaurants holding court through the night, making notes in his little book.

He was the blackest of sheep. His father came up from the Lower East Side to prosperity, greatly admired for his piety and plain dealing. Supreme Court Justice Louis D. Brandeis and Governor Smith attended a testimonial dinner in 1919 honoring the man called Abe the Just for his evenhanded arbitration of a garment district dispute. That, of course, was the year his son fixed the World Series.

When Arnold was three his father discovered him one night standing next to his older brother, a knife clutched in his hand. "I hate him," Arnold said. Harry was bright, cheerful, and well liked. Arnold was not. "You hate me," Arnold said. "You all love Harry."

Arnold often cut school, where he was indifferent to all subjects except arithmetic. He found his way into street crap games. At fourteen he was a serious gambler who understood the odds and never bet against the percentages. He financed this early gambling by borrowing the money and jewelry his pious father set aside before going to Temple for prayer. Arnold always returned the property before Shabbat ended Saturday evening.

As Eliot Asinof recounts in *Eight Men Out,* Rothstein at an early age "used money to make money." He began lending it at 25 percent interest and sent around the notorious Monk Eastman to collect from slow payers. He befriended Tammany Hall politicians, who protected two Rothstein gambling dens in the West Forties. He spent $100,000 converting a Saratoga mansion into a gambling hall, where the rich

159

could drop hundreds of thousands in a single night. Some of the money financed international drug dealing. The money simply rolled in, all of it dirty.

Damon admired Rothstein. Part of this represented the simple-minded tendency to find glamour in crime, to feel important for knowing the dirty little secret. Under the sharp Broadway exterior, the expensive, flashy wardrobe, Damon remained something of a rube. A mutual friend told Fowler that Damon "had several coats of sophistication, self-applied. But the varnish wore thin at times; the grain showed through. And then Damon seemed the small-town boy, standing in front of the village poolroom to watch the boys and girls go by."

The expedient code Damon absorbed in youth cost him the respect of some of his peers. As Ring Lardner, Jr., has pointed out, Ring, Sr., Grantland Rice, and Damon all were provincials who found fame in New York. But Ring's midwestern upbringing included reading of the children's classics and almost daily bouts with the King James Bible. Rice so embodied the code of southern honor that his probity seemed aberrative in the twenties, and his most famous verse—the one about the Great Scorer—is mawkish to later generations.

When Rice went overseas in World War I, he entrusted $75,000 to a family friend, a lawyer, for Mrs. Rice's care if anything should happen to him. Rice returned to find the lawyer had blown the money on bad investments. Rice took a couple of stiff drinks. Then he said, "It was all my fault. Mine entirely. I should not have placed so much temptation in the man's way."

So it is small wonder that both Lardner and Rice, who gambled and drank and were seldom hidebound, "couldn't understand what they regarded as a moral deficiency" in Damon, or that Ring, Jr., "got the impression in my early years that there was something vaguely shady about him."

By 1928 the word was around that Rothstein was slow paying off some of his bets, which was not very bright, particularly in a man Damon memorialized as The Brain. Lou Clayton, of Damon's favorite song-and-dance team, Clayton, Jackson and Durante, won $11,000 in a crap game run by Rothstein and could not collect until he threatened to pass the word along Broadway that Rothstein was a welsher, one of the few issues about which Broadway took a stern moral view. Rothstein paid off. But there were other rumors of slow pay, and in the fall of 1928 Tex Rickard told Fowler that Rothstein was going to be rubbed out.

160

A few weeks later, Fowler, who was then managing editor of the racetrack sheet, the *Morning Telegraph,* heard that story corroborated by a reporter named Johnny O'Connor, "one of the best-informed men on Broadway." Fowler's publisher told him the *Telegraph* was not interested in the troubles of a gambler, so Fowler tipped off his friend Walter Howey, the *real* Walter Burns, who, for some despicable sin in an earlier existence, was managing editor of the *Mirror.* Howey returned the call to say he had checked with Damon "and Damon said that you and O'Connor should change your bootlegger or, better still, quit drinking."

A few nights later, on November 4, Rothstein was sitting in Lindy's when he took a phone call from Samarra, directing him to the Park Central hotel, where he was shot in the belly in an argument over his leisurely payoffs. He lingered for two days before dying. He left an estate of $3.2 million and would have won almost another million on Herbert Hoover, had he lasted through the election, so it seems another twist in his character that he had developed, in the sporting phrase, fishhooks in his pockets.

Damon just a year later covered the trial of George McManus, who was accused of Rothstein's murder. It is accepted that Damon knew a great deal more about the affair than he ever admitted. He clearly did not think much of the State's case.

> McManus is one of four persons indicted for the crime [he wrote]. Another is Hyman Biller, an obscure denizen of the brightlights region of Manhattan Island, who probably wouldn't be recognized by more than two persons if he walked into any joint in town, such is his obscurity.
> Then there is good old John Doe and good old Richard Roe, possibly the same Doe and Roe who have been wanted in forty-nine different spots for crimes ranging from bigamy to disorderly conduct for a hundred years past. Tough guys, old John and Richard, and always getting in jams. McManus is the only one on trial for the killing of Rothstein, probably for the reason he is the only one handy.

Damon referred to the jurors as "the twelve good men and glum," noted it "would have been a violent shock to the enormous vanity of the dead gambler . . . to hear men who have lived in the very neighborhood he frequented shake their heads and say they didn't know him," and observed that some of the State's witnesses busied

161

themselves in the phone booths, demonstrating "it is a severe handicap to summon a man to such a remote quarter as the Criminal Courts Building along toward post time."

The case didn't even go to the jury. The judge directed a verdict of not guilty, and once again Damon could drink deeply the satisfying but dangerous brew of I-told-you-so.

The twenties were not entirely given over to carnality and tacky crime, and sometimes its events brought out the better side of Damon's innocent-abroad nature. When Charles Lindbergh on May 21, 1927, became the first person to fly solo across the Atlantic, the nations of the West practically tripped over each other in the rush to honor him. The man, the event, the times came together in an outburst of adulation without parallel. The technology of communication made instant, mass hero worship possible. People were tired of kidding themselves that life could be an extended holiday; perhaps they felt bad about themselves, and here was very proof that they could be brave and good.

The voice of Silas Bent was never more lonely than when he suggested there was an element of hysteria in this, fomented by the press, which found "The appetite grew by what it fed on."

Bent noted, "To the mere hop-off by Lindbergh, the *Times* gave three first-page, eight column streamers and thirty-seven columns of space, including more than a page of pictures, while it could spare but one column to a jail sentence for Harry F. Sinclair, millionaire prime mover in the Teapot Dome scandal." When Lindy, as he was quickly dubbed, landed in Paris, the Cincinnati *Post* printed "a two-line first page block letter headline five and one-half inches in height." The profoundly cynical Arthur Brisbane publicly fretted, "Pray that it may not occur to the daring youth to fly back again. . . . Regard for his mother doubtless will help hold him back."

A single issue of one Sunday newspaper devoted one hundred columns of text and pictures about Lindbergh's return to the United States. New York's welcome was a print orgy. The *Times* gave it 15 pages; the *American* 10; the *Herald Tribune* 9; the *World* 8, the *Mirror* and *The News* 23 and 16 pages respectively.

The *Evening World* called the Lindbergh flight "the greatest feat of solitary man in the records of the human race," but Bent really took out after the *Times:*

"What was the greatest story of all time?" the newspaper asked.

162

"Adam eating the apple?" (Readers of the Bible may have recalled that this story was told in less than 700 words.)

"The landing of the ark on Ararat?" (Amply reported in less than 400 words.)

"The discovery of Moses in the bullrushes?" (Fully covered in less than 300 words.)

But Lindbergh's flight, the suspense of it, the daring of it, the triumph and glory of it—these are the stuff that makes immortal news.

So Damon was hardly being fulsome when he covered Lindbergh's arrival in Washington:

A bashful-looking, long-legged, gangling boy, with cheeks of pink and with a cowlick in his hair that won't let the blond locks stay slicked down, came back to his home folks today one of the biggest men in all the world.

Lindy!

My heart, how young he seemed!

And how weighty, how absurd the Colonel Charles Augustus Lindbergh seemed as you gazed at him sitting there, as slim as your finger . . .

Lindy flew to New York:

"Back again, as he left, in a spidery little buggy of the breeze, something like the one he jockeyed across the Atlantic to his trysting spot with Destiny in France.

And this old town went mad—quite mad!

The mumble of millions of voices rose in clamor at his return, louder than the loudest winds above, or the waves below the track he traveled through the long night of his flight. . . .

Ah, say!—

Are those young eyes that stare at the tall towers of our town and the roaring crowd about to shed tears? . . . Well, let him cry, let him cry, the boy is entitled to a few tears!

Damon sandwiched this lachrymose interlude between a couple of fights elevated by the era into Homeric epic, the heavyweight title matches involving Dempsey and Gene Tunney, who offended Damon by fighting with his brains, by battling from Greenwich Village to

163

Greenwich, Connecticut, where he married into society, by chatting with George Bernard Shaw and announcing that he read Shakespeare and Omar Khayyám and by fastidiously keeping apart from the scum of the earth, the fight mob.

"If Mr. Tunney takes a good stout shot of some kind of invigorator and keeps the old bean with him . . . he might be able to pull and haul in there with Jack Dempsey for the full ten rounds," Damon predicted about the Philadelphia fight which would be watched by more than 120,000 people, in 1980 still the record for sentient presence at a heavyweight championship. "I give him an outside chance to stick the ten."

He gave Tunney another outside chance to win, "which is so far outside it is practically over in Maryland, or about the same distance as some of the spectators will be from the ring."

And after the fact, it was not so much that Tunney won, in Damon's ringside account, as that Dempsey lost:

> They all go the same way.
> Another once-great champion joined the big parade of the has-beens, the never-ending parade tonight.
> Jack Dempsey, called "the Manassa Man Mauler," was so badly out-boxed and out-classed . . . by Gene Tunney, once of the United States Marines . . . that toward the finish he seemed more a third-rater than one of the greatest champions that ever lived.

This was an event of transcendent importance in the twenties. The New York *Times,* which on a cataclysmic news day eight years earlier had used four eight-column headlines on the front page to report the Armistice, the overthrow of the German Empire, and the flight of the Kaiser to Holland, gave over *three* eight-column front-page headlines to announce that Tunney defeated Dempsey.

A few days later, Damon discounted rumors of a fix. There was too much "smart money" on Dempsey, he believed: "Mr. Nick the Greek from the Far West Coast; Mr. Doc Gulch of Atlantic City; Mr. Fred Perry of New York and Havana, and numerous other gents who can at least spell 'cat' took what is known in the parlance of the profession as 'a bath.'"

The rematch in Chicago on September 22, 1927, became boxing's first two-million-dollar gate and, when Dempsey dropped Tunney but neglected to obey the newly written rule about going to a neutral corner, the Battle of the Long Count. The referee delayed counting while he shepherded Dempsey across the ring, and Damon caught the wild drama of the moment:

> Down on the canvas for the first time in his boxing career, sniffing at the resin dust there, with the murderous old Manassa Man Mauler glowering over him with evil intent, Gene Tunney, the fighting marine, got up and carried to victory. . . .
>
> He got the decision . . . at the end of ten desperate rounds . . . with 150,000 men and women still fairly limp from the excitement of the seventh round. . . .
>
> It was in that round that Dempsey swarmed all over the big blond New Yorker—knocking him down not with one punch but with a wild rain of smashes on Tunney's pale body as he hung over the ropes. Tunney fell on his broad back, then he sat up, his pallid features pinched with the strangest expression of bewilderment and, it seemed to me, embarrassment. . . .
>
> Once he got to his feet, Tunney began running backward as only a skillful boxer in distress knows how to run, back, back, back he went, with the glowering Dempsey fairly growling in anger. . . .
>
> The bell ending the seventh round found Tunney out of immediate danger. . . . Then, as calmly as a delicatessen owner slicing up his bologna, he proceeded to cut Dempsey up with his spearing left. . . .

However sporting, gaudy, eyepopping, or dispiriting the event, history leaves little doubt that the jewel in New York journalism of the twenties was the *World,* presided over through most of the decade by the swashbuckling redhead Herbert Bayard Swope, and described by a contemporary as "a bright and glistening candle in the singularly materialistic and conscienceless times."

Westbrook Pegler called him "all gall, divided into three parts—Herbert, Bayard and Swope," but to those New Yorkers who felt with E. B. White that "Life has never seemed the same since the *World* took the count," it was the *World* of Swope, not Pulitzer's *World,* they revered.

A decade after Pulitzer's death, the *World* was phthisic, its mass readership reduced by competition from the tabloids, the popular magazines, and the movies.

With fewer financial resources than had been available to Pulitzer,

165

Swope recast the publication; in John K. Hutchens' view, "The *World* was an extension of Swope's personality as newspapers have not often been since the heyday of personal journalism." Swope demonstrated that in spirit *the World it was the old world yet.*

Its sports coverage was dull, its brightly written foreign news was spotty, its real estate section was as supine and its Sunday supplement was about as bogus as any in the land, but the *World* proclaimed cockily that it did "not believe that all the news that's fit to print is worth reading."

"The *World* was a newspaperman's newspaper," James Boylan wrote, "brilliantly written, tautly edited, politically and commercially independent, effervescent, irreverent, combative, liberal. No man who ever spent more than a few days under its beckoning golden dome at 63 Park Row, it seems, ever erased the fact from his memory."

Swope invented the op ed page, the page opposite Walter Lippmann's editorial page with the Rollin Kirby cartoon. FPA's "The Conning Tower" ornamented the op ed, but its most respected voice belonged to Heywood Broun. Laurence Stallings, coauthor of *What Price Glory?*, wrote book reviews, Woollcott covered the drama, Quinn Martin films, and Deems Taylor music; it was heady stuff for a daily newspaper and Swope did not attempt to square the circle by appealing to both the discriminating and the gum-chewer.

What resulted, Boylan said, was "no longer a newspaper for every New Yorker, but rather for those New Yorkers who read, went to plays and parties, took an interest in issues and 'kept up'—in other words, a kind of elite, but a numerous enough one to keep the circulation in the neighborhood of 300,000."

Without money or the staff to rival the *Times,* Swope's philosophy was "to pick out the best story of the day and hammer the hell out of it." He shared Pulitzer's crusading spirit and the *World* won Pulitzer prizes by exposing the Ku Klux Klan—with a jump of 60,000 in circulation—and Florida's slave-labor peonage system. The Klan in those days was a potent political force, not entirely a ragtag collection of crackpots and losers. Swope's reporters included Dudley Nicholas, William L. Laurence, Ernest K. Lindley, St. Clair McKelway, and Norman Krasna, who later distinguished themselves in fields as various as the movies, science reporting, punditry, magazine journalism, and network radio comedy but remained *World* men to the end.

Swope did not plead the Dana defense, which was that whatever Providence allowed to occur, he was not too proud to print; not for the *World* the editorial alibi that vulgarity and vacuity are the people's choice. "What I try to do in my paper is give the public part of what it wants," he said, "and part of what it ought to have, whether it wants it or not." This is a concept so stunning in its simplicity it seems not to have been thought of again.

Swope regarded journalism as "a priestly mission." He declared that no one from the advertising department should set foot in the eight-floor city room. Swope quoted Pulitzer, "Accuracy is to a newspaper what virtue is to a lady." Few, in those days, scoffed at either concept.

Damon said Swope "carried the power of the press like a flaming beacon when he was a reporter and fairly intimidated his way to the news." A staffer recalled that Swope, the editor, "attacked the news wich such zest the staff was galvanized—also partly paralyzed and partly amused." Swope's attitude toward the news was possessive. He looked out the window one wintry day and suddenly cried, "Who's covering my snowstorm?" Swope believed the front page of a newspaper was "the mirror of the world in which a man lives."

Staff loyalty was traditional. A *World* reporter in 1915 was fatally injured in the crash of a Boston-to-New York train. His last words, as he was carried from the wreckage, were, "Call up the New York *World* right away and tell them there is a wreck here—a big story. Also tell them I'm sorry that I won't be able to work the story because I'm smashed up. Call up my mother, too." The *World* remembered him with a plaque in the city room.

"Swope's ethical code," E. J. Kahn observed, "would have driven a tabloid right out of business. He refused to let the *World* print anything about divorce cases until they reached the courts. It was also part of his ethics that when a divorce case involving well-known people got that far, the *World* would write about it, even if one of the principals happened to be Ralph Pulizter."

Life around Swope was great fun. Parties at his Long Island estate ran through the night just about every night; unlike their neighbors, the Swopes didn't need to hire night watchmen because someone was always awake. Ring Lardner said the house looked as if it had been built by a man with a scroll saw and plenty of time.

After a few days as a house guest, Scott Fitzgerald had the inspiration for Gatsby's incomparable parties. One night the governor of Maryland was a dinner guest and an overserved celebrant burped loudly. After a moment of silence, Dorothy Parker said sweetly, "The governor will pardon you."

Swope instructed his staff, "In general, boil over whenever wrong is done the little fellow." Langston Hughes recalled that in the 1920s "the Negro was in vogue." A kind of condescension settled in, beginning with *Shuffle Along,* called "a honey of a show," which featured the ill-starred Florence Mills, Hall Johnson the choirmaster, and music by Eubie Blake and Noble Sissle.

167

Whites flocked to Harlem's Cotton Club, which discouraged black patronage, and preachers opened up shouting churches as sideshows for white tourists. But the black remained an invisible man in the metropolitan press, except in the *World*. It does not seem much, but when Swope ordered the word Negro capitalized, it was a giant step. He inaugurated a column of news about blacks. The response on the part of other newspapers was revealing: Their advertising departments spread the word that the *World* was becoming a Negro newspaper, read only in Harlem.

In a period of stultifying political complacency, the *World* raised its voice on other fronts, protesting, for example, the suspension of five duly elected Socialist members of the New York State Assembly. Dudley Nichols called Swope a man "who loved nothing better than pushing the strong around and giving a hand to the weak."

But nothing better defined the *World's* place in the journalism of the period than the tribute paid it by *The New Yorker* magazine, which was founded in 1925 and quickly became an indispensable periodical for the literate American. *The New Yorker* said in a promotional advertisement that it hoped to match the *World's* qualities of "intelligence, reasonable good taste, honesty, courage, good news sense, freedom from oppressive sensationalism, respect for the rights of privacy and, above all, interest, interest, interest."

The *World* was not free from the era's excesses, a screwball interest in the occult, for example, and the dead hand of Pulitzer sometimes seemed to guide its coverage of crime and scandal. And even in the era of gargoyle journalism, it was not alone in radiating a sense of lightness, a sense of fun which has all but vanished from the metropolitan press.

E. B. White, on arrival in New York, "burned with a low steady fever just because I was on the same island with Don Marquis, Heywood Broun, Christopher Morley, Franklin P. Adams, Robert C. Benchley, Frank Sullivan, Dorothy Parker, Alexander Woollcott, Ring Lardner, and Stephen Vincent Benét." Most of these were *World*-lings, but White also "would hang around the corners of Chambers Street and Broadway"—the *Sun* building—"thinking: somewhere in that building is the typewriter archy the cockroach jumps on at night."

Archy made his first appearance in the *Sun Dial* column of Don Marquis one morning in 1916. He wrote on the Marquis typewriter hurling himself "with all his force upon a key, head downward, and his weight and the impact of the blow were just sufficient to operate the machine, one slow letter after another. He could not work the capital letters . . ." Archy's first communication began:

> expression is the need of my soul
> i was once a vers libre bard
> but i died and my soul went into the body of a cockroach
> it has given me a new outlook on life
> i see things from the under side now.

Seeing things from the under side, Archy was free to comment on the fads and idiocies and big questions of the period, introducing such raffish companions as Mehitabel, "the dissolute feline who was a dancer and always the lady, *toujours gai.*" This inspiration, illustrated by George Herriman, creator of *Krazy Kat,* gave Marquis plenty of elbowroom for social comment; he was a gifted writer and in book form *archy and mehitabel,* the stuff of a daily newspaper, remained in print, edition after edition.

Even the *American,* which was determinedly lowbrow, printed verse all over the place, by Damon, James Montague, George Phair, and others. In 1924 Damon brought John Kieran of the New York *Herald* in for a visit with Fowler, the well-known managing editor.

Kieran was an anomaly, an erudite sportswriter whose interests included nature studies and Latin. He was tired of the *Herald,* which had so fallen from the ideals of its great founder as to cater to the carriage trade. Kieran, with a more ambitious program in store, wrote sports for the *American,* digressing one day to comment on a man who was arrested for smoking in Madison Square Garden after a no-smoking edict had been imposed by humorless authority:

> He might have committed a dozen crimes
> Untouch'd by the laws of the land.
> But he smoked one night at a Garden fight,
> And they hanged him out of hand.
> Yes, they hanged that man in the cold gray dawn
> And they gave three rousing cheers
> As he plunged in space to a resting place
> Where he'll smoke for a thousand years.

Franklin P. Adams conducted perhaps the most widely quoted column of the time, which featured not only his own Samuel Pepys diary but contributions from a stable of talented contributors. He joined the *World* on January 2, 1922, introducing himself with an ode "To His Lyre," which began with a phrase from Homer and concluded:

> Then aid me, Lute, beginning now!
> Give me theme for colophon or leader;
> And some day there may grace my brow
> The laurel from some Grateful Reader.

Laurels were deserved, as on the May day in 1926 when FPA commented on the Joyce Hawley–Earl Carroll vis-à-vis:

> To my office and read a tayle from Chicago, how that Joyce Hawley's mother hath said that when she was a child of ten, she would pour her father's brandy in her bath, deeming it would make her grow, albeit the mother did not say what it would maker her grow into. Oh,
>
> > Gentle Joyce was as sweet as candy;
> > She always bathed in her papa's brandy;
> > And when she grew up she was hale and hearty
> > And had a fine time at Earl Carroll's party.

"The block seemed to tremble" under the feet of the young E. B. White as he walked past FPA's house in West Thirteenth Street between Sixth and Seventh—"the way Park Avenue trembles when a train leaves Grand Central." The giants, the lighthearted versifiers, the crusaders, perhaps most of all the little cockroach made "buying a newspaper . . . quietly exciting in a way that it has ceased to be."
For White, looking back in 1950, the problem was obvious:

> In 1916 to hold a job on a daily paper, a columnist was expected to be something of a scholar and a poet—or if not a poet at least to harbor the transmigrated soul of a dead poet. Nowadays, to get a columning job a man need only have the soul of a Peep Tom, or of a third-rate prophet. . . .
> Archy used to come back from the golden companionship of the tavern with a poet's report of life as seen from the under side. Today's columnist returns from the platinum companionship of the night club with a dozen pieces of watered gossip and a few bottomless anecdotes. Archy returned carrying a heavy load of wine and dreams. These later cockroaches come sober from their taverns, carrying a basket of fluff.

"Hugh Leamy, Jr., of *Collier's* was recently wed to Jimmy Montague's daughter . . . James Watts, who last played in *Patience,* is now in London, where he just inherited a million dollars . . . Five pounds of matzohs were expressed to F. Ziegfled in Paris . . . Frank Carson, the editor, escaped from St. Luke's hospital to go whoopee-making the other middle-of-the-night . . ."

It seems a basket of fluff, all right, the matter Walter was spinning for the *Graphic* in 1928, but Gresham's law has its applications in journalism, too, and as McKelway wrote, "the effect of the new type of column was startling. People began to talk about it everywhere."

Apart from his column-writing, Walter's duties as drama critic did not bring to mind William Archer: "Herman Shumlin made his bow as an independent producer of plays at the Klaw theater with *Command Performance,* which proved to be highly enjoyable . . . It kept the auditors in a merry mood when they weren't suppressing heart throbs."

Walter offended the parsimonious brothers Shubert, who controlled half the theaters in the city. "A certain columnist has been barred from all the Shubert openings," he wrote. "Now he can wait three days and go to their closings."

He announced he would be in the audience when the Marx brothers opened in *Animal Crackers* at a Shubert theater. The Shuberts posted guards. The Marxes had their own money in the production and saw no reason why Walter shouldn't attend. They dressed him up as Harpo, fright wig, outsize coat, and cane. When the stage manager asked about the clone, Groucho explained, "Oh, Harpo sometimes throws a fit. We keep an understudy ready at all times." Walter watched the first-night performance from the wings.

Walter spent a lot of time at his speakeasy rounds. At a burst of laughter, he would join the party and demand, "What's the gag? Is it anything for the column?" McKelway reported that newspaper and theatrical people who summered near the Winchells at Long Beach got in the habit of hiding behind a cement wall to avoid him. He grabbed men by their arms or coat lapels, demanding, "Got an item? Gimme a gag!" Arthur Caesar, a movie writer, once jeered as Walter approached in a restaurant, "Look at him—the mental mendicant."

"Winchell got to know all sorts of big people," McKelway wrote, "and most of them encouraged him in his work. . . . Prohibition was on and the boom was rising; the magic word everywhere was tolerance, when people stopped to think at all, but most of the time, nobody stopped to think."

Emile Gauvreau, stopping to think, believed "No paper but Macfadden's tabloid could have nursed such a prodigy who, by some form of self-hypnosis, came to feel himself the center of his time." Walter was supported in his conceit by surveys indicating his column was responsible for one-third of the *Graphic's* readership.

Magazines sought him out, including *Vanity Fair* and the literary *Bookman,* for which he wrote an article explaining Broadway with the help of his dictionary:

> As a standard of moral comparison it is at once an entice-
> ment and a hell, a Circe's cavern of lasciviousness and soul-
> destroying delights, an unholy place where producers are
> seducers of women, where stars without talent are made
> meretriciously overnight, where pure girls succumb to rich
> admirers for diamond brooches, furs, imported automobiles,
> apartments and other luxuries—a Sodom and Gomorrah all
> within the confines of a garish district extending from just
> below Forty-second Street to Columbus Circle at Fifty-ninth.

Such sociological moonshine, along with analyses of Daddy and Ruth and the Reverend Hall evaporated in the heat of one blazing cause.

This was the matter of Sacco and Vanzetti, two immigrant anarchists convicted of murder in a payroll robbery and believed innocent by many liberals. It was called the case that will not die as it dragged on for six years after the men were convicted in July 1921. It inspired international demonstrations, a famous poem by Edna St. Vincent Millay, Maxwell Anderson's play *Winterset,* and the silencing of the *World's* preeminent voice in what instant historians saw as the symbolic end of that great newspaper.

Heywood Broun anchored the *World's* op ed page, the torchbearer of Pulitzer's liberal tradition. Broun, whose amiability was legendary, seemed transformed by the Sacco-Vanzetti case. Years later, he told his son that Sacco and Vanzetti marked a kind of dividing line which made previous jihads children's crusades. He wrote in fury as Massachusetts justice implacably rejected appeals:

> "The decision is unbelievably brutal," said the chairman of
> the Defense Committee, and he was wrong. The thing is
> worthy to be believed. It has happened. It will happen again,
> and the shame is wider than that which must rest upon
> Massachusetts. . . . Scratch through the varnish of any judg-
> ment seat and what will you strike but hate thick-clotted from

172

centuries of angry verdicts? Did any man ever find power within his hand except to use it as a whip?

The *World*'s editorial position on the case was moderate. Broun was having none of that: "What more can these immigrants from Italy expect? It is not every prisoner who has a president of Harvard university throw on the switch for him."

Broun absolved, with acid, the presiding judge. ". . . in no usual sense of the term is this man a villain," he wrote. "Although probably not a great jurist, he is without doubt as capable and conscientious as the average Massachusetts judge, and if that's enough to warm him in wet weather, by all means let him stick the compliment to his ribs."

From his cell, Vanzetti produced a remarkable statement:

> If it had not been for this, I might have live out my life talking at street corners to scorning men. I might have die, unmarked, unknown, a failure. Now we are not a failure. This is our career and our triumph. . . . Our words—our lives—our pains—nothing! The taking of our lives—lives of a good shoemaker and a poor fish-peddler—all! The last moment belongs to us—that agony is our triumph.

Against such eloquence, Masachusetts justice only called up memories of Salem. Broun wrote that when the judge pronounced sentence, "a woman in the courtroom said with terror, 'It is death condemning life!' The men in Charlestown prison are shining spirits, and Vanzetti has spoken with an eloquence not known elsewhere in our time. They are too bright, we shield our eyes and kill them. We are the dead, and in us there is not feeling or imagination nor the terrible torment of the lust for justice."

When the management asked Broun to lay off Sacco and Vanzetti, and he responded with another column, the *World* killed it and explained its position in an editorial. There was a somewhat civilized public exchange between Broun and Ralph Pulitzer, centering on the writer's right to write and the editor's right to edit, and Broun departed. He rejoined the *World* briefly after three months' absence, but the wound was uncurable, and Broun left the *World* for good not long before the *World* left the world. It was not cause-and-effect, but the symbolists had their metaphor. FPA later wrote, "I want it on the record that firing Broun, for anything, was a mistake."

And how did Damon react to the crisis of conscience occasioned by Sacco-Vanzetti? According to Gene Fowler, unpardonably.

173

The *American* in late August 1927 offers no record that Damon was concerned with the story at all. He was writing about the Dempsey-Tunney rematch in "The Mornin's Mornin'" damning Tunney with faint praise on the day of the execution: "I think Mr. Tunney is a great fighter of his type and style. He is strictly a counter-fighter, waiting on the other fellow's leads, which is the dullest and most uninteresting style in the world if it chances that the other fellow will not lead. . . ."

But Damon, in his all-over-the-paper mode, often published a sports column while he was covering a big news story. "The Mornin's Mornin'" appeared even as he reported the Hall-Mills and Snyder-Gray trials.

Fowler wrote that Damon was dispatched to Massachusetts and on exeuction eve filed a report beginning, "They're frying Sacco and Vanzetti in the morning."

Fowler claimed a horrified editor tossed out the story, to Fowler's recollection the only time Damon's copy was not used. The execution was covered for the *American* by two correspondents of Universal News Service, a Hearst agency.

Damon was not insensitive, and it does not seem likely he would have misread the mood of the occasion so badly, no matter how xenophobic the Hearst press. It may be that Fowler's memory played him tricks and that he reported old shoptalk, a good anecdote at the bar, as fact.

But Damon was capable of baring his manly chest for his readers. During the Snyder-Gray trial he wrote: "It has taken nearly two weeks to try a matter that the citizens of Pueblo County, Colorado, could have settled in two minutes under any cottonwood tree on the banks of the Arkansas, if all the State of New York has developed is true. But the citizens of Pueblo County are forehanded and forthright gents."

Fowler called the mindlessness of the twenties "the world's last holiday from fear." But Scott Fitzgerald in 1929 found New York

> bloated, glutted, stupid with cake and circuses, and a new expression, "Oh yeah?" summed up all the enthusiasm evoked by an announcement of the last super-skyscrapers. My barber retired on half a million bet on the market, and I was conscious that the head waiters who bowed me, or failed to bow me, to my table were far, far wealthier than I. This was no fun—once again I had enough of New York.
>
> We were somewhere in North Africa when we heard a dull

distant crash which echoed to the farthest reaches of the desert.

"What was that?"

"Did you hear it?"

"It was nothing."

"Do you think we should go home and see?"

"No—it was nothing."

The New York *Times* average of the prices of 25 industrial stocks had climbed in an almost uninterrupted march from 110 at the beginning of 1924 to 338.35 on January 2, 1929. It wobbled through the summer and began a dizzy plunge to 275 at the end of Black Tuesday, October 29, the most devastating day in the history of the exchange. By July 8, 1932, that average stood at 58.46, about the amount it *lost* in the terrible days of autumn 1929.

Among those who were not hurt by the crash was Walter. He was making $500 a week on the *Graphic,* and when market-playing friends asked him what he put his money into, he said, "Rubber bands." He was cagey enough to keep his money in three or four banks, and you did not have to know him very well before he would flip open a bankbook and say, "Take a gander at that."

Damon needed money, not so much because of the crash as because he always needed money, and the legend is that he needed a specific amount to pay for an appendectomy when, if he followed his own advice about the best way to approach a job of writing, he pulled a chair up to a desk facing a blank wall in a lonely room, and began typing. What he typed was: "Only a rank sucker will think of taking two peeks at Dave the Dude's doll, because while Dave may stand for the first peek, figuring it is a mistake, it is a sure thing he will get sored up at the second peek, and Dave the Dude is certainly not a man to get sored up at you."

That is the first sentence of "Romance in the Roaring Forties," the first of Damon's Broadway fables. It appeared in the July 1929 *Cosmopolitan,* the opening episode in what became a saga.

So in a time of national desolation, Damon had found a new direction for a career, and Walter was about to find a new shop, where he would make, and write, a peculiar kind of history.

ten

THE IMPROBABLE and endearing protagonist of Evelyn Waugh's *Scoop* had once seen "a barely intelligible film about newspaper life in New York where neurotic men in shirt sleeves and eye shades had rushed from telephone to tape machines, insulting and betraying one another in surroundings of unredeemed squalor."

It is true that along with its famous camaraderie, the newsroom inspires the kind of malignity associated with faculty life. By the early nineteenth century, American newspapers routinely employed what one historian called "the grossest epithets found in the English language."

The founding fathers of American journalism battled each other in the gutter. The elder Bennett called one rival "this impudent loafer of literature, this lazaroni of politics," and described the *Sun* as "our highly respected, dirty, sneaking, driveling, contemporary nigger paper." In turn, opposition papers variously called Bennett "daring infidel, habitual liar, Prince of Darkness, profligate, venal wretch, a turkey buzzard, rascal, rogue, common bandit and a polluter of the press."

Viewed against this larger background, Walter's feuds and knifings are less aberrative than they appeared to McKelway and other critics; they are almost part of a grand tradition.

Life with Gauvreau went from batter to worse. There were frequent shouting matches between editor and columnist, bizarre enough to attract attention even in the circus of the *Graphic* city room. Gauvreau hurled a bust of Napoleon at Walter. Walter called Gauvreau a goddamned cripple and shoved him down a flight of stairs.

In 1928 Jimmy Walker told Walter that Hearst was interested in hiring him. Nothing came of that, but Walter was sure he could get more money from Hearst than he was earning with Macfadden. Another columnist came to his rescue with a fraternal scam.

Mark Hellinger was a famous Hollywood producer when he died at forty-four, a man for whom a Broadway theater is named. But it was written of him, "The man was born and bred a newspaperman, and he only went to Hollywood to get some sucker money." This is something of an exaggeration. Hellinger came from a family in comfortable circumstances, and his father, a lawyer, was horrified that his son would want to be a newspaperman.

Hellinger inspired affection. Paul Gallico recalled:

> They wrote him up as a big tipper and a picker-up of tabs and dinner checks. It was true enough, but there were so many more things to say of Mark Hellinger. . . . He was sweet. He was kind. He was gentle. He was honest, and he was good. He worked hard. He never double-crossed his friends. He was rich in talent, and with his talent he enriched his times— when he died, he left too large a hole to fill in the hearts of many, including my own."

Beginning in the early twenties, Hellinger and Walter ran together. There was never any rivalry between them. If Walter was the first Broadway columnist, Hellinger was the first Broadway reporter, according to his biographer, Jim Bishop. As a columnist for the *News,* Hellinger was often under pressure to compete with Walter as a gossip. Instead he wrote columns of fiction, often starting and ending with the phrase "Episodes, Roscoe, episodes," and perhaps tacking on a couple of harmless gossip items as shirttails. "It was," Bishop wrote, "a weak compromise but it worked."

Hellinger and Walter "sat out the long nights in the small clubs, trusting and confiding in each other as they trusted and confided in no one else. And no matter where they set out to go, Hellinger, with his black slick hair, snap-brim hat and twinkling blue eyes, always murmured, 'Adventure, Walter, adventure.'"

Beneath a take-charge personality, however, there was a pit of black dogs, and Jim Bishop estimated that Hellinger put away a bottle of brandy every day in the last fourteen years of his life.

As young men, Hellinger and Walter signed promissory notes for each other. Walter said Hellinger was the only person he lent money because he always knew he could get it from Hellinger's father. And when Hellinger died, Walter wrote, "People who hardly knew him liked him, and those who knew him loved him." He signed off the column, "Adventure, Mark. Adventure."

In 1928, when Walter was trying to quit the *Graphic,* Hellinger persuaded Swope to fake a letter saying he was anxious to hire Walter. Walter showed the letter to a Hearst executive who promised him a job if he could break his contract.

The *Graphic* was an incubator, breeding gossip columnists and temperament. Walter turned to Ed Sullivan, then the sports editor, and asked for his help in getting Gauvreau off his back. Sullivan spoke with an advertising executive in the Macfadden organization. A couple of days later Gauvreau called Sullivan on the carpet, asking him why he went over Gauvreau's head. Gauvreau told Sullivan Walter had informed on him. When Sullivan confronted Walter about this duplicity, Walter explained lamely that Gauvreau had held his feet to the fire. This was the root of the celebrated Winchell-Sullivan feud, which bloomed for decades, attracted the attention of grown men, and consumed jeroboams of ink.

Walter was ever resourceful. Giving up on Gauvreau, he turned his guns on Macfadden, waking the physical culturist in the small hours, demanding to be released. When cutting into vital, healthful sleep didn't prove to be enough, the story goes that Walter threatened to report that he and other witnesses had seen the eminent vegetarian eat meat.

That did it. A publishing empire tottered. Macfadden passed the word. Gauvreau called to his office a young, second-string drama critic named Louis Sobol and told him Walter was out and that Sobol would replace him.

In the fall of 1978, Sobol reflected on those times. He is a jockey-sized man, bald and mustached, with a caricaturist's target of a nose and horn-rimmed glasses, not much changed in appearance from the half-column cut which accompanied his column in the *Journal-American*. His wife Peggy, a former show girl and publicist, was with him in a party of three in an almost-deserted French restaurant, and there was a melancholy to the scene. Sobol for decades was an important Broadway columnist, something of a gentleman in a rough trade, something of a stylist. "His manner and his way are neither blatant nor pugnacious," Gene Fowler wrote of Sobol. "His modesty and his decency should not be mistaken for badges of weakness."

Gauvreau had brought Sobol from the New London, Connecticut, *Day* to the *Graphic*.

> Back in the twenties [Sobol recalled], there were often two or three Broadway openings in one night. I was the second critic behind Walter. Norman Krasna was my backup, and my assistant was Jerry Wald, later radio columnist for the *Graphic* and after that a big Hollywood producer.
>
> I was editor of the *Graphic* syndicate. I handled Walter, Sullivan's sports column. We went in for the sensational, all right, but we had fun. I did a whole series on Daddy and Peaches Browning. I ghosted articles for Queen Marie.

I was very much a newcomer from Connecticut, though. Broadway was the most exciting place in the world. I was writing a play which was produced later, but Walter wrote a *column*. He was a big man. I started in awe of him. Unfortunately, that faded when I knew of his peculiarities.

I had an office next to Walter's. He'd shout over, "What do you think of this? Listen, is this a good line?" I'd okay him. Once in a while, I'd correct him. He was completely ruthless in those early years. He'd rap people if he was on the outs with them.

Sobol broke off. Peggy looked at him affectionately.

"Remember the time *you* were angry with someone and you said, 'Tomorrow, I'll make an issue of this in my column'?" she asked. "But you never did."

Sobol regarded his cigar.

"Did I ever take myself that seriously? I guess I did, I guess we did. We were spoiled, you see. Press agents would grovel in their shoes."

They had been taught to do that by Walter, whose reaction to being dismissed from the *Graphic* was abandon. He ran to his office and cleaned out his desk and hurried to the arms of Hearst, barely taking the time to hand Sobol some releases for the next day's column.

Walter was supposed to work for Hearst's *Journal*, but A. J. Kobler, publisher of the *Mirror*, argued the column would be more effective in a tabloid. It didn't make much difference to Hearst, who was heard to say Walter "appealed to the younger degeneration," and it made no difference to Walter, so long as he got his $500-a-week salary and the $500 bonus for signing. By 1929 it was a close race to determine which of Hearst's New York newspapers was in the most trouble—the *American,* the *Journal,* or the *Mirror.*

Walter Howey was managing editor of the *Mirror*. He wanted to run Walter's column on the front page. Walter talked him out of this, figuring the column would lose its form and flavor there, so Howey made do with daily front- and back-page promotions. On June 10, 1929, Walter made his debut in the tabloid that would be his flagship for the next thirty-four years: "The Sig Thayers (Emily Vanderbilt) romance has wilted already . . ." began the historic document. "As soon as they get their respective decrees, Sonny Whitney and Mrs. Edgar Warburton will be sealed."

"Half true," McKelway pointed out. "The first item was correct, the second incorrect, and contained a misspelled name, but it was gossip, and it was good gossip." The most popular columnist on the *Graphic,* "The King of Broadway," proved just as popular on the *Mirror:* "The

179

Jack Mulhalls have phffft! . . . The daughter of Walter J. Kingsley (by his first wife) was secretly sealed in October to Maurice O. Smith, the stork due in August . . ."

The gossip rolled on:

"Vincent Bendix gave his squaw 5 million for the divorce . . . Charlie Sherman, who was shot, stabbed and socked at the Abbey, is in Florida, aw better . . . What former newspaper woman has lost her mind, claiming she is being 'framed'?"

He was "Little Boy Peep," easily the most influential man on Broadway. "I knew I was a big shot," he said, "when people who called me a son of a bitch behind my back began asking me for favors."

Walter's exultation over his manumission was short-lived. That very summer of 1929 Hearst himself brought Gauvreau over as managing editor of the *Mirror,* with a $10,000 bonus and an understanding he would keep an eye on Walter. Walter said, "I thought I had escaped that man, and here he was following me."

The gossip was a flood:

"The one lad Peggy Joyce loved married another and Peg's heart is bleeding . . . Peaches Browning had her legs done over again . . . The doctor who lost $11,000 at chemin de fer a fortnight ago will have to be operated on before the winners can get it."

"The night clubs, which were controlled by protected racketeers, fed the gossip columns of the period and all sorts of one-line implications floated through the syndicates to be reprinted by provincial editors," Gauvreau wrote. "Winchell held his readers for months in readiness to rejoice over blessed events which often failed to happen. The reckless, midnight women who believed themselves pregnant after reading his column occasionally telephoned in pleasant surprise to have him guess again."

Walter made his radio debut on January 18, 1932, over a forty-two-station hookup, with a program called "New York by a Representative New Yorker," and although he didn't think he would make it on radio "because I talk too fast," he was an immediate success. In 1932 William A. Paley, president of the Columbia Broadcasting System, matched Walter with a sponsor, Gimbel's department store, for broadcasts over CBS's New York outlet, WABC.

The flamboyant George Washington Hill, president of the American Tobacco Company, whose advertising advances set back civilization by light years, heard Walter and liked the sound of that driven voice. He hired him for "The Lucky Strike Magic Carpet," which featured bands from cities scattered around the country, an electronic wow in the early thirties.

Touted by a promotional campaign that included billboards and newspaper ads, Walter soon was popularizing a tag line, "Ohhhhkaaaay, Aaaaaaamerica," introducing his famous greeting, "Good evening, Mr. and Mrs. America and all the ships at sea," and adding entertainment news to the mix.

He wrote a column examining his attitude toward the broadcast:

> It will be fun for me at least to resume radio gabbing on Sept. 9 . . . There is a wallop in the breathlessness and nervousness that grip you waiting for your guest star to show up . . . the crowding in of sensational sentences in the few minutes allotted . . . The problem of keeping from faltering or stumbling over a swift sentence, a syllable to a sequence containing too many s's . . . It will be a thrill again to hear that heart-thumping, march-tempoed "Give My Regards to Broadway" . . . the tap on the shoulder from the time-keeper . . .

Walter wrote, "Gotta have excitement. Gotta have a reason for being incessantly charged with zip . . . Never believed the theory that too much work laid a guy low . . . It's a short life at most . . . That's why I want to crowd all of it in before some kid with a new idea comes along."

His column sometimes reflected one source of those thrills, that sense of excitement, although Klurfeld says fancy occasionally dictated an item:

> Nursed the sheets till late, being weary from a strenuous tear the night before, having hoofed at a White Light place with Bobbie Folsom and other charming wenches. So to breakfast with Lovey Kent, who is as sweet as her Christian surname . . .
>
> Up betimes and broke fast with a baby doll from "Artists and Models" . . . In the rain to keep a rendezvous with Mary Thomas, who coryphees for a living . . . Later to visit Vivien and Pearl at the Commodore. The house detective reluctant to permit me to remain, but fell for my police card.

June Winchell's objections, according to Klurfeld, put an end to the parading of the cuties, if not to Walter's infidelities. If the language seems a pale imitation of Adams, and paler still of Pepys, it should be noted that Adams himself, when not reporting arguments with his

181

wife, frequently talked about beauties he encountered on his rounds. Given access to a typewriter and a woman, it seems to be a failing of some men.

In 1924 the Winchells had adopted a baby girl they named Gloria. "Walter was secretive about this aspect of his life," Klurfeld wrote, "but I believe Gloria had been born out of wedlock and had been the infant in June Magee's room when June and Walter first met."

Frank Mallen, a *Graphic* editor, remembered in *Sauce for the Gander* that Walter borrowed his phone to call Gloria each night. "He would bid her a fond and tender good night. Sometimes he'd tell her to say good night to me and hand me the receiver. I liked this, talking to her. There was a caress in her gay voice saying good night that momentarily transported me out of the harshness of newspaper life."

Gloria's early years were spent in a Broadway atmosphere reminiscent of a Runyon fable. The two floors above Billy LaHiff's tavern were rented to a polyglot crew that included through the years Damon, Dempsey, Toots Shor, Hellinger, Sullivan, and Bugs Baer. Gene Fowler, seeking an ambience as close to the city room as possible, sat himself down with his #5 Underwood next to the meat block in LaHiff's cellar kitchen and in twenty-one days wrote his first novel, *Trumpet in the Dust*.

When Walter was short of rent money, LaHiff waved it off. He enjoyed the sight of Gloria's baby carriage in the hallway. "It gives the joint class," he claimed.

In 1927 Walter reported in his column that his wife had given birth to a girl they named Walda, after his side of the family. He promptly announced he would save at least fifty dollars a week. The bankbooks were on public display. "Look at those numbers," he gloated. It was a measure of his success that even as the economy curdled, he and his family vacationed in Florida instead of Long Island, a boon to Gloria's health, which was precarious.

June didn't often accompany Walter on his nightclubbing. She was, a friend remembers, a kind of earth mother, devoted to the children. One Winchell critic claims she avoided being seen in saloons with Walter so she would not be confused with his tarts, and, in spite of her show business background, or perhaps because of it, she did not enjoy partying through the night. There were exceptions, however, as Walter reported in a column September 4, 1930:

> "What's on your mind this very minute?" June asked me as we sat watching the floor show at a Harlem hot-spot. "I was just thinking," I said. "I know," she snapped, "but I'm curious just what goes on in your mind."

182

"I was merely looking at people and thinking how a person can be sitting with the one he or she adores and never realize that only a table away sat someone Who Also Mattered . . . Over there, frinstance, is a woman with her sweetheart . . . They are going to be married soon . . . Two tables away sits the guy she really loves and with whom she keeps rendezvous whenever she can get away . . . She probably can't help it . . .

"At that other table is a horse from a different stable. The woman with him isn't his wife . . . His wife is in a 46th Street hideaway right now with The One She Goes For. Got it? . . . Must be terrible to be found out . . . And a guy is a sap to wise a pal, too, even when he knows he is being crossed . . . They never appreciate the tip . . . Instead, they usually quit talking to you . . . Women-Flesh being All That Matters."

Apart from the tangled syntax, the banality of the Broadway sophistication must have made the home fires and the kiddies look compelling to June. But Walter's gossip, the sense of blind omniscience, dazzled the crowd. By 1931 he was on the cover of *Time* magazine, where self-parody was in full cry:

Walter Winchell is no ordinary scandal-snooper. Famed is he in theater lobbies, speakeasies, nightclubs. From one gossip center to another he travels to get column material. Alert, the Winchell ear hears all. Amiable, the Winchell disposition makes friends easily, elicits scandal scraps. Then, at three or four in the morning, he goes back to his typewriter and two-fingers what he has learned, adding here and there the result of an imaginative mind.

Broadway offered *Blessed Event*, whose title was a Winchellism, starring Roger Pryor as a ruthless columnist. First-nighters at the Longacre Theater inspected Walter for symptoms of mortification.

"Nonsense!" Woolcott declared. "Winchell's emotions . . . probably were an ingenious and gratified surprise at finding himself, at thirty-five, already recognized as enough of a national institution to be made the subject of a play."

Walter achieved the ultimate. He was parodied by Ring Lardner:

A. Lincoln and Gen. McClellan are on the verge . . . Jimmy Madison and Dolly Payne Todd are THAT WAY . . . Aleck Hamilton and Aaron Burr have phfft . . . The Geo. Washingtons (she was Martha Lorber of the Follies) have moved into

their Valley Forge snuggery for the Old Man Shiver days . . .
Arthur Brisbane has signed up to do a daily column for
William ("Randolph") Hearst . . ."

Walter's version of Broadway clashed with the standard established
by a famous predecessor. O. O. McIntyre, called Odd, was.

McIntyre died in 1936 and is forgotten now, but his biographer
estimated that McIntyre was read by more Americans than any writer
who ever lived. Using the totemic 4.8 readers per newspaper favored
by advertisers, he put that figure at 104,000,000. *"Gone With the Wind*
broke all book-publishing records when it sold a million copies in six
months," Charles Driscoll noted scornfully. "That many people
finished reading a column by O.O. McIntyre every morning for years
before the rising sun had silvered the finial of the gleaming Chrysler
tower."

McIntyre was born in Missouri and raised in Gallipolis, Ohio, a
small town he made famous. His column, generally published as "New
York Day by Day," offered a picture of the big city the outlanders
wished to see: unbelievably glamorous, unbelievably dangerous, a
haven for small-town-boy-makes-good, a reservoir of the defeated and
lonely. An editor wrote, "Odd was the first newspaperman . . . who
realized the people of New York all originated somewhere else."

McIntyre's sentences often were as fanciful as that one. "All of the
jazz leaders are small town products," he wrote. McIntyre's New York,
J. Bryan III wrote in *The Saturday Evening Post,* "is not to be found
on Manhattan Island, but in some Cloud-Cuckoo Land on the other
side of the Looking Glass. . . . Here Harlem adjoins Chinatown, and
Greenwich Village is across the street from Hell's Kitchen."

But McIntyre gave his readers satisfaction. "I often wonder why
people from smaller cities have an urge to come to New York to live
someday," he claimed. "Indianapolis . . . has everything New York
has except the ocean and perhaps grand opera. Indianapolis people
live in greater comfort and have closer friends and neighbors."

McIntyre avoided gossip. He never wrote about the rich or famous,
by name, unless he could find something good to say. He frequently
wrote about two notable American preoccupations: dogs and death,
sometimes combining the two, as in his most famous column, "A
Letter to Billy, in Dog Heaven," a paean to his departed Boston bull.
("It has been more than a year now since you went away, and I miss
you more than ever. I think it was largely because you faced the Last
Terror with such magnificent valor. A patient little sigh, a twitch of
your nubbin tail, and it was all over." Among those who informed

184

McIntyre they were moved by that column were Ellen Glasgow and W.C. Fields.)

McIntyre had married Maybelle, his childhood sweetheart. At the height of his fame they bought a house they called Gatewood back in Gallipolis, with the stated object of returning someday. Someday. For, once arrived, the laureate of the good life in the small town never left New York, except for annual visits to Europe, where McIntyre purchased suits designed by a Paris tailor "chiefly known for his creations for women."

Far from the dream house in Gallipolis, McIntyre and Maybelle had lived in the Hotel Majestic on Seventy-second Street and Central Park West, for which McIntyre served as publicity director before his column got rolling. He turned that family hotel into a celebrity hostelry for the likes of Fritzi Scheff, "breaking hearts and box office records with her little drum and singing of 'Kiss Me Again'"; Bud Fisher, creator of "Mutt and Jeff"; Sarah Bernhardt; Lillian Russell; Pavlova; Nijinsky; Sigmund Romberg; Edna Ferber; and George S. Kaufman.

When McIntyre was told that dogs were no longer welcome on the premises, he turned livid and moved, that very day, to the Ritz-Carlton, "generally considered the best address in the world," where he lived for seven years without making a complaint, before moving to 290 Park Avenue. A humble dig of nine rooms with two French maids and a chauffeur, it was almost up to Indianapolis standards.

McIntyre's favorite restaurant was the exclusive Colony, of which he wrote so often that, in Lucius Beebe's observation, "dog wagons and saloons called 'the Colony' began appearing all over rural America." If McIntyre mentioned old-fashioned preserves in his column, or jellies or apple butter, "boxes and barrels of sweetmeats from all parts of the United States" flowed in. "There were thousands of men and women who sent whatever they thought might please the columnist who pleased them so easily every day," Driscoll wrote.

With all this, McIntyre was a nexus of neuroses and insecurities, a hypochondriac who suffered the last twenty years of his life without consulting a doctor. He read about the evils of tobacco, bought a sample of something called No-Ta-Bac and liked it so much he kept a quid of the product in one corner of his mouth and a wad of tobacco in the other.

McIntyre was an agoraphobe. Walking past Madison Square or Union Square, he might bolt from his companions and seek shelter in a doorway, or rush, shaking, back to his apartment. He developed a fear of crowds, of leaving home, then a fear that someone might slap

185

him on the back or pick a piece of lint from his coat, so that "during his last years . . . he rarely went out without a person walking closely on each side of him." He demanded theater seats on the aisle, so he could flee at the approach of nameless dread.

McIntyre also was, in a word of the day, effeminate, and he resented it when this was pointed out. He was homely, insecure, and suffered from what Jungians on the street called an inferiority complex. He had recurrent nightmares of dying in poverty, even as he earned more than $3,000 a week, of finding himself on the main street of Gallipolis, naked. Criticism made him bleed.

Variety might say, "McIntyre put the Broadway column on the newspaper map, making it possible for the rest to follow—which they did—long after," but clearly Walter, the aging urchin with the boudoir secrets and gags about men who lifted their pinkies, pointed the way toward a new kind of column and represented a threat to the tormented McIntyre.

"There are men in New York who have been identified by Winchell, by means of crystal-clear euphemisms, as homosexuals," McKelway wrote; "there are people whose attempted suicides he has reported; there are married men and women who, in spite of Winchell's stated intention not to let his column hurt happy marriages, have been linked with others of the opposite sex; there are couples whose separation has been reported when they were thinking of no such thing, whose impending marriage has been announced when it was not being considered by them; there are individuals whose affectionate regard for someone has been reported when they weren't sure of it themselves."

Driscoll explained that McIntyre believed he was above that sort of thing, and that his homely offerings would prevail over any mix of gags and digs. But poison-pen letters about Walter reached the desks of Hearst executives, sometimes in the green ink McIntyre occasionally favored. Some of the letters, contents unknown, were addressed to Walter.

Soon Walter's column contained lines like "The very odd McIntyre has a Rolls-Royce, but to hear the literati tell it, it is a Rolls-down hill . . ." or, "Scallions to O.O. McIntyre who complains to your superiors when you twit him but hands it out himself." After musing "My racket is hardly different from the newsie on the corner . . . We both peddle papers," Walter wrote in September 1930, "Wonder if people out of town still waste a lotta time by hating N. Yorkers . . . The McIntyre influence . . . Maybe I should change provincialism to pro-Winchellism."

It is a measure of Walter's instant celebrity that Hearst didn't lean on him in favor of the beloved small-towner with the hundred million readers. What Hearst did was address both columnists and advise them to lay off each other; they were both members of the same family.

Danton Walker, later a Broadway columnist for the *News,* found his competitors "by and large, a rather venomous lot, forever clawing at each other, and, as Tallulah Bankhead put it, 'As vain as a bunch of Goddam bathing beauties.'"

Walter's skirmishing with McIntyre, an American institution, and his public brawling contributed to a widely held notion that he was virtually friendless. Americans seem particularly susceptible to a belief in the laws of compensation—beautiful women must be dumb, the rich must be unhappy, or else life is so *unfair.*

So during Walter's decades of success, all that money, that power, the company of the eminent and notorious, yes, the company of beautiful women, there had to be some compensatory factor, and the usual explanation was that he was lonely and driven.

McKelway commented, "Winchell has written more words on the subject of friendship than any other modern gossip-writer, but the people he calls his friends do not number more than seven or eight and most of these are new rather than old." Well, seven or eight true friends and the love of a good woman might be considered good fortune in the shallow and atavistic world of the saloon columnist.

At least one of Walter's friendships endured for decades, and the relationship was symbiotic. Irving Hoffman was a bright boy from the Bronx who quit DeWitt Clinton High School at the end of his junior year because he found teachers boring. He attended the 1924 Democratic convention at the age of fourteen and drew caricatures of Franklin D. Roosevelt, Al Smith, and William Jennings Bryan, which he sold to the *World,* establishing himself as a contributor to other papers as well. He soon was submitting quips and items to Walter.

Hoffman became a successful publicist. He also wrote a column, "The Tales of Hoffman" for the *Hollywood Reporter.* Hoffman resisted syndication because he did not wish to compete with his friends, the gossip columnists. In a line of work not celebrated for its ethics, he maintained standards by refusing to publicize his clients in his column. Bob Thomas says that movie studios kept Hoffman on a retainer of $25,000 a year solely because of his access to Walter, and that, of course, was only one source of income for Hoffman, whom Damon described as "a tall, loose-jointed fellow, a man-about-tables, a squire of dames, a bon vivant, a raconteur and all that truck."

He read books, reviewed movies and plays for Walter. Some say he contributed greatly to the Winchell style, even creating some of the

187

neologisms. He was one of just two people—June Winchell was the other—who could criticize Walter freely. Hoffman proofread the column and made last-minute changes without Walter's approval.

And with all this, says Peggy Sobol, Hoffman was "the most thoughtful human being I've ever known." He was there in time of trouble; he cheered up bedridden or hospitalized friends with gags and cartoons. His nearsightedness was the stuff of countless anecdotes. Entering a night club with a young woman on his arm, he bumped into a friend, drew him aside, and asked fervently, "Is she pretty?"

Louis Sobol said Hoffman once found himself addressing what he thought was a speakeasy peephole. "You know me," he said. No response. "Sure, you remember. I've been here with Hellinger, with Winchell." Then he realized he was talking to a mirror.

Hoffman defended his wisecracking reviews by saying, "There's no reason why I should be as dull as the play." When a producer attacked his nearsightedness after Hoffman sank his product, Hoffman said, "Yes, but there's nothing the matter with my nose."

By the early thirties there were generally cheerless reviews of the American melodrama which offered a montage including bankers as suicides; jobless men; families without food; New Yorkers sleeping on subways, sleeping in Central Park, living in shanties called Hoovervilles. Henry Ford said, "There is plenty of work to do, if people would do it." Will Rogers said, "The working class didn't bring this on, it was the big boys who thought the financial drunk was going to last forever." President Hoover said, "With only local and unnecessary exceptions, there has been no starvation."

A month before the 1932 election, Walter wrote, "I do wish the various parties would stop submitting their ballyhooing to me about their respective candidates. I don't like any of them—and won't devote any part of the column's praise to them. I don't care whether Roosevelt wins or Hoover loses. I know too much about politics to care."

Later, as Walter played Dutch uncle to the nation, it would be charged he never voted. Robin Harris, a young reporter who was Walter's sometime roommate, said he once accompanied Walter to the polls. "I remember it because it was the first time I voted," he said. "It was at the Great Northern Hotel on Fifty-seventh Street, and if Walter didn't vote, I don't know what the hell he did."

McKelway, among others, expressed wonder that Walter, the gossip columnist, transformed himself from a man indifferent to politics to an invited guest at the White House. It happened, McKelway wrote, "under the very eyes of his readers, and without causing them to blink

188

or shudder, he has become a cosmopolitan thinker who can with a straight face cable advice to a British Prime Minister."

It was remarkable, all right, but Walter was tripping political turns not long after joining the *Mirror*.

On November 4, 1932, an item began, "A Columnist's Sec'y Jots Down a Few Notes . . . The day after your item appeared about that bank forcing its employes to contribute money to its Hoover fund, it returned the money to them, saying they didn't want 'certain newspapermen' to think they were intimidating their staff, etc. . . . So score another for the column, Mister . . ."

The day before the election there was a vintage example of the bewildering new mixture Walter was beginning to brew:

> The Associated Press will concede the country to FDR if he carries his own state . . . That news service, which has always brought its Washington staff to New York for Presidential elections, won't this time . . . Norman H. Davis of New York will be Secretary of State if Roosevelt wins . . .
>
> It's a boy over at Count and Countess Jonel Jorgelescoes and this pillar predicted the heir would be born on Nov. 1 . . . The doctor said it would arrive November 6, and the hospital figured November 15 . . . It was born Nov. 1st! . . . The Condé Nast divorce, Mr. Knickerbocker, was also recorded here originally, considering how often you claims scoops.

In the week after the election, the column noted, "Josephberg called. He said some people voted Republican but most people voted sensibly . . . Guinan called to say that she has a suspicion that many a politician who hears his country calling is a ventriloquist."

Walter was working and playing in Miami that winter when Giuseppe Zangara, as balmy as an offshore breeze, took aim at the President-elect in Bay Front Park and mortally wounded the mayor of Chicago. Walter hustled to the jail where he fed an overwhelmed sheriff a line already hackneyed by the movies, "Get me in there, and I'll put your name in every paper in the world!"

He obtained an exclusive interview with Zangara but foolishly left it with a pile of other stories at the Western Union office. Other newsmen obtained it. Walter not only lost his scoop but was asked by Gauvreau to pay the eleven-dollar wire charge. Hearst personally reimbursed Walter.

And then on March 5, 1933, just back from Havana, where he had

189

been writing about boxing and gambling, Damon filed from Washington, D.C.:

> On a dark, dour day in one of the darkest, dourest hours in the nation's history, Franklin Delano Roosevelt becomes President of the United States and sends a message of hope and cheer booming out across the land into the ears of 120,000,000 anxious people.
>
> He stands bareheaded in spite of a bitter breeze that hints of snow. . . . The people are curiously silent much of the time during the ceremonies—silent, and watching and listening . . .

Watching and listening, Walter soon was addressing "The Love Letters of Walter Winchell" to the President and Mrs. Roosevelt and noting "Franklin Delano Roosevelt's maw is plenty Okay America. She isn't ashamed to be seen dunking her cake in her coffee," suggesting the PR people were in touch with either Walter or the President's maw.

Walter even suggested a President's Day, to be celebrated "on Sunday, April 30—the day before May 1—the day when Communistic Reds land on all the front pages with their activities. . . . But most of all to show President Roosevelt how grateful we all are to him for his action and results."

What made Walter's transformation into political personage particularly hard for his critics to accept, of course, was his reputation as what Westbrook Pegler later called "a gent's room journalist" and what the Toots Shor set would call his palship with criminals. Walter documented these activities himself.

It was as necessary for a Broadway columnist to associate with gangsters as it was for a Washington correspondent to hang around with members of Congress. The gangsters were dangerous, to boot.

Walter had been summoned to Miami in 1929 to interview Al Capone, who gave audiences. Capone let it be known that he felt put upon by the authorities and was blamed for crimes of which he was innocent. He showed Walter some of the thousands of letters he claimed he received from Mr. and Mrs. America, many of them requesting money. Capone saw himself as a man who supplied the public with needed services.

Walter's interview did not harm Capone and it added to Walter's growing reputation as a man who was inside *everything*. The impression was reinforced by Walter's friendship with Owney Madden, who in the twenties and early thirties was described as "the most powerful man in New York. He was another Mayor."

Madden was a short, tough customer from Liverpool, who came to New York in youth and settled in Hell's Kitchen, where he proved himself the real stuff by getting arrested more than forty times before being sent to Sing Sing for murder. He was paroled in 1923, just as the good times rolled, and he quickly schemed and brutalized himself to preeminence in the kingdom of prohibition. He controlled booze, nightclubs, boxing, and local politicians.

Madden strolled over to Walter in a barbershop one day and said he liked his copy. They were soon seen everywhere together. Madden pressed a Stutz roadster on Walter, who made the mistake of protesting he could not accept it, since he was a newspaperman and it would appear to be a bribe. Walter never forgot the look of contempt that crossed Madden's face.

"What could a punk like you ever do for me?" Madden asked. Walter later claimed he gave Madden $2,000 for the car.

Madden's power was concentrated on midtown and Broadway. The less rewarding territory uptown was ruled by Arthur Flegenheimer, alias Dutch Schultz, whose deathbed statement as he lay riddled with mob bullets, "A boy has never wept, nor dashed a thousand kim," remains as runic as *Finnegans Wake*.

Being a mob boss is a little like being a politician or a dictator; who is to protect you from your friends? Vincent Coll, a Schultz lieutenant, tried to muscle in on the territory. Schultz ordered a swift and deadly justice, but accuracy comes no more easily to the gunman than to the newsman, and the mob rubbed out Coll's brother Peter by mistake.

Coll responded by kidnapping Sherman Billingsley, owner of the Stork Club, which Walter was making famous. Billingsley was beaten daily, according to Klurfeld, until friends paid a $25,000 ransom. Then Coll kidnapped Big Frenchy DeMange, a Madden partner, for a $35,000 ransom.

Coll next went after Schultz himself, attempting to ambush him as Schultz paid a visit to an East Harlem clubhouse. Coll swept by in a limousine, just the way it was done in the movies, spraying the premises with machine-gun bullets. He didn't get Schultz, but he killed a five-year-old child playing in the streets.

This was a pretty kettle of fish, even by the debased standards of the mob, and Coll now found himself in the unhappy position of "M," sought by the underworld as well as the police.

Mary Louise Cecilia "Texas" Guinan was one of prohibition's chosen children, playing hostess at nightclubs where she strived for Bartlett's with such phrases as "Hello, sucker," "the big butter-and-egg man," and "Let's give the little girl a great big hand." Her establishments, of course, were funded by the mob, and she had connections and frequently supplied Walter with tips, one of which found its way into his column on February 8, 1932: "Five planes brought dozens of machine guns from Chicago Friday to combat the Town's Capone . . . Local banditti have made one hotel a virtual arsenal and several hotspots are ditto because Master Coll is giving them a headache."

That very night, as Coll attempted a phone call from a drugstore telephone booth on West Twenty-third Street, having apparently been set up, he was dotted with machine-gun bullets and killed. The mob didn't miss this time, proving that it is relatively easy to shoot a man in a phone booth.

Walter had a big skewp, as he would call it, his prediction hitting the streets just about the time Master Coll did. Walter didn't have much time to enjoy the moment. He received a phone call indicating the mob's displeasure with the story. There was no sense kidding around. Walter called Madden, who phoned back a little later to say he had spoken with Coll's killers and they were sore, but he thought Walter would be safe. Just to be sure, he would send over a bodyguard.

For the next couple of weeks, the bodyguard accompanied Walter wherever he went, while the columnist wrote nervous items, including his own epitaph: "Here lies Walter Winchell—with his ear to the ground, as usual." He reflected, "'Where children are—there is the golden age,' said a wiser man long ago, but Victor Hugo's classic rings in my ears, and I wish that I had fathered the proverb so that after the brigands have blown me down, my babies would think I could write."

Walter suffered a nervous collapse. He took his family to California for a six-week vacation. The sunshine helped. But when he returned, death paid a call.

Gloria Winchell, always in precarious health, contracted pneumonia. There was not much medicine could do about it, and the illness filled her lungs and killed her. Klurfeld said Walter "never fully recovered from the tragedy." Until June Winchell made him quit, he wrote about it in the column. A reader sent him a cheap ring in Gloria's memory, and, except for a wristwatch, it was the only jewelry he ever wore. He kept Gloria's shoe on his desk at home, and he would touch it before he went to work.

Decades later, when Frank Mallen wrote his memoir of the *Graphic,* he dedicated it "To a Beautiful Angel, Gloria Winchell, Who Left This World on a Christmas Morn at Age 9 to Brighten the Celestial Palace."

Gangsters and speakeasies and darling, doomed children and hard-boiled newspapermen with soft hearts. It was life anticipating a kind of art, and as Walter stirred the brew for the column, Damon borrowed it by the tankard, for the magazine and book publishers, and for the silver screen, where nobody except a chump could miss it.

eleven

WHAT IS arguably the greatest and most influential American movie ever made is a newspaper movie.

Orson Welles' *Citizen Kane,* of course, is more than a movie about newspapers. When it opened in New York in 1941, one critic wrote, "Seeing it, it's as if you never really saw a movie before; no movie has ever grabbed you, pummeled you, socked you on the button with the vitality, the accuracy, the impact, the professional art, that this one does."

Exactly thirty years later, Pauline Kael called *Kane* "a shallow work of art, a *shallow* masterpiece," but it "is perhaps the one American talking picture that seems as fresh now as the day it opened." François Truffault named *Kane* among all movies as "probably the one that has started the largest number of film-makers on their careers."

Kane is a free adaptation of the life and times of Hearst, and it was largely written by Herman J. Manckiewicz, a former newspaperman and a friend of Hearst, who in 1926 had summoned an old newspaper buddy named Ben Hecht to Hollywood with a classic telegram that ended: MILLIONS ARE TO BE GRABBED OUT HERE AND YOUR ONLY COMPETITION IS IDIOTS. DON'T LET THIS GET AROUND.

Mankiewicz achieved enormous success in Hollywood, writing scores of movies, and he kept bringing his friends west. Kael writes, "If the first decade of the talkies—roughly the thirties—has never been rivaled in wit and exuberance, this is very largely because there was already in Hollywood in the late twenties a nucleus of the best American writers . . . most of [them] had a shared background: they had been reporters and critics, and they knew each other from their early days on newspapers and magazines."

Many of the movies made in the thirties and forties, particularly the screwball comedies, as Kael notes, had newspaper backgrounds, movies like *It Happened One Night,* which enshrined Clark Gable as a star; *Mr. Deeds Goes to Town,* with Jean Arthur as a girl reporter; *Woman of the Year,* in which Katherine Hepburn is a syndicated pundit; *Theodora Goes Wild,* with Irene Dunne as a smalltown novelist whose escapades entrance the local press; *Viva Villa!* with Stu Erwin as a correspondent; and *His Girl Friday,* the best of *The Front Page* remakes, with Rosalind Russell as a female Hildy Johnson.

This journalistic presence accounted for much of the movies' flair. Many were hard-boiled films, so tough they stopped just short of cynicism, perhaps in deference to the box office. Before people thinking of themselves as film-makers took over, the wise-guy attitude of the city room influenced Hollywood. Ben Hecht so enjoyed using Walter Howey as Walter Burns that he used him again, as Fredric March's managing editor in *Nothing Sacred,* describing him as "a cross between a Ferris wheel and a werewolf." When, as a disciplinary measure, Mankiewicz was assigned to write a movie about the canine hero Rin Tin Tin, he reacted with the insouciance of a cub reporter. He turned in a script which ended with the dog carrying a baby *into* a burning building.

But Hollywood was essentially a moneymaking machine, many of its best men and ideas subverted for reasons of commerce by men at the top with little talent except for accounting. The guiding principle was nicely caught by the unspeakable Sammy Glick, the protagonist in Budd Schulberg's Hollywood novel *What Makes Sammy Run?*

In the process of knifing his mentor, a man of merit, and impressing the studio's money-men from New York, Sammy says, "After all, pictures are shipped out in cans. We're in the canning business. Our job is to find some way of making sure that every shipment will make a profit."

The tip-off that Sammy is headed for the top is an item in Walter's column: "When rising young columnist Sammy Glick celebrated his twenty-first birthday at the Algonquin last night . . ."

The mixture of fact and fancy worked both ways. Even as Hollywood plumbed the depths of sensational journalism with movies like *Five Star Final, The Picture Snatcher, Scandal for Sale, Night Club Scandal,* and *Design for Scandal,* Walter and Hollywood made use of each other.

After appearing in a short subject, *The Bard of Broadway,* with Madge Evans, Walter wrote a story for Darryl F. Zanuck, who in 1933 had just left Warner Brothers to build Twentieth Century-Fox. It was called *Broadway Through a Keyhole,* and it dealt with a triangle involving a gangster, a chorus girl, and a singer.

Garbled word reached the notoriously bad-tempered star, Al Jolson, that the movie was based on his marriage to Ruby Keeler. One night as Walter and June attended the fights at the Hollywood Legion Stadium, Jolson, who was present with *his* wife, rose and swung at Walter.

There is confusion over what happened next. Walter did, or didn't, swing back. June or Ruby swung a shoe. The aggrieved Jolson displayed bruised knuckles the next day and asked, "Does this look like I hit him in the neck?" He spoke as a husband outraged by Walter's alleged intrusion on his marriage. "You know," he said, "we're just plain folks, very much in love with each other." This was a few years before the obligatory Hollywood divorce.

Sweet are the uses of publicity. Although Walter denied it was all a stunt, he accepted $10,000 from Zanuck for the attention the fracas attracted. He warned that those who wished to emulate Jolson by punching him on the nose, or neck, "will have to wait their turn in line."

Broadway Through a Keyhole was a long way from *Citizen Kane,* but the potboiler is more the measure of Hollywood than a work of art. To the groan of publicity mills, Walter made two movies with Ben Bernie, a bandleader with whom he conducted a running feud, phony for a change. These were *Love and Hisses,* written by an ex-newspaperman named Art Arthur, and *Wake Up and Live.* His performances drew respectable notices, and Bob Thomas writes that Walter banked $75,000 from each movie.

But he was uncomfortable making movies, rising early to sit around a set, and he returned to New York with the conviction that studio life was uncongenial for him. It is significant that the show business encounter that most warmed the heart of the old trouper had been a week in 1931 headlining at the Palace for $3,500.

He gossiped, danced, and sang a little. He later told Klurfeld, "All the years of playing the hick towns, getting the rebuffs and hoping that some day you'll play the Palace . . . for me [it] was better than being elected to the White House."

If acres of former newspapermen supplied Hollywood dialogue, the demand for story lines seemed insatiable. Damon provided plots he said derived from *Cinderella* and *Snow White,* although the philosophy informing Damon's fairy tales indicates that the violence and corruption of the underworld and racetracks simply expresses dishonesties fundamental to society.

The idea wasn't openly expressed in Damon's fables, but it was a leitmotiv easily accepted by an America which saw the air leaking from the balloon. The times demonstrated that reputed financial wizards of just about any stripe operated with a duplicity so basic it seemed almost naive.

Damon added to his weariness at the way of the world in 1933 when he covered the Senate investigation of the House of Morgan. "Morgan, the mighty," he reported, "one of the richest men on the face of the globe, pays no income tax in 1931 or 1932. He does not remember about 1930. . . . He knows nothing whatever about income tax matters concerning his firm." It was sport, watching the Senate, many of whose members were indebted to Morgan, lift him from the prosecutorial hook.

Damon had been similarly bemused when he covered Al Capone's trial for income tax evasion in 1931, hearing that Capone testified he carried all his money on his person. Damon "cheerfully yields the palm he has borne with such distinction for lo these many years as the world's worst horse player to Mr. Alphonse Capone" after Capone testified he had lost $217,000 on the ponies "up to closing time this afternoon."

Damon didn't lose anything like that amount at the track, but he lost enough to help stir the creative juices. In a reflective moment many years later, Damon wrote his son, "I think my greatest misfortune was in getting caught in a current that demanded a certain standard of living, and it took money to meet that standard."

Along with closets full of clothes from Nat Lewis's Broadway haberdashery and the stacks of bench-made 5½B shoes the pixielike boxing writer Hype Igoe broke in for Damon, and along with the gambling—he often returned penniless from a day at the races—Damon was now supporting two households. His marriage, so long desperately unhappy, crashed in a series of domestic wars.

Damon tried to draw Gene Fowler into the skirmishing. He charged that Fowler, the most worldly and circumspect of men, supplied Ellen with the name of a show girl Damon was seeing. Fowler admired Damon as a writer but didn't think much of him as a man. He brushed aside Damon's baseless accusation. When Damon, in his rage, threatened to get drunk, Fowler, with great forbearance, talked him out of it.

In truth, Damon was no better at covering his tracks than most erring husbands. Damon, Jr., heard Ellen discuss Damon's "Broadway shenanigans" with her friends. One day his mother dispatched the maid to investigate when she spotted "an eye-sore yellow roadster" parked outside a store. The car was familiar to Damon, Jr., and his sister since it was often sent to pick them up for outings.

"'Was it her?' my mother inquired darkly," he wrote.

197

"'Yes, she was in the auction room.'"

With such clues, it wasn't long before even the children knew.

The breakup was witnessed by Damon, Jr., one day in 1928, when the battle between his parents raged from room to room of the Riverside Drive apartment. Damon finally stormed to a closet, opened the door, and pointed dramatically to a bottle Ellen had squirreled away. Damon packed his clothes. His son wrote, "He went to another woman."

This left Ellen free to kill herself with liquor in just three years time. She and the children moved to Bronxville, a New York suburb, and she drank herself to death for reasons no heart but hers understood. Damon, Jr., came home from school on November 9, 1931, to find the house full of his mother's friends and his father there. His mother was dead. He and Damon went upstairs to talk. Damon wept, the first time his son had seen a man cry.

Already the inheritors of touchy temperaments, the children had been shaken and divided by the end of the marriage. Mary sided with their father, but Damon, Jr., blamed him for walking out when the going got rough. Both children felt rejected, because they were.

Damon was living in a small penthouse at the Hotel Forrest on West Forty-ninth Street, off Broadway. There was no room for the children, so they went to live with Ellen's relatives in Washington before Mary married Dick McCann, a young sportswriter, and Damon, Jr., was sent to military school.

Damon discussed none of this in his column, the compulsion for public confession not yet having seized the land. But on March 9, two years earlier, he had slipped in a personal note: "With these few lines, I am now shoving off to the Polyclinic hospital to lend my presence to a pastime that seems to be known as appendix-snatching." He pointed out that Polyclinic was just across the street from Madison Square Garden and said that on fight nights the doctors simply opened the windows "and the odors of some of the fights creep in and chloroform the patients."

Whether it was release from a miserable domestic situation, the new love that shortly appeared in his life, or the unpredictable call of the muse, Damon entered on a period of great accomplishment.

He had written only a few magazine pieces between the end of World War I and 1929, but "Romance in the Roaring Forties" did more than pay off the doctor's bill; it opened the mysterious floodgate of creativity. "Romance" was only the first of four Broadway stories to appear in *Cosmopolitan* in 1929; in 1930 there were six magazine appearances, four of them in *Collier's;* in 1931 nine stories were published in *Collier's* and *Cosmopolitan,* and that same year *Guys and*

Dolls marked the first collection of Runyon stories. He produced fiction at about that pace through the decade.

Damon was a hypochondriac, wary of drafts, rich in nostrums, but his stories, his column, his reporting, and his social life kept him too busy to take serious interest in his health. Doctors removed his tonsils in 1931, warning him that his throat was in tough shape and might cause trouble in the future, but he was gripped by busyness and assumed his sore throats and the growing huskiness of his voice were complications of an "allergy to tobacco," nothing serious enough to cause him to quit cigarettes.

Nothing caused him to give up a good line. When Gallant Fox, Earle Sande up, won the Kentucky Derby the previous year, Damon began his account with a farewell appearance of his most popular verse in its most famous form:

> Say, have they turned back the pages
> Back to the past once more?
> Back to the racin' ages
> An' a Derby out of the yore?
> Say, don't tell me I'm daffy,
> Ain't that the same ol' grin?
> Why, it's that handy
> Guy named Sande
> Bootin' a winner in!

But Damon didn't dwell in the past. In 1932 he married a show girl from the Silver Slipper. She called herself Patrice Amati Del Grande Gidier, was twice divorced and twenty-five years old. The ceremony was performed by Mayor Walker, who had been drinking. The happy couple moved to the Parc Vendome apartment house on West Fifty-seventh Street. It was, for Damon, for a time, perhaps the greatest happiness he ever knew. Patrice accompanied him on his Broadway rounds. She estimated that in ten years of marriage they ate no more than ten meals at home.

As long as the money came in, there is little indication that Damon was bothered by literary critics who paid no more attention to his fiction than to the work of other writers for the mass magazines of the thirties and forties.

In *A Gentleman of Broadway,* Edwin Hoyt surveyed a broad field of university professors, few of whom thought that Damon contributed any enduring fiction. But one observation offers a clue to the popularity of the stories, particularly when it is remembered that they appeared during the depression and World War II. "His sentimentalized falsifications," in this view, "may represent the kind of peasant wish fulfillment that created fairy tales in the face of an intolerable existence."

The stories are slick, conventionally plotted, and often provided with an O. Henry ending. But it remains debatable if they are entirely "falsifications." Damon knew the underworld well, and against the charge that he romanticized his characters must be weighed the photographic evidence of the great gangster funerals of the period, with their vast floral displays and lachrymose sentiments.

It remained for an English critic, E. C. Bentley, to claim that Damon made "one of the richest contributions to comic literature in our time," and that evaluation holds up to the extent that the phrase "Damon Runyon character" continues to serve as a description.

The plot of "Romance in the Roaring Forties" is typical Runyon, a few twists and a kicker at the end. Its protagonist is Waldo Winchester, the gossip writer. "Waldo Winchester's" name surely evokes Walter's, although it's doubtful that Damon knew Walter in 1929 except by reputation. Waldo is merely described as "a nice-looking young guy who writes pieces about Broadway for the *Morning Item*."

Waldo falls in love with Miss Billie Perry, a dancer at Missouri Martin's Sixteen Hundred Club. But Billie is the girl friend of Dave the Dude, a menace. Dave kidnaps Waldo, but so great is Dave's love for Billie that he arranges for her marriage to Waldo. The ceremony, however, is broken up by Waldo's ever-loving wife, an acrobat named Lola Sapola, who looks four feet tall and five feet wide and punches out, among others, Dave the Dude.

Since the clergy and the guests are assembled, Dave the Dude and Billie are married. At the end, the narrator reveals that he is the one who tipped off Lola Sapola that her husband was about to embrace bigamy and Billie, a secret he will keep "because maybe I do not do Dave any too much of a favor at that."

Apart from its historical interest as the first of the Broadway tales, "Romance" indicates something of Damon's cautious attitude toward gossip columnists. Damon loved inside information. He knew, literally, where many bodies were buried. But he regarded gossip as something for women. Waldo writes "about goings-on in night clubs, such as fights, and one thing and another, and who is running with who, including guys and dolls.

"Sometimes this is very embarrassing to people who may be married and are running around with people who are not married," the narrator concedes, "but of course Waldo Winchester cannot be expected to ask one and all for their marriage certificates before he writes his pieces for the paper."

200

The comic touch is somewhat surer in "Madame La Gimp," another story Damon published in 1929, his first story to be sold to Hollywood. A bunch of Broadway guys and dolls, including Dave the Dude and Miss Billie, help a twenties version of a bag lady pass herself off as high society to impress the titled family of her daughter's fiancé. The reader is in on the little joke when various deadbeats are announced at a reception as eminent Americans.

The narrator becomes O.O. McIntyre; Big Nig is Willie K. Vanderbilt; Tony Bertazolla from the Chicken Club is Mr. Al Jolson; Rochester Red is Otto Kahn, the financier; Nick the Greek is Heywood Broun "and gets very sore when I describe Heywood Broun to him," and Guinea Mike is "Vice President of the United States, the Honorable Charles Curtis." All ends happily, not only for the young woman and her fiancé but also for Madame La Gimp, gussied up for the occasion, who rekindles passion in the heart of an eminent jurist with whom she'd been in love decades earlier.

Not all the tales have happy endings, which shatters one misconception about popular fiction of the period. "Little Miss Marker," another movie sale and the one which made Shirley Temple famous, deals with a little girl who is left as a marker, that is, as security against a bet, with a hardhearted bookie called Sorrowful Jones. When her father, the gambler, does not return to claim her, she becomes Sorrowful's charge, and she gradually gives the old grouch a reason for living until she is hospitalized with pneumonia. Surrounded by gamblers and touts, she struggles for life:

> Now, very faint, like from far away, comes a sound of music through a half-open window in the room, from a jazz band that is rehearsing in a hall just up the street from the hospital, and Marky hears this music because she holds her head in such a way that anybody can see she is listening, and then she smiles again at us and whispers very plain, as follows: "Marky dance."
>
> And she tries to reach down as if to pick up her skirt as she always does when she dances, but her hands fall across her breast as soft and white and light as snowflakes, and Marky never again dances in this world.

Hollywood fixed up that ending, you can bet, and it avoided occasional flashes of the Runyon vision which were as dark as conventions of popular literature allowed. In "The Lily of St. Pierre," a lovely little French-Canadian waif is seduced, abandoned, and left to die by the loathsome Louie the Lug, who is then dispatched by Jack

201

O'Hearts, who loved Lily, although Louie, at that, dies game, without ratting; in "That Ever-Loving Wife of Hymie's," Hymie Banjo Eyes, a horse trainer, is repeatedly betrayed by his self-centered tramp of a wife.

But if, as one critic observed, Damon's stories relied on the timeworn device of making an enemy of society behave like St. Francis of Assisi, they were constantly, enormously popular, and magazine editors were avid for more. In 1934 Damon made his first trip to Hollywood to work on the screenplay of *Little Miss Marker*. He also received $30,000 from Twentieth Century for "Gentlemen, the King," in which hoods named Izzy Cheesecake, Jo-jo from Chicago, and Kitty Quick from Philadelphia are sent to an unnamed country in Europe to kill the king, only to discover the king is a charming little boy. They pull a good old American Double X. Warner Brothers paid Damon another $30,000 for "The Old Doll's House," in which a rich, reclusive old maid, through a neat plot twist on loan from Dickens, saves a killer from the electric chair. By Damon's ambiguous lights, this is morally all right since the saved man is a more-or-less good killer who got rid of three bad killers.

Damon's stories were cockeyed morality tales. There was little regard for the sixth commandment; taking a life was as likely to be funny as anything else. No Marxist peered at man's existence through a more sharply ground economic prism; all the world is out to Get the Money. The morality boiled down to a woozy application of the Golden Rule.

Much of this made sense to Americans in the thirties. Bankers and economists marched to the witness stand and indicated they didn't know what the hell was going on. It was, in many ways, a terrible time, a decade which opened with a depression and ended with the threat of fascism.

And yet there was a curious sense of purpose in American life. Thrown back on their own devices, Americans talked with each other and discovered each other. Keeping up with the Joneses pretty much meant providing three squares a day. Americans were too busy hustling to seek fulfillment or to ask if they were happy. There were plenty of dissidents, and the voice of the crackpot was heard in the land, but the case can be made that a good many people were having a better time of it than they did during the vapid hedonism of the twenties.

In the depths of a deepening depression, the New Yorker's mood could be jaunty, almost cocky, as A. J. Liebling indicated in a drumroll of the city's charms, written during those dark days: "It is one of the oldest places in the United States but doesn't live in

202

retrospect like the professionally picturesque provinces. Any city may have one period of magnificence, like Boston or New Orleans or San Francisco, but it takes a real one to keep renewing itself until the past is perennially forgotten. . . . The Revolution was fought all over town, from Harlem to Red Hook and back again, but that isn't the revolution you will hear New Yorkers discussing now. . . ."

Liebling believed "Native New Yorkers are the best-mannered people in America . . . New Yorkers are modest . . . New York women are the most beautiful in the world. . . . The climate is extremely healthy . . . and the average life expectancy so high that one of our morning newspapers specializes in interviewing people a hundred years old and upward."

Not everyone agreed with Liebling even then, and metropolitan comity in the eighties is one with S. Klein's, but he isolated a facet of the city's charm that endures: "The finest thing about New York City, I think, is that it is like one of those complicated Renaissance clocks where on one level an allegorical marionette pops out to mark the day of the week, on another the skeleton death bangs the quarter hour with his scythe, and on a third the Twelve Apostles do a cakewalk. The variety of the sideshow distracts one's attention from the advance of the hour hand."

The skeleton death paid its call on the New York *World* in 1931, for reasons that baffled and infuriated survivors the rest of their days. Pulitzer had made it clear in his will that he expected the *World* to endure: "I particularly enjoin upon my sons and my descendants the duty of preserving, perfecting and perpetuating the *World* newspapers, to the maintenance and publishing of which I have sacrificed my health and my strength, in the same spirit in which I have striven to conduct it as a public institution, from motives higher than mere gain."

But he left the largest interest in the newspaper to his son, Herbert, who had little apparent interest in journalism. Joseph, Jr., who had the best head for publishing, was maintaining the St. Louis *Post-Dispatch* as a paper worthy of his father's memory. Ralph, as publisher of the *World,* tried, although he could not get along with Swope, who departed the paper in 1928.

There is doubt that Swope could have saved the *World* even had he stayed. Some argue his restless energies contributed to the paper's decline. The heirs would not spend money to make money. When the *World* turned a profit, none of it was plowed back into the product. A jittery business office raised the price of the paper, losing readers it didn't regain when it returned to the two-cent level. Too late, employes learned the *World* would be sold. A frantic, last-ditch effort by the men of the *World* to put together a syndicate to buy it failed.

The English of the old man's will was unmistakable, but ways will be found to break wills, and the *World* was sold to Scripps-Howard for $5 million, becoming the *World-Telegram* and, in 1950, the *World-Telegram & Sun,* which critics said only proved the *Telegram* had absorbed the two most individualistic newspapers in New York and still remained the *Telegram*. Still later, the bastardy wound up as part of the *World Journal Tribune,* a short-lived concoction that carried as its masthead a melancholy reminder of New York journalism's decline and fall.

He was not precisely a victim of the depression, but Mayor Walker was forced to resign in 1931 amid charges of great wrongdoing. He came out of it all with not much more than a bloody nose. The mayor who saw the old town through the depression, Fiorello LaGuardia, proved to be as much showman as Walker, and with a longer attention span.

And Broadway remained a great show during those years. Robert Sylvester, a saloon columnist for the *News,* recalled, "It is completely understandable that back in the boom of the 1920s, night life and booze joints should have flourished. Yet why did they come to full flower in the Great Depression, when New York night life and the general metropolitan color was at its most colorful?"

Part of the answer was supplied by John Bruno, proprietor of the Pen and Pencil, who told Sylvester in the late sixties, "I served steaks for $1.95 when I opened in the early 1930s, and I made more money then than I can make with a steak for which I've got to charge you seven dollars."

The best-known of the New York nightclubs during this *belle époque,* probably the most famous nightclub in the world, was the Stork Club, and it owed its fame more to Walter, its unpaid publicist, than to Sherman Billingsley, its proprietor. From the day Texas Guinan suggested to Walter that he might want to give a great big hand to Billingsley, who had just opened the Stork, and Walter responded with a compelling claim in his column, "The New Yorkiest place in New York is the Stork Club," to a final break between the two men decades later, Walter plugged the Stork relentlessly.

Regiments of out-of-towners, wanting to eat and drink at the *New Yorkiest place in New York,* smoldered at the memory of being turned away at the velvet rope, which served as a moat, because they chewed gum or because their shoes were brown or because, well, frankly, they didn't look right.

A nice touch, the velvet rope. The story is that on opening night only a handful of customers appeared. But Billingsley put up the rope, turned away latecomers, and word got around the next few days that it was difficult to get into the Stork. Human nature and Walter did the rest. Billingsley, who reportedly had been spending $10,000 a month to keep the Stork operating, later said that after Walter's plugs "I started banking $10,000 a week."

It was not only the Stork that Walter made famous but a table *at* the Stork. This was Table 50, to the left as you entered the Cub Room, the Forbidden City of the Climber, and by the late thirties, it became about the only beat Walter had to cover. The hustling gossip who once prowled the nightclubs, restaurants, and streets demanding items was now an oracle who let his kind of news come to him. It was at Table 50 that Grace Kelly told Walter about her engagement to Prince Rainier, that Lana Turner and Artie Shaw announced their divorce, and that, according to Herman Klurfeld, Ernest Hemingway reported after a two-hour luncheon with Spencer Tracy the movie star's lament, "Sometimes I think that life is a terminal illness."

Walter expressed concern to Billingsley after a gangster was murdered in the place where Walter got his hair cut, the Hollywood Barber Shop at Broadway and Forty-seventh Street; Billingsley obligingly installed a barber shop on the second floor of the Stork. Walter complained about his sinusitis. Billingsley installed airconditioning.

Billingsley kept his prices high. He sent complimentary champagne to big spenders, Stork Club ties to deserving males, Stork Club perfume to women who might pass the word and the scent around. In terms of profit and publicity, it was all like a perpetual motion machine, the famous coming to the Stork to become more famous and spending money for the privilege.

It was too good to last, of course, and it didn't, but in a city where restaurants have the life expectancy of a running back in the National Football League, the Stork endured for more than three decades. In its heyday, as McKelway wrote, "People sit at the Stork Club bar for hours waiting for Winchell to come in so that they may have the opportunity to compliment him."

If the Stork had a rival all those years, it was John Perona's El Morocco. Perona and Billingsley, of course, were don't-invites. Ernest Cuneo, who was Walter's lawyer, recalled discussing the difference between the two establishments:

> We agreed El Morocco was the base of the idle, untalented rich. The Stork was the racetrack and showplace of the

205

Meritocracy, the winners, the career people of both sexes. I said, "Women are the profession of idle men, and the relaxation of the warrior."

"That's a good line," said Walter.

"It's not mine. It's George Bernard Shaw's."

"Well," he said, scribbling it down, "I'll give it some circulation."

Clearly, the Stork's atmosphere was heady.

Toward the end of his life, Damon became a regular at the Stork Club, during those small hours when he and Walter were constant companions. But it is a measure of basic difference between the two men that the eating establishment Damon made as famous as Walter made the Stork was a delicatessen.

This, of course, was Lindy's. The original Lindy's, founded by Leo Lindemann, a former busboy, and his wife Clara, a cashier in her uncle's restaurant when she met Leo, mirrored Broadway for thirty-six years before it closed, after serving an estimated fifty million patrons. They opened the place at 1626 Broadway, just below Fiftieth Street, on August 20, 1921, a month after Dempsey knocked out Carpentier.

"Broadway's lighting was all gold and silvery then," Lindy once told Meyer Berger of the *Times*. "But mostly silvery—more like a Great White Way." Al Jolson, an early regular, suggested that Lindy install tables for customers. There were fifty legitimate theaters in New York, and both the stars and the hungry young beginners found Lindy's. As speakeasies crowded out the grand hotel dining rooms and carriage trade restaurants like Churchill's and Shanley's, Lindy's flourished.

Arnold Rothstein conducted business at Lindy's. "You're giving our place a bad name," Clara told A. R. Lindy informed his cashier he'd be fired if he took messages for the gambler, but the cashier was afraid of Rothstein and, on that fatal November night, he passed the word to Rothstein that he was wanted at the Park Central. When the police came around after Rothstein was murdered, Damon helped take the heat off, and the Lindys never forgot that kindness and more than repaid it.

Repeal closed the Palais Royal and the Silver Slipper and the other big speaks, and Broadway began its descent into frankfurther joints and penny arcades and shooting galleries. For reasons not entirely clear, some wrangle between the Lindemanns and a partner, the Lindys moved out of the original establishment during the depression

206

and opened larger quarters across the street at Broadway and Fifty-first.

They were given an early boost, even in those hard times, when Eugene O'Neill's marathon *Strange Interlude* opened around the corner, a play which started in the afternoon, sprang audience and cast for refreshments, and resumed in the evening. Both audience and performers discovered Lindy's, perhaps the only restaurant in the world serving breakfast for show business people and the press after lunch for normal folk.

But it was Damon in his columns, and changing only the first initial in his fiction, who imprinted Lindy's on the national consciousness. "One evening along about seven o'clock, I am sitting in Mindy's restaurant putting on some gefillte fish," begins "Butch Minds the Baby." "One night The Brain is walking me up and down Broadway in front of Mindy's restaurant," begins "The Brain Goes Home." "One evening, along toward seven o'clock, many citizens are standing out on Broadway in front of Mindy's restaurant," begins "Little Miss Marker."

Reading "Personally I do not care for coppers, but I believe in being courteous to them at all times, so when Johnny Brannigan comes into Mindy's restaurant one evening," the cognoscenti knew Mindy's was Lindy's and Brannigan was Johnny Broderick, the legendary Broadway detective who was so fearless that, unarmed, he cowed the allegedly toughest guys in creation.

Among Lindy's patrons was Moe "The Gimp" Snyder, a hood who was married to Ruth Etting, the singer. He demanded Lindy serve him only female lobsters. When the Gimp was jailed for shooting Miss Etting's piano player, the Lindy's crowd sent him messages of cheer, and he suggested they form an Eastern Defense Committee and hold a rally for him at Madison Square Garden. Chuck Green, a jewelry salesman Damon called the Doorway Tiffany, said, "The Gimp must think he's Sacco and Vanzetti."

Even as the good times mounted for Damon and Walter, however, their papers foundered. It was more than a matter of depression economics: The *News* continued to sap Hearst's readership and advertising. More than that, as A. J. Liebling wrote, "It might easily have been argued that the *Daily News* was the best newspaper in New York" in 1933.

Liebling offered as one argument the *News* coverage of the bank holiday affecting twenty-four states, which the *News* wrapped up in a half dozen paragraphs, plus telephone interviews with officials in each of the stricken duchies.

"Any one of the million and a half readers of the *News* who went this far with the story, which was under his nose as he opened the paper on the subway," Liebling commented, "was better informed than a *Times* or *Herald Tribune* reader on the same day could have been without an excursion into the financial page and a determined exercise of his powers of deduction."

Liebling attributed this to "the editorial skill of . . . Joseph Patterson, who had a gift of putting complex propositions in simple words."

He went on to pay tribute to the *News* comics and sports section and to those departments which recognized "that most people are constantly embarrassed, never sure of themselves, silly about children, worried about blackheads, mixed up about their sex lives and eager for reassurance."

Against this powerhouse, the *Mirror* seemed not much more than a firecracker. Although its circulation was the highest in the Hearst chain, it was in the constantly difficult position of trying to catch up with the *News*. It had a certain honey, to paraphrase Gertrude Stein, but it didn't pour.

As Ring Lardner, Jr., remembered it:

> There was very little connection between working for the *Daily Mirror* in 1935 and the great newspaper tradition of the 1920s that persisted into the thirties on the *Trib* under [Stanley] Walker and to a lesser extent on the other non-tabloid papers.
>
> It was not enough, in that tradition, to get the facts straight and relate them coherently under a lead that stated the essence of the story in a provocative way. The best reporters were also literate, entertaining, and so individual that devotees could recognize their style without a by-line. They brought knowledge and values of their own to the material they covered, and they included in their numbers at one time or another most of the worthwhile writers of all kinds in the decades that followed.

Lardner's estimate was that the *Mirror* "competed for many years with the *Daily News* largely on the strength of Walter Winchell's column," but this is something of an overstatement. The *Mirror* was not without other strengths, notably a lively sports section presided over by Dan Parker, a tough, funny writer who was most often singled out in memory for his honesty, which may be a comment on the lodge brothers. There was a widely followed horse-race specialist called

Tony Betts, who as Anthony Zito was a copyboy on the *World* under Swope, for whom he retained a reverence. After a day at the races with Swope and Bernard Baruch, he told *Mirror* readers, "You have the feeling you are in the presence of great Americans like Thomas Jefferson and Benjamin Franklin."

Bob Considine called the *Mirror* sports department "one of the most-admired and best-read (except by proof-readers) in the land," complete with an office eccentric who chose to spend his *vacation* traveling with the St. Louis Browns, the original New York Mets.

Hearst was increasingly desperate to make a go of the *Mirror*. He assigned Arthur Brisbane, his mouthpiece and leading columnist, to talk with Walter Lippmann and Heywood Broun about joining the organization, an idea to tickle the gods. Lippmann listened politely and politely declined, as did Broun.

The interview with Broun took place at Brisbane's palatial Fifth Avenue residence. Broun noticed a painting of Albert Brisbane over the fireplace.

"What a marvelous face your father had," Broun said. "It reflects the calm outlook of a man who is right with himself."

"Yes," said Brisbane. "He looked that way because he never had to work for Hearst."

Brisbane, like many men, wanted it both ways. He told Fowler, "Mr. Hearst is a great big safe, and I am the only one who has the combination." Brisbane's syndicated column, "Today," was read by thirty million readers. It was known that he would praise any show on Broadway that advertised in the *American*. He had been a first-rate reporter, but in the 1930s he seemed to entertain no great belief beyond adding to his millions. This does not always comfort a man.

This latter-day Brisbane shocked Emile Gauvreau, who remembered being guided as a young man by Brisbane's column "to second-hand bookstores where I picked up the works of Samuel Johnson, Racine, Heine, Montaigne and the rest of the immortals. It was through Brisbane that I learned enough to know why Homer, Dante, Goethe, Cervantes and Shakespeare are the greatest writers that ever lived."

In October of 1934 Hearst in a ruthless ploy dismissed Kobler as publisher of the *Mirror* and installed Brisbane. It was an experience Gauvreau never forgot, an avalanche of words and ideas through dictaphone messages that wore down batteries of secretaries. So ingrained was the habit, Gauvreau wrote, that Brisbane after a hard day at the office forgot himself one night while addressing a banquet of utility magnates and began: "All caps gentlemen uncaps colon a great writer named caps Sir James Barrie uncaps has said that quotes

209

life is a lesson in humility unqotes period." A secretary jerked his sleeve and returned him to reality.

Brisbane admired, in addition to money, power. In those days, this translated into an admiration for Mussolini, who used to be a newspaperman himself, and a wait-and-see attitude toward Hitler. Brisbane was full of strange ideas. One day he said to Gauvreau: "When I look into the city room, during the few hours when we are busy, I see thirty or forty persons trying to do something. What are they all doing? Although this may not mean anything to you, I only see a handful with blue eyes. The rest look like a lot of white-collared butterballs. It annoys many when I talk about blue eyes, but any man who ever amounted to a damn in history had them, or gray eyes, even men from dark races like Napoleon from Corsica, Caesar from Rome. Here is a short list: Washington, Jefferson, Lincoln, Roosevelt, Edison, Henry Ford. Look up the rest."

Brisbane believed that Christ was an agitator and that Nero was the greatest man who ever lived "because he had the courage of his convictions and used the ignorant rabble to achieve his own ends." Brisbane's beliefs weren't important, of course, not even to him. Hearst paid him $260,000 a year for weathervane thinking. In Gauvreau's phrase, "You changed your editorial mind as Hearst changed his, like throwing off an old hat." As recompense, Brisbane frequently quoted his salary on meeting someone for the first time: "Perhaps you didn't know I make," etc.

The *Mirror* was selling more than 600,000 copies daily. Brisbane believed circulation should be at least 1,500,000. Going after it, he unretired Marie Manning Gasch, the original Beatrice Fairfax, a love-and-marriage columnist at the turn of the century. He also resurrected Nell Brinkley, an illustrator of the same period. These three old parties mounted a campaign, in the middle of the depression, outlined in a Brisbane memo: "Young ladies and gentlemen, don't fail to read the love and marriage page in tomorrow's *Mirror* and daily thereafter. Nothing is important but (capitals, quote), LOVE (uncaps, unquote) nothing is important but (full capitals) LAWFUL MAR-RIAGE (uncaps) Stop So read the *Mirror's* (quotes) Love and Marriage (unquote) page Stop Get Married as soon as you can (Caps) Have a baby."

The slogan didn't send circulation soaring. Neither did Brisbane's history lessons as he recalled the grand days of the *Journal* and the Spanish-American War:

"My God, sir, where the hell were we getting war news in 1898?" he bellowed at Gauvreau. "I read it off the bulletin boards of the papers that could pay for it, with my binoculars, and then dished it up to the

210

people in better fashion than my competitors could present it! People were sitting on the curbstones reading it! A million was nothing. We can do it again." He recalled favorite headlines: "Peeping Dowager Names Actress," and one he wrote himself: "The Bull That Butted the Train Off the Tracks!"

Brisbane was as appalled as Hearst by the Roosevelt administration and its taxes, but he was anxious not to offend municipal authorities who taxed his real estate interests. He ordered Gauvreau to fire on Christmas Eve a reporter who had been with the *Mirror* from its beginning but who had unintentionally upset the tax people.

When Gauvreau protested, Brisbane ·interrupted himself while dictating an editorial on "the beautiful character of Christ" to exclaim, "You mean you can't fire him on Christmas Eve! Say—say, this is the funniest thing since 'The Old Homestead.'" Then he stuck his great granitic face in Gauvreau's. "'Fire him now,' he murmured, his lips a narrow line. 'You're not married to him, are you?'"

Gauvreau fired the reporter.

There were great waves of cost-cutting. The Hearst empire was in serious trouble. The pressure on Brisbane grew. Brisbane was pleased when the *Times* honored him with an editorial on his seventieth birthday, but he was furious when his business friends, whose opinions he had solicited, responded with such comments as "After looking through every page, I can't find any reason why you call it a newspaper," and he was chilled when Hearst telegraphed, "Dear Artie. Congratulations. You are now putting out the dullest newspaper in the world."

Brisbane despised and admired Walter.

"I don't understand a word of his jargon," he told Gauvreau. "It is something that has caught hold of our modern degeneration, as Mr. Hearst calls it, and Winchell is cashing in on it while it lasts. . . . Yesterday he pulled out a bagful of clippings from his pockets, things people were writing about him, and he wanted me to read them! Does he think we're working for him?"

Brisbane read Walter's columns carefully, with an eye out for libel. He said he always read Swift afterwards, as an antidote. Shakespeare described Walter's column, said Brisbane: "'A tale told by an idiot, full of sound and fury, signifying nothing.'"

But he was fascinated by Walter's rise to fortune. Between the *Mirror,* syndication, and radio, Walter was making about $185,000 a year. Brisbane would ask Gauvreau to tell again about hiring Walter for $100 a week and commissions in 1924. "That money came too fast to him," Brisbane said, shaking his head.

On another occasion, he said, "That fellow Winchell is a barrel of copperheads. But I notice his eyes are blue."

In 1934 and 1935 Walter was up to those blue eyes in the crime, the case, and the trial of the century. On March 1, 1932, Charles Augustus Lindbergh, Jr., not quite twenty months old and the first-born of the transatlantic hero and the former Anne Morrow, was kidnapped from the Lindbergh home near Hopewell, New Jersey. The reaction was nationwide: shock and horror. A psychiatrist called it "an intense feeling of individual and personal affront at this crime against an adored citizen of the world."

It was almost enough to take minds off the depression. Newspapers printed every rumor, every lead. Everyone offered to help, from President Hoover to Al Capone, serving eleven years for tax evasion, who told Brisbane he would get the child returned to the Lindberghs in return for his freedom.

On March 12 the body of the baby was found in a shallow grave near the Lindbergh home. He had been dead since the night of the kidnapping. The heartlessness of it, the fact that the kidnappers held out hope to the Lindberghs, assuring them the baby was well, triggered a fury expressed in a *News* editorial: "The damnable fiends, the inhuman monsters. . . . Until the killers are tracked down and brought to justice, the children of America will not be safe."

On September 16, 1934, Walter told his radio audience that ransom bills were turning up in Manhattan and the Bronx. He addressed the borough's bank tellers. "Boys," he said, "if you weren't such a bunch of saps and yaps, you'd have already captured the Lindbergh kidnappers." But McKelway wrote, "Banks had turned over bills to the police as early as December, 1935," and noted that Walter twice falsely reported that ransom money had turned up in local restaurants.

Three days after Walter's radio tip, however, police picked up Bruno Richard Hauptmann, a German-born carpenter, at his Bronx home, nailed when an alert filling station attendant copied down Hauptmann's license number after being given one of the bills. Hauptmann went on trial the following year.

"It was on the Hauptmann case that Winchell was given an opportunity to display his talents as a reporter of an actual news story," McKelway wrote. "He wrote close to seventy thousand words on this case." McKelway, a hard marker, didn't give Walter a passing grade.

On January 6, 1935, Walter apologized to Mr. and Mrs. America for offering a column prepared "several days in advance" because he was in Flemington, New Jersey, "cub-reporting the saddest drama ever staged." Cub-reporting or not, Walter's name led the list of correspondents covering the trial. Wrote George Waller in *Kidnap,* "No less than three hundred . . . some of them famous novelists turned reporter for the trial—Walter Winchell, Edna Ferber, Arthur Brisbane, Fannie Hurst, Damon Runyon, Kathleen Norris, Alexander Woollcott, Adela Rogers St. John. . . ."

Samuel Leibowitz, the noted criminal lawyer, offered radio commentary on the case, but it was a commentator named Gabriel Heatter who built a nationwide following there, and his "There's good (or bad) news tonight" later became a catch phrase.

On January 7, 1935, Walter worked at being Man About Town and Country, but, writing from Flemington, his heart wasn't in it. After gossiping "Virginia Kent, daughter of the Atwater Kent radio man, is the reason Franklin Roosevelt, Jr., is not as hot as he was over Ethel du Pont. . . . The Jack Farleys (he's Jim's brother) have phffft. . . ." he confessed, "I just can't get into the mood of writing trivia about people, except those at the trial. . . . It's the only news worth while writing about, and in my opinion the public isn't interested in anything else. . . .

"The Philadelphia papers and Damon Runyon, who are seated directly behind Hauptmann, reported on their front pages that Hauptmann turned to them and in a thick accent asked, 'Where is dot Vinchell sitting?' We were pointed out to him. . . . The reports continue, 'Hauptmann then said, "He should not be allowed here. He is not a nice man."' We were never cordial to suspected murderers."

Brisbane, who didn't doubt Hauptmann's guilt, fired off a telegram to the Hearst papers: "We are constantly referring to the prisoner as 'the German.' If he were Irish we should not drag in the Irish, and if he were Jewish, we should not drag in the Jews. THE GERMANS ARE THE LEAST MURDEROUS OF ALL RACES. Their average in murder is much lower than ours, on the average about ten to one. . . ."

Damon, as Walter pointed out in his column, "wrote about 8,000 words the first day, in long hand," beginning, "Bruno Richard Hauptmann, cold, silent, more the type of Old World criminal, with a record as a 'bad guy,' goes on trial for his life. . . ."

Forty telegraph and cable operators sat shoulder to shoulder in the courthouse garret, prepared to transmit a million words a day. Foreign accents mingled with the homely syllables of stage and screen stars, politicians, celebrities, and those whose life would be ruined if they missed an important event—a title fight, a World Series, a Broadway opening, a spectacular murder trial.

The trial lasted six weeks and was argued in a million and a half words, which filled thirty typewritten volumes. Amid all the logorrhea, Hoyt reports, Damon "was again congratulated from all sides. . . . He added more weight to his reputation as the most colorful newspaper writer in America."

Colorful, yes, but Damon could play the violin, as in reporting Mrs. Lindbergh's testimony: "She takes the things in her slender fingers, a faded piece of flannel that was a chest protector for her ailing child and a dingy white sleeping suit, fondling them lovingly for a moment. Then, in a quiet, cultured voice that tears at every heartstring in the packed courtroom . . . she says, yes, those were Baby Charles's."

The trial induced a kind of fever dream of journalistic frenzy, a drive for a scoop, a beat, an exclusive angle. The Associated Press, as the verdict neared, sent out a false flash. Damon, writing on February 14, got it right: "Bruno Richard Hauptmann must die the week beginning March 18. . . . He is found guilty tonight of murder in the first degree, without recommendation, and is immediately sentenced . . . to be executed. . . . The jury is out from 11:16 this morning to 10:40 tonight, a surprising length of time to many, in view of a charge from Justice Trenchard that made conviction seem a certainty."

The sensational press, with which hypocrisy can be a virtue, was by no means done with the Lindberghs. Having wept over their tragedy, the tabloids now staked out the Hopewell home, in spite of the Lindberghs' pleas for privacy.

Still grieving over the death of her firstborn, Mrs. Lindbergh gave birth to another son. He was about two years old when a resourceful *Mirror* photographer, peering through the curtains of a black wagon, snapped a picture of Mrs. Lindbergh and little Jon Morrow walking happily from his private schoolroom. Brisbane approved the *Mirror's* front-page headline:

FIRST PUBLISHED PHOTO
OF 2ND LINDY BABY!

The photograph was profitably sold to other newspapers. "It was widely reported that Colonel Lindbergh considered this publicity a final, unpardonable assault on his privacy," Gauvreau wrote. When Lindbergh and his family fled to exile in England, Brisbane complained: "The departure of Colonel Lindbergh and his family . . . is not a good advertisement for this country, its police and its system of justice, but it is an advertisement that the country deserves. If you had a small boy constantly threatened with anonymous letters, and had already lost your only other child, kidnapped and murdered, you also might move out."

Walter believed he had proved himself a pretty good reporter during

214

the Lindbergh trial. He devoted a column, "No. 13 on the Jury," to a listing of nineteen scoops he claimed.

McKelway didn't think much of the claim. "There were two scoops with qualifications," he wrote, "one scoop, which was never confirmed, is hardly a scoop; two scoops printed the same day by other papers; six scoops which had been printed from four days to seven weeks earlier in the *Times;* seven scoops which cannot be considered as scoops in the accepted meaning of the word, and one scoop in which he misquoted his own editor."

But the trial of the century would soon be overwhelmed by history. This time Walter was on target in warning Americans about the implications of some of those events, although McKelway didn't even give Walter credit for this, and it is one of life's ironies that Walter and Damon became friends just as Walter's horizons broadened beyond the Broadway in which Damon increasingly found shelter as well as home.

twelve

"SOCRATES, YOU know, in ancient Athens, drank the hemlock because he was accused of corrupting the youth of the city. But these degenerates who write rock and roll, they've corrupted the youth of the world."

The speaker is Mitchell Parish, a solid, hearty figure with close-cropped whitish hair, a small mustache, and snapping blue eyes. For years he contributed verse to Walter's column, bittersweet froth that began with lines like:

> Last night between the midnight and the dawn,
> I walked the quiet avenues of sleep.
> And everywhere I looked, the blinds were drawn . . .

Or:

> At last the tide has turned, you thought that never
> Would I unforge the chains that held me bound . . .
> That I would play the abject fool forever . . .

Often, the verse ended with a snapper, as in "Nostalgia:"

> The days when we had everything so good,
> Would you go back to them? Like hell you would.

Transitory stuff, surely, but Mitchell Parish also wrote what Walter called The Anthem. That is, he wrote the lyric. The music he was given to work with was unforgettable and inimitable. It was written by a young Indiana University law school graduate named Hoagland Carmichael, who later confessed he had "that horrible thought, that queer sensation that this melody was bigger than I. It didn't seem part of me. Maybe I hadn't written it at all."

His old college roommate, gesturing to indicate dust falling from the sky, suggested the title, and the song survived in the mid-1920s as

216

an instrumental. "Just a little tune, Don," Carmichael told a band-leader named Don Redman in Detroit. "You might want to play it."

For three years the tune bounced around in upbeat, jazzy arrangements. In 1929 Parish, a rising young lyricist, was commissioned to put words to the music. ("That will date me," Parish said in 1978. "Not that I care, but my girl friend thinks I'm thirty-two.")

"Walter Winchell heard a piano rendition of the tune by a *Sepian* at the Black Feet café in Greenwich Village, and he got a new kind of love, so he tells me," Carmichael recalled in a memoir, *The Stardust Road*. "Contemporary newsmen were forced to put down their drinks while Walter held them by the lapels and whistled the first four bars. In this way, *Stardust* became known as the Walter Winchell song."

It is a great popular song, great as a piano solo, a saxophone or trumpet solo, or played on a comb, or a capella in the shower, great in lush, full orchestra rendition. Sinatra once recorded only the verse. In 1955 *Time* magazine noted, "In Italy it is called *Polvere di stella,* and it ranks with *O Sole Mio* as an all-time favorite. In Japan, it is called *Sutaadasuto* and is one number record stores are not afraid to overload. In England, no song has sold more copies." For a quarter of a century, Carmichael's royalties from "Stardust" averaged $25,000 a year.

"Stardust" represents a popular, forgotten conceit that it was fun to spend a night dancing with a person of the opposite sex in your arms, cheek to cheek, moving to a melody that was easy to whistle, which was decorated with words, often banal but sometimes graceful, examining the phenomenon of romantic love.

In 1978, Mitchell Parish expounded on the song in the Victorian atmosphere of the Friars Club bar in mid-Manhattan. He is by no means a one-shot lyricist, having also written the words for "Deep Purple," "Sweet Lorraine," "Stars Fell on Alabama," "Don't Be That Way," and "Volare," but he is aware that "Stardust" is special.

"It became a synonym or symbol for popular songs," he said. "Whether a short story, article or cartoon, if they want to mention a song everyone knows, they use *Stardust.* Not too long ago, *The New Yorker* ran a cartoon of a bartender hollering at a drunk, 'No, I do *not* want to hear you sing *Stardust.*'" This was about fifty years after the song was written; it is not clear if the same future awaits "Kiss Me All Over."

The growing popularity of radio and music on radio helped "Stardust." It also was helped, Parish believes, because it was not an overnight hit, played so often people tired of it. "Stardust" was given time to grow. And Walter's role was crucial.

"He was important in promulgating the song in his column," Parish

217

said. "He couldn't quote the music, but he quoted my lyric. He raved about the tune. Over a period of forty years, he must have mentioned *Stardust* hundreds of times. You couldn't get that publicity for millions of dollars."

Walter didn't pay his contributors except in plugs, and by the time the lyricist of "Sophisticated Lady," "The Lamp is Low," and "Stairway to the Stars" began sending Walter sonnets, Parish was not exactly desperate for recognition. He became a contributor because he admired the column.

"It was full of information and gossip, especially Broadway news," Parish said. "He told you about the goings and comings. I liked the verses he printed at the top of the column. I thought they had real merit. They weren't Auden or Spender or Robert Frost, but he published verses of substantial merit, Don Wahn included."

Don Wahn was a pen name for a Winchell contributor named Phillip Stack, a shy clerk at Brooklyn Edison. O. Henry might have written his story. Stack began sending verse to Walter in 1924 and, attributed through the decades to Kid Kazanova, The Melancholy Don and, most often, Don Wahn, his doggerel frequently topped the column. Often, it floated a lambent moon, fragrances, snatches of melody, regret, bitterness. The belief was that show girls and debutantes found wisdom and release in Stack's verse, "Broadway Rhapsody," for example:

> I am for Broadway when the moon is low
> And magic weaves along the fabled street
> For I can search for ghosts of long ago
> When time was slow and violins were sweet.
> And few there are who note the haunted eyes
> That hint of dreams too gossamer to last
> And few there are when youth and beauty dies
> Who bar the benediction of the past. . . .

Stack's infant son had died, then his wife died in childbirth, reason enough for the Don to be melancholy. For a period he quit his contributions. When Walter finally located him by phone, Stack said he had recently remarried and was too happy to write. This passed. Stack's verses appeared in *Esquire* now, and on greeting cards.

In 1948 he submitted a verse for Walter which began:

> You who are prone to dream . . . remember this . . .
> That lighted inns loom starkly on the day,

That mystery can fade from out a kiss . . .
That love can wear the trappings of decay.

The verse ended with a couplet:

This is a world of never-ending strife,
Dreams are a one-way passage out of life.

This seemed no gloomier than some of the Don's earlier pronouncements until Walter received a call from either the police or the
Associated Press, accounts vary, asking him if he knew a Phil Stack.
He was told that Stack, learning he was incurably ill, had just jumped
to his death on Thirty-fifth Street. Walter explained that he would be
of no help in identifying the body, since he had never seen his
contributor of more than twenty years. For all he knew, the Melancholy Don might have been, like Homer, a committee.

By printing verse from contributors, Walter encouraged a dying
tradition. Time was when poetry sprouted all over American newspapers, from the editorial page to the sports section. In the Chicago
Tribune, Bert Leston Taylor's "A Line O' Type or Two," generally
regarded as the progenitor of the twentieth-century column, danced
with verse.

Even the determinedly lowbrow Hearst press offered verse of a
spectrum so broad, both geographically and artistically, as to encom-
pass "The Man with the Hoe," written by an Oakland school principal,
and the works of Nick Kenny, a *Mirror* troubadour discovered by
Damon and the author of the observation that snow is the dandruff of
God.

Walter continued to encourage poetry and Mitchell Parish, already
famous, began contributing to the column to take the place of the
pseudonymous Stack. Walter printed his first offering with a public
note, "Come again, dear man," and soon Parish joined Walter on his
rounds.

Walter's readers learned about romance in all its aspects, not just
the divorces and infidelities and passing passions. In what McKelway
called his "Self-Immolation of a Columnist" phase, Walter wrote
considerably about his family, never with more emotion than on July
27, 1935, when he reported the birth of Walter, Jr. He said "The Thrill
was the most enjoyable I've ever known."

Walter seemed the proudest of fathers, displaying a prose snapshot
to millions: "His tiny ears are up against his well-shaped head. Dark
blue eyes. Black hair. Exceptionally good chest expansion (according

219

to the nurses). He rolls both his huge eyes at the same time. There isn't a blemish on his sturdy little body. He seldom cries. He gurgles. And coos." And so forth.

The great human interest story of the time was the birth of the Dionne quintuplets, and when Dr. Allan Roy Dafoe, the cantankerous country doctor who delivered the quints, visited the most cosmopolitan city in the world, Walter spirited him to the Winchell apartment to examine the heir. Walter confessed to trepidation as the doctor stoically looked over the infant.

Dr. Dafoe smiled and said, "He's perfect," adding inaccurately, "He's just like Marie." Walter reported, "I never felt so good about anything in my life."

Not that he ignored Walda, whose recorded sayings were what might be called average cute. "Walking down the street with a warm little hand clasped in yours," Walter explained to his readers, "is a thrill only a daddy knows. Your child is clinging to you, so dependent and trusting—so safe with your firm grip to guide her. There really isn't a more thrilling thrill than that of a little girl's warm hand in yours, as you swing along. Have a baby and start living."

He was right in step with Brisbane's crusade. Before Walter, Jr.'s, birth, his father let readers eavesdrop on a naming-the-baby colloquy:

"If it's a boy, I think Reid Winchell would be nice," the mother remarked.

"Sure," replied the father. "And if it's a girl we can call her Sue Winchell."

The way it really happened, as June Winchell explained to a press agent when Walter, Jr., was about twelve and already in trouble, is that "his father came into the room right after he was born and said he was going to call him Walter Winchell, Jr., and I agreed. It was the most terrible thing I've ever done. It destroyed the boy."

Walter was candid in occasional columns called "Mr. and Mrs. Columnist at Home," which he began writing in 1934. In one of them June discussed Walda's meeting in the park with nine-year-old Gloria Vanderbilt, about whose person a sensational custody battle raged.

"Poor Walda. She has her little aches. Dorothy told me that when Walda and the Vanderbilt child, who is nine, first met, Walda went up to her and said: 'What is your name?' and she replied: 'Gloria.' Walda's bottom lip started to quiver and her chin dropped—but she steadied herself—and never mentioned the incident to Dorothy or me, poor thing."

"Yes, I know. I've received several lovely poems from people about that line I ran the other day—about 'Gloria would have been eleven.' One came from a Cleveland newspaperman—a lovely thing."

"Don't run them—none of them—don't do it!"

"Oh, honey—I won't—I know . . ."

June censored the column, after publication. She sometimes circled items in red crayon, with marginal comments such as "This makes me very proud of you." Walter reported a family battle, in which June demanded:

"Don't put me in the paper—don't make me say things I didn't say. People will think I'm silly or something. Walda, come here. Be careful what you say in front of Daddy—he'll put it in the paper!"

"Oh, cut that out. Everything I said, you said! Maybe not on the same day—but you said those things. It's a good idea for a column, and I'm going to do it every now and then—and what do you think about that? It's intimate, personal, inside stuff about us—and several people have written in to say they like it. Get me some orange juice."

June's influence prevailed, and there were fewer mentions of Walter's family in his column. In 1937 he bought a sixteen-acre estate in Westchester County, outside New York, inspired at least in part by fears the children might be kidnapped. An iron fence guarded the property, electronic devices were installed to set off sirens against intruders, and only a few close friends knew its exact location.

For a time, the city boy expressed wonder at the joys of the country, the rolling hills and fresh air. This amused friends who had a hard time picturing The King of Broadway contemplating crabgrass.

He played the role of commuter-in-reverse, returning to the household at the end of his day, just as the children started theirs. But with increasing frequency he spent his nights in the city, explaining "the cooing pigeons in the country" kept him from sleeping, in spite of drawn blinds and air-conditioning. "It was more fun," Klurfeld wrote, "for Walter to sleep with shapely city 'doves' in New York." But he drew the blinds on his private life.

J. P. McEvoy interviewed Walter for a 1938 article in *The Saturday Evening Post*.

"Winchell loves privacy. Not your privacy, but his," he wrote.

. . . When I suggested that maybe I ought to have a chat with his wife and a look around his home if I was going to write something about him, his roar of protest frightened me: "No, sir! You can say anything you like about me, but you've got to keep my family out of this."

That from Walter Winchell?

"But, Walter," I said, "you've made a national reputation and a tremendous fortune out of other people's private affairs."

"That's different," he said. "That's business."

"But this is business. How can I write about you if I don't know something about your interests outside of work?"

"I haven't any interests outside of work."

"But what do you do when you're not working? You go somewhere, don't you?"

"Certainly. I go home."

"Well, where is that? In the city? In the country? Do you live in a house? Or a flat? Or a cave? Have you got a wife, children, relatives, friends?"

"What's all that got to do with it? Anything you want to know about me I'll tell you, but a man's got a right to his private life."

Whee! And he didn't crack a smile.

McEvoy, who called his article "He Snoops to Conquer," sent an envoy to speak with Walter's secretary at the *Mirror:*

"I can't give out any information about Mr. Winchell," she said.

"Does he work here?"

"I can't say."

"When did you see him last?"

"I don't remember."

Life was kind to Walter, but shock waves echoed through the Hearst empire by the middle thirties. Gauvreau departed the *Mirror,* after writing an insufficiently anti-Communist book about Russia. Brisbane fired him with regret. It was, for Gauvreau, a poignant moment, a farewell to the ruin who had led him to Shakespeare and Dante.

"Someone has said," Brisbane told Gauvreau, "that it's not in the least likely that any life has been lived which is not a failure in the secret judgment of the person who lived it. Not much that I have written will be remembered for long after my obituary appears on the front pages. . . . I pointed out to you the conclusions that Swift reached about mankind. Don't pin your hopes too high on anyone."

Brisbane died on Christmas day 1936. Tributes came from Roosevelt and LaGuardia. His death was on the front pages, all right, and the *Times* carried the story over to an inside page under a five-column banner. His estate was estimated at $25,000,000. His son-in-law reported Brisbane's last words were, "Everything is for the best in this best of all possible worlds." But the old cynic was right. His millions of words were interred with his bones.

Brisbane had offered none of his money to Hearst, who had very much been his benefactor. At seventy-four, as Swanberg noted, Hearst was finally learning the financial facts of life: "The day of reckoning was at hand. The castles, the Van Dycks, the tapestries, the swimming pools, the tourism à la Hearst, had taken their toll. The Organization was staggering under a load of debt to stockholders, newsprint companies and twenty-eight different banks."

It may have been that the unaccustomed concern with financial niceties, along with a growing dread of Roosevelt, had shaken Hearst's already capricious judgment, but he selected as Brisbane's successor the most unlikely candidate, and this was Damon Runyon.

The new column was called "As I See It." It would not run in Brisbane's slot on the front page; that space was retired, like the uniform number sanctified by an athlete. But Damon was asked to be cerebral, which is often as calamitous for a working newsman as it is for an actor. The problem, as Hoyt noted, was that Brisbane "could invest a baseball game with the importance of a secret meeting between heads of state. Damon could reduce an earth-shaking event to the level of a heavyweight wrestling match in Keokuk."

Damon tried. He suggested executing dope peddlers, bemoaned gangsterism, and passed along a recipe for a kind of Mickey Finn. But he was relieved when Hearst took him off the Brisbane beat after two months. He was given a new column with the title "The Brighter Side," which endured to his death. As the title suggests, he was no longer expected to be solemn.

Damon was no longer a sports columnist, but he was still around for the big events, of course. Amid ever more ominous rumbles about the vanishing *American,* Hearst dispatched his usual wrecking crew of reporters to cover the James J. Braddock–Joe Louis heavyweight title match in Chicago in 1937, including Damon, Bugs Baer, Sid Mercer, Ed Frayne, Lewis Burton, and a couple of young sportswriters named Bob Considine, who liked practically everybody in journalism except Damon, and Jimmy Cannon, who was a Damon enthusiast.

Cannon, a product of Greenwich Village, became the definitive New York sportswriter, developing a style as personal as, but entirely different from, Damon's. When he was a young copyboy at the *News*, one night the wild-eyed visitor who haunts all newsrooms turned up, demanding to see the editor. Cannon politely asked for his name.

"The stranger fixed him with a crazed eye.

"My name?" he roared. "Why, I am God."

Without missing a beat, Cannon stuck out his hand. "Glad to meet you," he said. "I've heard a lot about you."

Now, on fight night, there were rumors only the intercession of the Almighty would save the *American*. Damon wrote his lead, "Joe Louis knocks James J. Braddock as cold as a frozen haddock in the eighth round tonight to become the 15th heavyweight champion of the world since John L. Sullivan's time and the second Negro to win the title. . . ."

A Western Union wire broke down.

"Dammit," growled Sid Mercer. "Get that wire fixed or I'll miss an edition."

"Get that wire fixed," said Cannon, "or he'll miss a newspaper."

The words were prophetic. Two days later the *American* went out of business and was merged to become the *Journal-American*. It was clear that Hearst had no choice, or he would not have allowed that to happen to his mouthpiece, the flagship of his tottering empire. Matters were so desperate that Hearst's salary was cut from half a million dollars to $100,000. Others, who could less afford it, also took paycuts, and hundreds of Hearst employes were fired.

Damon joined Walter on the *Mirror*.

Walter welcomed him in the weekly column allegedly written by Walter's secretary: "I guess you know about George Gershwin. Understand he's desperately ill . . . And they don't know what's the matter yet . . . I knew you'd get a kick out of hearing about Runyon, Ripley and others coming over to the *Mirror*, that's why I phoned."

It is difficult to imagine anyone buying the *Mirror* simply to read Damon. Without questioning his adroit touch as a sportswriter and the fire he brought to courtroom reporting, without questioning his credentials as a newsman, one can still realize that the column of general comment may be the most difficult to write. Damon had been a columnist since "The Mornin's Mornin'" first appeared in 1914, and now, devoting an entire column to an attack on midwestern coffee, there were days when he appeared in danger of becoming what Edmund Wilson called "the kind of columnist who depends entirely on a popular personality . . . who merely turns on the tap every day and lets it run a column."

Mark Hellinger warned, "Ten years is about as long as any columnist can take it"; all the more remarkable, then, that in the 1930s the great days for Damon's column lay ahead.

It is easy to believe that Walter was the first thing readers turned to when they bought the *Mirror*. Brisbane had complained that the *Mirror* had "more columns than a Greek ruin." Staffers, who called the paper "a quail and crime sheet," said that with everyone except the rewrite men conducting a column, there was no room for news beyond page eight.

And yet, although it is as dated as gossip must be, Walter's column, sharing the page with Damon, catches the eye: "The next marriage threat in the Roosevelt tribe is the baby of the family (John) and Adelaide Muffett Brooks, whose young groom fell from their 14th floor home in Park Avenue several months ago . . . Be prepared for an exciting flash regarding the Leopold Stokowskis. Her chums in the Orient (from which she returned via San Francisco Thursday) fear they will go to the courts . . . Anagrams for 'A. Hitler' is 'A liar.'"

However limp that may appear in the reflective eye of history, Alexander Woollcott called Walter "the most celebrated, most debatable, most enterprising and most intrusive journalist of our time. . . . I suppose it would be easy to assemble evidence in support of the contention that Winchell is lacking in taste. He has a more valuable asset. For want of a better term, let us call it zest."

Damon's column undoubtedly suffered from inattention. He was busy on other fronts, publishing more than thirty short stories between 1933 and 1940 in national magazines, a half-dozen collections of those stories appearing in the United States and England. He commuted to Hollywood to work on movie versions of those stories. He even found time to collaborate with Howard Lindsay, coauthor of *Life with Father,* on a play called *A Slight Case of Murder.* Mark Hellinger was heard to remark, during the play's first intermission, "This is going to be a slight case of getting out of here as fast as I can," and the remark got back to Damon, giving him another grudge.

The writing of *A Slight Case of Murder* was outside anything in Lindsay's experience. They started working in Damon's Parc Vendome apartment late at night. They took time out to visit a hunting and boxing camp in the Maryland countryside, where Damon kept hunting dogs. Damon snored prodigiously, then accused Lindsay of keeping him up all night by talking in his sleep. The playwrights ventured to Damon's Florida retreat, just in time for a rare and fearsome cold snap. The mansion was a showplace, but it had no central heating.

Along the way, Lindsay met some of Damon's underworld friends. Little Augie Pisano, who may have murdered a man named Greenfield; Al Capone's brother, Ralph; an ex-bootlegger named Bill Dwire and the purported killer of Vincent Coll all dropped by. One night Lindsay attended a dinner tossed by underworld figures in Damon's honor. He later reported that no one on Broadway talked the way Damon had them talking.

Murder was successful enough to achieve a Hollywood sale, $50,000 for Damon and Lindsay. Around this time MGM asked Damon if he would write a story suitable for Eddie Cantor.

"Sure," he said, "but I need thinking money."

"Thinking money?"

"My mind doesn't work very well until I get a check."

He was paid $5,000. He came up with an idea in which Cantor was a desk clerk who was aided in his work by a seal. Damon received another $15,000 for writing a treatment. MGM decided against the movie. Damon kept the idea and the $20,000.

Damon took his money where he found it. A favorite charity of Mrs. Hearst was free milk for the children of the poor. Back in the twenties, Damon came up with the idea of promoting fights to benefit the Milk Fund. These were commercial, and sometimes artistic, successes, and the bookkeeping was imaginative. Damon, as always, was close-mouthed, but his colleague, Bill Farnsworth, liked to shock younger reporters by pointing to a Cadillac Farnsworth had bought after a Milk Fund fight.

It used to be an axiom that the man who controlled the heavyweight champion of the world controlled all of boxing. A ticket speculator named Mike Jacobs broke the stranglehold of Madison Square Garden on the Sweet Science by tying up promotional rights to Joe Louis's fights.

His organization was called the Twentieth Century Sporting Club, and it was revealed by an enterprising journalist that Damon, Farnsworth, and Ed Frayne, sports editor of the *American,* each owned 25 percent of Twentieth Century.

This put the boys in the dilemma of reporting their own promotions. In journalism school that might be viewed as unethical, at least a conflict of interest, but in the avaricious world of Hearst the revelation apparently stirred no emotion except admiration, and Damon, Farnsworth, and Frayne managed to control their qualms.

In addition to fight promotion, movie- and playwriting, the Broadway stories and his columns, Damon worked other veins. A couple of them were outgrowths of work he did for special sections of the newspaper. He had started as far back as 1923 with sketches called

"My Old Home Town," fictive memories of his Colorado boyhood. These were interrupted when Damon and such other contributors as Bugs Baer and Fowler learned that their work was being pirated. You did not fool around with Damon on money matters.

Another series, "Our Old Man," purported to be the philosophies of the narrator's father, but the columns were clearly more Damon than Al Runyan, a chance for Damon to speak more frankly than he might feel free to do in his own name. There was, for instance, a day when Our Old Man stepped into a church to get out of the rain and was called on to speak. This gave Damon-as-Al safe conduct for a comment on the hypocrisy of the self-satisfied:

> Our Old Man said he often attended various churches although he did not belong to any one. He said he often wished he could join some church but that he felt it would be improper, if not false pretense, for him to do so until he had completely adjusted his conduct and his thought to the teachings of the church. He said he was going to wait until he was dead certain he could sit in church on Sunday accepting the teachings in his mind and heart without feeling on Monday that he might be tempted to skin a neighbor in a business dicker.
>
> He said he was certainly delighted, however, to see so many of his fellow citizens who had obviously arrived at the adjustment of which he spoke. He said they must have arrived at this adjustment, else they would not be there. He said he was sure they would not be assembled in that holy place accepting the sacred teachings if they were men who collected rents from the poor for rat-ridden, disease-breeding shacks, or who double-crossed their pals or swindled their customers.
>
> Or if they were men who mistreated their wives, or indulged in riotous living, or profited at the expense of the unfortunate in any way.

That was about as close as Damon got to stirring up the clientele. He continued to view life through the prism of ambivalence he had picked up in boyhood, through which the distinction blurred between the law and lawfulness.

In the midthirties Hearst ordained a crusade against the underworld, and Damon seemed an obvious choice to carry the banner, a man who "has studied and written about the racket game and the racketeer . . . the last score of years," as a promotional blurb put it. Damon's conclusion, however, was that government and business

227

exemplified the really big rackets, the Ohio gang of President Harding and "the bankers who made a racket of the banks as disclosed by the evidence in scores of cases in the last few years." Compared to them, Damon said, Al Capone was "a small timer."

In general, Damon kept a public peace with society. When the columnist Leonard Lyons asked him why he appeared to believe one way but to write another, Damon looked at him with steely eyes, smiled his mirthless smile, and said, "I never bite the hand that feeds me."

The most successful of Damon's forays into the special section of the Hearst Sunday newspapers were the Joe and Ethel Turp stories, which were told as letters written by a young husband in Brooklyn. They were unremittingly warmhearted, and one of them, "A Call on the President," became a movie in 1939. (". . . She ses I bet anything the President of the United States would give Jim the Mailman back his job if we tell him about it. I ses Ethel sugar plum, the President of the United States lives in Washington and he is a busy fellow, and I do not think he would have time to see us even if we went there, and she ses now there you go rooting against yourself like you always do. . . .")

Hollywood paid Damon $5,000 for that one-page sketch, which appeared in Hearst's *Pictorial Weekly*. When Frank Nugent of the *Times* called the movie "as transparent as Runyon himself," Damon explained his approach in a column: "It is a method founded on the ancient formula of make 'em laugh and make 'em cry, of which a chap named Charles Dickens was the all-time master hand. It is a highly commercial method, largely employed by fiction mercenaries of the typewriter after they abandon the idea of being Voltaire. We adopted it as soon as we discovered that the theory that two could live as cheaply as one was walnut shells.

Hollywood stayed in touch with Broadway.

Hellinger returned from California to make the rounds with Walter, having produced his first big movie success, *The Roaring Twenties*, with Jimmy Cagney, Priscilla Lane, and a newcomer from New York named Humphrey Bogart.

Walter asked Hellinger if he noticed any changes along Broadway. "Not at all," Hellinger said. "Ten years ago, we'd be saying goodbye to Billy LaHiff instead of Toots; ten years ago we'd go to Texas Guinan's, today it's the Stork Club; ten years ago, we'd get a kick out of rubbing shoulders with gangsters; today, it's J. Edgar Hoover and his boys; and to prove that things haven't changed a bit, Walter, you just asked for the check—and I paid it."

Walter and J. Edgar Hoover were all but rubbing *noses*. Through the bifocals of hindsight, Hoover—particularly in his later years—appears as a Wizard of Oz, nine-tenths puffery. It is difficult to see him as the colossus he once seemed, swinging for decades through the jungle of celebrity like a Tarzan, beyond the reach of mere presidents, and Walter was his Edgar Rice Burroughs.

Hoover had taken over the grubby Federal Bureau of Investigation in 1924, when it was only a murky little corner in the scandaled labyrinth left over from the Harding administration. He cleaned it up. The Bureau remained as unknown to the general public as the Bill of Rights until, in the 1930s, the FBI was called on to crack down on the wave of kidnappings, bank robberies, and other lawlessness which seemed to plague the America of the depression.

A cornered thug coined the phrase "G-Man"; some genius of publicity came up with the idea of a Ten Most Wanted list of criminals; the times obliged with villains named Dillinger and Pretty Boy and Machine Gun and Baby Face and even Ma Barker, and before America knew it, it was listening to "The FBI in Peace and War." Walter was Hoover's prophet.

Hoover brought Walter to Washington for a tour of FBI headquarters. He wrote Walter that he had addressed a newspaper editors' convention after Hauptmann's arrest:

> I pointed out, without, of course, mentioning the name specifically, how a well-known columnist had refrained from printing a truly national and international scoop on the Lindbergh case for twenty-four hours, in order not to harm the investigation. . . .
>
> Of course, you know who that person is. The entire speech is "off the record," but I thought the editors should know that there was at least one columnist who put patriotism and the safety of society above any mercenary attitude in his profession.

Gauvreau disputed that claim. He also had received a note of commendation from Hoover. No matter. Walter had *his* letter framed and placed over the desk in his office. Hoover seldom held a news conference, but he played the press like a piccolo.

The little drama of Waiting for Lepke should have put Walter and Hoover's friendship on the front pages. Louis Buchalter was a product of the Lower East Side, where his mother lovingly called him Lepkeleh, or Little Louis. What the stocky, shy little fellow became was head of Murder, Inc., a vice and extortion racket which preyed on industrial New York. In a time of vast unemployment Lepke offered his enforcers steady work at up to $150 a week, a nice salary and you couldn't beat the hours. Murder was the ultimate bargaining point. Between 1922 and 1933 Lepke was arrested eleven times, but he always went free, often through the brutally simple device of ordering potential witnesses rubbed out. "You're forty-five years old?" he asked one of them. "You have lived too long."

In 1936 Lepke was arrested on charges of racketeering in the fur industry. He was freed on $10,000 bail by a Tammany hack who was later convicted of selling justice. Lepke jumped bail and walked the streets of Sodom on the Hudson for two years, disguised somewhat by a little added weight and a mustache.

But District Attorney Thomas E. Dewey, en route to the governor's chair and, as he believed in his heart of hearts, the White House, offered a reward of $25,000 for Lepke, dead or alive. The FBI matched the offer, with the fussy proviso that it wanted Lepke alive.

Alive is what Lepke wanted to be, and he figured that he would not be shot if he turned himself in with Hoover's friend Walter in attendance. He also believed the federal government, which was after him on a drug-smuggling charge, would be more lenient than the State of New York, which was thinking in terms of the electric chair.

Walter's friend and collaborator, Irving Hoffman, received a phone call in which he was told, "Lepke wants to come in. He's heard the New York cops will bump him off and say he was trying to escape. He wants to surrender to Winchell, no strings attached."

The identity of the caller was a mystery, or Hoffman made it a mystery, but he passed the word along to Walter, who called Hoover. Letting the Bureau run itself, Hoover went to New York for the surrender. If the FBI chief was not in the class of Bernard Baruch, a man in Murray Kempton's phrase who could hear the sound of film being put in a camera ten miles away, he did not object to a little personal publicity.

Walter and Hoover waited for two weeks; negotiations for the surrender were complicated. Phone-call arrangements for the surrender fell through. Walter finally lost patience and told the caller that if Lepke didn't turn himself in within twenty-four hours, the deal was off.

Finally, on the night of August 25, 1939, the meeting of the nation's top cop and the man Dewey described as "probably the most dangerous criminal in the United States" took place, engineered by Walter, who described it the next morning in the tradition of the great scoop:

230

The surrender of public enemy "Lepke" Buchalter to the government last night took place while scores of pedestrians ambled by, and two police radio cars waited for lights to change, near Twenty-Eighth Street and Fifth Avenue.

The time was precisely 10:17 P.M., and the search for the most wanted fugitive in the nation was over. The surrender was negotiated by this reporter, whom G-man John Edgar Hoover authorized to guarantee "safe delivery."

Following instructions, Walter had picked up Lepke on Madison Square. He drove to the designated drop, where Hoover was waiting, disguised in sunglasses.

"'Mr. Hoover,' we said, 'this is Lepke.'

"'How do you do?' Mr. Hoover said affably.

"'Glad to meet you,' replied Lepke. 'Let's go.'"

The story was fragrant with irony. When Walter called the city desk with his scoop, he was told the Nazis had just invaded Poland. Even the *Mirror* recognized that the start of World War II was a bigger story than the surrender of the nation's top exterminator. When Walter called home, as he often did in moments of triumph, June told him Walter, Jr., had just hurt himself in a fall and why wasn't Walter ever around when his son needed him?

And finally, it was later learned that Lepke surrendered on the command of Walter's neighbor in the Majestic, Frank Costello. Costello, whom Walter called Francisco in his familiar way, was a criminal of far greater puissance than Lepke. Walter liked him and had introduced him to Hoover. It was all like playing cops and robbers. Costello backed Frank Erickson, widely identified as the nation's leading bookie. Erickson sometimes gave Costello tips on races which Costello relayed to Walter to tell Hoover, who was a follower of the bangtails. When Hoover warned Costello that if Lepke didn't surrender, the FBI would "declare war on the underworld," Costello persuaded the fugitive to turn himself in. For all the maneuvering, Lepke wound up in the electric chair.

Walter was turning his and his readers' attention toward a more frightening kind of criminal, identified in the idiom of the day as the international gangster. "Winchell has been engaged more recently," McKelway wrote in 1940, "in a campaign that he calls 'The Winchell Column Versus The Fifth Column,' in which he directs the attention of his readers to various hairdressers, hat-check girls, press agents, etc., whom he accuses of waiting hopefully for Nazi parachutists to come and spying busily the rest of the time."

That was a curiously flip sentence to be writing in 1940.

It would be more than two decades before Hannah Arendt isolated the process as "the banality of evil," but even in the late thirties it was known that the ragtag and disaffected, undoubtedly including some hairdressers, etc., were precisely the sort of people Hitler recruited in the early going. History makes it easy to root for the good guys, at least in part because we know who the bad guys are. When Walter started his campaign against the Nazis, many Americans were not so sure about the villains.

Walter's employer was a great admirer of Mussolini. "He is a marvelous man," Hearst wrote after a 1931 visit with Il Duce. "It is astonishing to see how he takes care of every detail of his job." The German press quoted Hearst as saying, "If Hitler succeeds in pointing the way of peace and order, he will have accomplished a measure of good not only for his people but for all people."

Hearst claimed he was misquoted, but he was impressed with Nazi "efficiency," particularly in handling labor. Brisbane was judicious: "Hitler is a youngster, confident of his power to dictate to the people of Germany. Perhaps he will succeed."

That, of course, was the Hearst press, which the discriminating could dismiss as sensational. But *Time* magazine was as middle-class as orthodonture and the mortgage, and in 1934 Henry Luce was saying, "The moral force of Fascism, appearing in totally different forms in different nations, may be the inspiration for the next general march of mankind." Italians, *Time* reported, "were fired by the excitement of [Mussolini's] purpose," as "Fascism has all but conquered all of Europe and half of Asia." Mussolini appeared on *Time's* cover a record five times by the midthirties, supported by generally favorable notices.

As for Hitler, *Time* believed, "Even to intelligent Germans, it began to seem that the Hitler regime might be useful in getting Germany's international dirty work done." Did Germany break a treaty? *Time* tolerantly called that "Hitler's exit from the jam-closet, sticky-faced" and chuckled "Germany has been naughty but is not to be spanked." *Time* accepted Hitler's version of the inevitability of Hitler: "The Treaty of Versailles all but wrote into its text the eventual arrival of Adolf Hitler upon the world scene."

Time's coverage of foreign affairs was described by two adjectives often applied to Walter's column—"lively" and "gossipy." It was, said Dwight MacDonald, filled with every virtue "except such dull ones as honesty and accuracy."

Racism and anti-Semitism were not left to the street-corner thug, of whom there were plenty. *Time* punctiliously noted the birthname of

232

Jews who had changed their names, without examining the reasons why they may have thought it prudent to do so. To *Time,* the premier of France was always "Jew Blum."

Mussolini's invasion of Ethiopia, according to *Time,* was heralded by the Italian people "who were saying, in their own way, 'We hold these truths to be self-evident.'" *Time* described Ethiopia as "the hell-hole of creation," called its soldiers cowards, and smirked that its women were "fashionably tallowed with Ethiopian grease."

The more sensitive writers who toiled for Luce in the 1930s often fled to the back of the book, as it was called, the arts and sciences sections, to escape the biased taint of its national and international departments. But the master's touch was everywhere.

Time clearly approved of a skit in George White's *Scandals* which offered the most cosmopolitan city in the world Hailie Selassie as a character who cries, "'Boys, our country am menaced! What is we gwine to do?' From then until the curtain falls amid applause which almost stops the show, His Majesty and guardsmen execute a hilarious tap dance."

Yet one did not have to be a premature anti-Fascist, or even a liberal, to see the dark road ahead. The wickedness was apparent to any working newsman with eyes. Westbrook Pegler, who died so far to the right he fell off the edge and who incidentally despised Walter, returned from Germany in 1933 horrified by "the ferocity of Hitler's Ku Klux." To those curious as to exactly what Hitler's anti-Semitism meant, Pegler explained:

> The German child who is a Jew is compelled to listen to the most unspeakable vilification of his parents, and the child's first attempt at spelling out public notices on the billboards will inform him that he is not a human being like other children, but a beast whose parents are not human beings, either, but loathsome animals. . . .
>
> It is absolutely certain that their childhood, the few hours of innocence which are given to all of us and which civilized people try to invest with beauty and joy, has been destroyed by a man with a mustache, adopted from the makeup of a famous comedian. . . . It would be a mistake to call him a baby-killer. You can't torture a dead child.

Pegler, of course, did not foresee the death camps.

The "moral force of Fascism" took a somewhat different form in Spain, and there was pressure on American Catholics to support Franco. To *Time,* the Spanish Civil War did not match Loyalists and rebels but Reds and Whites, and Franco's program was "Back to Normalcy for Spain." Scripps-Howard, on the grounds that it might offend readers, suppressed a column written by Pegler, a Catholic. His conclusion: "If I were a Spaniard who had seen Franco's missionary work among the children, I might see him in hell but never in church."

No signal pierced the dark night of the thirties more strongly, more consistently, than Walter's. Through his broadcasts and more than eight hundred newspapers, he reached millions. He emulated Pulitzer, although it's unlikely he thought of it that way, with his gossip, the hula dancer, enticing his audience to the cathedral of his polemic.

Walter was at home in the gutter, and he went after the Ratzis, as he called them, the swastinkas and swasticooties, with allegations of homosexuality. He compared Hitler to the "yoo hoo boys of the swishy set," calling him "Adele Hitler," asking, "Didn't you scream at the way Hitler lifted his eyes in yesterday's *Mirror?*"

He preached, "People will not bow before the swastika 2000 years from now, but they will kneel before the Cross. If a tomb cannot hold a man's soul, a concentration camp cannot hold his spirit. Men will follow a rosary where they cannot be driven by a whip."

He was Little Boy Peep, the insolent, even dangerous tattler:

> Paul Rocky (the Rocky twins, whoopsy dancers) is now a German film idol! And a devoted chum of Adolf . . . His real handle is Paul Rosenberg, a Joosh boy, and Hitler knows it . . . Stephanie Hohenloe, Nazi Germany's most important official hostess, en route to join Capt. Fritz Wiedman, new Nazi consul in San Francisco, is a Jewess. Her mother, a noted Jewish beauty (during the Kaiser regime) now wears a swastika on her necklace as she makes the social rounds.

If all this seems petty or obvious, it was enough in April 1933 to get Walter's picture in the Nazi's *Völkischer Beobachter,* which identified him as "A New Hater of the New Germany," and said, "His listeners and readers are morons."

Walter identified the man many of the disaffected turned to in 1933: "Fritz Kuhn, who poses as a chemist for a motor magnate, is Hitler's secret agent in the United States." The motor magnate was Henry Ford. Like Hitler, Kuhn would have been a figure of fun, if he had not been so dreadful. He was bowlegged and bullnecked with a coarse, jut-jawed face and the cold eyes of the fanatic, the prototypical storm trooper with a comic-hall German accent: "De Joos, dey are persecuting me again. . . ."

Kuhn was born in Munich on May 15, 1896. He was not exactly kicked out of Germany, but he was encouraged to leave after stealing three thousand marks' worth of clothes. He emigrated to Mexico in 1922. Five years later he was in the United States, and he was naturalized in Detroit in 1934, already swaggering around in his blue-gray uniform, head of the German-American Bund, "heiled" by his followers.

The German-American Bund traced its origins to the Chicago unit of the Teutonia Club in 1924, which became the Friends of Hitler Movement and, in 1933, Friends of the New Germany. By 1936, the organization was the German-American Bund, and Kuhn was its *Bundesführer*. It was backed by Nazi money and controlled by the Foreign Section of the Nazi party, which was spending an estimated $300 million a year to promote world revolution. There may have been manicurists and press agents in the ranks, but they were not kidding around. It is given to all men to dream and Bundists divided the United States into three districts, each with its own *Führer* or *Gauleiter*. Fifty-seven Bund cells, according to an undercover agent calling himself John Roy Carlson, "were subdivided into *Ordnungsdienste* (uniformed state troopers); *Jungenschaften und Mädchenschaften* (the male and female Hitler Youth Corps); *Frauenschaften* (women's auxiliary), and the *Deutsche Konsumverband,* or the German-American Business League, which . . . published a business guide boycotting anyone not in sympathy with it."

This was during the depression; there were a good many desperate people looking for simple solutions. Both left and right promised answers while democracy, as always, said "maybe." The first amendment guarantees the promulgation of bosh—even in the enlightened eighties oddball prophets wander the land—and Bundists were not in touch with reality. "Germans in America, too, have experienced their Versailles," wrote a Nazi of Scot ancestry. "A man will arise and rally them, a German Thomas Paine."

The Bund spawned fronts to cover its activities. The overseas section of the Nazi party claimed that in 1936 it maintained twenty thousand German organizations in the United States. It had its friends in Congress, on Park Avenue, and in the pulpit. Kuhn's view of Christianity was skewed; he argued that Christ was an Armenian.

Much of the potential for terror was on paper, of course, but Walter's warnings were not fantasy. His sources were good, and beginning in 1936 he was joined by a young man from the Bronx named Herman Klurfeld who began contributing gags as a sixteen-year-old schoolboy and, by his own estimate, wrote more than four thousand columns for Walter over the next twenty-seven years. The ease with which Walter switched from gagman to political pundit demonstrated both the strength and weakness of his operation.

Klurfeld first enjoyed success with Walter by offering witty observations on behalf of a notoriously solemn bandleader named Enoch Light. Klurfeld made Light the wit of Lindy's. Then Walter tired of running items about the bandleader, and none appeared for a couple of weeks. Light accosted young Klurfeld. "Hey, kid," he demanded, "what's become of my sense of humor?" That line has been attributed to others, including Arthur Murray, the dance instructor, but Klurfeld insists Light originated it.

Henny Youngman one day supplied Klurfeld with a string of one-liners which Klurfeld passed along to Walter. "They were returned with a note saying, 'This is Jack Waldron's entire act,'" Klurfeld recalled. "I was a kid. How was I to know?"

Klurfeld also was a serious young man, "raised on *The New Republic*." He began writing anti-Nazi material. There was no shortage of sources, he remembered; other newspapermen like Meyer Berger of the *Times* contributed stuff they couldn't get into their own papers.

The main source was Arnold Forster, general counsel and director of the Anti-Defamation League of B'nai B'rith. In 1938, not long out of St. John's law school, Forster and some friends got into a scrap with demonstrators shouting anti-Semitic slogans. Forster took to hauling soapbox orators from Columbus Circle into court, where the charges often were dismissed. Once, Forster told a newsman years later, the judge told the angry young lawyer, "If you want free speech stopped in Columbus Circle, you better dig up Columbus and get him to do it. I won't."

"He was right," Forster said. "Incidentally, the judge's name was Cohen."

Material from Forster, newspapermen, and other sources often stacked a foot high on Walter's desk. Klurfeld mined it, inaugurating a section in the column called "The Headliners," items about figures in the news which anticipated the "About People" columns in newspapers of the seventies. He often ended the section with a quote from Hitler, Goering, or other Nazi leaders topped, of course, with a wisecrack.

"That's when Walter decided he didn't want my stuff going anywhere else, in 1938. He asked me to come to work for him,"

Klurfeld said recently. "He asked me what I was making. I said $25 a week. He said, 'I'll double it.' That's when I made my big mistake—I should have told him $100."

Klurfeld's employment with Walter was a well-kept secret for almost twenty years. In the beginning Walter paid him in cash, so there would be no record he didn't do everything himself. Klurfeld believes this was self-defeating. "All those years, people assumed Walter had a huge, secret staff," he said. "It would have been better if they'd known the truth."

There were more than monetary rewards for Klurfeld.

"The most memorable part of my relationship with Walter wasn't the business part of it," he recalled one summer's day in the Boca Raton condominium where he was living in 1979. "It was the quiet afternoons and evenings, sometimes mornings, at his apartment in the St. Moritz or the Majestic."

Sometimes Walter cooked. One night he prepared pot roast and potatoes for the two men. As they were leaving the kitchen, he spotted a slice of uneaten bread on a plate. He put it back in the breadbox. "You can never tell when I'll need that again," he said. Klurfeld thought he might be kidding, but he saw that he wasn't.

When the two men rode through Broadway at night in Walter's car, they sometimes played a kind of numbers game, betting on the next code number to come over the police radio. One night Walter won $40, just about Klurfeld's salary. As they rode up in the elevator at the Majestic, Walter said, "I bet you think I'm going to return that money to you." Klurfeld said, "Yes." "Well," said Walter, "I'm not. It will teach you a lesson about gambling."

For the young contributor there was a rewarding sense of power, however anonymous. One of Klurfeld's jobs was to write page four of the Sunday night broadcast, generally a word about Nazis and their sympathizers. One night he was stuck for an item when he noticed the galleys of a new book. It was called *Under Cover,* by a writer using the pseudonym of John Roy Carlson, who had joined various Nazi and right-wing groups around the country. A score of publishers had rejected the book, but Klurfeld liked it and wrote a rave. The chance review ignited a literary explosion.

"Published in 1942," an E.P. Dutton publicist wrote in 1979, *"Under Cover* had to be reprinted again and again, thanks to the zeal with which Walter Winchell called attention to it. There was a never-ending demand for it, slowed only by the war-time lack of paper the publisher could obtain.... Eventually, it sold close to a million copies."

The Steuben Society already had sponsored a *Deutscher Tag*

celebration in a Madison Square Garden draped with swastikas when Walter commented on the Bund's boldest push for publicity in 1939: "The Ratzis are going to celebrate George Washington's birthday at Madison Square Garden—claiming G.W. to be the nation's first Fritz Kuhn . . . There must be some mistake. Don't they mean Benedict Arnold?"

Twenty thousand Bundsmen and their sympathizers attended the rally under the eyes of two thousand police. The first amendment bent, but it did not break, as speakers denounced Jews under a thirty-by fifteen-foot portrait of Washington flanked by United States and Nazi flags. A young Jewish hotel worker who dashed on stage as Kuhn was speaking was beaten and his clothing was ripped by storm troopers. It was almost like the old country. There were thirteen arrests, most of them involving pickets outside the Garden.

Dorothy Thompson, the internationalist columnist for the *Herald Tribune* and the original Woman of the Year, was escorted out by the police when, as Walter said in nominating her for a Pulitzer prize, "she laughed at the idiocies . . . during the Ratzi's demonstration of how to bite the hand that feeds you."

If Walter was not alone, he was out front in all of this, and the crusade was not without danger, personal and professional. One December night in 1935 he was set upon by two thugs as he emerged from the barber shop. They ran off after bloodying Walter's face and loosening a tooth. They were never identified, and Walter had more enemies than the elder Bennett, so it was not easy to narrow the list of suspects, but he claimed they were Nazi sympathizers.

A more substantial threat was posed by Walter's employer. Hearst was disturbed by Walter's growing stridency about the Nazis. In March 1938 he instructed his editors, "Please edit Winchell very carefully and leave out any dangerous or disagreeable paragraphs. Indeed, leave out the whole column without hesitation, as I think he has gotten so careless that he is no longer of any particular value."

Editors immediately reacted by slashing the column, many of them deleting any item that wasn't Broadway gossip. Klurfeld wrote that Walter resigned five times between April 1 and April 15. "As a matter of fact, he resigned four times in three days." But the contract with Hearst was ironclad. Hearst knew that Walter had a standing offer to go to the *News* for more money; he also knew that surveys indicated Walter accounted for one-third of the *Mirror*'s circulation. For his part, Walter, outwardly so brash, fretted, "What if I lose my column? Then I'm no different than the loudmouth in the bar."

Others were bewildered by Walter's sudden defense of the Jews. Not only was he a non-practicing Jew, he had for years used the column for dialect stories which offended some readers.

> Mefoofsky of the germant district [one item began] was plodding his weary way down Seventh Avenue when a Jewish fairy in shining white garb appeared before him.
> "Mefoofsky," said the fairy, "I got me de power to give you anyt'ing your heart desires. But I ain't got much time, so make vun veesh. Go ahet!"
> Mefoofsky blinked his orbs and breathlessly said, "So I'll take a beelyun dollars, seex hotels mitout no mortgages, all de moovink peecture companies, enough stocks they should fill a fife-ton truck . . ."
> "Here, here, here," said the fairy. "I said you should make vun veesh, not twelf!"
> "I know, I know," alibied the sheepish Mefoofsky, "but how do I know vut you got in stock?"

Bob Thomas reports that one eminent Jew asked Walter to lay off his defense of Jews since "obviously, you know nothing about Jewry and might be misunderstood." But there seemed an element in Walter of what a jurist called the "foul weather Jew," that is, a Jew who is not particularly concerned with his religion until it is threatened.

In spite of all the sniping at his embattled outpost, from Hearst, from coreligionists, and from his targets, Walter continued firing away at what seemed to be a self-perpetuating parade of dangerous crackpots, including the Reverend Gerald B. Winrod, a Kansas fundamentalist who left the United States virtually penniless but returned from a visit to Germany with money enough to pay off his debts and a conviction that "Nazism and Fascism are patriotic and nationalistic."

According to Carlson's *Under Cover,* William Dudley Pelley, who organized his Silver Shirt storm troopers the day after Hitler assumed power, was once called "the most dangerous man in America." He called "on every Gentile in these prostrate United States to form with me an overwhelming juggernaut." His slogans were "Christ or Chaos" and "For Christ and Constitution." Congressional investigators estimated Pelley received more than $160,000 in donations over two depression years.

But the most ominous voice on the surreal landscape belonged to the Reverend Charles E. Coughlin, who from the Shrine of the Little Flower in Royal Oak, Michigan, spawned the National Union for

239

Social Justice, with principles based on fascism. Although he was condemned by the Catholic hierarchy, Father Coughlin was an enormously effective and popular radio orator with a simple creed: "The only unbiased source of truth is Father Coughlin." His weekly magazine, *Social Justice,* reached a circulation of more than one million and his more devoted followers formed the neighborhood Christian Front movement, aimed at combating communism, which, since all Jews were Communists, put the handwriting on the wall.

It was not easy to dismiss these variants on the *Führer;* the great sweep and moan of the depression turned them up by the bucketful. Men with Faulkneresque names like George Deatherage and Colonel Eugene Nelson Sanctuary, women like Elizabeth Dilling and Mrs. Leonora St. George Schuyler, quondam officer of the Daughters of the American Revolution; professional hate merchants like the Reverend Gerald L.K. Smith and Joseph Kamp; organizations like the Silver Shirts, the Black Shirts, the Gray Shirts, and of course the KKK, peddling their publications in meeting halls and on street corners and in living rooms, small towns to metropolises; warning about conspiracies, takeovers, how the depression was *organized* and *controlled,* updating the Protocols of the Elders of Zion, or simply extolling fascism, warning that Communists would unleash niggers to rape wives, sisters, mothers, daughters, warning of Asiatic conspiracies that mysteriously absolved the Japanese, who were on a civilizing mission to China—so much nonsense that it was hard to keep track.

But Walter kept after them, the Klan, the Nazis, the shirts of many colors. He had infinite resources; there was never any shortage of material piling up on his desk.

He was not quite obsessive about it. There was always plenty of gossip and gags. But he was remorseless in his pursuit of alleged perpetrators. He kept after Fritz Kuhn, who finally was arrested and charged with forgery and grand larceny in his handling of Bund money. Kuhn insisted the leadership principle allowed him to do as he pleased with the funds; it was ridiculous expecting a *Bundesführer* with big things on his mind to bother with bookkeeping.

Kuhn was convicted and sent to prison, where he had to be segregated because other inmates wanted to kill him. Kuhn wept. In 1943 he was deprived of his citizenship, and two years later, he was deported to Germany.

It was never easy to know whom to take seriously; if this group was a small collection of the ragtag, that one could fill the Garden. Joe McWilliams, for example, born on a Cheyenne Indian reservation in 1904—what was there to make of him?

McWilliams went to New York in the twenties, peddling mechanical gadgets of his own invention. A newsman remembered him in the thirties as "a good-looking guy, kind of a frustrated actor." In 1933 McWilliams attended the Communist Workers School and later was affiliated with the Trotskyites. Jewish friends took him to Florida two years later to recuperate from rheumatic fever.

In 1939 he made a sudden turn to the right. He formed a very tough group called the Christian Mobilizers, ex-convicts, rapists, pimps, strong-arm men, all good Aryans, of course. He announced formation of an American Destiny Party, its symbol the covered wagon.

He was an orator. He told his audience, "This is another revolution. A revolution for a nationalist America. Don't let anyone tell you anything different. It's a revolution against the Jews first, then against democracy, then against both the Republican and Democratic parties. Both are rotten. Both useless. . . . We are fighting for a Christian Aryan America."

Walter called McWilliams Joe McNazi and Joe McJerk and outraged him by quoting from McWilliams' off-the-record speeches "to a few criminals in Bronx basements." Others called him "the Little Führer of Yorkville," a predominantly German section of Manhattan's East Side. A picture magazine ran an article about McWilliams asking, "Is this the American Hitler?"

A newsman who had known him earlier sought him out and asked him about the article. McWilliams said, "Listen, I'm getting paid $200 a week for this." The newsman asked him where the money came from. McWilliams said, "I don't know. But it's a living."

Walter appealed to Mayor LaGuardia and the police, charging that McWilliams was inciting riot. McWilliams was arrested, found guilty of disorderly conduct, and freed when he promised not to do it again. Walter commented, "That's like taking Hitler's word when he says he wants peace."

McWilliams, of course, couldn't last long without hearing the sound of his own voice, and he soon was back talking about "kicking the kikes out of America." He was arrested again. After a psychiatric examination determined that he was sane, or anyway capable of understanding what he was doing, he was imprisoned. He left New York after he was released and turned up in Chicago as an industrial engineer. Walter's column followed him. McWilliams went to Akron. So did the column, remorseless.

Even his enemies conceded that Walter was a big man on the American scene. He was no longer simply an ex-hoofer turned gossip columnist. It was not just that he pursued evildoers like some comic strip superhero. He was dealing with members of Congress, with the

Prime Minister of England, with the President of the United States.

After all these activities and the outbreak of he greatest war in history, it seemed remarkable that Walter found time for the late-blooming friendship with Damon, that he would prove himself the truest of friends and become a comforting presence in seeing Damon through the wreck and tragedy and pain of his final days.

thirteen

WINCHELL KEPT me out until broad daylight two nights hand-running, mostly just walking around. I do not mind awaiting daylight in some pleasant deadfall but walking around is no good for me, and Walter cannot show me that it is of any benefit to him, either. Because he walks around a heap, he always has a beef about not feeling any too well, and he gets balder by the minute.

Of course, I was onto Winchell while he was walking me around. I knew he wanted company and that he wanted to talk. I made the ideal companion inasmuch as I am unable to articulate and he did not have to listen to my replies.

That explanation of the friendship between Damon and Walter, which Damon offered in a column, comes pretty close to dissembling, for by the time the two men became close it was Damon who desperately needed the companionship, while Walter, whose career was in full cry, had a wide choice of comrades of both sexes.

There is no indication that the two did much more than nod in passing in the earlier years, although Walter often mentioned Damon with a line or two of praise in his column. As the 1940s opened, they did not even share a city.

Damon was out in Hollywood, on what seemed to be a semipermanent basis. He went out there with a screenwriter named Leonard Spigelgass he'd expressed interest in working with. Spigelgass had come east to meet Damon. The rendezvous took place at midnight at Lindy's. "That figured," Spigelgass later wrote. He joined Damon, Patrice, and a Broadway mob including Leonard Lyons, finding "the dialogue was fast, special, and a little out of my line." He didn't think he had a chance for the job, didn't know if he wanted it, and didn't think Damon much took to him.

They met again the next afternoon in Damon's Parc Vendome apartment to discuss "Butch Minds the Baby" and "Tight Shoes," stories which Damon had sold to Universal Pictures.

After being chewed "by three of the most badly-behaved cocker spaniels on record," Spigelgass "went into Damon's study, surprised to find that it was Louis XVI and very formal, when I'd expected a cluttered desk and pictures of Jack Dempsey and Joe Louis." The meeting started off badly. Neither man liked the other's ideas on "Tight Shoes"; Damon believed great pictures had been made out of "Little Miss Marker" and "Madame La Gimp"; but he didn't like "Princess O'Hara," which Spigelgass had produced. Neither did Spigelgass.

"I kept sizing him up, those chilly eyes and that florid complexion," Spigelgass wrote, "the loud Glen Urquhart plaid suit and the lavish Charvet tie, the gold cigarette case and his cold and incisive voice."

But things began to work as the two men discussed "Butch Minds the Baby," each applauding the other's suggestion, then topping it. Damon showed Spigelgass a New York the tourist may miss, including a traveling crap game, and then the two men set off for Hollywood. They rode out on the Century (nobody flew in those days), and Spigelgass recalled that when they reached Chicago the following morning:

> We were met by every sports writer, jockey, prize fighter . . . baseball player and wise guy in town. They had a gala luncheon for [Damon] at the Blackstone, and I saw happen there what I'd seen in Lindy's and at the Yankee Stadium . . . and in little candy stores where bookies hung out, and at the opening nights and in Washington—the same thing all over again, the adoration of men and women who looked upon Damon as their best friend, who respected him, told him their secrets. . . . I guess Damon knew more dirt than any man living, and I guess Damon told less.

Wherever the train stopped across the country, Spigelgass wrote, it was like that, "guys got on, jockeys who were retired, or ball players who were tubercular, or just characters on the lam, and they looked at him with love."

Spigelgass said Damon "thought screenwriting was one of the hardest jobs in the world, said he could never do it. He never did, either. Best I ever got out of him were occasional lines of dialogue. The rest, I assure you, I stole hook, line and sinker from his stories." Damon believed screenwriting required the attributes of "a novelist, a playwright and a civil engineer."

Damon loved the movies. "I think he saw every picture ever made,"

244

Spiegelgass reported. Damon hated message pictures; he thought the movies were meant to be "fun and jokes and tears." He claimed he preferred movies to the stage because there were no intermissions "when many of the customers surge from their seats up the aisle and back again with charming disregard of courtesy and the comfort of non-surgers."

Damon, not thinking he would like Hollywood, stayed until 1943. He sold "Little Pinks," the story of a busboy with a hopeless love for a self-centered and crippled show girl, for $15,000. He was hired as producer, and he did all right. He kept within his budget, which studio heads appreciated, and he let his staff alone, which is not taught in Producer's College, although it is almost universally approved by writers, directors, and actors. Spiegelgass wrote, "Literally, he understood more about people than anybody I ever knew." *Time* said, "He sees every scene through the eyes of the average movie audience."

Damon faced the traditional struggle of a New Yorker adjusting to southern California, which had no night life to speak of. He kept the shades drawn all day in his one-story house in Beverly Hills. There was no Lindy's or Stork, so he made do with Mike Hyman's, Chasen's, and Prince Mike Romanoff's.

Louis Sobol had taught Damon gin rummy back in New York and he became an addict. He said that Hyman's, "'way, 'way out in California," as he always located the state, was "the gin rummy capital of the world for a short time." This ended when "Hyman examined the books and found he was losing more at gin rummy than the joint was taking in." Damon believed there was "no such thing as 'a friendly game of cards' in which money is involved. A man who tries to take your money is not your friend."

He offered a couple of reminiscences:

> . . . I used to sit by the hour in Romanoff's completely entranced by the voice of John Carradine delivering Hamlet's soliloquy or some other Shakespearean dialogue while leaning against the bar all alone.
>
> At the same time, Monty Woolley might be reading aloud to himself in a nearby booth, usually something in philosophy, and I could turn from one to the other at my pleasure. It was better than going to the library.

Damon affectionately recalled the five Goetz brothers, "all New York City born and all connected with the movies," his favorite being Harry who in 1924 had "produced *The Crimson Stain Murders* with

Maurice Costello, the Clark Gable of the day. Harry personally hand-colored portions of the film. Whenever a murder was to be committed, the murderer's eyes flashed red and Harry hand-tinted the negative himself."

Damon found George Burns to possess almost as singular a talent:

> I am a tough guy to make laugh [he wrote]. I have a dead pan and a soul above laughter, or even chuckles, except on very great provocation. . . .
>
> Yet there is one man who utterly devastates me when he opens his bag of tricks at a private gathering. He has me laughing up and down the scale. His power over my risibilities is something extraordinary. . . .

Burns, Damon noted, had the same effect on Jack Benny, who "literally falls right on the floor laughing at George. What appeals to Jack about George's performance is the seriousness with which George goes about it. He goes at it like a dog. . . . He would not work as hard on stage for a large salary as he does for nothing at a party."

Damon recalled that Burns even upstaged Al Jolson, sent him reaching for his hat, and Jolson, Damon felt, was "one old champion they have yet to equal. . . . He was one of the few performers I ever saw who could hold the stage as long as he pleased without tiring the audience. An hour is a pretty long stretch, but that was duck soup for Joley. . . . You have to talk to veteran actors to get a true measure of Jolson's stage stature in his prime. He was not the most popular man among them that ever lived, but I never heard one deny that he was the greatest of all the entertainers they had ever known."

Damon was idiosyncratic in his tastes. He had no more than two and a half cheers for California's celebrated climate. Like Mark Twain, who believed that California's boosters were weather-vain only because they had never lived in New England, Damon was a man for all the seasons:

> Autumn is the dependable season in the Big Town, and the most glorious anywhere in the whole world. . . . You can go to sleep on the New York autumn, so to speak. Spring and summer and winter are tricky. Autumn is solid as the rock.
>
> For winter and the earlier spring, give me Dade County, Florida. Yes, sir. Yes, ma'am. There is a piece of the spring when Maryland is not hard to take but shifty. I mean, you cannot lay a price on it. The Dade County spring is just wheat in the sun as far as weather is concerned.

For summer, southern California. Well, I will throw in northern California, too, so no one there can feel slighted. Summer in southern California is 100 proof. It is 18-karat. I am aware that Californians set up certain pretensions for their state as a winter resort, and I have often wondered why when they have so much summer merchandise to sell.

It rains out there in the winter.

Toward the end of his life, Damon wrote his son, "I wish I might have continued to live in Beverly Hills and stayed in the movies. I enjoyed life out there and enjoyed making pictures."

The feeling was reciprocated. Spigelgass said Damon "was one of the greatest, sweetest, most intelligent men that ever lived. And if that's sentimental, then it's sentimental."

It was also not a unanimous verdict. Damon's hideous death, his courage in the face of it, and his accomplishments cannot brighten the dark side of his nature. Jimmy Cannon admired Damon not much this side of idolatry, but he once told an acquaintance about a fight manager's experience with Damon.

The manager was down at the heels and desperate for a big payday in New York. He handled a fighter of promise, and he needed a publicity break. He ran into Damon and suggested lunch. Damon eyed the manager's frayed cuffs and collar and runover heels. He said certainly, why didn't they go to 21?

The manager, gulping, agreed. Damon suggested starting things off with mock turtle soup. The manager said no, he'd make do with a cheese sandwich. Sweating, he touted his fighter as Damon ate his way through extensive and expensive courses. At the end, Damon let the manager pick up the tab and never wrote a word about the fighter.

It may be difficult to work up sympathy for a fight manager, but not even those colleagues who were beneficiaries of Damon's enthusiasm and guidance remained admirers, and not necessarily because they were ingrates.

Damon championed Bugs Baer and got him work with Hearst. It was a felicitous move. It was Baer who wrote that staple for a comedian facing an unappreciative audience, "What would you charge to haunt a house?" And he flirted with immortality when he observed that "Paying alimony is like buying oats for a dead horse."

So fecund was Baer that, at the urging of a syndicate man, he began moonlighting a column for the *World* in 1931 under the name Graham Wire. Damon, whose training in frontier print shops taught him to read copy upside down, came across Baer as he was writing "Wiregrams" one day in the *American* office.

"You give me away," Baer warned, "and I'll break your arm."

Damon's discretion, to say nothing of his resourcefulness, was immediately tested. A Hearst lieutenant was so taken with "Wire-grams" that he decreed the organization must hire the writer away from the *World,* and Damon was dispatched to approach "Wire." Damon sweated some, but he returned to the lieutenant with the word that "Wire," while grateful, had promised his old mother that he would never, never work for Hearst. It was a plausible out.

Damon's flawed character was most evident in his handling of his children. Bob Considine put the matter succinctly, writing, "My wife and I had reason to believe he treated his daughter, son-in-law, and Damon, Jr., with something considerably less than paternal affection. He just didn't give a damn."

Considine also had reason to be grateful to Damon. Surveying the younger sportswriters, Damon had told a Hearst official, "One of them, a chap we've already got—Considine. I think he will be a corker when he gets his sights adjusted. He is terrifically ambitious and a hard worker."

In spite of that assist from the star of the organization, Considine found Damon "as thin-skinned as an aging Met soprano." He wrote that Damon "was fussed over by owners and headwaiters at Lindy's, to which he gave great if passing fame as the Mindy's of his Broadway stories." Considine was wrong about that. Lindy's was only made of clay, but Mindy's—Mindy's is here to stay.

In what seems naïveté at the least, Considine could not understand why Damon, at the summit of his fame, was so difficult. The Considines entertained Mary and her husband at dinner. In the course of the evening, Considine paid tribute to Damon, saying, "I'd like to be able to cover a range like that."

The next time he saw Mary, she reported that her father was angry with Considine.

"'What did you tell him?' I asked.

"'What you said,' Mary said. 'That you were out after his job.'"

Considine could look after himself, but the Runyon children were another matter. Mary, in her brother's phrase "that gentle little girl of yesterday who'd sought only affection and attention," suffered a nervous breakdown not long after she became a mother. She spent much of the rest of her life in institutions, occasionally visiting her father and brother in their separate locations. Damon did not do much more than pay the bills; but, of course, by then there was not much more he could have done.

The two Damons endured a father-and-son relationship in which there was more talk than communication and not all that much talk. Damon, Jr., was an adult before he learned that his name really was Damien, the saint's name most closely approximating the name his parents wished him to inherit.

The boy demonstrated his confusion and anger over his parents' warring and their divorce by performing indifferently in school, an area in which his father hoped he would do well. He attended a parochial school with something of a military curriculum. In a rare show of parental concern, Damon withdrew him when he discovered the teachers laid hands on the boy.

When Damon remarried in 1932, it was determined that Damon, Jr., would attend Riverside Military Academy in Gainesville, Georgia. The academy maintained winter quarters in Hollywood, Florida, and Damon thoughtfully pointed out that since he and Patrice wintered in Florida, Damon, Jr., would be able to visit them on weekends and vacations.

Damon, Jr., spent three and a half years at Riverside before quitting. The old man's demonstrations of close order drills in various New York apartments may have had their effect; young Damon was outstanding in military performance, but he did poorly in some of the academic work, drawing artillery barrages from home.

He already had made up his mind to quit when his platoon won a close-order competition. He received the first military efficiency medal awarded a cadet officer of his rank. The ceremonies were witnessed by ten thousand persons, not including his father, although the commandant telephoned Damon, asking him to attend.

But Damon did come to Riverside a few days later, at his son's request. Damon, Jr., told him he was leaving school. Damon took the news "with amazing calm," misunderstanding his son's intentions. He told his son he could attend any school, then any college in the United States. He made it clear that he thought of his son's college career in terms of Harvard, Princeton, or Yale. But Damon, Jr., was determined to be a newspaperman, starting immediately.

"You understand," Damon said, "that once you leave home, there's no turning back." Leave *home!* "I will give you the best education I can afford, but after that, you're on your own."

Damon, Jr., understood. His father spelled it out. "Any school in the United States. Any place you choose where you think you'd be happy, and there'll be no more of those letters from home."

"It's a little late to think about that," the son said.

Within two weeks, Damon, Jr., was working for United Press in Cleveland, where Mary and her husband lived. Damon visited from time to time. "We talked," Damon, Jr., wrote, "but often we were silent for long stretches of time. We never really discussed family or related problems."

Parent and child viewed the past differently. Damon recalled the presents showered on Damon, Jr., and Mary at Christmas, "the most fabulous gifts from people in the world of sport." Damon, Jr., remembered "many of these fabulous gifts were overwhelming to a small child and sometimes downright frightening."

Damon, Jr., didn't return home, and he and his father did not write each other, not even at holiday time, for eight years, not until Damon was a dying man and the son had fought and lost battles with the bottle that saw him fired from successive jobs, saw him in the gutter, hospitalized, suffering from delirium tremens, on point of suicide.

Damon's idyll with Patrice, for that's what it appeared at least from his point of view, wound down. It seemed as much a matter of the difference in age as anything else. But women were, if not enemies, aliens to Damon.

His writing about women frequently was marked by unflattering generalities. Sociologists *manqués* in the press corps insisted, back in 1927, in treating Ruth Snyder as a type, rather than as an individual, and in Damon's copy she was often "the blonde," a woman "who is thirty-three and looks just about that, though you cannot tell much about blondes." He called the seamy tragedy "the old, old yarn— Friend Husband, a nonstepper, Friend Wife, full of go."

Damon even proposed a verity: "Mankind at last has a clue, developed by the Snyder-Gray trial, as to the approximate moment when a blonde becomes very, very dangerous. Gentlemen, if she asks you to try out a few sleeping powders, that is the instant you are to snatch up the old chapeau and take the air."

All very hard-boiled and witty, but Damon didn't propound any theory about Gray as Everyman, beyond observing that he was the eternal chump. It was easier to consign women to a category; hadn't Damon sighed to his young son ". . . you can't live with 'em and you can't live without 'em"?

The dolls who parade through Damon's fiction are a various lot. There are *naifs* like Lily of St. Pierre and Clarice Van Cleve, who so entrances Sam the Gonoph, Liverlips, and Jew Louie that they wind up brawling in defense of the goalposts as they save her from Gigolo Georgie in "Hold 'Em Yale." There are bag ladies. There is the murderous old Widow Crumb of "Lonely Heart." There is Mousie. Itchky Ironhat of "Old Em's Kentucky Home" prefers his fourteen-

250

year-old racing mare to his shapely wife because "Em never wishes for any thick sirloin steaks such as Mousie adores."

The gorgeous "Dark Dolores," the channel swimmer, disposes of three killers by promising to marry the one who overtakes her as she swims out in the Atlantic. They drop off, one by one.

In general, women in Damon's fiction complicate a man's life and are about as reliable as a toss of the dice. (The dice with which Sarah Brown, she of "the one hundred percent eyes," wins Sky Masterson are loaded.) The best women, in Damon's stories, are pretty and keep their mouths shut.

Through many of the stories, there is a barely concealed antagonism toward women, who interfere with a guy's fun, his gambling, carousing, and skullduggery, an "instinct to get the woman down," as Edmund Wilson wrote of Hemingway, or "a fear that the woman will get the man down."

Damon wrote a column about "my friend" who said that "after he got shed of his second wife, many of his acquaintances came around to tell him that it was a good job because she was no account and they had known it all along, but they didn't want to tell him for fear of hurting his feelings." Telling the "friend," Damon suggested, might have saved him a lot of money and not made him "the laughing stock of tables at the Stork and Toots Shor's and El Morocco's and Child's."

Damon and Patrice had drifted apart in Hollywood. He gave up the Beverly Hills house and rented the entertainer Gertrude Niesen's Holmby Hills residence. He attended Hollywood parties alone. He spent much time with Prince Mike Romanoff, discussing the art museums of Europe, in Romanoff's recollection, and Spengler and Kant.

Damon's favorite of the movies he made with Leonard Spigelgass was *The Big Street,* released in 1942 and based on "Little Pinks." The big-nosed little busboy becomes Henry Fonda, and the shrewish showgirl is Lucille Ball, and when she dies in his arms, the Runyon character called Professor B utters the curtain line: "It is well-known to one and all on Broadway that a citizen never loses what he'd filed away in his ticker."

Damon filed Patrice away in his ticker. The outbreak of World War II found them on the West Coast. Damon was sixty-one. Patrice shortly found work ferrying bombers to the East Coast. She was closer to the action than he was. Perhaps this prompted his reflection on one of war's ultimate injustices: "Old men do all the talking. Old men scheme all the schemes. Old men give all the orders. . . . Surely, they must know how and when it is best for youth to die."

251

Damon produced *When Irish Eyes Are Smiling*, starring the crooner Dick Haymes and June Haver. The movie made money for Twentieth Century-Fox, but by that time Damon had more serious things on his mind.

Gene and Agnes Fowler had long been concerned by a huskiness which made Damon hard to understand, nattering at him to consult a doctor. The story is that Damon took Nubbin, a cocker spaniel he acquired while renting Miss Niesen's house, to a veterinarian. Damon's opinion of doctors was mixed, and while he was there he asked the vet to take a look at his throat. The vet was alarmed by what he saw.

That may be legend, but by early 1944 Damon's throat was so painful that he consulted Dr. Hayes Martin, a New York throat specialist, who ordered him hospitalized.

What the doctor found was a cancer which had spread so thoroughly that Damon's larynx was removed in two operations, beginning on April 10. Damon did not leave the hospital until June. He made one more trip west, returning to New York for good in September.

He was hospitalized for another operation, this time on the lymph glands. There were more operations and treatments with radium. From now on, Dr. Martin said in one of those ominous medical pronouncements, it was "simply a matter of management."

Alone with anger and fear, of course, the death sentence shook Damon's self-regard. The worldly gambler with all the inside information had been a sucker, had blown the biggest stakes of all. He had waited too long to see a doctor. In a situation where he would be, at best, on the short end of the odds, the bet was off the books, he was the kind of wise guy he despised, holding the short end where there was no betting because the odds against him were incalculable.

Damon's hour now was testament to a final lesson learned from Montaigne, his great instructor, "that no man shall be called happy until after his death . . . the earlier acts of our lives must be proved on the touchstone of our last breath."

Whatever his emotions, however, Damon kept them pretty much to himself. He certainly did not display them publicly. He could not talk now, except to whisper words. He carried a little pad of paper captioned "Damon Runyon Says" and penciled his end of the conversation, sometimes in capital letters for emphasis. "Stop shouting," the producer Mike Todd once told him.

So widespread was the cancer that surgeons removed Damon's trachea. A tube in the throat served for eating and drinking. He breathed through another tube which emerged near his collarbone and was covered by gauze to prevent foreign objects from entering his lungs.

Damon was cavalier about this. "I am taking certain medical treatments that have deprived me completely of my sense of taste," he began one column, "a condition I am assured is temporary but which is giving concern to some of my friends." The column turns into bleak comedy as his friends learn Damon cannot taste garlic, stuffed cabbage—a Runyon favorite—horseradish, salt and pepper. They ply him with beverages—beer, chartreuse, champagne, bourbon, but, he says, he can taste none of them. Suddenly the friends realize he is drinking up all their liquor. He sneaks off. "'Let's sing *Sweet Adeline,*' a friend was saying as I departed."

Damon wrote columns about friends who suffered on medically ordered diets, Leo Lindy and Jimmy Durante, who was

> the saddest spectacle I ever witnessed.
>
> When he did not have two white quarters to rub together in his pants pocket, he dreamed of a day when he could step into a restaurant and order all the food he pleased.
>
> Now he's making maybe $200,000 a year, and he has been limited as to food by his croaker or MD. "It's ironical," I said.
>
> "No," said Jimmy. "It's gall bladder trouble."
>
> "Do you mean you can't even have pasta fagioli?" I asked.
>
> "Oh," groaned Jimmy.
>
> "Or lasagna?" I queried.
>
> "Oh, oh," moaned Jimmy.
>
> "Your doctor's a sadist," I said.
>
> "No, he's a Presbyterian. . . ."

Damon cut a little closer to the nerve when he wrote a column called "No Life." In it, the doctor remorselessly reduces his patient's food and beverage list—no orange juice, no grapefruit, no sorghum, no wheatcakes, no sugar; it gets worse—no coffee, no candy, no herring, no gefillte fish, no goulash; it keeps getting worse—no salami, no highly seasoned Italian food and, ultimately, of course, no cigarettes. "Doc," the column ends, "a guy might as well be dead, hey?"

Damon stuffed himself with food. He needed the nourishment, but it also seemed as though chewing was one of the few pleasures left to him. For a time he gained weight. He wrote joyously of accompanying trenchermen from the fight mob, a gaggle of managers, to Ratner's, down on Delancey street. They were "chaps who can look the most pickled of herring in the eye without quailing. . . . I dislike persons

253

who are timid in the presence of herring, the king of fish, or anyway the president of them."

If there was solace for Damon besides the companionship of his friends and the all-night action of Broadway, it was in his reconciliation with his son. Patrice was in Miami at their Hibiscus Island home, and Damon was living alone at the Hotel Buckingham on West Fifty-seventh Street when he returned to the hospital in September 1944 for the operation on his lymph glands.

Damon, Jr., "was allowed five minutes to work out the puzzles of five lifetimes." His father was drowsy with drugs. The son talked enthusiastically about his new job with Cincinnati radio. For the first time since he was a little boy, he held his father's hand.

After Damon, Jr., returned to Cincinnati, he and his father began corresponding. In Damon's first letter, he wrote that Damon, Jr., was wise to settle in a smaller city. "A New Yorker has no community life outside of night clubs and they are expensive and tiresome," he wrote. But then, in his dissatisfaction, Damon had also claimed he wished he lived in Scranton, Pennsylvania.

He adjured his son, "Watch your health. That is about the only advice I have to give nowadays. No one takes advice anyway."

Damon, Jr., certainly didn't. He lasted just five weeks on his new job before getting drunk and getting fired. His father did not hear from him for eight months. Then Damon, Jr., wrote that he "had reached an island of safety by falling into the hands of Alcoholics Anonymous" and Scripps-Howard.

Damon supposed many a great career could have been saved if AA had existed in the old days. He added that "I have only a little time left, as you may surmise from my ailment, but I will go happy if I know you have conquered your enemy."

As he never did publicly, he described for his son the desperate course of his private battle:

I will be 65 in October. I get around all right and feel pretty well, but I live under a shadow. I have to see a doctor every week. I do my daily column and a Sunday feature and last month I wrote two fiction stories for *Collier's*.

I have to keep plugging away at an age when I thought I would be in retirement, because my illness practically broke me. I went to Hollywood at a salary of over $2,000 a week largely as a matter of satisfying my vanity—I thought it was wonderful to be able to command that kind of income at 63— forgetting that it only added to my normal income and increased my taxes.

254

Well, the upshot was that the government took most of it, and when I became ill and the big money was shut off entirely, the doctors and the hospitals cut up what was left. I am now living not only on borrowed time but practically on borrowed money.

Although he poor-mouthed, Damon didn't whine. "But having seen others similarly afflicted," he wrote, "I know that I have no kick coming."

In the first period of his illness, in 1944, Damon's column began appearing irregularly. He told his readers he was running out of things to say. He had been a writing machine all his adult life, "writing others out of the paper," but now he had to husband his energies.

He wrote his son that *Cosmopolitan* offered him $5,000 a story for twelve stories a year, "which strikes me as a trifle ironical as it comes at a time when I could not possibly muster the energy for even a third that much work, while in the period of my greatest activity, when I might have been able to do it, they paid no attention to me."

But somehow, as Edwin Hoyt says, Damon seemed to draw "new life from some hidden source" after January 1945, "life and zest which he poured into his column." He was writing for the *Journal-American* now, which had more space for columns than did the tabloid *Mirror*.

"I never liked doing a column until lately," he wrote Damon, Jr. "I could always make more money with much less effort on fiction. But lately, for some reason, I have taken a fancy to columning, trying to prove, I think, a theory that people seem more interested in people and in things that happen to people than in politics."

Biographer Tom Clark's enthusiasm for Damon's last columns surpassed Hoyt's. He called them "one of the delights of our literature, pieces sometimes as free-roving, conversational and bright as the essays of Addison, sometimes as intelligently reflective as those of Montaigne. If the art of the essay—a form defined perfectly by one great practitioner, Samuel Johnson, as 'a loose sally of the mind'—has reached greater sophistication in this century, it is hard to see where."

Well, it is unnecessary to bring out all that heavy artillery to honor Damon's final accomplishments. Damon knew better. Not long before he died, he visited with John Kieran, the erudite sportswriter he'd helped find work on the old *American*. Kieran ascended, becoming sports columnist for the *Times* and something of a national institution on the radio program *Information Please,* when listeners marveled that a sportwriter knew as much about Plutarch as about the fundamentals of the single wing. On the strength of that celebrity,

Kieran signed to write a syndicated column of general interest. It shortly failed.

> "I could have told you" [Damon wrote]. "I could have told you that beauty and tranquility and quiet rumination have no market nowadays. . . . You write too much like those old-time essayists. . . . Did you ever read a fellow named Addison?"
> "Certainly," said John.
> ". . . Well, he would be a bust today. You couldn't give his stuff away. You couldn't give Lamb's stuff away. Or Montaigne's. Or any of those other old guys who are now called immortals. If an editor printed some of Voltaire's writings, he would get thrown in the jailhouse and the paper would be boycotted."

If there is an implication that John and Damon would write up to Chuck and Mike, given the opportunity, it is a harmless conceit. Many writers delude themselves that circumstances use them cruelly. Damon went along with that fantasy to the extent of writing a column about a "successful" man ready to chuck it all and write a novel until he remembers his obligation to "Harriet. His good wife Harriet. Then he sighs heigh-ho and picks up his oar again and resumes pulling."

Damon's column took on a vitality and dash which removed from the category of a bad joke pieces called "The Brighter Side" written by a dying man. He indulged in reminiscence, recalling John Kelly, the baseball umpire and boxing referee, who found a glass eye and returned it to the notorious gate-crasher, "One-Eye" Connelly, "thereby gaining the name 'Honest John'"; he revisited the Harlem hotel that had been headquarters for the New York Giants many years earlier, discovered it had since been raided as a place of prostitution and was now guarded, at taxpayer's expense, by a cop who asked incoming couples if they were man and wife, "a question that I guarantee you would have been considered impertinent, inconsequential and, indeed, irreverent in the days when I lived there. . . . The old Giants . . . would have dropped a loaded bat bag on his head and gone about their business. I mean of playing baseball."

He even kicked up his heels a little, seeing a blonde bombshell from Hollywood named Marilyn Maxwell singing at a stage show, so far away she appeared naked in a flesh-colored gown, "largely an optical illusion," Damon sighed. "But I have reached a stage where optical illusions are not bad at all."

And now the time arrived for Damon and Walter to become friends, the most consequential friendship of their turbulent lives, Damon and Pythias, a classics-minded Broadway habitué called them.

Walter was at the crest of his career. While Damon was bringing a little bit of Broadway to Hollywood, Walter had been doing the same in Washington, where he was a big enough man to serve as a kind of meteorologist as FDR tested the climate for his third-term run in 1940.

McKelway devoted a chapter of *Gossip* to an examination of Walter's inaccuracies. He dissected five Monday columns for the month of April. (Walter's newsiest stuff usually appeared on Monday. He knew, like Theodore Roosevelt, that Sunday generally is a slow newsday, the western world being deep in prayer, so that Monday morning is the time to break a story.)

"In these five columns," McKelway wrote, "were 239 separate items. Of these, it was discovered that 108 were unverifiable because they were what gossip writers call 'blind' items, in which no names are mentioned, or were expressions of opinion, or were items in which the persons concerned refused to confirm or deny. Thus, 131 items of the 239 were verifiable. Of these, 53 were completely accurate, 24 were partially accurate and 54 were completely inaccurate. . . .

"In other words," McKelway summed up, "on verifiable items, Winchell was not quite half right in the month of April." Herman Klurfeld, reminded of this finding in 1979, was unperturbed. "That's about par for the wire services or most newspapers," he said.

Some of the WWobblies, as they were later called, are ludicrous in that hindsight with which all men are blessed at birth, Walter writing on September 7, 1931, "After having her molars fixed so they will photograph better, Barbara Stanwyck will make no more flickers"; writing on March 29, 1937, "Adolf and Benito have phfft!"; writing on September 18, 1938, "The local stores will be selling television sets for as low as $3.95 by October 1."

McKelway chided Walter for setting down "prophetic items every which way on a coming event, like a man betting on all the horses in a race." He chose as his example various items Walter wrote about Roosevelt's political future: "You can safely bet that FDR positively will not run in 1940." "FDR's choice for President in 1940 is Senator Barkley of Ky." "F.D.R. will run a third term." And so forth.

What McKelway didn't know was that Walter was writing his predictions about Roosevelt more or less on orders from the White House. They were conveyed to Walter by a man named Ernest Cuneo, a Columbia University graduate, lawyer, and journalist who had been introduced to Walter by Leonard Lyons, the columnist. Cuneo had been an aide to LaGuardia, about whom he wrote *Life with Fiorello*

257

many years later, and he was close to those advisors to FDR called The Brain Trust.

It was determined that, more than any political foe, the tradition that no president sought a third term was Roosevelt's chief campaign problem. One way to solve this was to talk it to death, which Walter was good at, manufacturing a flotilla of possible Democratic successors to the president.

"I can't remember how many were 'nominated' by broadcast and column," Cuneo wrote. "Byrd of Virginia, Wheeler of Montana, Earle of Pennsylvania, Bankhead of Alabama, Bailey of North Carolina, Barkley of Kentucky. It got so ridiculous that *The New Yorker* commented, 'Nominate your friends for the Presidency. It makes a harmless, inexpensive and delightful little Christmas present.'"

Ultimately, of course, Walter and the electorate settled on FDR.

Cuneo wrote that Walter was unaware of his power, although when Walter again responded to a White House call by urging his readers and listeners to demand that Congress appropriate funds for a two-ocean navy, 1,200,000 letters swamped the Congressional post office. "Unequivocally, both State and the White House credited Walter with the victory," according to Cuneo.

Cuneo was with Walter when they ran into Joseph P. Kennedy, ambassador to England, who said that Lindbergh's report on Germany's air superiority prompted Prime Minister Chamberlain to hand over Czechoslovakia to the Nazis in the Munich pact. Kennedy also told Walter that England had decided its fleet could do no more than defend the home waters, never mind the colonial outposts. It was a great scoop for Walter although, according to Cuneo, it marked the end of Kennedy's usefulness to FDR.

As war with Germany appeared imminent, Walter cabled Chamberlain with "a layman's suggestion" that the prime minister declare war not against the German people but "against Adolf Hitler personally and his personal regime."

Walter printed his suggestion the next day in his column and the day after *that* was able to report Chamberlain's statement that "'Great Britain did not declare war against the German people, but against Adolf Hitler and the Nazi regime' . . . The suggestion was sent to the Prime Minister in a cablegram, acknowledgment of which has arrived."

This sort of thing infuriated McKelway, who noted that Walter "considers himself an important influence in current affairs—private, national and international." When Walter wrote about the meaning of Thanksgiving, in broad, democratic strokes, McKelway pointed out that exactly one year earlier he had used the same space to observe, "The most interesting person I've seen in ages is a 16-year-old girl from Ohio, whose specialty is making a muscle in her shapely chest wiggle."

McKelway was indignant. "You can't tell how Winchell manages to shift his gaze without a hitch from the wiggling chest of a sixteen-year-old girl to the dignity of man; you can only watch him shift, as you watch a trick play on a football field."

But it was mostly the body politic that interested the public Walter those days. Klurfeld estimates that by the eve of World War II, Little Boy Peep devoted "about 90 per cent of his broadcast and 50 per cent of his column . . . to political events and trends at home and overseas."

Walter's capacity to rouse indignation was just about without parallel. His war against Nazis and racists carried him into the halls of Congress, where he trained his big guns on the powerful voices of the America First movement. "I do not know," cried Senator Wheeler, "but it is possible that Walter Winchell is in the pay of the British government."

Not at all, replied Walter, "but like all Americans I am in its debt."

He called his congressional foes Assolationists and Reprehensibles and worse. He went after Senator Robert Reynolds of North Carolina, chairman of the Senate Military Affairs Committee, a favorite of Fritz Kuhn, and, Walter said, "a jackassolationist." Reynolds said, on the eve of World War II, "Democracy is finished in Europe. Hitler and Mussolini have a date with destiny. Why not play ball with them?" Walter commented, "Reynolds has always been consistent. He has always been wrong. . . . He invariably commands more attention than respect."

When Reynolds inserted columns from a pro-Axis, Italian-language newspaper in the *Congressional Record* shortly before its publisher's naturalization was revoked, Walter printed the story. Not long after, Reynolds was retired from public life.

If Walter was not, in Jimmy Durante's phrase, "duh toast of duh intellectuals," he was greatly admired for the enemies he made. He brawled with Representative Martin Dies of Texas, first chairman of the House Committee to Investigate Un-American Activity, which was established in 1938. Since it is every man for himself when it comes to defining "un-American," the committee enjoyed a broad mandate, and it soon appeared that Dies' concern was more with supporters of Roosevelt than with native fascism.

Walter noted that "the committee has spent $675,000 and has not drafted or suggested a single line of corrective legislation." He said,

"We must be a fun-loving people, or Dies would not have been in public life all this time." He called Dies "one of a dime-a-dozen statesmen of no particular stature. . . . He got his first appropriation by convincing the gullibles that America was threatened with overthrow by the Communists. Whom did he pin the plot on? Stalin? No. Trotsky? No, no. . . . He named Shirley Temple."

In an eerie anticipation of events, Dies demanded equal time to answer Walter. He was given the opportunity on March 26, 1944, opening his mouth to dig his grave. He charged that Walter led a "smear bund" aimed at destroying "reputable and loyal citizens" by linking them to Nazi agents. He quoted Walter's observation that "Many of Hitler's pals have been arrested, but too many have been renominated."

Walter answered with "A Newspaperman's Declaration of Independence," saying, "Far from retracting a single statement, I stand by every one of them." Dies spoke loudly of investigating Walter, but nothing ever came of that and, a few weeks after the exchange of broadcasts, the congressman announced his retirement.

Walter tangled with isolationist leaders like Representatives Clare Hoffman of Michigan and Hamilton Fish of New York. He battled with the inflexible Senator Robert A. Taft of Ohio, who would soon be perceived as Mr. Republican. FDR supplied Walter with a couplet: "Senator Taft is a horse's aft." Editors blue-penciled the item. Walter tried again a few days later. Again it was deleted. The thing dragged on for days, until Walter wailed, "I got it from FDR. How can it be in bad taste?" Those were, in some ways, more innocent days. Finally Walter wrote "Sennnntfffftttttisahuzzzzzsaffft!" which made no sense to most readers, although Walter translated it for the curious.

It is important to emphasize that Walter's war on many fronts was a lonely one. The major newspapers and newspaper chains, the news magazines and respected commentators like Walter Lippmann supported Wendell Willkie, Roosevelt's opponent in 1940. Walter bucked the no-third-term tradition and isolationist sentiments which were perfectly acceptable to moderates, as well as the fascist and anti-Semitic forces which were not.

In Washington his column appeared, when it appeared, in the *Times-Herald,* which was published by the bad-tempered Eleanor "Cissy" Patterson, sister of Joseph Patterson, cousin of Colonel McCormick, and a character even by family standards. Cissy had her crosses to bear—marriage to a womanizing Polish count, a fling with an honest-to-God cowboy, and a term as Drew Pearson's mother-in-law. She and Walter had once been pals, but they broke over his support of FDR and her isolationist fervor.

In one month she killed 19 of 28 Winchell columns. He took out an ad in the rival Washington *News,* noting "a certain Washington newspaper whose initials are the *Washington T-H* omits considerable material from the column. . . . The omissions are usually about certain so-called Americans, pro-Nazis and pro-Japs."

Walter and Cissy uttered insults about each other unprintable in those more decorous times. When Walter served in the Navy, Cissy said, "There isn't a night goes by that I don't get down on my knees and pray they take that bastard . . . off shore duty and put him on a destroyer that will sink."

Walter's naval career spawned great controversy. He had retained deep affection for the Navy since World War I, another bond with FDR. Like many important men, Walter regarded himself with awe. Once he entered the oval office to find the President conferring with Admiral William D. Leahy, his chief of staff. The President asked Walter what was on his mind.

"I'd rather tell you alone," Walter said.

"Walter," FDR laughed, "if I can trust the admiral, you can trust the admiral."

Walter applied for active duty the day after Pearl Harbor. The Navy felt he was more useful behind a typewriter and a microphone. Walter persisted and used his White House connections and was commissioned a lieutenant commander. Klurfeld was with him as Walter, in uniform, made out his will. "Apparently," Klurfeld wrote, "he was ready for any eventuality, including a sneak attack on the Stork Club."

In fact, Walter fought his bloodiest battle in Lindy's. He was there in uniform when he got in a fight with another patron, grabbed a ketchup bottle and fetched his adversary a blow on the head that left him unconscious and bleeding. A friend of Walter's raced out and found Johnny Broderick, the Broadway detective, who arrested Walter's foe, and the incident was kept out of the newspapers.

Walter worked four days a week for the Navy, continuing with his column and his broadcasting. He produced a show at Madison Square Garden, raising a million dollars for Navy Relief. He was sent on Top Secret orders, all wartime orders being Top Secret, to South America as a kind of goodwill ambassador. On the first airplane flight he had ever taken, Walter made fourteen landings in three days before reaching Brazil. He was groggy but game, although he later reported he spent Christmas day in bed with a bellyache.

At a press banquet in Rio de Janeiro, he raised a cup of coffee in toast: "Never above you. Never beneath you. Always beside you." In a radio broadcast, he told his audience, "Brazil and my country—the twin Gibraltars of freedom—will stand guard in the Western hemisphere . . . more than good neighbors, good brothers."

Admiral Jonas H. Ingram commented, "I was amazed by the quantity and accuracy of the stuff Walter picked up. . . . He did a lot to correct the bad impression made by those movie stars and opera singers" who previously served as goodwill ambassadors.

None of this satisfied congressional detractors who suspected Walter of somehow using his Navy post to further his career, although he served without pay. Not long after his return, he answered his critics on his Sunday broadcast with an unfortunate choice of words, "You bet I'm prejudiced against those in high office who guessed so wrong before Pearl Harbor. They're still guessing wrong. What worries me most are all those damned fools who re-elected them."

The uproar was national. Walter had profaned the Sabbath and, worse, questioned the ultimate wisdom of the electorate. Congress demanded and got a congressional investigation. Walter's superiors told him he was to make no further answer to his detractors. Walter wrote a letter resigning his commission and took it to the White House. He submitted it in person to the President of the United States. FDR glanced at it, crumpled it, and tossed it in the wastebasket.

"Now, Walter," he asked, "have you heard any good jokes lately?"

Secretary of the Navy Frank Knox, a newspaperman himself, appeared before Congress to defend Walter. A sketch of Walter's naval service, in the sort of terms applied to John Paul Jones, was read into the *Congressional Record*. But in the end, Walter was placed on inactive status.

Michigan Representative Clare Hoffman, an isolationist, was jubilant. "No longer will Navy men wince at the spectacle of a Broadway gossiper sporting lieutenant commander's stripes while he snoops about night clubs for sexy tidbits," he cried. Walter saw it differently, explaining, "I am now free to carry on—no longer strangled by gold braid."

The ferocity of those battles with Congress was only one demonstration of the celebrity Walter had achieved. He felt betrayed when McKelway's articles appeared in *The New Yorker* in the spring and early summer of 1940, but the six-part profile was the longest the magazine had ever printed. (Years later, Harold Ross, *The New Yorker*'s editor, passed McKelway in the halls and muttered, "I always thought that damned Winchell series was too long.")

John Crosby, the radio critic of the *Herald Tribune*, even saw Walter as a kind of thermometer, measuring the national temperature. "When the United States is worried, his rating is high," Crosby wrote. "When the United States is serene, his rating is low."

Eminence made Walter hard for some people to take. He was like that rooster in George Eliot which believed the sun rose so that it might hear him crow. Indeed, Walter stood with friends outside the St. Moritz on Fifty-seventh Street one night, waving his latest Hooper rating and crowing "Cockle-doodle-doo!"

Jimmy Cannon called Walter "the thrilling bore." Once Cannon and a young woman were in a party at Table 50 as Walter conducted a monologue. After about fifteen minutes, Cannon whispered to the young woman out of the corner of his mouth, "Would you like another drink?"

"Jimmy," snapped Walter, "you're not listening."

That was often, after a few thousand words, the case, and "You're not listening" was one of Walter's more frequently used expressions. In an exasperated moment Cuneo once demanded, "For God's sake, Walter. Don't you ever talk about anything but yourself?"

"Name a more interesting subject," said Walter.

Not for Walter any posturing about the terrible price of fame. He loved it. He liked to drop into out-of-the-way bars and restaurants and see the stir his presence caused. If there was no stir, he would tell the bartender, "I'm Walter Winchell." Then there was a stir, and he could depart.

McKelway wrote that Walter and a companion once stopped at a roadside restaurant for coffee. Walter, winking at his friend, asked the waitress, "Do you read the *Mirror?*"

"No," she said, "I take the *News.*"

"Ever listen to the radio?"

"Sometimes."

"Ever listen to Ben Bernie or Walter Winchell?"

"Nah," said the girl. "What I really like is Hawaiian music."

Walter and his companion left. As they got in the car, Walter said, "Can you imagine that dumb biddy?" Still later, as they drove along, Walter said, "Huh!" and his companion asked him what he meant. "I was just thinking about that dumb biddy," said Walter. "Can you imagine it?"

To a friend who explained he had missed the column the previous morning because his mother had died, Walter was all sympathy. "That's all right," he said. "You can read it in the library."

If this self-preoccupation irritated some people, others found it understandable, even endearing. In 1979 Cuneo recalled that there was a certain fascination in watching and listening to Walter: he was

263

like a natural force, there was a childlike purity to his self-centeredness, almost an innocence.

All the more wonder that Walter and Damon became friends, since Damon could be testy with the self-important. But Damon needed a friend for the terrible hours of the night and dawn as he waged his losing, sucker's battle. And there was more to the friendship than the fact that one talked, the other listened. Walter worshiped talent, particularly writing talent. Damon worshiped success. Each man gave the other what he looked for.

They spent hours together at Table 50. Damon rode with him through the New York streets while Walter chased police calls. They saw murders and stabbings and fires. One night on an East Harlem street they saw a terrible fight between a legless derelict and a drunken Hispanic youth who had been tormenting him.

The legless man grabbed the youth and began choking him. The legless man had powerful arms. He growled around the cigar stub clenched in his mouth, "Watch him go to sleep." Walter wanted to break up the fight. Damon restrained him, writing on his note pad, "I've never seen a man choked to death." The youth broke free and ran off, the legless man scuttling in pursuit. Damon called it "the most bizarre incident I've ever witnessed in all my years on Broadway."

The small hours are a time of trouble. Damon seemed to find a dark release in this. It brought out the instincts of the amateur psychologist:

> The women of the lower East Side of New York when in pain or fright cry out, "'Oh-h-h, O-h-h. O-h-h," subdued and wailingly.
>
> The women of midtown, the so-called Roaring Forties, taking in the Broadway night sector, cry more shrilly and sharply from the head, "eeee-eee-eee," the tonal quality being more characteristic of women of the United States generally. I mean thus do women cry in Pueblo, Colorado, or Los Angeles.
>
> The women of Harlem cry "ooo-ooo-ooo," long drawn and throaty and eerie when it rises out of the quiet night. . . . You note these things riding through the streets of the big city in the early hours of the morning with Winchell.

Occasionally celebrities rode with Walter. Klurfeld recalled sitting wide-eared in the back seat, "not much more than a kid," while Hedy Lamar told Walter about her love life. Myrna Loy, according to McKelway, dropped off to sleep the one time she joined Walter on his night ride. McKelway observed, "The celebrities seldom go more than once."

Ennui was not the only reason for this. Peggy Sobol remembered that when she and Walter answered a police call, it was to find a dead baby in a garbage can. "Once was enough for me," she noted delicately.

In *The Damon Runyon Story,* Ed Weiner wrote that Orson Welles joined Damon and Walter one night. Welles chided Walter for driving recklessly. Runyon agreed, scribbling that less than an inch "stood between us and a headline reading, 'Runyon and Winchell Killed.'"

Walter sat on that for a moment. Then he asked, "What do you mean, 'Runyon and Winchell'? Do you think you should get top billing?"

Damon scrawled that he hadn't given the matter much thought.

"'Walter Winchell, noted news columnist and commentator, accompanied by Damon Runyon . . .'" was the lead Walter foresaw.

Damon held up his hand. "I've got a bigger following than you," he wrote. "I should get first mention."

"Oh, is that right?" Walter asked. "Did you know my Hooper rating was over 25 this week?"

"What about seniority?" Damon asked. "Besides, I know more newspaper editors than you, and they would give me a break."

At length Welles, who did not hide his light under a half-bushel, leaned forward from the back seat and asked where his name fit into all this. The two newsmen regarded him with scorn—an actor. They agreed that it would be either, "Winchell, Runyon and Welles," or "Runyon, Winchell and Welles." Welles would run no better than show.

Damon told Welles, "I can personally guide you through all Winchellville, inch by inch, from having been briefed by him so thoroughly, though he claims I never listen to him."

Walter drew an X on the sidewalk to call the attention of his companions to a particular location. He said that one day a jealous barber sat there with his girl friend in his arms after he had taken a swipe at her with his razor. He was rocking her, crooning to her. When the police arrived and lifted the girl from his arms, her head fell off.

A tale told after midnight, all right. There is a danger to the constant exposure to the desperate and defeated in the small hours. It often makes cynics of policemen and firemen and reporters. Four o'clock in the morning does little for the soul. The view of humanity is seldom reassuring, and it can produce that weariness of the imagina-

265

tion which drives some writers to seize on the neurotic and psychotic and make them metaphors for humanity.

That was now the climate of Damon's private, emotional country, although the men of Table 50 often deferred to him as arbiter. The womanizer is, by definition, a great cuckold, and one night Walter and Billingsley were sitting around lamenting the suspected infidelities of their current girl friends. Damon took all of that he could stand and then, drawing on his vast knowledge, scribbled in the kind of language favored by schoolboys with chalk that the body of woman is not damaged by lovemaking. This was accepted as higher wisdom.

Sometimes, almost helplessly, Damon wrote, "Walter, you're full of shit" as the monologue descended on his head like a waterfall. One night, with Leonard Lyons present, he went too far, wisecracking about the alleged illiteracy of the radio audience. Walter angrily walked away. The next day he received a note from Damon:

Dear Walter:

The remark about the radio audience not reading books was intended as a rib as Lenny says and you are not to file it away in the serious department as you seemed inclined to do last night.

Don't you know that if I had a single thought that tinged on the uncomplimentary about you that is the one thing I would make certain not to say? Or about your work.

Any time I make a crack that sounds belittling it is probably an effort to steam you up and I want you to remember that it is from the tip of the tongue and never from the heart.

In affection,
Damon

Most of the time, the kidding *was* affectionate. Damon and Walter were walking along Broadway in the pre-dawn when Damon pointed out a spectacular shooting star arching in from the Atlantic.

"Jesus," said Walter. "It might fall on me."

"Why don't you double the population of the world," asked Damon, "and make it 'us'?"

The cancer was progressing. Damon did not, in public, cry aloud. Friends noticed that there were nights when he sat on the edge of Table 50 so he could dash to the men's room when the pain became unbearable. His gluttony alarmed Walter. Often the night would end with his spooning down gobs of ice cream, and Walter finally went to

266

Damon's doctor about it. The doctor said Walter should encourage Damon to eat all he liked.

"But why?" asked Walter.

"But why not?" said the doctor.

Even when illness forced Damon to drop the column for a while, he returned with a wink. "I was in the hospital recently for a sort of check-up," he wrote on November 14, 1945. He complained about the hospital regimen which upset his routine and which, he believed, was devised for farmers. "What proof can they offer it does a man any good to be awakened at 8 A.M. and put to sleep at 9 P.M.," he wrote, "when all his life he has slept till noon and gone to bed at 4 A.M.? Let us be fair about this."

He wrote about sports. Not the sports he once *had* to cover like golf, about which he thought the word "courage" should never be used. "The only thing about golf that requires courage," Damon wrote, "is the clothes." And he seemed to agree with Montaigne that any young man preferring tennis to a wrestling match was not likely to amount to much.

But boxing continued to grip him. He saw a mustached Mexican heavyweight and mused, "Every man will steal something, if it is only an idea or wife or a sweetheart. I am not a fellow that would heist any of those things or money or a horse or a cow. But there was a time when I could not trust myself around a heavyweight contender. . . . Thinks I to myself, Gee, what a man could do with that 'tash and a few reliable tankers out in Los Angeles where there are 150,000 sports-loving Mexicans."

He was outraged when he saw a heavyweight imported by his old pal James J. Johnston held to a draw in his American debut. "I gathered that [Johnston] has the quaint idea that when you test a heavyweight you test him against a tough opponent. . . . This idea of Johnston's went out with high-button shoes. It is quite corny though very honest. You fight that kind with a new heavyweight in Tincan, Wyoming, where it will not get bruited about if anything untoward happens. . . . In St. Nick's before a metropolitan mob, you fight Sam Accordion, who folds easily."

Damon saw Rocky Graziano knock out Al Davis in four rounds and scribbled a note to Johnston, "There is your second Ketchel," referring to Stanley Ketchel, the Michigan Assassin (1886-1910), who was remembered by the old-time fight fans the way the *World* is remembered by old newsmen. "I like fighters who keep blasting away," Damon explained, "and who have to be pried from their opponents."

Damon sprang to the defense of his friend Hype Igoe, who died in

1945, and about whom "the younger sports writers" suggested a naiveté. Hype, Damon said, appreciated a fake fight as much as anyone did. He affectionately recalled his friend at ringside "doing a little soft shoe dance in the manner of the old vaudeville dance teams and singing softly . . . 'Oh, Daniel O'Leary and Barney McCoy. . . .' It was Hype's way of saying the [fight] was in the nature of a dance."

Damon confessed, "I dearly love a good, fast fake fight. I think a fake requires more finesse than the real thing, is just as exciting for the suckers and is less calculated to blind the participants or render them punchdrunk. I prefer a fake that I know in advance to be a fake because then I can study the technique from start to finish, but I am just as happy when they pull the scamus on me unexpected-like to give me a sudden, unlooked-for thrill."

Damon attended his first night baseball game. "It struck me as more of a show, an exhibition, than a regularly scheduled game . . . but probably that was due to my unfamiliarity" with the proceedings. He was astonished at the surprise expressed when it was learned that Brooklyn College players were involved in a basketball scandal.

He wrote, "From all I have been hearing along Broadway and from persons connected with the game itself, including one of its foremost coaches, I was rather under the impression that chucking the games was a fairly familiar practice." Damon was out front on that story; the lid blew off half a dozen years after he was in his grave.

Damon defied his doctors and pulled himself from his bed to attend FDR's funeral in Washington. He wrote a widely reprinted account, an improbable dialogue between a father and his teenaged son, in which the boy asks about the dead president's human qualities and the father confesses he had always hated Roosevelt but saw now, through his son's eyes, how wrong he had been. It is all too pat, and the reader may feel Damon could have filed the story without ever leaving the Hotel Buckingham in New York.

Damon's true feeling about politicians, at least toward the end of his life, might have been reflected in a comment he made to Walter, who had returned from a trip to Washington disillusioned and furious about Harry Truman. "I would rather meet a heavyweight champion than a President anytime," Damon wrote. It was an opinion that would enjoy great vogue among literary innocents by the 1960s.

Damon's heart went out to the common soldier. He advised servicemen to organize and demand a bonus after the war, quite apart from any veterans' benefits they might receive. To critics, he said, "I must reply that I consider cash a nicer reward than the apple stands we so generously bestowed on our heroes of 1918."

268

He suggested and pushed for a national lottery. He objected to bestowing nicknames on generals. He excoriated General George S. Patton for slapping the face of a wounded man. He demanded respect for the serviceman:

Q: And what was your contribution to the war effort, Mr. Runyon?

A: I never called him GI Joe.

The Court: If there is any more applause from the spectators, I will order the bailiffs to clear the room. . . .

Q: Would you mind telling us your reason for never calling him GI Joe?

A: I always considered the term with reference to its more familiar connotations in American city talk in which for over 40 years a Joe was a Jasper, a joskin, a yokel, a hayseed, a hick, a clodhopper.

Q: Well, then, would you inform the court what you did call him?

A: Soldier.

Westbrook Pegler took issue with Damon, "who is to our native slang as Henry Mencken is to our more substantial and enduring, if quaint, forms of expression." Pegler traced "Joe" in its common usage to a reporter's observation that the 1930 Brooklyn Dodgers would start the season with "Dazzy Vance and a lot of guys named Joe. . . . That I believe is the true origin of the expression 'a lot of guys named Joe' from which soldiers in turn adopted their 'Joe' and with about the same meaning."

But Pegler had not heard the word used to mean "a Jasper, a joskin, a yokel," although "I have been around many of the places where [Damon] has been, during the same time, always with an ear stretched out."

Damon affected great injury: "I am hurt because it is one of my own pet expressions. I often use it to describe a neckyoke, or rustic. If Mr. Pegler did not hear it, it follows that he never paid any attention to what I might be saying. . . . I thought he was practically hanging on my every word."

Dying, Damon was still able to summon up indignation at editors who cut his column "until the sense of it is lost and the writing technique crippled or destroyed. . . . I could shorten the whole business if necessary or even boil it down to fifty words because no man can teach me any tricks about keeping 'er short. But that is not the idea of the column I write. . . . The idea is to make it long enough to entertain the reader for a few minutes."

He was able to report to Damon, Jr., "of a sudden my column took fire with the boss people, including Mr. Hearst, and he is prodding the editors to make sure and get it in the papers, which only makes it necessary for me to keep on a regular schedule instead of doing it when I felt like it."

Damon pleaded poverty and spoke of obligations, but the reason he kept writing, although he was in pain and gulped sedatives all day long, the reason he fought his way to the typewriter daily, was that more than forty years and sixty million words after he started he was a newspaperman to his marrow, as committed to the calling as a saint is to his God.

"You say you don't know if you will ever be anything more than a better than average reporter," he wrote Damon, Jr. "Well, my boy, I think that is better than being king. I do indeed."

His peers, including Bugs Baer, whether they were aware of the price he was paying or not, agreed that Damon's final columns were his finest. Some are brilliant. In "Death Pays a Social Call," Damon apotheosized death as a "large and most distinguished looking figure" who weeps because "'No one wants to chat with me. I am so terribly lonesome.'"

In "Why Me?" Damon wrote of the resentment and fear felt by the victim of a fatal illness:

"Why me?" he keeps asking himself, dazedly. "Of all the millions of people around, why me?"

It becomes like a pulse beat—"Why me? Why me? Why me?"

Sometimes he reviews his whole life step by step to see if he can put his finger on some circumstance in which he may have been at such grievous fault as to merit disaster.

Did he commit some black sin somewhere down the years? Did he betray the sacred trust of some fellow human being? Is he being punished for some special wrongdoing? "Why me?"

He wakes suddenly at night from a sound sleep to consciousness of his affliction and to the clock-like ticking in his brain—"Why me? Why me? Why me?"

Damon was hard-boiled. "Trust no one," was his advice to the young. "If every person in the world was taught from birth to trust no one, it would eventually be a universal state of mind and people would know no other. No man would make a deal of any kind with another man without guarantees that would preclude the double-cross with which most of us are familiar. Widows would not be swindled by their late husbands' best friends." He quoted the Book of Job for support.

He offered to "the youth of the land . . . my best advice in three words":

> Get the money.
> I said that is my advice. Get the money.
> Get it honestly, son, I said. The hazards and inconveniences of dishonest dough are too numerous to make it worth while. You not only run the risk of going to the can, but there is the matter of conscience that produces sleepless nights and waking hours of fear and brooding like an income tax full of lies.

He advised getting the money "by hard work and application" or "in a soft berth that requires little effort" or "fall in love with an heiress, if you must fall in love, and vice versa to the girls.

> Yes, I know the good book states that "Love of money is the root of all evil," but it also says "Money is a defence," and that is what I am talking about, money as a defence—a defence in youth against that irksome love in an attic or a housing project, in middle age against the petty laws and regulations that annoy Mr. and Mrs. Mugg, and in old age against fear and disrespect.
> Son, I said, get the money.

Along with Walter, Damon watched the days dwindle down with Paul Small, a theatrical agent, and Eddie Walker, a fight manager, and Walker's wife. But when Damon, Jr., made the mistake of suggesting about someone, "I understood he was close to you" Damon turned to his typewriter and wrote, "No one is close to me. Remember that."

He continued paying his respect to women.

"Ladies," he wrote, "I do not say that some of you are liable to get killed. No, I don't say that. I do not even say you may be badly hurt, but what I do say is that you are building up greater hatred for your sex than is necessary when you sit at a restaurant table and haul out your make-up kit and start fixing your make-up while hungry gentlemen are standing by."

He wondered why women complaining of the wartime cigarette shortage did not take up the cigar, "most aristocratic of all smokes."

271

He answered himself. "I doubt that women, who are clumsy enough in smoking cigarettes, could ever acquire that exquisite aplomb" needed to smoke a cigar.

A reader asked Damon why he never wrote about his wife. Damon said that he used to do so, "thinking that this was a real homey touch to my column and gave my readers the impression that I was a fireside man just like them and had the same household adventures."

But, said Damon, he had received a letter from his wife's lawyers in which she pointed out she was not "a public character" and that such columns were an "invasion of privacy" and "no part of the matrimonial deal." Damon was asked to avoid "all the cliches of married relations that column writers are prone to present to their readers, including good cooking, unpunctuality, basic inability to understand intricate public problems, make-up, idiosyncrasies of dress and all the rest."

Finally, said the lawyers, according to Damon, "She wishes to inform you that referring to her as the ever-loving, the storm-and-strife, the ball-and-chain, the old lady, the boss or any other term of flippancy or disrespect will be deemed by her particularly flagrant."

At a time when the world seemed lit by what were called triumphs of the human spirit, Damon's courage and tenacity were beacons. In the words of a great contemporary, he not only endured but prevailed. His afflictions were those of Job, a book he all but parsed. The progression of the cancer brought days and nights of unbroken agony. "The pain is terrific," he wrote his son. The Internal Revenue Service dunned him for back taxes. In June of 1946 he and Patrice were divorced. He gave her the best of everything, the once-happy home on Hibiscus Island, his racing stable, half the income from his literary properties. She agreed to pay the taxes and to pay for Mary's institutional care. The day he learned about his divorce he seemed unusually grave at Table 50. His companions were sympathetic. He scribbled a note: "What a day. My horse Scribe came in at Jamaica— paid $10.20."

A young magazine editor, assigned to work on an article with Damon, said, "I want the old Runyon." Damon eyed him for a moment. Then he wrote, "The old Runyon doesn't live here any more."

He could still be testy with his son. He wrote Damon, Jr.:

> I notice you do a lot of thinking about yourself and your problems. Sometime when you are in a mood for thought, give one to your old man who in two years was stricken by the most terrible malady known to mankind and left voiceless with a death sentence hanging over his head, who had a big career

stopped cold, and had his domestic life shattered by divorce and his savings largely dissipated through the combination of evil circumstances. All this at sixty-five years of age when most men's activity is completely ended. Try that on your zither some day, my boy.

Again: "I do not know your problems . . . but I do know it is a good thing I never permitted similar bedevilments to pull me down to a standstill. . . . Stop squawking."

Damon fought his incurable wound like James's Milly Theale, with "a kind of ferocity of modesty, a kind of . . . intensity of pride." Only occasionally the mask slipped away, and he revealed his terrible loneliness. He wrote a sad little column about soldiers and sailors and their girl friends in a Broadway arcade. There was a machine "purporting to register the steam in a kiss. 'Naughty.' 'Hot stuff.' 'Exciting.' 'Cold.' 'Sour.' Although I waited around quite a while, no one took a crack at it. I suppose I could have tried it myself, but no one would be interested in my score. Not even myself."

Damon was too ill to enjoy the ride as New York entered one of its great periods. The Broadway theater flowered; fed by wartime prosperity, night life was never livelier, not only the Stork and El Morocco, but the Copa and the Diamond Horseshoe and Fifty-second Street jumped with jazz. It was a time, John Cheever wrote, "when the city of New York was still filled with a river light, when you heard the Benny Goodman quartets from a radio in the corner stationery store, and when almost everybody wore a hat."

Damon's son paid him what proved to be a final visit. As the two men sat in Damon's rooms at the Hotel Buckingham, Damon suddenly scrawled the unanswerable question: "Why did your mother drink?" Damon, Jr., believed his father really meant "Do you still blame me?" He fumbled with an answer, saying alcoholism was the combination of many factors, that his mother doomed herself, and that Damon did the only thing he could do when he walked out.

A little later, Damon, Jr., prepared to leave. It was afternoon, but Damon had gone to bed, perhaps to avoid goodbyes. But the phone rang and woke him. Then his son said, "Goodbye, Dad."

"His lips formed the words, 'So long, son.'

"He broke just a little—he put his arm around my shoulder and squeezed."

Bill Corum, a Hearst sports columnist and, decades earlier, Damon's roommate on baseball road trips, paid him a visit. Damon began to weep. He turned away from his old friend. After a time, he crossed over to his bed table, lifted the cloth and looked down. When

273

Damon left the room, Corum examined the bed table. There was a full-length picture of Patrice beneath the cloth, placed under the light.

Sometimes Damon's later columns were compassionate:

> If I had my way, no person under 60 would suffer so much as a toothache or know one little sorrow. I do not agree that sorrow and suffering are any help in life. I know they are inevitable, but let them come to the old, not the young. . . . When [calamity] reaches a man in his late years, at least he has no kick coming on the basis of prematurity, for in the language of the Bard of Broadway—
>
> I've had my fling,
> And here's the thing—
> It's all even.

Damon couldn't understand the debate about what to do with Hitler, the Japanese leaders, and other assorted war criminals: "You just take them out as you catch them and string them up to trees or under trestles or however you can get a stout hitching post, or you put them in front of hitching posts if more convenient, and bing-bing-bing, it is finished."

He confessed, when readers caught him in grammatical lapses, "I should have gone a couple of grades further." He was overwhelmed with letters after he wrote about a tonic which allegedly grew hair. He believed betting should be permitted on all "sports events, or elections, or anything else of a comparable nature."

He dined one day at the Café Royal, "the haunt of the artistic element on the East side" and was told the novelist Fannie Hurst was dining in the back room. "I said, 'All right, tell her Runyon is dining in the front room.'"

He wrote a marvelously funny column about a Broadway figure's run-in with Jim Moore, the terrible-tempered proprietor of Moore's restaurant in the West Forties, where Damon spent great moments with his buddies, eating at a table in the kitchen. The Broadway fellow ordered corned beef hash *without* onions and, although he was an old customer, Moore grew furious. "'Get out of my house!' roared Jim Moore. 'And never darken my doors again. I don't want anyone in here that don't know better than that.'"

Damon was irritated by public opinion polls. He thought he might say to a perfect stranger who started asking him questions, "Would it surprise you to know that I am thinking of kicking your pants until

274

your nose bleeds?" After watching the fights on an invention called television, he wrote, "I can tell you now that in a couple of years from this date, everybody will be squatted comfortably at their own firesides viewing through this medium, the spectacles of the day."

Death was ever closer. Damon said he was now "pally with pain," but the dying man turned to the kind of device used by beginning columnists who seek attention. If you don't attack pets or the flag, you write, "American women of this generation are the worst house-keepers the world has ever known. They are incrediby bad." He meant women from eighteen to thirty-eight, Damon explained. They complained, he said, about not being able to get domestic help for a three-room apartment "they could 'do' in twenty minutes every day if they had any gumption."

Damon recalled women "of the old days" who could "clean a 14-room house, making five or six beds, doing all the other drudgery around the joint, besides attending to the marketing and the cooking without sitting down from sun-up to sun-set."

Damon believed that making the bed "is one detail of housekeeping that . . . is overdone." He thought beds should be made every three days or so "to shake the bedbugs out of the sheets." A made bed, he noted, is unmade every night. "I have never heard of any great good coming out of a made bed," he wrote.

Damon concluded that he was "a better housekeeper than any woman of today, a better cook."

The response was as might be expected. A few weeks later Damon was writing, "Dear me, dear me . . . if it is not just my hard luck to be personally incapacitated at a moment when I might be making a package off the dames by betting them on my abilities as a house-keeper."

An angry reader demanded to know how "a half-decent woman" could be expected to keep house for a lout "with his feet on the table and maybe playing with a dirty dog?"

"She is entitled to a fair answer," Damon wrote. "Well, then, ma'am, is he barefooted or does he wear shoes? In the former case, I think it is permissible, but in the latter, he is out of line. The shoes may get in the oatmeal. . . . As for the dog, it should be washed every morning before breakfast. That is one of the duties of the expert house-keeper. . . . Plain laundry soap will serve in the washing, if toilet soap is unavailable."

Damon's time was just about up. He and Walter had raced through many nights, covering fires. The contrast between the life and beauty of the flames and the destruction they wrought fascinated Damon. "Of all the sounds that rise out of a big city night, those attendant upon the alarm of fire are the most terrifying," he wrote.

He described the efforts of a woman to return to a blazing building to rescue her baby. Then "The woman plumped herself down on the sidewalk in a sitting posture and sat there moaning until some of the other women showed her the baby, unharmed, and then she sobbed out of sheer relief and joy. The smoulder which was in the basement and had filled the street with odorous smoke was extinguished, the spectators and the police departed, and then the quiet of the morning was broken by the easy ding-dong of the bells of the home-going trucks saying 'All right now, all right now.'"

Walter devoted his vacation in July 1946 to spending the nights with Damon, who wrote, "I think Winchell is about to collapse and will have to spend the rest of his vacation in bed. . . . He did not know that I was an assistant Caliph when he was still writing little squibs for the *Vaudeville News*. . . . At the start of Winchell's vacation we would not fold until 9 or 10 o'clock, but here lately he has been calling King's X an hour earlier, until now he is down to 6 A.M. . . . I think he will have to take a vacation from his vacation."

Darryl Zanuck, the film mogul, rode with Damon and Walter one night and suggested they write a movie based on their adventures. Walter said it would be "a sort of *Grand Hotel* of New York." Damon suggested a title, *Proceed With Caution*.

But there was no time.

One night at Table 50, the regulars discussed a black-bordered notice which had appeared in *Variety* annually for thirty years, placed by a casting agent in memory of the man who had helped him early in his career.

"When I am gone," Damon wrote on his notepad, "I hope somebody remembers me even a little while." Given time to think, he later expanded the thought: "You can keep the things of bronze and stone, and give me one man to remember me just once a year."

His friend Jimmy Walker died on November 18, 1946. Doctors would not allow Damon out of bed to attend the funeral. He was confined to his room at the hotel. The weight he had added gorging himself was eaten away; he dropped from 190 to not much more than 100 pounds. Walter was in Florida, but he called Damon nightly. "Runyon being ill is like New York Bay—with the Statue of Liberty dark," he wrote.

Damon emerged from his room just once more. He and Mike Jacobs, the fight promoter, walked to Columbus Circle where they planned to build an arena to compete with Madison Square Garden.

On December 6 a group of friends took Damon for a drive. When the car stopped in front of Memorial Hospital, Damon panicked. He scribbled, "What's this?" He was told it was vital that he be hospitalized. "Where's Walter?" he whispered. "Where's Walter? He wouldn't let you do this to me."

He let it happen.

He wrote Patrice from his hospital bed. He wrote his son. He wanted no funeral service. No display of his body. No flowers. A woman had "come into my life, late. . . . If she likes, I wish she might be permitted to commune with me after I put my checks back in the rack." He wrote final instructions for the disposition of his remains. For a time, he had said he wished his ashes to be scattered in Biscayne Bay, but in conversation with his son and in his column, he had countermanded that request.

The pain-killers were not much more than placebo. The coma into which he lapsed December 7 was as kindly as sleep. His son rushed to the bedside from Cincinnati, fighting his way past a palace guard of Damon's friends, sporting and show business people. Damon never regained consciousness. He died in the early evening of December 10.

Mythology bloomed. The *Times* obituary, noting CHRONICLER OF BROADWAY GAVE STREET'S LINGO TO NATION, missed his birthdate by four years and accepted Damon's fancy that he enlisted in the Spanish-American War at fourteen.

Over at the *Mirror*, Dan Parker had Runyon in the press box at the Kentucky Derby of 1930, taking a drag on his cigarette and proceeding "as if taking dictation," to write "A Handy Guy Like Sande." Then Parker asked:

> Where will we find another
> Even with half his skill?
> Would that he had a brother
> To pick up his writing quill.
> Would we could turn the years back
> To the '20s once again
> With his stuff each mornin'
> The sports page adornin'
> And Damon bootin' 'em in!

Hollywood stars, Broadway characters, what a columnist called "we of the theatre and us of the press," underworld figures and politicians paid last respects at Frank E. Campbell's. In an episode right out of Damon's fiction, his son, seeking privacy, sneaked Damon's ashes from the funeral parlor after some hugger-mugger involving two cars, one of them to throw pursuers off the trail.

On December 18, as Damon had wished, John F. Gill, chief pilot, and Captain Eddie Rickenbacker, the World War I flying ace and president of Eastern Airlines, lifted off a twin-engine transport from LaGuardia airport. Damon, Jr., and his wife were passengers. At three thousand feet, the plane made its turn over the Statue of Liberty.

Captain Rickenbacker took the heavy bronze urn from Damon, Jr. The plane steadied over Broadway, and at Times Square Rickenbacker tipped the urn.

fourteen

ON THE SUNDAY after Damon's death, as Walter later wrote, "I threw away the last page of my newscast and extemporized, 'Mr. and Mrs. United States! A very good friend of mine—a great newspaperman, Damon Runyon, was killed this week by the Number Two killer—Cancer. Let's do something about this terrible thing. Let's fight back! Will you please send me a penny, nickel, dime or a dollar? I will turn all your donations (no expenses deducted of any kind) over to the cancer fighters."

Walter said he intended the money, "maybe $50,000," to be used to "dedicate a bed to Damon in a New York hospital. . . . But the millions poured in."

Those millions overwhelmed Walter. He was, after all, a columnist, not a cache. He turned the money over to the American Cancer Society. But he'd promised "no expenses deducted of any kind," and, according to Harvey Katz in *Give! Who Gets Your Charity Dollar,* the Cancer Society set aside a sizable portion of the money it received for administrative costs, fund-raising, and other expenses. Meanwhile, postal authorities warned Walter he could be in trouble for personally handling charitable contributions.

So Walter established the Damon Runyon Memorial Fund for Cancer Research, with operating costs to come from the Walter Winchell Foundation, which he bankrolled himself.

The Fund's goal, in the words of its annual report, is to "act as a catalyst in the development of greater knowledge in connection with the cause and control of cancer. . . . The best means of attaining this objective is by supporting post-graduate Fellowships for doctors engaged in basic research, in the hope of building a cadre of scientists who would continue work in this field."

From the beginning, the story of the Fund was rich in touches of Broadway, show biz, and Damon Runyon characters.

An early contributor was the convicted labor racketeer Joseph "Socks" Lanza, who sent $250 from prison, with a covering note from his lawyer: "Socks would be glad to raise much more if it could be arranged for him to circulate more freely." When Milton Berle was Mr. Television in the early 1950s, he pioneered the charity telethon, raising about a million dollars in each of five annual twenty-two-hour broadcasts for the Cancer Fund.

In columns and broadcasts, Walter ceaselessly promoted the Fund and its works. He wrote about children who put on a play in the basement of a Harlem tenement, charging two cents admission, and solemnly presented him with eleven dollars in pennies in four milk bottles. He wrote about Richard Rodgers and Oscar Hammerstein II, who set aside certain orchestra seats for *South Pacific, Mr. Roberts,* and *Carousel,* the proceeds going to the Fund. In a modified form, that practice continues. The Fund offers seats for Broadway shows for the box-office price plus a tax-deductible contribution.

Walter proclaimed that every journalist in the country was an honorary chairman of public relations for the Fund. He appointed Dan Parker president and Leonard Lyons vice president. For years, the list of Fund officers included names like Joe DiMaggio, Jimmy Durante, and Ed Sullivan.

The Fund took money where it found it. There were benefit baseball games, drag races, a Damon Runyon Memorial Handicap at a Miami racetrack. There was income from land in Maine and from the property on which Grauman's Chinese Theater was located in Hollywood.

Walter was the dynamo which got the fund rolling, but he gave off sparks as well as energy. Leonard Lyons resigned as a Fund official after fighting with Walter, and so did Arthur Godfrey and John Charles Daly, the host of television's *What's My Line?*

With the decline of Walter's influence the Fund, once one of the most publicized charities, became The Quiet Charity. In the eleven years beginning in 1968, some 78 percent of the Fund's contributions came through wills and bequests, a perhaps ominous indication that its big supporters were dying off.

And yet the Fund's files bulge with testimony from former Fellows. One scientist wrote, "My tenure as a fellow . . . was undoubtedly one of the most critical periods in establishing the future direction and success of my scientific career"; another professional, after mentioning awards and honors that had come to him, commented that "to a great extent my success can be attributed to the opportunity I had as a post-doctoral fellow of the Fund."

Cancer seems obdurate. But an enormous amount has been learned about it after more than a quarter-century of the kind of research sponsored by the Fund. The year before he died, Damon wrote a column about cancer, "One Disease That Doesn't Make Sense":

> Cancer is not a penalty disease like many others. For instance, heart trouble, which often comes of high living and excitements, or a broken-down stomach, the result of over-indulgence in the wrong kind of food and drink. . . .
>
> If a man knows a physical affliction is due to his own indiscretions, possibly in the face of medical warnings, he has no particular kick coming. He asked for it, as the saying goes.

Damon nowhere mentioned that he was suffering from cancer, and in 1946 its link to cigarette smoking had not been established, so there was no sense of *mea culpa* in the reflection about indiscretion in the face of medical warnings. He quoted "a sawbones on the Pacific Coast" as telling him that "if the human race lived long enough, everybody would have cancer." But Damon noted that the disease also strikes the very young.

Damon also included a scenario, a movie for the theater of his mind. "One of these days a goggly-eyed, anemic and very poor young fellow puttering around in the pursuit of his experiments, will unveil the mystery of cancer and find the cure, and it will probably be so simple that everyone will say, 'Well, for goodness sake, why didn't someone think of that before?'"

That view seems simpleminded in the 1980s, when prevailing medical opinion holds that cancer wears many veils, and that any cure will be arrived at in slow, painful steps. But man's history is told largely in terms of conflict, and generations fed on movies and television respond to the image of the lonely cancer fighter waging war against disease, like one of Shakespeare's bloodied kings rallying the troops.

The irony of Damon's death was not lost on Bob Considine, who wrote: "He was mourned by millions, this lonely and often irascible man. It is inconceivable that any outstanding pundit of Walter Lippmann's stature, or even Ernie Pyle or Ernest Hemingway, could have served after death as the rallying point of the remarkable cancer research fund that bears Runyon's name."

Walter may have exaggerated the extemporaneous nature of his appeal for money. The idea for the Fund came from J. Edgar Hoover. As time and agony ran out for Damon in New York, Walter and the G-Man were patrolling the nighttime streets of Miami Beach.

Dade County was not yet the drug capital of western civilization, and business was slow. Walter mentioned Damon's losing struggle and Damon's remark that he hoped to be remembered, and Hoover came up with a thought about endowing a bed in Damon's name for newspapermen stricken with cancer. He emphasized to Walter that neither his name nor that of the FBI was to be connected with the project.

A publicist named Irving Mandell recalls that the day after Damon died, Walter came down from his Miami Beach hotel suite and announced simply, "Damon's dead," and suggested they take a stroll. Mandell says they hit up every bookie within the area of a couple of blocks and returned with $5,000. Walter wouldn't touch it. He told Mandell to send the money, in the form of a certified check, to Walter's secretary in New York.

Mandell says, "That's how the Runyon Cancer Fund got started, and don't let anyone tell you different," and it seems to be a beginning so in line with Damon's life that it is undoubtedly true.

If Damon's name was the rallying point for the Fund, only Walter's power made it possible. That power was at its maximum. In 1946, and for much of the decade to follow, he continued riding the treacherous wave of public opinion like a surfer. In 1944 Charles Fisher had published *The Columnists: A Surgical Survey,* examining the careers of Dorothy Thompson, Drew Pearson, David Lawrence, Lippmann, Pegler, and other specialists in telling people what to think.

The first words in the book are "On any given day some twenty-five million Americans reverently fold back their newspapers to the Brains Page and gasp in unison over the diverting, although conceivably apocryphal report that Miss Millicent Rogers sleeps in a night dress lined with chinchilla fur."

Fisher believed "The successful columnist of our time engages the instant daily attention of a greater number of clients than any author who ever set quill pen to paper or explored the keyboard of an Underwood with burning forefingers." He claimed, "Miss Harriet Beecher Stowe reached a meager million of her contemporaries with *Uncle Tom's Cabin;* Mr. Walter Winchell reaches twenty-five million of his with a note upon Miss Rogers' nightwear." Forget the gaffe which returns Mrs. Stowe to the maiden's state; the point is that in 1944, in a book examining the allegedly unparalleled power and influence of the syndicated columnist, Walter's name led the list.

Walter had been convulsed in 1938 by a gallimaufry of a Broadway show called *Hellzapoppin',* created by a couple of old vaudevillians named Ole Olsen and Chic Johnson. The critics hated it, but Walter kept plugging *Hellzapoppin'* on radio and in his column, and it ran for 1,404 performances. In 1955, in the face of barrages from the critics' shore batteries, he helped something called *Ankles Aweigh* stay afloat for 176 performances. It starred Jane Kean, his girl friend of the moment.

If he pushed "Stardust" on its way in the 1920s, he remained powerful enough three decades later to boost the comedy team of Dan Rowan and Dick Martin from the inns of Hobbs, New Mexico, and Portland, Oregon, to the Copa.

Walter hailed his share of flops and hopeless books, plays, and songs, and one successful comic recalled without malice that after Walter called him one of the best comedians on radio, "I was out of work for two years," but, as Fisher reflected, "even Zeus can throw a wild thunderbolt at times."

It was by the 1940s not a case of Walter and Klurfeld, with an occasional assist from Ernest Cuneo and a few other contributors, attempting to cover a world which was no longer restricted to Broadway. Walter had accumulated a staff of stringers which numerically rivaled that of any metropolitan newspaper. Viewed sympathetically, which he seldom was, he was a kind of city editor, screening the contributions of his beat men.

These were, of course, press agents and publicists, and they crawled for Walter. They were paid space rates—publicity for a client. Walter awarded "orchids" of praise in his column and "scallions" of criticism. "If you got an orchid for a client," one publicist recalled in 1979, "you earned a month's salary in a day." Something like an international exchange rate developed. An agent supplied up to five news items, pieces of gossip, gags, for one orchid.

Agents ordered stationery headed "Exclusive to Walter Winchell." One publicist sent Walter an item attached to a pair of hip boots, with a note explaining, "If you don't use this item, I'll have to wear these because of my tears."

Walter could be generous, as Bob Thomas noted in *Winchell*. When the evangelist Aimee Semple McPherson opened to slow business at the Capitol Theater, a press agent overheard the manager tell her he was going to cancel the engagement and announce that she was ill. "Oh no," said Miss McPherson. "God wouldn't like that."

The press agent hustled that line to Walter, who thought it was the best item he'd heard that year. The press agent was rewarded with a column carrying every plug he submitted.

Walter could be capricious. If a publicist submitted a borrowed or inaccurate item, his name went on Walter's Drop Dead list. The publicist and his client became nonpersons, barred from mention in the column for a predetermined time. There was seldom possibility of parole.

Walter frequently was abusive and profane. Klurfeld recalled in 1979 that one of Walter's two secretaries was so terrified of him that she seldom left the telephone in the *Mirror* office, even to go to the bathroom. Walter often "fired" her, rehiring her after she was properly contrite. Once, a few days after she had been "fired," Klurfeld suggested they have a drink. Her eyes filled with tears. "Oh, do you still want to talk to me?" she asked. Klurfeld said, "She figured if she wasn't working for Walter, she was no longer of any interest."

Walter was unquestionably king of the columnists, with right of first refusal. He loved to see items he'd rejected turn up in Ed Sullivan's or another rival's column. He called the other Broadway columnists his wastebaskets.

Press agents joked nervously about Seven O'Clock Stomach, the jitters with which they awaited the first edition of the *Mirror,* when they turned to page ten to see if their client made the column. An agent was in a restaurant one night when friends belittled Walter. He turned his eyes skyward. "Please, Walter," he cried. "I'm not even *listening!*"

Robert Sylvester wrote of an approach he called "the weep," a note attached to the press release explaining that if the item weren't used the publicist would lose the account, or that his wife was ill and needed an operation. One desperate fellow, Sylvester reported, sent an ill-dressed child to a columnist, envelope in hand. "My daddy's sick in bed again," she was instructed to say, "and mommy said I should help him get well by bringing you this envelope."

"It was considered," Sylvester wrote, "that this lowered the dignity of the craft."

Publicists sometimes wrote entire *columns* for Walter—"Things I Never Knew Until Now," for instance, with plugs for a movie or show artlessly lodged among the trivia.

There were dangers in this. Once a publicist cribbed an entire column from a booklet he'd picked up at a bank. The booklet's author demanded money and a public apology. Walter was in a rage: *America might discover he didn't write the column all by himself.*

That lawyer was found who brings surcease to the afflicted, and he discovered that the publisher had changed the cover of the book without reapplying for a copyright, meaning the copy was in the public domain. Walter was off the hook. The publicist went on the Drop Dead list.

Publishing other men's work as your own is irresponsible at the least, but Walter did not invent the practice. The ghost-writer has long haunted the American landscape. The president of the United States who consistently wrote his own stuff went out with Coolidge.

Many talented newsmen have firsthand experience with publishers who can't write and businessmen who can't think and executives who claim they're too busy to do either, and giving them something to say is, as twentieth-century life goes, a relatively harmless way of making money.

But Walter pioneered as the ghost-written newsman. His associates are at pains to point out that he was a terrific editor who made major contributions with the blue pencil.

This defensiveness reveals an alarming lack of historical perspective. The public relations man has been part of American journalism about as long as the reporter, although this is seldom discussed at First Amendment seminars.

It can be argued that as Benjamin Franklin is the patron of American printers, Tom Paine and Sam Adams, publicists both, were premier American journalists. The press agent, noted Professor Alfred McClung Lee, "appear(ed) shortly after or with the periodical press and before the reporter."

In spite of the axiom that "the wisdom of the serpent is a somewhat more useful quality than the harmlessness of the dove" in dealing with press agents, the puff and pieces of special pleading muted the glory of the free press. In 1869 the *Times* printed an editorial "substantially as written" by President Grant's brother-in-law, a spokesman for the Fisk-Gould gang.

In 1844 a critic complained that "any enterprise that depends on advertising must have special men hired solely for the purpose of 'working the press' for notices, free advertising and the like."

It took an Act of Congress in 1887 to cut off free railroad passes for "trustworthy" reporters. The railroads then resorted to straight cash payments, prompting Chicago's ineffable Eugene Field to publish his going rates, including $1.50 a line for "complimentary notices of wives and children of railroad officials."

All this was symptomatic of a society in a hurry, with little time for the niceties. As things settled down, press agentry became more sophisticated. Ivy Lee, progenitor of the moderns, transformed the image of the elder Rockefeller from monopolist and wrecker into that of a benevolent old gentleman who handed out dimes to urchins.

"Any item is a puff which is of more interest to the firm or person mentioned than to the general public." That definition was handed down by C.H. Taylor, Jr., the publisher, to reporters on the Boston *Globe* in 1890.

But in 1926 Silas Bent found that 60 percent of the stories in the *Times* of December 29 were "suggested, created or supplied by some sort of publicity agency." He noted that his count did *not* include sports or society stories "to give them the benefit of a doubt they are not . . . supposed to deserve; nor did I count some fifty real estate items, all of which bore the earmarks of interested activity."

The percentage was pretty much the same for the *Sun* of that period, and Stanley Walker found that 42 of 64 local items in one newspaper "were rewritten or pasted up from press agent material."

That, of course, was the journalism which was Walter's kindergarten and Damon's training school. As times and tastes changed and Walter moved toward an end not even his enemies would have wished for him, he enjoyed a special relationship with two of his contributors, Frank Farrell, a columnist, and Irving Mandell, a publicist.

Farrell is very much a New Yorker, a man about Manhattan, a public relations consultant, speech writer, and self-described troubleshooter as the seventies waned for firms like Reynolds Metals and the Chase Bank. But he was best known to newspaper readers as a columnist, feature and entertainment writer for the *World-Telegram and Sun*.

No trace of his native Brooklyn remains in his speech, which is establishment. His russet hair is touched with gray. He has led a tumultuous life. The son of a hard-drinking Irishman, he was getting out of bed at 5 A.M. when he was six, supplementing the family income with a newspaper route. His mother died when he was seven, and he doubled his income by assisting the milkman, rising at four, before delivering the newspapers.

Later, on his way to school, he dropped off at church to serve as altar boy. At the end of the school day, he hustled out to Fort Hamilton to exercise polo ponies for Army officers, one of whom, George S. Patton, saw young Farrell as West Point material.

He was fourteen when his father died, adding a further complication to the Horatio Alger challenge. One of Farrell's brothers was married and preoccupied with his own financial battle; another brother had shipped out to sea. There was a younger sister. Farrell boarded her with a family in Connecticut and took a fourth job to pay her bills. He worked as a soda jerk from 5 P.M. to midnight. He learned that he could get along on four hours sleep, a pattern that has stayed with him.

The alternative in those days was the orphan asylum, which Farrell wished to avoid. He lived alone in a furnished room, forging his father's name to report cards which were good enough to earn him a scholarship to Bishop Loughlin Memorial High School.

When Farrell was fifteen, he won a statewide contest with an essay, "George Rogers Clark and the Winning of the Northwest Territory."

286

The publicity about that led to work as a school correspondent for the daily press. He quickly discovered that he could cover the same sports event for more than one newspaper, at space rates. He was something of an athlete, an outstanding juvenile horseman, a track and basketball star, so he sometimes reported events in which he starred.

When Farrell was earning $85 a week, he gave up the milk route. Otherwise, life continued along spartan lines. He became a full-time sportswriter for the Brooklyn *Times Union,* depending on the definition of full-time. By selecting early morning courses, he put himself through New York University without telling his editors. He was graduated with a degree in banking and finance and was in law school when World War II intervened.

It was a different New York then, somewhat more casual.

In '35 or '36 when I was going to law school at night, I wanted a day job [Farrell recalled one evening in 1979]. So I switched to the city desk and became a midtown reporter. At 8 A.M., I'd meet the Twentieth Century coming in with all kinds of Hollywood stars, very glamorous. I'd interview the famous who were staying at the Waldorf.

I became feature editor in 1939 after they offered me the society editor's job. I said, "I don't wear lace on my underwear, and it's a disappearing department. In a very few years, there'll be no society, anyway." They asked me to take over the columns. "You mean I'll be Pegler's editor?" I asked. I was told, "Why not? You're in law school anyway."

Pegler and I had many skirmishes. I was on to him. When I had covered the Yale-Harvard game, I'd write the running story, put a top on it for the late edition and write the overnight. I finished. The others finished. Pegler stayed on and on. He was the most painful writer I've ever known. I don't know how he lasted so long. One year, I waited just to see it. They put out all the lights in the stadium. The poor Western Union operator was lighting candles Pegler'd brought with him, knowing he wouldn't be finished. How long, after all, does it take to write one goddamned 750-word article?

Pegler, by the time Farrell became his editor, was off the sports beat, having, as he put it, gone cosmic. Used to his ways, Farrell said that if Pegler missed his deadline and there was a question about the column, "I'd call him at 4 A.M. to check it. I was a brash little brat of

287

about 25. Pegler was not one to fight in the open. He was thin-skinned and easily cut. But behind his typewriter, he was an artillery barrage."

In the late thirties Farrell began running into Walter at cocktail parties and receptions. One day Walter drifted over to him and said, "I've been reading your stuff, and it's just great." Farrell said, "I began writing columns for him then, things I couldn't put in the *World-Telegram* because they were a total departure from my style for Scripps-Howard."

Farrell went underground, becoming what was later called an investigative reporter, a line of work that in one form or another occupied much of his attention for the ensuing decade. He joined the German-American Bund, coming away with a series of eighteen articles. "They were too hot for Scripps-Howard to handle and they said 'Give it to Naval Intelligence and the Dies Committee.'" Farrell believes much of the material turned up in John Roy Carlson's exposé *Under Cover,* "but I couldn't do anything."

It was not a time for the peeves of authorship. Farrell enlisted in the Marines the day after Pearl Harbor. For four years with the 1st Marine Division, he warred through Guadalcanal, Tulagi, New Guinea, Palau, names all but forgotten but purchased at a bloody price. Farrell emerged with a chest full of medals he didn't wear, the Silver Star, the Bronze Star, the Asiatic-Pacific Campaign medal with six stars. He led assault waves and reconnaissance patrols.

The Silver Star citation noted that Farrell "voluntarily and with utter disregard for his own personal safety led numerous small patrols into enemy territory to secure vital information . . . On two occasions, he accomplished his mission at great risk of his life. . . ."

In January 1945, at his own request, Captain Farrell, as he was then, parachuted into the Chinese interior behind Japanese lines. He was assigned to harass Japanese shipping and communications. With the end of the war, he went after remnants of the Japanese Black Dragon network in China, discovering that the Germans had violated their surrender agreement and had worked with the Japanese, hoping to establish in the Orient a kind of Nazi government-in-exile.

With his two years of law school, Farrell was appointed special prosecutor and principal witness in the trial that followed. Twenty-one German agents and saboteurs drew sentences of from ten years to life.

One aspect of Farrell's military career is the kind that fuels Broadway cynicism, although he speaks of it without bitterness. He recalls, "I was on top of the world, writing about Broadway, heading

11 departments at the *World-Telegram*" when he shipped out to the Pacific. "And in four years, how many people do you suppose wrote me? Bette Davis, Walter, and perhaps four or five more. Every week, Walter sent me his columns with the names included for all the blind items and, at the bottom, the latest dirty jokes. Do you realize what it was like to be in the South Pacific and there was something for you in every mail you could show the other guys?"

Walter kept track of Farrell in his column. After two years on Guadalcanal, Farrell wrote, "Peculiarly, I don't want to come home; not yet, anyway. I think it would be pretty depressing. . . . For what I would find back there—and for what I would miss out here."

After the war Farrell wrote columns for Walter documenting the pro-Axis activities of Tokyo Rose and Kirsten Flagstad, the eminent soprano. He took over "New York—Day by Day," which, following O.O. McIntyre's death, fell into the hands of his biographer, Charles Driscoll, "who wrote about himself and his dog." Not everyone can do this five days a week. "The syndicate came to me and said, 'Look, he's running out of dog columns.'" Farrell had known McIntyre and his wife, and he was honored to take over the column.

Farrell slipped back easily into New York night life. He is a member of the Friars, the Dutch Treat, the Artists and Writers clubs, the New York Wine and Food Society. He squired beautiful women like Ann Miller, the dancer, and Ginger Rogers, who perhaps for purposes of sweet publicity named Farrell as one of the fourteen best dancers in the world.

There was a revealing blowup with Walter. Billingsley publicly badmouthed Frank Costello's wife and then, undoubtedly aghast, reported to Walter that Farrell made the injudicious comment. Walter, in Florida, called Farrell and asked him if he were trying to get himself killed. Farrell took the next plane to Florida, buttonholed Walter, and asked him why "after 20 years of friendship," Walter was ready to convict him "like a Hitler court."

The two men didn't speak for a couple of years. It was the sort of flare-up that often poisoned Walter's well. But he wrote nothing critical about Farrell. "He knew that I knew enough about him to crucify him," Farrell said, pointing out a first line of defense.

One night Farrell was in El Morocco with Elizabeth Taylor, then in the full bloom of her drenching beauty.

"When Elizabeth and I got up to leave, Walter came over. He asked, 'Are you going to be mad at me for the rest of your life?' I said, 'Well, you've got your Drop Dead list.' He said, 'Come on. Can't we shake hands?'

289

"I said, 'We'll shake hands first. Then you can shake hands with Elizabeth Taylor, which is what you wanted to do.'" Curiously, "That ended the feud."

Walter's power, his pettiness, vindictiveness, and occasional malignity overshadow in most memories the bursts of generosity and thoughtfulness which found their fullest expression in his friendship with Damon and his establishment of the cancer fund.

But in the fall of 1979 a white-haired public relations man named Irving Mandell sat in the Café Des Sports on West Fifty-first Street and, in an otherwise dispassionate appraisal of Walter's persona, recalled a couple of weeks with Walter that changed Mandell's life.

Mandell grew up in Newark. He was working for the old *Star-Eagle* as a fifteen-year-old schoolboy when he began monitoring the activities of the German-American Bund, which flourished in New Jersey. The Bund apparently was as mole-ridden as the Communist Party, U.S.A., would become in the 1950s. Mandell sent his notes to Walter.

He also sent Damon a story he'd written about a couple of men fishing, one of them with great success because he was baiting his hook with beer. Damon mentioned that item in his column. "You can imagine," said Mandell, "that set me up."

Some time later, Mandell was attending the fights at Madison Square Garden when he ran into Damon, who said, "Walter Winchell's here tonight. Would you like to meet him?"

Mandell glows at the memory. "I was a schoolboy," he said, "chatting with the two most famous newspapermen in America." Walter encouraged him to continue reporting on the Bund.

Mandell went off to a very tough personal war in Europe. He was decorated thirteen times. He became sports editor of *Stars and Stripes* *after* V-E Day, as he carefully points out.

"When I got out of the army," he said, "I went to Florida for a two-week vacation. I stayed fifteen years."

He landed a job as a sportswriter with the Miami *News*. He quit when the newspaper assigned him to the copy desk. "You know, sports writing is the best job on the newspaper, and after that. . . ."

He set up as a public relations man. It was tough going. He encountered Walter, who said he'd noticed Mandell's byline in the *News*.

"I told him I was now doing publicity. He said, 'You got many clients?' I said, 'One.' He said, 'You married?' I said, 'Yes.' He said, 'Tell your wife you're going to be with me the next couple of weeks.'"

It was as simple as that.

"At the end of that time, I had one of the biggest lists of clients in Florida. Walter took me everywhere, and he'd say to a prospect, 'This is Irving Mandell. You ought to go with him. I use his notes all the time.'"

The two men became close. That night in 1948 when Thomas E. Dewey learned he was not going to be president of the United States, Walter was doing, as Mandell says, "alleged color" on the election for ABC radio. Walter said, "Irving, these sons of bitches are giving me nothing but numbers. Write me something to say."

Mandell wrote under the gun, and Walter read the pages as they were handed to him and was heard by the vast radio audience to say, "Dewey will go down in history as one of our greatest admirals that son of a bitch Irving Mandell." ABC presented Mandell with a record of the utterance, and Mandell carried it with him and often threatened to play it back for Walter.

A little more than a decade later, Walter was broadcasting from Miami as Fidel Castro moved in on Havana. Castro was emerging as a folk hero to Americans at the time, puffed up as a kind of Robin Hood. Someone had given to Walter, for airing, a record Castro had made on his plans for a better tomorrow, which included no mention of the life and works of Karl Marx. Mandell, sitting with Walter as air time approached, said, "Walter, you know that son of a bitch is a Communist."

"'You've got to be kidding,' he said.

"I said, 'Get Hoover on the phone.'"

That, of course, was no problem for Walter, who told the G-Man, "I'm going to broadcast a tape Castro is sending me, and Irving tells me he's a Communist." According to Mandell, Hoover told Walter, "Irving is a very dear friend of Battista," the outgoing Cuban dictator. This was true enough, since Mandell cheerfully concedes that his client list included a good many Latin-American strongmen.

Mandell recalls, "Walter played the tape."

There is more to the story, of course, than the fact that Castro is a Communist and Battista wasn't. For a man who wrote about politics as much as Walter did, he was often thought to be ill-informed and even naive. He was also a great black-and-white man—not for him the nuance. Mandell's impression of Walter is shared by other of Walter's friends, although not by all of them.

"Walter was smart in merchandising what he produced," Mandell said, "and in getting an audience. I don't think he knew what he was doing half the time, but he was a very shrewd man." Ernest Cuneo

291

goes further. He wrote, "Walter had an IQ of brilliant proportions, nearly the equal of an Einstein."

Arthur Brisbane once advised a young journalist that if he would be successful "never lose your superficiality," and if Walter never heard the story, he absorbed the lesson, which helps explain the ease with which he moved from New Deal liberalism to Eisenhower conservatism and beyond.

Walter thought with his heart or, to put it more inelegantly, with his gut, and his political shift seems to have been based on chemistry. Even most of FDR's enemies admitted that he *looked* presidential and *sounded* presidential. He was, after all, up there for thirteen years. Walter idolized the patrician with the common touch, whose tenure in the White House coincided with Walter's metamorphosis from Broadway gossip to political gadfly, and who welcomed the poor boy from Harlem to the White House and shared secrets with him.

Truman was another matter. Many people had trouble adjusting to the man from Missouri with his haberdasher's clothes and flat, border-country accent and uninspired speech style, even during that brief period of sympathy and hope after the sun, the moon and the stars fell on him.

For Walter the honeymoon was brief. Cuneo arranged an Oval Office meeting between Truman and Walter. There is dispute as to exactly what happened. Irving Mandell's account has Walter entering the office to find Truman busy at his desk.

"The President finally looked up.

"Walter said, 'I'm Walter Winchell.'

"'So?'

"'I remember when a President sat in that chair,' Walter said and stormed out."

Other versions had Truman upsetting Walter with his profanity or making an anti-Semitic crack, either about a New York newspaper publisher or about Walter himself, a line Walter allegedly overheard when he stopped back to pick up his hat. Truman was accused of just about everything during his stormy presidency, but anti-Semitism was not often laid at his door.

Whatever the cause, and it may not have been much more than the clash of two feisty personalities, Walter was enraged when he stamped into the Stork Club, crying, "The man's no president! The man's no president!"

Walter was not so much for Dewey in 1948 as he was against Truman, telling friends, "I don't think either of them should win." The feeling was widely shared. The New York *Post* noted, "The radio

292

voice that Americans listen to most is not that of President Truman or Dewey but Walter Winchell's. In the midst of a presidential campaign, Walter is No. 1 on the Hooper rating list. His 23.1 rating is in dramatic contrast to the 2 or 3 points that political talks have averaged. Winchell's position as the veritable voice of America is even more remarkable in the face of the widespread belief that the end of the war had 'killed off the commentators.'"

Walter became an early, enthusiastic supporter of Eisenhower, visiting him when Eisenhower was president of Columbia University to urge that he run for the other presidency. Walter joyfully broadcast the Eisenhower inauguration from the White House steps. But he never confused Eisenhower with Roosevelt. To Walter there could be only one FDR.

Walter was a hard man to tune out, but trend-seekers could spot a blurring of identity. He became a voice in the crowd; it was no trick for a columnist to support Eisenhower, it seemed everyone was doing it.

The same thing was true of Walter's crusade against the Communists. Walter had attacked the Nazis while publishers solemnly considered fascism as a moral force. There was never any danger that Luce or Hearst or Roy Howard were going soft on communism. In effect, the once lonely crusader had slipped back in the pack.

But even A. J. Liebling, no admirer of Walter's, admitted "It is difficult not to agree with Winchell once in a while." He was commenting on Walter's public row with Andrei Vishinsky, in 1947 the chief Soviet delegate to the United Nations. As reported in the *Times,* Vishinsky, peeved at something Walter said, suggested he visit the Soviet Union to check out conditions for himself. Walter accepted, publishing a list of forty-one newsmen he'd take along, including Pegler, Jimmy Cannon, and Leonard Lyons, but adding, "I will go only if the Russian Government extends to me and the men I pick to go with me . . . the same courtesies that the Russian Tass men get over here—the right to go wherever they please and write what they please."

The trip never came off.

Walter then went belly up for Joe McCarthy, a final, dismaying apostasy for his liberal followers. Bob Thomas says Walter was threatened by McCarthy's forces, for during the war years, Walter had written flattering things about the Soviet Union.

But it is likely no threats were necessary. One of McCarthy's protégés was a young man named G. David Schine, whose father owned hotels, including the Roney Plaza, Walter's Miami Beach headquarters. The precocious G. wrote an anti-Communist broadside which the proud father thoughtfully placed in his hotel rooms, like a Gideon Bible. G. and a young lawyer named Roy Cohn were McCarthy's legmen. "Cohn took advantage of Walter," one of Walter's old friends recalled in 1979. "He sold him a bill of goods that he was going to save the country from communism."

Klurfeld argued that Walter frequently arrived at political views instinctively. With his sixth-grade education and casual reading habits, there was not much besides instinct and the counsel of advisers Walter could rely on as he told readers and listeners what to believe. There is no proof Political Science 101 would have helped either Walter or Coriolanus, but it couldn't have hurt.

Much of the time Walter reflected that anti-intellectualism endemic to American life and reflected in its journalism. "Of all horned cattle," Horace Greeley said, "the most helpless in a printing office is a college graduate."

The Front Page reporter asks a victim of a Peeping Tom, "Would you say he looked like a college professor?" No self-made merchant was more smug in his suspicion of formal education than Pulitzer, who was a good deal more thoughtful than most newspaper publishers because he had more to think with, and who argued, "the best college is the college of the world . . . the university of actual experience."

Professor Jacques Barzun found American newsmen "derisive, suspicious, faintly hostile . . . the democratic ego when faced with the intellect." By way of emphasis, Westbrook Pegler interrupted decades of interpreting the Constitution for his readers to proudly identify himself as a "misogrammarian, a dummy who does not know nothing, does not want to know anything and does not like intellectuals."

Although as glibly as any television talk show host Walter recommended books he hadn't read, there is no indication he believed books were the instrument of the devil, but he lashed out at eggheads, and he was capable of pronouncing Shakespeare okay because Shakespeare wrote for the groundlings, not the "high-domes."

The lashings-out were beginning to bore Walter's audience. As the fifties rolled along, nailing a suspected Communist in public life was a little like the late hit, or piling on, in a football game. Seven other people already had tackled him. The penalty was loss of interest.

Walter, who had derided Congressman Dies for coming up with Shirley Temple as a threat to the republic back in the thirties, stirred a brief sensation in 1954 with a blind item: "The number one star of television is a Communist." The accused was Lucille Ball, then at the height of her popularity with *I Love Lucy*. As her career teetered on the precipice of public fancy, she convincingly explained that in 1936 she had registered, just that once, as a Communist, to please her grandfather, an old-line Socialist. America forgave her.

Walter wrote with a snarl. In 1956 he cracked, "A vote for Adlai Stevenson is a vote for Christine Jorgensen," the latter an ex-GI who had undergone a sex-change operation. Twenty-six million Americans voted for Stevenson in 1956, and Walter's line reportedly alarmed putative sponsors.

Walter turned on a former protégé, a radio talk show man named Barry Gray, whom he called Borey Pink, but it was a tempest of only local interest, and readers and listeners across the land grew restless.

Walter's recklessness passed understanding. In 1951 television scored one of its first big hits covering Senator Estes Kefauver's hearings on organized crime. Walter denounced the committee for its treatment of his friend Frank Costello, who rewarded him with an exclusive interview. Walter pitched his questions underhand, although Costello conceded, "You can put down that I haven't sold Bibles all my life."

But Walter wrote a wisecrack about gambling which could only puzzle his readers as much as it pained his family. "The Kefauver committee is looking for Billy Koch, the bookie," he wrote, "but they'll have to dig him up to find him." That was Walter's farewell to the benefactor of his youth, the big-hearted uncle who had bought Walter the camera he needed for his first job in journalism. Koch had died of a heart attack shortly before the item appeared.

And finally, serving as metaphor for the fading gunslinger, there was the Baker affair. Josephine Baker was a black American entertainer who achieved enormous success in France between the wars. She returned to the United States with an act about which Walter raved after seeing it in Miami. She was appearing at the Strand Theater in New York when, on October 16, 1951, she and a party of friends dropped in for a late snack at the Stork Club. Service was slow, and Miss Baker, enraged, departed and later claimed she had been discriminated against and that Walter knew about it.

Walter had been in the Stork when she arrived but not, apparently, when she left. He was at first unaware of the problem. But then he sprang to the defense of his old pal, Sherman Billingsley, who had somewhat feebly denied Miss Baker's charges.

Walter being Walter, he soon was writing that Miss Baker was anti-Negro, anti-Semitic, a former supporter of Mussolini, and a "fellow-travellist." Since the Stork Club was not exactly celebrated as an equal opportunity provender, there was only one side for liberals, or even Ed Sullivan, to take, and after all those years they found Walter a sitting target.

Beginning in December 1951 the then-liberal New York *Post* ran a series of more than twenty articles about Walter. One estimate held that the series increased the *Post*'s daily circulation by forty thousand. It was an attempt at ax murder, clumsily enough done that the victim survived. The series also was soreheaded, since Dorothy Schiff, the *Post*'s publisher, had tried to hire Walter away from the *Mirror*. Walter had even dreamed up *The Lyons Den* as the name for Leonard Lyons' column, and Lyons frequently sought Walter's imprimatur for gags and items.

Under headlines like WINCHELL OVER HOLLYWOOD, WINCHELL ON THE AIR, WINCHELL'S MIAMI, WINCHELL & SULLIVAN (AND OTHER FEUDS), the articles were more bombs than bombshells. A team of seven reporters worked on the series. A couple of them uncovered Klurfeld as Walter's No. 1 ghost. Identifying himself as a shoe salesman, Klurfeld was uncommunicative, although the *Post*men pried out the information that he was "some kind of a writer" from a candy store proprietor.

In 1979 Klurfeld was amused by that memory. "All they had to do," he said, "was call my mother. She would have told them everything. She was proud of what I was doing, and she thought I should be making more money."

The series shocked Walter into unaccustomed silence, but only temporarily. Klurfeld suggested ridicule as retort, but Walter reached for the old standby—he began calling the rival paper the *Compost,* alleged that James Wechsler, its managing editor, was a Communist and directed the FBI's attention to the "presstitutes."

It makes for dreary reading, but Walter's feud with Lyons was treated gravely. Ernest Hemingway had just survived a plane crash when he wrote in a letter from Nairobi in February 1954: "Walter, if it were possible, could you and Lenny call the feud off and be friends? It would mean a great deal to me if you could. This is one of the things I thought of when the chips were down."

The feud continued.

The *Post* brought a million-dollar libel suit against Walter and his various employers. Hearst and ABC forced Walter to make a public retraction of statements that either the *Post* or Wechsler were Communists or sympathetic to communism. The affair was as violent as anything cooked up by Bennett, Dana, or Pulitzer and somehow shabbier. No one seems to have learned anything.

When Walter discovered that he was personally responsible for punitive damages in any libel suit, he was furious. He gave ABC an ultimatum—accept that responsibility or he'd quit. He thus talked

296

himself out of a lifetime $16,000-a-week contract. He retreated to the Mutual radio network, which was not one of the big three.

Walter's private life was unraveling. His mother's health had failed, and she spent a year in California. When she returned to New York in 1949, she was checked into Doctor's Hospital. Assured by her doctors that she was all right, Walter headed for Miami Beach. A few days later, Jenny Winchell, aged seventy-seven, fell or leaped from her tenth-floor window.

There already were troubles with Walda. She blossomed into a pretty young woman with reddish-gold hair. She won a Hollywood contract and attended a studio acting school. Adopting the stage name Toni Eden, she appeared on Broadway in *Dark of the Moon*. Walter praised her performance in his column, without identifying her as his daughter, and he was not alone in that praise.

They were sometimes photographed together at a restaurant table or dancing, Walter and his baby girl. Then she eloped with an Army sergeant, changed her mind shortly after the ceremony, and found herself sued for divorce. The marriage was annulled.

Walda fell in love with a young Broadway producer named William Cahn. Walter suspected Cahn of being more interested in the Winchell name than in Walda. Soon his column bristled with attacks on "that con producer." He warned his Broadway friends to avoid Cahn. The romance ended.

Walter was in Hollywood when Walda, who had been undergoing psychotherapy, disappeared from her room at the Hotel Gotham. "Walda is very, very ill," he told reporters. Walda returned to her mother, but Walter's feelings about her were now ambivalent. He told Klurfeld, "She is full of so many fears. I don't know where she gets those fears." Like many womanizers, Walter had trouble accepting a daughter who was no longer a child. He said, remorsefully, "The apple never falls very far from the tree."

Television damaged Walter in two ways. It brought gossip, live, into the living room. There was no need to turn to Walter to find out who was phfft! or infanticipating, since the injured or joyous parties turned up, late at night, to talk about it in detail previously reserved for the courtroom or the obstetrician's office.

And when Walter took to television himself, he did not travel well. For a time his Sunday night program was, to use the kind of bastard word he favored, simulcast; that is, broadcast simultaneously on radio and television. What viewers saw was a querulous, squirrel-cheeked, gray man, yammering with his hat on. (With his hat off, under studio lights, he was cruelly bald.)

In 1956 he attempted *The Walter Winchell Show,* a half-hour variety program. It was, according to historians, not a bad program, except for its host. In what was called a cool medium, Walter came across hot, aggressive, and loud. The hated Sullivan, tongue-tied and rigid, was what the audience preferred. The Winchell budget allowed just one "name" guest each week, perhaps most memorably Helen Hayes, who decided she was tired of doing dramatic monologues and instead would offer Lewis Carroll's "Jabberwocky."

Advertising agencies supervised entertainment programs at the time. Although there was no listing for a Lewis Carroll in *Red Channels,* the blacklister's bible, the agency man assigned to nail subversive references on the Winchell show demanded to see a copy of Carroll's contribution, since it did not appear in the script.

He was confounded when it was handed to him. "I can't understand a word of it!" he protested, his eyes narrowing.

Walter, conceding he had only a sixth-grade education, offered to interpret. He took one look. "Christ, this doesn't make any sense," he said. "Whoever typed it ought to be fired."

Miss Hayes and Mr. Carroll prevailed, but the Winchell show folded after thirteen weeks and Walter, who had crowed over his Hoopers, now threatened an exposé of the Nielsens, "the rating system which devastates and puts people out of work."

His only television success would be offscreen, narrating a television series called *The Untouchables.* It was cops and robbers and, after each broadcast, Walter called the producers with the verdict of the UN—the "underworld nobility."

By the midfifties Walter was in syndicate trouble. Only 150 newspapers were carrying his column, down from a high of around 1,000. One hundred and fifty newspapers is more than a respectable number—unless you were Walter Winchell, cock of the walk for three decades.

"Oh, well," he told Klurfeld, "you can't be Number One forever." But he was baffled. "I'm still writing the same type of column," he said. "I'm still doing what I have always done. I don't know what the editors want. I really don't know what's happening."

He began offering racetrack tips on his broadcast. He offered information on the stock market, attracting the attention of the Securities and Exchange Commission and financial columnist Sylvia Porter, who analyzed more than forty stocks recommended by Walter and concluded that while a buyer acting on Walter's information would have done all right, "he would have made out just as well or better if he had bought any of several hundred stocks which have gone up in an almost perpendicular line in this period of a rising market."

The coup de grâce was applied on October 16, 1963, when the *Mirror* folded, never having recovered from a six-month New York newspaper strike. A brief announcement killed the self-proclaimed "newspaper with a heart" in its thirty-ninth year, Volume 40, Number 99.

"I've lost my flagship," Walter said. The *Herald Tribune,* the hectic flush on its own cheek, dispatched Jimmy Breslin to the scene. Like everyone else in the devastated newsroom, he wanted to speak with Walter.

"He had no hat on," Breslin wrote, "but his blue television shirt was flashy. Winchell put a foot up on a chair and began to talk softly.

> "June 10, 1929," he said. "I walked right into this place and I was ready to swing."
>
> "Tell me about the big one with Lepke," somebody said to him.
>
> "It was on the corner of Fifth Avenue and Twenty-eighth Street between 10:20 and . . ." Walter reminisced briefly. Then:
>
> "What's left?" he was asked.
>
> "I'm sixty-six," he said quietly. "I've had an awful lot of action over the years."
>
> You don't have to worry about him. But the ones he was looking at, the ones who were standing by their desks and talking, they are the ones that were hurt when the *Mirror* went last night. Oh, they'll get jobs. But working for a newspaper can get to be a way of life more than a job, and now these people stood and talked and their way of life was gone.

There is something about the diurnal rhythm of journalism that is as seductive as it is wearying. Newsmen who give it up are seldom happy. Often they develop haggard, even guilty looks, as though whatever cushy job they have chosen is less honorable. They become belligerent and defensive and talk about how much money they are making.

Herbert Bayard Swope walked out on the *World* to a kind of leftover life as a publicist, and more than twenty years after he met his last deadline, he was rather forlornly writing, "I have been a newspaper-man all my life." Long after Gene Fowler had gone over to Hollywood gold, he insisted, while testifying in court, that he was a newspaper-man.

There was more than personal tragedy in the collapse of the *Mirror,* however. It was no monument to American journalism, but its disappearance took a little verve from metropolitan life. Bob Considine saluted Fred Keats, a handicapper of horses who "had not set foot in the building in years." Considine remembered "a saintly soul put down by Providence into the profane world of tabloid journalism," who edited Considine's copy so that Jimmy Braddock, denying he wanted a rematch with Louis, came out saying, "Heck's bells, I'm not going to let them make a football outta my head." Two *Mirror* journalists were members of the Henry the Eighth club, restricted to men who had been married at least five times.

The *Mirror's* society editor, writing as Barclay Beekman, was a badly nearsighted fellow named Howard Shelly, who stationed himself at the front door as the Metropolitan Opera opened its season and, by way of saving Hearst money, would tell the photographer whose picture to take. Often, after sticking his face into the faces of an arriving couple, he cried loudly, "They're nobody!"

And so, while sobbing for the *Mirror* was controlled, there was truth in the remark of the historian Theodore H. White to Breslin: "When a newspaper folds, we think immediately of the loss of jobs. I think of something much more important. The loss of a voice. This town's major industry is the word business. We make all the ideas for the whole western world." The *Mirror* was never much on ideas, but it was a voice.

Breslin was wrong when he said there was no need to worry about Walter. Along with other *Mirror* features, Walter's column moved to the *Journal-American,* where editors treated it indifferently, and in a couple of years it was cut back to just three truncated appearances a week.

Even by the standards of the sensational press, it was hard to call the *Journal-American* a newspaper. In a darkly prophetic piece called *Toward a One-Paper Town,* written on February 18, 1949, A. J. Liebling examined a copy of the *Journal.*

Not counting the sports and financial pages it contained eighteen columns of what might be called news—*Ex-Cop and Wife Die in Auto Crash, Red Trial Police Scan Spectators.* . . .

Eight columns—two on the first page and six on the second—were consecrated to the memoirs of Robert Stripling, recently resigned investigator for the House Un-American Activities Committee. . . .

There were also 34 columns of space occupied by the output of 26 columnists, including Bob Hope, Major General David P.

Barrows (retired president of the University of California), Cholly Knickerbocker . . . Mary Haworth, Betty Betz Bets *(the Teen Set)*, Dorothy Kilgallen, Louella Parsons, Paul Gallico, Louis Sobol. . . .

Considine, whom Liebling elsewhere identified as a "sixth string Pegler," was listed as editor of the Stripling biography, as well as author of his own column, "which means that he filled six columns, or a third as much as the paper's total of straight news."

Walter had leaped from a sunk ship to one that was dangerously overloaded. For all their popularity, columnists frequently suffered from insecurity, a sense that they didn't, well, quite belong. They were viewed by many in the newsroom with mingled condescension and envy.

Walter entertained occasional doubts that he was a newspaperman at all, and there is a probably apocryphal story that one day he tried to butt in on a conversation between two *Mirror* reporters who ignored him. When he demanded angrily, "What's the matter? Aren't I part of this newspaper, too?" one of the reporters replied, "Only in the sense that a barnacle's part of a ship."

Past the age when most men retire and are financially independent, Walter had no domestic life to shelter him. One day when he was still at the top of the hill, he turned angrily from the telephone with a complaint about the problems of raising children.

"You don't have any children, Walter," Klurfeld recalled telling him. "You have a column. You don't have a wife. You have a radio program."

There was an awful truth in the comment. Walter might have echoed Flaubert's remark about Madame Bovary and said of the column, *"C'est moi."* Life without his column would be an abyss. The column had shaped and measured his life. He had grilled friends and acquaintances about the column, treating with pity and disbelief any indication that someone hadn't read it.

Walter undoubtedly approved of the free spirit sentiment expressed in Rodgers and Hart's "The Lady is a Tramp": "I never miss Winchell, I read every line." But once when Walter was in Miami Beach, he came upon Rodgers and a couple of other men as the composer was in the middle of an anecdote. Rodgers didn't know Walter very well, but he politely backed off and started the story over to fill Walter in. Walter listened a moment, then held up his hand like a traffic cop. "Sorry. It's no good for the column," he said and strolled off.

This egocentricity was hard to put up with, but it is in the finest journalistic tradition. "Pulitzer expected employes to give their life's blood to the *World,*" Swanberg wrote. "Any indication that an employe did not place a *World* idea, headline or news story in the same category of importance as his wife, his children and his God aroused his instant indignation."

Walter might have escaped Pulitzer's ire, but his obsession with the column left him little to step down to. Walter had no hobbies. He had learned to swim when he was thirty-five—insisting that "all his friends watch him"—but he didn't play golf or the piano, or fish, cook, or ice skate. He was not much of a reader. In Robert Frost's equation, Walter's avocation and Walter's vocation were one, as his two eyes were one in sight.

Walter talked about writing an autobiography. It was even announced in the press. But he said privately he would never write it because he couldn't tell the truth about himself. Cuneo told Klurfeld, "Christ, Walter doesn't even *know* the truth about himself." Few of us do, of course, but Walter's past was haunted by ghosts. So many had written so much for him through the decades that autobiography would be an adventure in anthropology, puzzling over old bones.

Since Walter had trouble composing more than an item at a time, Frank Farrell believed that asking him to write a book would be like entering a sprinter in the Boston marathon, "but I'd like to know just how much he banked in advances for it."

Walter may have listened to Damon, who said he would never write his autobiography because "If I told the truth, a lot of people, including myself, might go to jail."

And finally, Boy Peep or no, Walter remained jealous of his privacy. When in 1955 his long-time friend and sometime source, Ed Weiner, wrote a biography of Walter, he went on the Drop Dead list. Walter appeared to okay the project, but he objected to the adulatory tone of the book. He said he didn't want his friends prettying him up, although this doesn't square with his outrage at criticism. He also indicated that nobody should write Walter's story but Walter. Weiner had been a friend for more than twenty years, and a kind of bodyguard, but he never returned from Coventry.

Walter's preoccupation with work at the expense of his family raises the similar charge often made against busy executives, but journalism is more than a business; it is a strident and demanding mistress. We are told that the bravos of *The Front Page* "have small respect for themselves or each other as husbands, fathers and lovers." In *City Editor* Stanley Walker warned,

It is true, and a bit sad, that the laudable ambition to marry often leads a newspaperman into such a maze of difficulties that he loses his hair, his digestion and his ability to work. A few seem to thrive on connubial existence, and they appear happy in their suburban homes, with their automobiles and their droves of children. But it is a tough assignment for most. The nature of a newspaperman's work keeps him from home until unheard of hours. His wife, though she may be sympathetic, doesn't always like it, and comes to regard his work as a stupid and probably rotten exercise.

Journalism was by no means Walter's only mistress. He remained sexually vigorous until his final illness. "Bending and stretching," he told Klurfeld, was his favorite exercise. There always were young lovelies in line, hoping for a big publicity break.

When Walter visited Hollywood, studio heads tossed him starlets, or even an occasional star. But once when he emerged from a Hollywood nightclub, a young woman shed her coat in the parking lot and rushed toward him, naked. She was followed by a photographer. Walter ducked back into the doorway. Walter figured this was a blackmail attempt, and thereafter he preferred the scant solace of the professionally circumspect call girl.

There was one more-or-less long-lasting affair. It involved a young show girl. Walter dispatched Frank Farrell to settle her hotel bill and relocate her in an apartment. She has since been described as sophisticated beyond her sixteen years, but Farrell laughs at that.

"She was just a country girl," he said. "Five minutes' conversation and you knew all she had to say. But she was a good listener."

This made her an almost perfect companion for Walter. The affair ended when he heard that congressional gumshoes were on the trail. Prurience in America at that time still descended from Puritanism, which Mencken defined as the suspicion that somebody, somewhere, is having a good time.

The young woman accepted the end of the affair indulgently and disappeared into matrimony. June Winchell never reacted publicly to her husband's infidelities, but she was an intelligent woman and not likely to have listened with much patience as Walter leaned on the old crutch of the difference between sex and love.

Walter once told Klurfeld, "The problem with having a mistress isn't the screwing part. It's having to eat dinner twice in one night." But Klurfeld notes that Walter was hardly Walter in June's presence, the brash know-it-all disappearing in favor of Casper Milquetoast.

More serious troubles than Walter's carousing afflicted the family. After Walda's difficulties, Walter, Jr., became a problem that ended in tragedy. He had been an intractable child, inordinately fond of guns.

Once he smeared himself with ketchup and lay at a suburban roadside to see how motorists reacted.

"How would you grow up," he demanded, "if you were Winchell's kid?"

He made news when he pistol-whipped three youths who trespassed on the Winchell estate. He joined the Marines but was discharged as underage.

As a fifteen-year-old, he had accompanied his father to an exclusive interview with the recently cashiered Douglas MacArthur at the Waldorf Towers and was so impressed he told Walter he was going to make journalism his career. The delighted father assigned Klurfeld to write a column about cub reporters.

But when the son picked up a newspaper job and his byline appeared as "Walter Winchell, Jr.," which, after all, was his name, his father was outraged, and Walt, as the son liked to be called, lost the job.

After bumming around the country, he married a young woman he identified as the daughter of a Nazi general. He donned a Nazi uniform and stalked Third Avenue bars. In one battle, he jammed a broken bottle into a man's face, and Walter paid heavy damages. June Winchell called Arnold Forster and asked him to start denaturalization proceedings against her son. The lawyer gently explained you cannot denaturalize a native citizen.

Walt, his wife, and their two young children drifted, like so many other searchers, to California. He worked for a time as a dishwasher. He applied for welfare, identifying himself as a writer. On Christmas Day 1967 he stepped into his garage in Santa Ana and blew his brains out with a .38. He was thirty-two years old.

Father and son had written each other at the top of their voices, but not long before he died, Walt wrote Gene Fowler a letter about his father. He said that no one had ever written an accurate portrait of Walter. "Dad reveres the newspaper game to the extent that nothing except patriotism and my mother have ever entered his heart," he wrote. "He's a champion, Gene, and there are damned few like him left around."

Walt's suicide echoed that of another famous father's son. Damon, Jr., having written *Father's Footsteps,* with its painful appraisal of alcoholism, was fired from the Miami *News* for drinking. In April 1965 Walter got him a job with Irving Mandell.

"He only worked for me a couple of days," Mandell recalled. "Then he disappeared. About a week later, he killed himself." He was forty-seven.

The temptation is to draw a moral from these self-immolations. Two inheritors of famous names, "juniors" at that, bob up in a society which worships fame as much as it does money, sons of fathers who are too busy or too selfish to be fathers. Drifting and seeking, perhaps unwilling to be no more than "a better than average reporter," the sons come to bloody, willful deaths on warm-weather littorals, unable to escape the harsh climate of the soul.

But in an age of overheard psychology, speculation is easy and wrong.

And curiously, the daughters survived. In 1979 Walter's daughter, divorced, lived in southern California with her daughter and declined to be interviewed. Damon's daughter lived in a retirement home outside Cincinnati.

Walt's death, the gunshot fired by the son he never found time to know, killed something in Walter. The family tragedy was acted out as Walter's professional life descended to farce and despair.

The *Journal-American* folded in 1968, victim of another newspaper strike, and Walter's column appeared once a week in a short-lived hybrid called the *World Journal Tribune.* After that newspaper disappeared, the onetime king of the columnists turned beggar.

Walter took out a full-page ad in *Variety,* pleading for a newspaper job. "Is the 2d Largest Newspaper Circulation in America *(Wall Street Journal)* in the market for an extra janitor?" he asked.

"N.Y. Morning Telegraph? Never claimed being a newspaperman, Mr. Editor. Always called myself a newsboy. Peddling papers. Why not audition the column for one month?"

There were no takers. Walter called that "the only real humiliation in my otherwise frenetic, frenzied, frantic, happy life."

He began making unsolicited public appearances. Until management shooed him off, he wandered on stage where the singer Eddie Fisher was appearing with a comic named Buddy Hackett, formerly a supplicant for space in Walter's column. Now Hackett told the audience, "Walter used to be the Lion of Broadway. Now he's a pussycat. Here, pussy! Here, pussy!"

People kicked, now that Walter was down.

It got so bad that he made up with Ed Sullivan. Sullivan wrote an article for *The Ladies Home Journal,* conceding Walter "invented the Broadway column and wrote it better than anybody." The next time the two met, they shook hands, and Sullivan's wife told Walter, "You're not seventy. You're two thirty-fives."

She was being kind. Klurfeld, unceremoniously cut loose by Walter in 1965, ran into him a few years later. "Old age hadn't crept up on him," he wrote. "It had pounced with a flying leap."

When a couple of press agents threw a seventieth birthday party for Walter, attendance was spotty. "Walter was so grateful," a guest recalled, "it was pathetic."

Variety finally picked up the Winchell column. Cuneo told Klurfeld, "Walter's office has become like something out of *Sunset Boulevard*. For no reason, a state of euphoria exists. He thinks nothing has changed. When he was in Chicago, he confided to me, 'Nobody has my phone number.' Well, who the hell wants it?"

Walter, always something of an insomniac, endured sleepless nights after his son's death. He announced he was going to his Scottsdale, Arizona, home "to get his bearings." He had bought the place as a retreat for June, whose health had become delicate. He was proud of it. A few years earlier, when Klurfeld acquired a modest home in a New York suburb, Walter asked him what it cost. Given a figure, he commented, "That's about what my driveway in Scottsdale cost me." But it was a continent away from Broadway.

Walter announced his retirement on February 5, 1968. "This is the time for me to step down," he said, perhaps a decade too late.

He and June had a year together before she died of a heart attack at sixty-four. Not long thereafter surgeons discovered and removed a malignant tumor from Walter. Tired of "putting around the putting green," he returned to New York in 1970 for an abortive revival of the *Mirror*.

But in 1971 he went back to Los Angeles for medical treatments. He entered the University of California Medical Center at Los Angeles on November 19, 1971. The cancer spread, and four months later, aged seventy-four, he died.

Walda asked the press for privacy as she buried her father next to her mother and her brother in Scottsdale. "His entire family is here now," she said. Only she and a rabbi attended the service. She explained that her father died "technically of cancer, but actually of a broken heart."

Walter's death was front-page news. The *Times* printed a lengthy obituary, misspelling Klurfeld's name and, he believed, underestimating his contribution to the Winchell *corpus*. He was told not to worry, the errors would be corrected in *his* obituary.

The tendency was to bury Walter's works with the man. As far back as 1940, McKelway was writing "No one says 'making whoopee' any more" and disparaging other of Walter's neologisms. But "making whoopee" was cited proudly by one television talk show host in 1979 as his euphemism for lovemaking. "Infanticipating" turned up on the *Today* show the same year, with a note that Walter coined the word.

All that is not much more than a historical footnote. Walter's presence is sensed in more important ways. No columnist in 1980 remotely approached his power. The day of the syndicated pundit seemed past—there are no authorities quoted the way Lippmann was quoted, or Dorothy Thompson or Pegler.

But if it's accepted, as McKelway argued, that gossip in the American newspaper is almost solely due to Walter, then his influence flourished. Newspapers like the New York *Times,* which scorned the idea of carrying a saloon columnist when Walter was alive, now run columns of gossip with such titles as *Notes on People,* items about the celebrated and notorious that fall into a grab bag because they are seldom, under any reasonable definition, news.

On February 18, 1980, *The New Yorker* printed a cartoon in which one young thing advises another, "Gossip should be declared a medium." Gossip is frequently excused as being fun although it is tacky. Given the sanction of print, however, it can be malicious, even malevolent.

The suicide in 1979 of Jean Seberg, the movie actress, was blamed by a former husband on a blind item which had been published a decade earlier. That item was written by Joyce Haber, a gossip columnist for the Los Angeles *Times.* The column identified Miss Seberg, without naming her, as carrying the child of a Black Panther, a radical group of the period.

Devastated by the story, according to her husband, the actress miscarried. She returned with her dead baby to her small hometown in Iowa, selecting an open coffin for the child so her old friends and neighbors could see that the baby was white. After years of deepening sorrow, Miss Seberg killed herself on the anniversary of the child's birth. Questions have been raised about that version of the story, but why were public prints speculating about the paternity of a child anyway?

Yet it seemed improbable in 1980 that a gossip column ever carried that kind of power to hurt. Gossip columnists still existed, but it was hard to figure out why. Who read them? Who cared what their readers thought? By 1980 gossip columns only looked like the kind of thing Walter used to do better.

McKelway in 1940 drew a conclusion that remained true four decades later:

> Newspapers have bigger circulations than they ever had before, and they have never been held in less esteem by their readers or exercised less influence on the political and ethical thoughts of the times.
>
> There is not a truly distinguished newspaper editor in the country. The editors of the greatest newspapers are anonymous; nobody knows who they are and nobody seems to care. Editorials in the newspapers have begun to lose their force.

No matter how well written they are, nobody seems to pay much attention to them.

McKelway saw gossip as contributing to this unhappy state: "The people see no sense in paying any attention to an editorial in a newspaper if the editorial reads as if a writer is posing as a leader of thought or an arbiter of manners when, as editor of the paper, he . . . has just recommended to them as one of the features of his paper a column by Winchell or some other gossip-writer."

By 1980 it seemed that not only the American's right to privacy, but his *desire* for it were memories. The public prints and airwaves were clogged with personal confessions, family secrets, discussions of finance and sex. Strangers at parties exchanged secrets that once were carried to the grave.

The day when Damon, dying of cancer, could keep his lip buttoned about his illness for more than two years while writing a daily column seems to belong to prehistory.

The face of journalism was transformed.

In 1978 the American Newspaper Publishers Association reported that there were 1,756 daily newspapers in the United States with a record circulation of 62,000,000 and with 400,000 employes, third in manufacturing behind the automobile and steel industries.

But that was almost one thousand *fewer* dailies than there were seventy years earlier, and 1978's newspapers, most of them in one-voice communities, reached 82 percent of American households, down from 124 percent in 1950, when people bought more than one newspaper. Readership surveys showed "significant losses in virtually all age groups."

Somewhere there is a reliquary for dead newspapers, located not far from Mencken's graveyard for dead gods, "All mighty gods in their day, worshipped by millions, full of demands and impositions, able to bind and loose—all gods of the first class."

For the dead newspapers bellowed and brayed, too, embracing this doctrine, that political party. The *World* is there, the *Telegram,* the *Sun,* the *Herald* and the *Tribune* and the *Herald Tribune,* the *Call* and the *Transcript,* the *Jeffersonian,* the *Express,* the *Man,* the *Star,* the *Continent,* the *Evening Globe,* the *Journal* and the *American* and the *Journal-American,* the *Gazette* and the *Daily Advertiser.*

There are dozens more in the pathetic grotto reserved for the departed of New York journalism.

Publishers, turning aside from their ledgers, wonder what went wrong. This paper died of bad business practices, this one became a bore. Surveys are conducted. Specialists are consulted. Comic strip sections expand. Promotions proliferate. New makeup is tried.

And new columnists are always hired, for an executive does not finish sophomore year in Publisher's College without learning that the hottest columnist, Walter in his prime, Damon in his, can be hired from a syndicate for a fraction of what it costs to feed and clothe one cub reporter.

In 1948 A. J. Liebling complained about "the small proportion of the personnel of the American press that is actually engaged in hunting for news, and the increasing distaste of publishers for practitioners of this pedestrian activity."

By 1980 New York City was down to three daily newspapers. The *Times* prospered. The *News* had fallen behind the *Wall Street Journal* as the daily with the largest circulation in the nation, and, like much of the metropolitan press, seemed hostage to the suburban captivity of the newspaper, as it struggled to find a new voice. The *Post* was so far gone in irresponsibility as to be "a force for evil," according to the *Columbia Journalism Review,* and was losing gratifying amounts of money.

New York as a three-newspaper town is a shame of the cities. One excuse is that the high cost of labor and antiquated union rules frighten off prospective publishers, the sort of problems the elder Bennett would have to walk around the block before solving.

On the lists of great or best newspapers, some names seldom change. The *Times* is always there, the Louisville *Courier-Journal,* the *Christian Science Monitor,* the St. Louis *Post-Dispatch,* and the Milwaukee *Journal*. None has ever been celebrated for the number of syndicated columns it carried.

Even if Walter and Damon returned to a journalism that was receptive to their talents, however, they would undoubtedly look for different beats. There is little that is exciting, enticing, or romantic about Broadway which once was home to them.

Discos discourage conversation in ways that nightclubs didn't, and such *mots* as are reported corroborate May Bertram's observation in *The Beast in the Jungle:* "What's the most inveterate mark of men in general? Why, the capacity to spend endless time with dull women— to spend it, I won't say without being bored, but without minding that they are . . . which comes to the same thing."

Stand on Fifty-seventh Street at sunset and look toward Times Square as the city lights come on, and it is deceptive. This was the beat of the men who invented Broadway. Ghosts of pretty, wicked girls and their escorts hustle out of cabs to warrens where they may find good food and drink and entertainment. Dusk just about anywhere is the kindest time of day.

But the reality offers a sleazy, frightening street of sex shows and fast food shops, a street given over to thugs, understandably nervous tourists, homosexuals and hookers who look like rejects from some Port Said bus terminal, junkies and drunks.

Perhaps that despond is transient. A better poet than Don Wahn or Damon surveyed Broadway as an old man, forever. In 1888 Walt Whitman wrote:

> What hurrying tides, or day or night!
> What passions, winnings, losses, ardors, swim thy waters!
> What whirls of evil, bliss and sorrow, stem thee!
> What curious questioning glances—glints of love!
> Leer, envy, scorn, contempt, hope, aspirations!
> . . . Thou, like the parti-colored world itself, like infinite, teeming, mocking life!
> Thou visor'd, vast, unspeakable show and lesson!

Just a couple of blocks off Broadway, right there in midtown, is that monument to Damon and Walter, the storied old speakeasy which supports research into the disease that killed them, and perhaps Damon's "goggly-eyed young fellow" will yet come up with something curative.

In the meantime, as an excited agent put it early in 1980, "Runyon is back!" There was a big Broadway premiere in March for Hollywood's latest version of *Little Miss Marker,* risen like the phoenix from her hospital bed. Plans were brewing for musicals based on short stories by Damon and for a musical version of *A Slight Case of Murder.* A standard edition of his writing was being discussed, like the New York edition of Henry James.

If that happens, of course, it will be a discovery for younger generations.

Frank Farrell recalled having drinks with three young advertising men in the late 1970s.

"Well," he observed, "as Walter Winchell used to say, 'Sex is the most fun you can have without laughing.'"

His companions smiled, and then one of them asked Farrell, "Who is Walter Winchell?"

bibliography

One way or another, all the following books are part of the preceding book. Most are quoted directly. Some contributed indirectly to the writer's understanding of time, place or situation. In a few cases, references wound up in the wastebasket only because the writer felt he was running out of space.

My particular thanks to Professor James Boylan of the Columbia University School of Journalism, who helped get this project under way through his generous loan of books, and to Richard Hill, librarian, and Charles Brown and Charles Benson of the Newspaper Reading Room of the New York Public Library.

Adams, Franklin P. *The Diary of Our Own Samuel Pepys*. New York: Simon and Schuster, 1935.

Alsop, Joseph and Stewart. *The Reporter's Trade*. New York: Reynal & Company, 1958.

Atkinson, Brooks. *Broadway*. New York: Macmillan Publishing Company, Inc., 1974.

Barris, Alex. *Stop the Presses*. South Brunswick and New York: A.S. Barnes and Company, 1976.

Beer, Thomas. *The Mauve Decade*. New York: Alfred A. Knopf, 1926.

Bent, Silas. *Ballyhoo*. New York: Boni and Liveright, 1927.

Berger, Meyer. *New York*. New York: Random House, 1960.

Boylan, James, ed. *The World and the 20's*. New York: Dial Press, 1973.

Breslin, Jimmy. *The World of Jimmy Breslin*. New York: The Viking Press, 1967.

Britt, George, ed. *Shoe Leather and Printer's Ink*. New York: The New York Times Book Company, 1974.

Carlson, John Roy. *Under Cover*. New York: E. P. Dutton & Co., 1943.

Carlson, Oliver. *Brisbane*. New York: Stackpole Sons, 1937.

———. *The Man Who Made News*. New York: Sloan and Pearce, 1942.

Carmichael, Hoagy. *The Stardust Road*. New York: Rinehart & Company, Inc., 1946.

Chapman, John. *Tell It to Sweeney*. New York: Doubleday and Company, Inc., 1961.

Churchill, Allen. *Park Row*. New York, Toronto: Rinehart & Company, Inc., 1958.

———. *The Great White Way*. New York: E. P. Dutton & Co., Inc., 1962.

Clark, Tom. *The World of Damon Runyon*. New York: Harper and Row, 1978.

Clegg, Charles & Duncan Emrich, eds. *The Lucius Beebe Reader*. Garden City, New York: Doubleday and Company, Inc., 1967.

Cobb, Irvin S. *Exit Laughing*. Indianapolis, New York: The Bobbs-Merrill Company, 1941.

Considine, Bob. *It's All News to Me*. New York: Meredith Press, 1967.

Dixon, George. *Leaning on a Column*. Philadelphia and New York: J. B. Lippincott Company, 1961.

Drewry, John E., ed. *Post Biographies of Famous Journalists*. A University of Georgia Press Book. New York: Random House (distributors), 1942.

Elder, Donald. *Ring Lardner*. Garden City, New York: Doubleday & Company, 1956.

Fisher, Charles. *The Columnists*. New York: Soskin Publishers, 1944.

Fitzgerald, F. Scott. *The Crack Up*. Edited by Edmund Wilson. New York: A New Directions Paperbook, 1956.

Fowler, Gene. *Skyline*. New York: The Viking Press, 1961.

Gardner, Gilson. *Lusty Scripps*. New York: The Vanguard Press, 1932.

Gatewood, Worth, ed. *Fifty Years in Pictures*. New York: Doubleday & Company, 1979.

Gauvreau, Emile. *My Last Million Readers*. New York: E. P. Dutton & Co., Inc., 1941.

Hale, William Harlan. *Horace Greeley*. New York: Harper & Brothers, 1950.

Hershkowitz, Leo. *Tweed's New York*. Garden City, New York: Doubleday & Company, Inc., 1977.

Hosokawa, Bill. *Thunder in the Rockies*. New York: William Morrow & Co., Inc., 1976.

Howe, Irving. *World of Our Fathers*. New York and London: Harcourt Brace Jovanovich, 1976.

Hoyt, Edwin P. *A Gentleman of Broadway*. New York and Toronto: Little, Brown and Company, 1964.

Hutchens, John K. and George Oppenheimer, eds. *The Best in the World*. New York: The Viking Press, 1973.

Kael, Pauline. *Raising Kane*. Toronto and Boston: Little, Brown and Company, 1971.

Kahn, E. J., Jr. *The World of Swope*. New York: Simon and Schuster, 1965.

Katz, Harvey. *Give!* New York: Anchor Press, Doubleday, 1974.

Kieran, John. *Not Under Oath*. Boston: Houghton Mifflin Company, 1964.

Klein, Alesander. *The Empire City*. New York and Toronto: Rinehart & Company, Inc., 1955.

Klurfeld, Herman. *Winchell*. New York: Praeger Publishers, 1976.

Langford, Gerald. *The Richard Harding Davis Years*. New York: Holt, Rinehart and Winston, 1961.

Larder, John. "The Secret Past of a Popular Author." *The New Yorker*, August 27, 1949.

Lardner, Ring. *The Best Short Stories of Ring Lardner*. New York: Charles Scribner's Sons, 1957.

———. *Some Champions*. Edited by Mathew J. Bruccoli & Richard Layman. New York: Charles Scribner's Sons, 1976.

Lardner, Ring, Jr. *The Lardners My Family Remembered*. New York, Hagerstown, San Francisco and London: Harper & Row, 1976.

Lee, Alfred McClung. *The Daily Newspaper in America*. New York: The MacMillan Company, 1937.

Lee, James Melvin. *History of American Journalism*. Boston and New York: Houghton Mifflin Company, 1917.

Liebling, A. J. *The Press*. New York: Ballantine Books, 1975.

Lindstrom, Carl E. *The Fading American Newspaper*. Garden City, New York: Doubleday and Company, Inc., 1949.

Mallen, Frank. *Sauce for the Gander*. New York: Baldwin Books, 1954.

Marquis, Don. *The Lives & Times of Archy & Mehitabel*. Garden City, & New York: Doubleday and Company, Inc., 1950.

Mencken, H. L. *A Mencken Chrestomathy*. New York: Alfred A. Knopf, 1949.

Montaigne, Michel de. *Essays*. Translated by J. M. Cohen. Penguin Books, 1978.

Mott, Frank Luther. *American Journalism*. New York: The Macmillan Company, 1941.

O'Conner, Richard. *The Scandalous Mr. Bennett*. Garden City, New York: Doubleday & Company, Inc., 1962.

———. *Heywood Broun*. New York: G. P. Putnam's Sons, 1975.

Oppenheimer, George, ed. *The Passionate Playgoer*. New York: The Viking Press, 1958.

Pearson, Drew. *Diaries*. Edited by Tyler Abell Holt. New York, Chicago and San Francisco: Rinehart and Winston, 1974.

Pegler, Westbrook. *'T Ain't Right*. Garden City, New York: Doubleday, Doran & Co., Inc., 1936.

Pilat, Oliver. *Pegler: Angry Man of the Press*. Boston: Beacon Press, 1963.

Rivers, William L. *The Mass Media: Reporting, Writing, Editing*. New York, Evanston, San Francisco, London: Harper & Row, 1975.

Rogers, W. G., and Mildred Weston. *Carnival Crossroads*. Garden City, New York: Doubleday and Company, Inc., 1960.

Runyon, Damon. *The Best of Damon Runyon*. New York: Pocket Books, Inc., 1940.

———. *Damon Runyon Favorites*. New York: Pocket Books, Inc., 1943.

———. *Short Takes*. New York: McGraw-Hill, 1946.

———. *Trials and Other Tribulations*. Philadelphia and New York: J. B. Lippincott Company, 1947.

———. *A Treasury of Damon Runyon*. Selected by Clark Kinnaird. New York: Modern Library, 1958.

———. *From First to Last*. London: Pan Books, 1977.

———. *On Broadway*. London: Pan Books, 1977.

Runyon, Damon, Jr. *Father's Footsteps*. New York: Random House, 1954.

Seitz, DonCarlos. *The James Gordon Bennetts—Father & Son, Proprietors of the New York Herald*. New York: Beekman Publishers, Inc., 1974.

Seldes, George. *Lords of the Press*. New York: Julian Messner, 1946.

Smith, H. Allen. *The Life and Legend of Gene Fowler*. New York: William Morrow and Company, Inc., 1977.

Snyder, Louis L., and Richard B. Morris, eds. *A Treasury of Great Reporting*. New York: Simon and Schuster, 1949.

Sobol, Louis. *The Longest Street*. New York: Crown Publishers, Inc., 1968.

Spigelgass, Leonard. *Damon Runyon*.

Stagg, Jerry. *The Brothers Shubert*. New York: Random House, 1968.

Stallman, R. W., and E. R. Hagemann, eds. *The New York City Sketches of Stephen Crane*. New York: New York University Press, 1966.

Stone, Candace. *Dana and the Sun*. New York: Dodd, Mead & Company, 1938.

Stone, I. F. *In a Time of Torment*. New York: Vantage Books, Random House, 1965.

———. *The I. F. Stone's Weekly Reader*. Edited by Neil Middleton. New York: Random House, 1973.

Stone, Melville, E. *Fifty Years a Journalist*. Garden City, New York: Doubleday, Page & Company, 1921.

Stuart, Lyle. *The Secret Life of Walter Winchell*. New York: Boar's Head Books, 1953.

Swanberg, W. A. *Citizen Hearst*. New York: Charles Scribner's Sons, 1961.

———. *Pulitzer*. New York: Charles Scribner's Sons, 1967.

———. *Luce and His Empire*. New York: Charles Scribner's Sons, 1972.

Sylvester, Robert. *Notes of a Guilty Bystander*. New Jersey: Prentice-Hall, Inc., 1970.

Talese, Gay. *The Kingdom and the Power*. New York and Cleveland: World Publishing Company, an NAL book, 1969.

Taylor, Bert Leston. *The So-Called Human Race*. Arranged by Henry B. Fuller. New York: Alfred A. Knopf, 1924.

Thomas, Bob. *Winchell*. New York: Doubleday & Co., Inc., 1971.

Villard, Oswald Garrison. *Some Newspapers and Newspaper-men*. New York: Alfred A. Knopf, 1926.

Walker, Danton. *Danton's Inferno*. New York: Hastings House, 1955.

Walker, Stanley. *City Editor*. New York: Frederick A. Stokes Company, 1934.

———. *Mrs. Astor's House*. New York: Frederick A. Stokes Company, 1935.

Wanger, Jean. *Runyonese*. Paris, New York and London: Stechert-Hafner, Inc., 1965.

Weiner, Ed. *The Damon Runyon Story*. New York, London and Toronto: Longmans, Green and Co., 1948.

———. *Let's Go to Press*. New York: G. P. Putnam's Sons, 1955.

Wheeler, John. *I've Got News for You*. New York: E. P. Dutton & Co., Inc., 1961.

Winchell, Walter. *Winchell Exclusive*. New Jersey: Prentice-Hall, Inc., 1975.

Winslow, Susan. *Brother Can You Spare a Dime?* Assisted by Wendy Holmes. New York and London: Paddington Press, Ltd., 1976.

Yardley, Jonathan. *Ring*. New York: Random House, 1977.

index

Adams, Abbie Reinhardt, 144
Adams, Franklin P., 49, 89, 169–70, 173
Adams, Henry, 70
Adams, Maude, 32
Adams, Satir C., 144
Albee, Edward F., 81
Alexander, Grover Cleveland, 106
Anderson, Maxwell, 172
Arendt, Hannah, 232
Arthur, Art, 196
Asinof, Eliot, 159

Baer, Bugs, 25, 125, 157, 182, 247–48, 270
Baker, J. Frank, 91
Baker, Josephine, 295
Ball, Lucille, 294–95
Barzun, Jacques, 294
Beaverbrook, Lord, 19
Becker, Charles, 49
Beebe, Lucius, 185
Beer, Thomas, 50
Bennett, James Gordon, 36, 48, 51, 176
Bennett, James Gordon, Jr., 38
Benny, Jack, 246
Bent, Silas, 51, 110, 119, 137, 138, 147, 153, 154, 162, 285
Bentley, E.C., 200
Berger, Meyer, 23, 206, 236
Berkeley, Sir William, 34
Berle, Milton, 280
Bernhardt, Sarah, 41–42
Bernie, Ben, 196
Betts, Tony, 209
Bierce, Ambrose, 21, 42, 48
Billingsley, Sherman, 191, 204, 205, 266, 289, 295
Bishop, Jim, 177

Blaine, James G., 43
Bonfils, Frederick G., 62
Boorstin, Daniel, 55
Boylan, James, 166
Bradley, William, 92
Brady, Diamond Jim, 31
Brandeis, Louis D., 159
Brando, Marlon, 20
Breslin, Jimmy, 299, 300
Brinkley, Nell, 210
Brisbane, Arthur, 52, 64, 87, 112, 120, 121, 162, 209–11, 213, 214, 222–23, 225, 232, 292
Broderick, Johnny, 207, 261
Bromfield, Louis, 25
Broun, Heywood, 151, 166, 172–73, 209
Brown, Ned, 50
Browning, Edward West, 146–48
Bruno, John, 204
Bryan, J., III, 184
Buchalter, Louis "Lepke," 23, 229–31
Bulger, Bozeman, 89, 117
Burke, Billy, 31
Burns, George, 246
Burns, Tommy, 98
Byrd, Admiral, 134

Caesar, Arthur, 171
Cahn, William, 297
Cannon, Jimmy, 223–24, 247, 263
Cantor, Eddie, 76, 226
Capone, Al, 22, 190, 197
Capone, Ralph, 226
Carlson, John Roy, 237
Carmichael, Hoagland, 216–17
Carpentier, Georges, 119
Carroll, Earl, 148, 170
Cashman, Harry, 85

Castro, Fidel, 291
Chadwick, Henry, 36
Chamberlain, Neville, 258
Chaplin, Charlie, 76
Cheever, John, 273
Churchill, Allen, 32, 33, 37
Cicotte, Ed, 107
Clark, Tom, 141, 255
Clayton, Lou, 160
Cobb, Irvin S., 117, 148, 148–49
Cohn, Roy, 294
Coll, Peter, 191
Coll, Vincent, 23, 191–92
Compton, Betty, 134
Condon, Glenn, 82
Considine, Bob, 209, 223, 248, 281,
    300, 301
Coolidge, Calvin, 125
Corum, Bill, 273–74
Costello, Frank, 231, 295
Coughlin, Rev. Charles E., 239–40
Crane, Stephen, 31, 43, 47, 50
Creelman, James, 50
Crosby, John, 262–73
Cuneo, Ernest, 205, 257–58, 263–64,
    291–92, 302, 306
Custer, George Armstrong, 53

Dafoe, Dr. Allan Roy, 220
Daly, John Charles, 280
Damon Runyon-Walter Winchell
    Cancer Fund, 15, 16, 25, 279–82
Dana, Charles Anderson, 29, 37, 38,
    48
Davis, Clarke, 52
Davis, Rebecca Harding, 52
Davis, Richard Harding, 28–31, 33,
    37, 45, 46, 50, 52, 105
Day, Benjamin H., 35
DeMange, Big Frenchy, 191
Dempsey, Jack, 84, 117–21, 163–65,
    174, 182
Denison, Lindsay, 49
Dewey, Thomas E., 230, 291, 292
Dickens, Charles, 125
Dies, Martin, 259–60
Doyle, Larry, 87
Drieser, Theodore, 43
Driscoll, Charles, 184, 185, 186, 289
Durante, Jimmy, 253, 259
Dwire, Bill, 226

Eagels, Jeanne, 137
Eastman, Monk, 159
Ederle, Trudy, 134
Edward, Prince of Wales, 135
Edwards, Gus, 75
Eisenhower, Dwight D., 293
Elwell, Joseph, 114
Erickson, Frank, 231
Etting, Ruth, 207

Fallon, William, 159
Farley, Francis, 136, 142
Farnsworth, Bill, 226
Farrell, Frank, 286–89, 302, 303,
    310
Fay, Larry, 25
Fields, W. C., 185
Finch, Frank "Doc Bird," 64, 65,
    66–67
Firpo, Luis, 121
Fish, Hamilton, 260
Fisher, Charles, 282
Fitzgerald, Scott, 132–33, 167, 174
Flegenheimer, Arthur, see Schultz,
    Dutch
Floto, Otto, 62
Foch, Marshal, 106
Ford, Henry, 188, 234
Forster, Arnold, 236, 304
Fowler, Agnes Hubbard, 84, 104–5,
    106, 117, 126, 129, 130, 252
Fowler, Gene, 64, 65, 66, 83–84,
    102–3, 104–5, 117, 119, 124,
    127–28, 129, 134, 154, 156–58,
    160–61, 169, 173, 174, 178, 182,
    197, 209, 252, 299, 304
Fowler, Gene, Jr., 84
Fowler, Jane, 84
Fowler, Will, 84
Fraser, Sir John, 135
Frayne, Ed, 226
Frohman, Charles, 31
Frost, Robert, 302
Fulton, Fred, 117–18

Gallico, Paul, 177
Gasch, Marie Manning, 210
Gauvreau, Emile, 151–52, 171–72,
    176, 178, 180, 189, 209, 210,
    211, 222, 229
Gibbons, Tom, 120

Gibbs, Surgeon, 50
Gibson, Charles Dana, 29
Gibson, Jane, 139
Gill, John F., 278
Glasgow, Ellen, 185
Goddard, Morrill, 43–44
Godfrey, Arthur, 280
Goebel, William, 48
Goetz, Harry, 245–46
Goldberg, Rube, 119
Gould, Jay, 38
Gowdy, Hank, 106
Gray, Barry, 295
Gray, Henry Judd, 154–55
Greeley, Horace, 35, 48
Green, Chuck, 207
Green, Rita, 78–79, 80, 81–82
Guinan, Mary Louise "Texas,"
    191–92
Gunther, John, 84

Haber, Joyce, 307
Hackett, Buddy, 305
Hall, Rev. Edward W., 137–38
Hall, Mrs. Edward, 137–39, 141, 154
Hammerstein, Oscar, II, 280
Hanafusa, Dr. Hidesaburo, 18
Harding, Warren G., 125
Harris, Benjamin, 34
Harris, Robin, 188
Hauptmann, Bruno Richard, 212
Hawley, Joyce, 148, 170
Hayes, Helen, 298
Hearst, George, 41, 42
Hearst, Phoebe Apperson, 41, 42
Hearst, William Randolph, 20, 29,
    31, 41–49, 51, 84, 100–1, 104,
    112, 135, 137, 142, 157, 158,
    176, 179, 180, 186–87, 189, 194,
    207, 208, 211, 223, 224, 232
Hearst, Mrs. William Randolph, 142
Hecht, Ben, 102, 153, 195
Heenan, Frances "Peaches," 147–48
Hellinger, Mark, 22, 176–77, 182,
    225, 228
Hemingway, Ernest, 296
Henry, O., 33, 83
Hill, George Washington, 180
Hitler, Adolf, 232, 234, 258
Hoffman, Clare, 260, 262
Hoffman, Irving, 230, 287–88

Hoover, Herbert, 188
Hoover, J. Edgar, 23, 229, 281–82
Howe, Irving, 71
Howey, Walter, 161, 179, 195
Hoyt, Edwin P., 53, 59, 125, 141,
    199, 214, 255
Hughes, Charles Evans, 102
Hughes, Langston, 167
Hutchens, John K., 166
Hutton, Barbara, 24

Igoe, Hype, 197, 267–68
Ingersoll, Col. Robert, 71
Ingram, Adm. Jonas, 262
Irwin, Will, 38, 49

Jacobs, Mike, 226, 276
James, Henry, 70
Jeffries, James J., 98
Jessel, George, 74
Johnson, Jack, 98–100
Johnson, James L., 267
Jolson, Al, 195–96, 206, 246
Jorgensen, Christine, 110
Joyce, Peggy Hopkins, 136

Kael, Pauline, 194
Kahn, E. J., 100, 167
Kean, Jane, 283
Keaton, Buster, 125–26
Keeler, Ruby, 195–96
Kefauver, Estes, 295
Kelly, John, 256
Kennedy, Joseph P., 258
Kenny, Nick, 219
Kessler, Mr. and Mrs. George, 95
Ketchel, Stanley, 267
Kiernan, John, 169, 255–56
Kinnaird, Clark, 68, 124
Kipling, Rudyard, 153
Klurfeld, Herman, 73, 75, 80, 114,
    181, 182, 191, 192, 196, 221,
    226–27, 238, 257, 259, 261, 264,
    284, 294, 296, 297, 298, 301,
    302, 303, 305
Knickerbocker, Cholly, 86
Knox, Frank, 262
Kobler, Albert J., 135–36, 179, 209
Koch, Billy, 114, 295
Kofoed, Jack, 120

Krasna, Norman, 166
Kuhn, Fritz, 234–35, 240, 259

LaGuardia, Fiorello, 204
LaHiff, Billy, 182
Langford, Gerald, 29, 30
Lanza, Joseph "Socks," 279–80
Lardner, John, 19, 64, 120
Lardner, Ring, 84, 89, 108, 118–19, 160, 183–84
Lardner, Ring, Jr., 160, 208
Laurence, William L., 166
Leahy, Adm. William D., 261
Le Corbusier, 132
Lee, Alfred McClung, 120, 285
Lee, Ivy, 285
Lewis, Alfred Henry, 94
Liebling, A. J., 40, 202–3, 207–8, 293, 300, 309
Light, Enoch, 236
Lindbergh, Anne Morrow, 212, 214
Lindbergh, Charles, 162–63, 212
Lindbergh, Charles, Jr., 212
Lindeman, Leo "Lindy," 206–7
Lindemann, Clara, 206
Lindley, Ernest K., 166
Lindsay, Howard, 225–26
Lippmann, Walter, 112, 166, 209
Louis, Joe, 119, 226
Luce, Henry, 232, 233
Luciano, Charles "Lucky," 23
Lyons, Leonard, 228, 243, 257, 266, 280, 296

MacArthur, Charles, 102, 153
McCann, Dick, 198
McCarthy, Joe, 293–94
McCormick, Col. Robert R., 109, 112
MacDonald, Dwight, 232
MacDonald, Ramsay, 134
McEvoy, J. P., 221–22
Macfadden, Bernarr, 143–45, 176, 178
McGraw, John J., 87, 88, 95
McIntyre, Maybelle, 185
McIntyre, O. O. "Odd," 184–86, 187
McKelway, St. Clair, 17, 72, 76, 115, 166, 171, 179, 186, 187, 188, 205, 212, 215, 219, 231, 257, 258–59, 262, 263, 264–65, 307–8
McKinley, William, 45, 48

McManus, George, 161
McPherson, Aimee Semple, 283
McWilliams, Joe, 240–41
Madden, Owney, 23, 190–91, 192
Mallen, Frank, 142, 182, 192
Manckiewicz, Herman J., 194, 195
Mandell, Irving, 282, 286, 290–92, 304
Marie, Queen of Rumania, 134, 145
Marlowe, Julia, 32
Marquis, Don, 168–69
Martin, Dr. Haynes, 252
Martin, Quinn, 166
Marx, Groucho, 171
Mathewson, Christy, 87, 106
Maxwell, Marilyn, 256
Mencken, H. L., 30, 120
Mercer, Sid, 89, 224
Millay, Edna St. Vincent, 172
Miller, Webb, 106–7
Mills, Eleanor, 137–38
Mitchell, Charley, 87
Montague, James J., 91
Montaigne, 130
Moore, Jim, 274
Morgan, J. P., 197
Mott, Frank Luther, 35
Munsey, Frank A., 110
Mussolini, Benito, 232, 233

Nadel, Dr. Marion, 15, 16, 18, 24
Nesbit, Evelyn, 49
Nicholas, Dudley, 166, 168
Northcliffe, Lord, 49, 109, 110
Nugent, Frank, 228

Ochs, Adolph, 46–47
O'Connor, Johnny, 161
Ogilvy, Lyulph Stanley, 63
O'Malley, Frank Ward, 49
Oursler, Fulton, 149, 150

Paley, William A., 180
Parish, Mitchell, 216–18, 219
Parker, Dan, 208, 277, 280
Parker, Dorothy, 167
Patterson, Eleanor "Cissy," 260–61
Patterson, Capt. Joseph Medill, 109, 110–11, 136–37
Patterson, Thomas MacDonald, 62
Patton, Gen. George S., 286

Payne, Phil, 136–37, 142
Pegler, Arthur, 114
Pegler, James Westbrook "Bud," 71, 84, 114, 133, 165, 190, 233–34, 269, 287–88, 294
Pegler, Julia Harpman, 114
Perona, John, 205
Pershing, General, 106
Phair, George, 119
Phillips, David Graham, 49
Pisano, Little Augie, 226
Porter, Sylvia, 298
Pulitzer, Albert, 38, 43
Pulitzer, Herbert, 203
Pulitzer, Joseph, 36, 38–39, 43, 44, 45, 48–49, 50–51, 167, 203
Pulitzer, Joseph, Jr., 203
Pulitzer, Ralph, 173, 203

Raft, George, 25
Ralph, Julian, 49–50
Raymond, Arthur L. "Bugs," 87–88
Redman, Don, 217
Reid, Whitelaw, 38
Remington, Frederic, 45
Renoyan, William, 53
Reuben, Arnold, 129
Reynolds, Robert, 259
Rice, Grantland, 89, 160
Rickard, Tex, 119, 120, 160
Rickenbacker, Capt. Eddie, 106, 278
Rodgers, Richard, 280, 301
Rogers, Will, 188
Romanoff, Prince Mike, 251
Roosevelt, Franklin D., 18, 112, 190, 211, 257–58, 260, 261, 268, 293
Roosevelt, Theodore, 39, 44, 50, 51, 102
Rosenthal, Herman, 22
Ross, Harold, 262
Rothstein, Arnold, 22, 159–61, 206
Rothstein, Harry, 159
Rous, F. P., 18
Runyon, Alfred Lee, 53–54, 55
Runyon, Damon, 15–16, 18–26, 83–108, 116–24, 138–42, 148, 153–55, 157–65, 173–75, 192, 196, 198–207, 213, 223–27, 243–56, 264–78
Runyon, Damon, Jr., 67, 94, 97, 103, 126, 127, 128, 130, 158–59,

197–98, 248–50, 254, 255, 270, 272, 273, 278, 304
Runyon, Ellen Egan, 66–69, 85, 88, 96, 104–5, 106, 117–18, 126–27, 129–30, 158–59, 197–98
Runyon, Libbie J. Damon, 53–54
Runyon, Mary Elaine, 96, 97, 127, 158–59, 198, 248, 305
Runyon, Patrice Amati, 199, 243, 250, 251, 254, 272
Ruth, Babe, 125

Sacco, Nicola, 172–73
Sande, Earl, 122–24
Schiff, Dorothy, 296
Schine, G. David, 293–94
Schultz, Dutch, 191
Schurz, Carl, 38
Seberg, Jean, 307
Secker, Alice Louise, 111
Shelly, Howard, 300
Shor, Toots, 182
Shubert, Herman, 171
Simon, E. M., 25
Sinatra, Frank, 20
Sinclair, Harry F., 162
Smith, Al, 134, 159
Smith, H. Allen, 156
Small, Paul, 271
Smith, Red, 65
Snyder, Louis L., 17
Snyder, Moe "The Gimp," 207
Snyder, Ruth, 154, 156, 250
Sobol, Louis, 115, 178–79, 188, 245
Sobol, Peggy, 178, 179, 188, 265
Spas, Mary Louise, 147
Spigelgass, Leonard, 243–45, 247
Stack, Phillip, 218–19
Stallings, Laurence, 166
Stanton, Dr. Frank, 25
Steffens, Lincoln, 48
Stengel, Casey, 121–22
Stevens, Henry, 139
Stevens, Willie, 139, 143
Stevenson, Adlai, 295
Stimson, Sara, 21
Sudenberg, Johnny, 118
Sullivan, Ed, 143, 178, 182, 305
Sullivan, John L., 87, 99
Swanberg, W. A., 39, 40, 42, 44, 47, 51, 142, 223, 302

Swift, Kid, 59
Swope, Herbert Bayard, 49, 100,
    113, 153, 159, 165–68, 177, 203,
    299
Sylvester, Robert, 204, 284

Taft, Robert A., 260
Taft, William H., 144
Tammen, Harry, H., 62
Tarkington, Booth, 30, 135
Taylor, C. H., Jr., 285
Taylor, Deems, 166
Taylor, Elizabeth, 289–90
Temple, Shirley, 21, 201
Thaw, Harry K., 49, 148
Thenuz, Col. Reflipe W., 46
Thomas, Bob, 189, 239, 283, 293
Thompson, Dorothy, 238
Tibbetts, Harry, 131
Tinney, Frank, 148
Todd, Mike, 252
Toner, Johnny, 131
Truffaut, François, 194
Truman, Harry, 268, 292–93
Tunney, Gene, 163–65, 174

Valee, Rudy, 149
Valentino, Rudolph, 149
Van Loan, Charles E., 69, 84–85, 88
Vanzetti, Bartolomeo, 172–73
Villa, Francisco "Pancho," 101
Villard, Oswald Garrison, 44, 47
Vishinsky, Andrei, 293

Wagner, Jean, 59, 94
Walker, Eddie, 271
Walker, Mayor James J., 113,
    133–34, 135, 176, 199, 204, 276
Walker, Stanley, 109, 113, 134, 135,
    146, 149, 156, 287, 302–3
Walter, Danton, 187

Ward, Josiah, 63
Waugh, Evelyn, 176
Wechsler, James, 296
Weiner, Ed, 53, 265, 302
Weiner, Jack, 74
Welles, Orson, 194, 265
West, Mae, 25
Wheeler, John N., 92
Wheeler, Senator, 259
White, E. B., 24, 165, 168, 170
White, Stanford, 44, 49
White, Theodore H., 300
Whitman, Charles, 49
Whitman, Walt, 310
Willard, Jess, 98–100, 117–18, 119
Winchel, Chaim, 71
Qinchel, George, 71
Winchell, Gloria, 182, 192
Winchell, Jacob "Jack de," 71–72
Winchell, Janet "Jenny," 72, 73, 297
Winchell, June Magee, 115, 181–83,
    188, 196, 220, 221, 303, 304, 306
Winchell, Walda, 182, 220, 297, 305,
    306
Winchell, Walter, 15, 17–18, 21–24,
    26, 53, 70–82, 113–16, 143, 148,
    150, 171–72, 175–84, 186–93,
    195–96, 204–6, 208, 211–22,
    228–42, 257–67, 276–77,
    279–95, 297–301, 305–7
Winchell, Walter, Jr., 219–20, 303–4
Winrod, Gerald B., 239
Woollcott, Alexander, 105–6, 137,
    141–42, 154, 166, 183, 225

Yardley, Jonathan, 87
Youngman, Henny, 236

Zangara, Giuseppe, 189
Zanuck, Darryl F., 195, 196, 276
Zenger, John Peter, 35

321